LATIN POETS
AND
ROMAN LIFE

LATIN POETS AND ROMAN LIFE

Jasper Griffin

This impression 2004
This edition published in 1994 by
Bristol Classical Press
an imprint of
Gerald Duckworth & Co. Ltd.
90-93 Cowcross Street, London EC1M 6BF
Tel: 020 7490 7300
Fax: 020 7490 0080
inquiries@duckworth-publishers.co.uk
www.ducknet.co.uk

First published in 1985 by Gerald Duckworth & Co. Ltd
© 1985 by Jasper Griffin

A catalogue record for this book is available
from the British Library

ISBN 1 85399 430 8

VXORI FIDISSIMAE ATQVE OPTIMAE

Contents

Preface

The first three chapters of this book are amended versions of articles which appeared in the *Journal of Roman Studies*: 'Augustan poetry and the life of luxury' in *JRS* 66 (1976), 'Propertius and Antony' in *JRS* 67 (1977), and 'Genre and real life' in *JRS* 71 (1981). Chapter Eight is an amended version of an article which appeared in *Greece and Rome* 26 (1979), Chapter Nine of one which appeared in *Literary and Artistic Patronage in Ancient Rome*, edited by Barbara K. Gold, published by the University of Texas Press in 1982. I should like to thank the editors of those publications for their kind cooperation.

For various kinds of help and encouragement I am indebted to Professor Hugh Lloyd-Jones, Dr Oliver Lyne, Sir Ronald Syme and Professor Paul Zanker. Mrs Carolyn MacNicol did most of the typing: Dr Robert Parker kindly read the proofs.

Balliol College, Oxford   J.G.

Introduction

This book aims to illustrate and clarify the relationship between Augustan poetry and the world in which it was produced and enjoyed. Many readers of Augustan poetry have difficulty with an obvious and central feature: the highly polished verbal style and the brilliant metrical expertise are accompanied by highly stylised conventions of situation and attitude. Yet behind the conventional devices – the pastoral scenes, the songs sung outside closed doors, the Greek myths – the reader feels the presence of emotional truth. How is this effect produced, and what is the relation of the finished poem to the raw stuff of life?

All art involves conventions. 'There can be no art without a convention which emphasises certain aspects of experience as important and dismisses others to the background. A new convention is a revolution in sensibility. It appeals to and is adopted by a generation because it makes sense of experiences which previously had been ignored.'[1] Living in a post-Romantic period, we find it harder than earlier generations to accept that universal truth. It is a small but striking instance that popular songs, which in the days of Gershwin and Cole Porter were written in rhyming verse, now generally do not scan or rhyme: the artificiality of such devices would be felt as incompatible with the anarchic spontaneity which such music now aims to convey. But the poetry of Horace and Propertius is conventional in a stronger sense than that, extending to the whole life of the poet and the world in which he moves.

For instance, love. Marchesa Origo, in her book about Byron's affair with Teresa Guiccioli, remarks that 'It is curious to note that the feeling, although quite unmistakably genuine, is all within the Italian convention of the period. Passion, jealousy, storms, reconciliations, protestations of eternal fidelity ... It is all, to English ears, curiously formal.'[2] That is perhaps a little overstated, in the sense that the England of Byron's time – the England of Harriette Wilson – was less unfamiliar with this stylised life of love than she suggests;[3] but certainly a modern English reader is surprised by it in Byron as he is in Propertius. What Propertius and Tibullus present in a largely serious manner, what Horace and Ovid

[1] W.H. Auden and Norman Holmes Pearson, Introduction to *Poets of the English Language* 2 (1950).
[2] Iris Origo, *The Last Attachment* (1949) 11.
[3] Cf. below p. 26.

depict with different kinds of irony, was the life of love – envisaged as an engrossing occupation.[4] If it is to be engrossing, it must offer variety and contain rejection and unhappiness as well as blissful satisfaction. Terence states the composition of this life:

> *in amore haec omnia insunt vitia: iniuriae,*
> *suspiciones, inimicitiae, indutiae,*
> *bellum, pax rursum ... (Eunuchus 59–61).*

'A love affair contains all these bad things: violence, jealousy, feuding, armistice, war, then peace again ...' Three hundred years later Tacitus comments on a *crime passionnel*: 'As is regular in a lover's quarrel, abuse, pleading, reproaches, reconciliation, and part of the night set aside for making love.'[5] That dry historical account could cover many of the poems of these authors, and of Catullus too; and it has to be accepted that the life of illicit love, of love outside marriage, had of its nature that character. The elegists indeed make it clear that they like the passionate scenes and the stormy reconciliations: 'A placid girl is what I'd wish my enemies',

> *hostibus eveniat lenta puella meis* (Propertius 3.8.20),

might be one of their slogans.

This conception of love is one which centres very much on pleasure. The life of enjoyment is exalted by the poets to a level where it can possess beauty, dignity, seriousness; where it can stand beside the ideal poetic world of the myths and measure itself against the supreme standard of death. In chapters Four to Seven I work out in detail a number of ways in which the pleasures of life are handled in verse, in a delicately varied scale of levels of stylisation. Thus the drinking of wine can be depicted in a straightforward manner, or exalted by such realistic devices of luxury as naming choice vintages, or such 'poetical' ones as the invocation of Bacchus and his retinue. It can provide a peg on which to hang quasi-philosophical poems about the modesty and moderation of the poet, who does not drink such rich wines as his wealthy friends and patrons; it can give a setting for the praise of Augustus, whether at a lively party (as in Horace *Odes* 1.37), or as we drink our sundowners on the land he has made safe for us (as in *Odes* 4.5), or – at another level – as Bacchic inspiration carries the poet away to sing of Caesar (as in *Odes* 3.25).

These chapters do not exhaust the motifs and attitudes of love poetry which can be related to the details of the life the poets led. The narrow

---

[4] On the introduction to Rome of the definite conception of the full-time lover, cf. E. Burck in *Hermes* 80 (1952) 166 = *Vom Menschenbild in der röm. Lit.* 193.

[5] *Ut adsolet in amore et ira, iurgia preces exprobratio satisfactio, et pars tenebrarum libidini seposita*: Tacitus *Annals* 13.44. Cf. below pp. 19f. on this conception of love.

crowded streets of Rome, cobbled or muddy, naturally found a counterpart in fantasy in the obsession of the lover with grass and *solitudo*; their foulness and stale air reinforced his yearning for the streams of running water which purl through poetic countryside.[6] The blank walls of the Roman town house, from which the beloved could not look down from a window, help to explain the vogue for the song at the door rather than the serenade proper. The discomfort of the Roman toga reinforced the longing for poetic nakedness. The busy life (*negotia*) which a Roman of good family was supposed to lead made the *otium* of poetry and love all the more delightful. The class society in which he lived and loved lent appeal to the world of myth, in which class was not important since all were heroes and heroines – even favourite slave girls being captive princesses (*Odes* 2.4). The difficulties of meeting a woman and being alone with her are reflected in the fantasy world where there are no obstacles to lovers being together. The crushing weight of public opinion and parental control gives impetus and spice to the imagining of a happier existence far removed from *patria potestas* and the Roman virtues. But the role of fantasy was not limited to escape. No less important was the refinement and glorification of real life, as the poets turned the man about town into a romantic lover, picnics into pastorals, and amours into Amor.

It is not only love poetry which can be brought into close relation to the realities of life. The motif of going away to serve the state in peace or war (Chapter Three), the way an elegiac poet envisages his own funeral (Chapter Seven), the myth of Pygmalion and the role of Jupiter in the *Aeneid* (Chapter Six), the society of the bees in the Fourth *Georgic* (Chapter Eight), the set-piece battles, in Ovid's *Metamorphoses*, of the suitors of Andromeda with Perseus and of the Lapiths with the Centaurs (Chapter Four), all lend themselves to being seen in a way which sets them closely into their background in Roman life and custom. It emerges repeatedly that the same material can be observed at different levels of stylisation in different poetical contexts, all the way from something like realism to high idealisation. The elegists are often found approaching a subject in ways characteristically different from Horace. The *Metamorphoses* can be seen to versify, at yet another level, many of the motifs which elegy and lyric derive from ordinary life. Some of the same material can be found in the *Aeneid*, handled in a way which illuminates the work of the other poets and is itself illuminated by them. And, not least important, vital aspects of Virgil's poetry can be understood in

---

[6] The *rus* is always presented in verse as the opposite of the venal and sordid city. It comes almost as a shock to read in the dry tones of the Digest (5.3.27) that 'many respectable men have brothels on their country estates', *multorum honestorum virorum praediis lupanaria exercentur*. 'Love in the country' is stylised in a way that veils that sordid reality: which, however, we ought to have been able to guess, it is so well in line with the thesis of this book.

relation with Roman ideas and practices: even some for which very exotic sources have been thought necessary by some scholars (Chapter Nine). The first chapter, much more heavily documented than the others, is a general attack on the doctrinaire separation, in some influential books, of life and literature: whether in the form of arguing that what poets say is 'explained' when we have produced literary precedents and models, or in that of the argument that Greek names and Greek practices, when they occur in Latin poetry, show the 'unreality' of what is described in the poem. The contention of this chapter is that life and literature are on the contrary indissolubly linked, with literature actually affecting life; and also that refined existence in Rome and the arts of pleasure really were radically Greek. The elaborate display of evidence set out in this chapter is meant to be taken as underlying the argument of the rest of the book.

The second chapter extends these general arguments to a spectacular individual case. The romantic life which Propertius describes himself as living is related to the career and *Liebestod* of Mark Antony; the role of propaganda and its effect on Antony being an important aspect. Antony was described as living a Propertian life and dying a Propertian death: an example of the intimate way in which the fictions of the poets are related to the rest of Roman society, including its politics.

The third chapter confronts another general theory which drives a wedge between poetry and reality: the theory that ancient poems depend upon and reflect the rhetorical genres of public speakers rather than the direct experience of the poets. It is argued that on the contrary these rhetorical patterns themselves were only a part of the furniture of the world available to the poets, along with many other kinds of experience; and that they are in no way privileged.

Chapter Four works out in detail the significance and the variety of the usage by the poets of the motif of wine, from quasi-realism to high stylisation. Horace is seen to use it differently from the elegists; and in particular an explanation is offered of his puzzling poems of Bacchic ecstasy and of transformation into a swan. The realities of the picnic and the party are traced to the elevated stylistic levels of the *Metamorphoses* and the *Aeneid*.

Chapter Five deals with the pleasures of bathing, swimming, nakedness: all the way from the banal realities of public baths and sea-side resorts, by way of Propertius' brilliant exploitation of the images of Cynthia swimming, boating, drowning, to such myths as those of Leander, Europa, and Hylas. Scenes in the *Metamorphoses* transpose the sea-side vamp and sea-side seducer on to the mythical level. The poets are seen devising means – mythology and other forms of fantasy – to confer dignity and beauty on the more or less sordid scenes in which in reality they might see women naked.

In Chapter Six devices are discussed by which the poets evade or play with the unpoetical idea of payment for love; with such myths as those of

Danae and Atalanta. The removal from the poetic world of the *leno* in favour of the *lena* is put into this connection. The love poets dwell upon two apparently contrasting themes: the rape of virgins, and passionate women who welcome love. It is argued that the two belong closely together, in contrast not only with virtuous wives but also with heartless professionals. The importance for the *Aeneid* of the philandering of Jupiter is explained; and the episode of Pygmalion in Ovid is taken as a model for Roman marriage.

Chapter Seven goes into the ways of exploiting the link between love and death: itself a cliché, it could be made to suit very different purposes and poetic personalities. The ideal funeral of a love poet is to be understood in the light of real Roman funerals. The anger and the fears of Cynthia's ghost derive from those of the Roman poor. The development of an erotic Elysium is related to ordinary beliefs, as are the death of Dido and her curse on Aeneas. The language and emotions of Roman epitaphs are closer than is often suggested to the reflections of the great poets.

The eighth chapter interprets the Aristaeus-epyllion in the Fourth *Georgic*. The bees possess the Roman virtues and are indeed a sort of image of Rome; but the omission of the motif of music from their description points up their lack of the arts in an impersonal and passionless society. That society goes on and can transcend death; but the artist Orpheus and his love are destroyed. The *Aeneid* will make similar points, with the Romans ('Others' possess the arts, says Anchises) forced to destroy Dido, Camilla, and the symbolic stag of Silvia, as the price of establishing the Empire.

In Chapter Nine the creation of characters in the *Aeneid* is analysed, and any strictly 'typological' account rejected. Various ways existed in which, in oracles and propaganda and rhetorical examples, one character and situation was seen in the light of another. The originality of Virgil lay in the way in which he used the variety of his sources: to present his main characters in a way which made them systematically complex. No single judgment on Aeneas or Dido or Turnus will do, and that is partly because we see Aeneas, for instance, at different moments in the light of our response to his model at that moment – Achilles, Hector, Menelaus, Paris, Jason, Augustus. So Virgil exploits for the central purposes of his poem common features of his society.

The last chapter makes a case for Roman drama, both tragedy and comedy, as more important than is currently thought for the work of the Augustan poets. Their reluctance to cite them as sources does not mean that they were not influential. Comedy contributed to elegy a world of impoverished lovers and a strong opposition to the values of respectable elderly persons; tragedy contributed the mythological narrative, and passionate laments of heroines. The *praetextae*, tragedies on Roman themes, must have been important for the origins of the practice of

treating Roman persons with the full panoply of Hellenic poetry.
It is my hope that the whole will be found to make a case, in general
and also in detail, for a certain approach to the work of the Augustan
poets; and that it will emerge that their poetry cannot be amputated
from an intimate connection with life. If it is, not only does it become less
interesting: what we say about it also ceases to be true.

CHAPTER ONE

Augustan Poetry and the Life of Luxury[1]

These delicates he heap'd with glowing hand
On golden dishes and in baskets bright
Of wreathed silver: sumptuous they stand – Keats

The Augustan poets raise in an acute form the question of the relationship between experience and convention, between individual life and inherited forms of expression. The problem, which haunts the *Sonnets* of Shakespeare and the poems of the Romantics no less than Horace and Propertius, has notoriously been answered in very different ways at different times. Scholars like Zielinski[2] and Wili,[3] for example, created romantic stories about Lydia and Cinara, working out Horace's feelings for them, the chronology of the affairs, and the way it all ended. In revulsion from these excesses, some influential modern writers go to an opposite extreme; they distinguish on the one hand 'Greek' or 'Hellenistic' elements, which are 'unreal' or 'imaginary', from 'Roman' ones which are 'real'. Thus, to give a few examples at once, Gordon Williams, in his important book, writes that 'Horace's erotic poems are set in a world totally removed from the Augustan State',[4] while R.G.M. Nisbet and Margaret Hubbard, in their indispensable *Commentary*, say 'The "love interest" of Horace's *Odes* is almost entirely Hellenistic',[5] and, of *Odes* 1.5, 'Pyrrha herself is the wayward beauty of fiction, totally unlike the compliant harlots (*scorta*) of Horace's own temporary affairs'.[6]

My argument will be that this view is over-schematic and makes a distinction false, in this form, to the poets and to their society. It will, I think, prove possible to argue this point without falling into sentimentality or self-indulgence. The aim is not to reconstruct the *vie passionelle* of the poet, but to discover the setting and the tone in which he means his poems to be read. We must decide what a poem is supposed

---

[1] This chapter is much more heavily documented than any of the succeeding ones. It has seemed appropriate to retain this documentation, to indicate the kinds of evidence which underlie the whole work and the way in which the rest could have been supported. Also more explicit confrontation with the views of other scholars serves to bring out the controversial nature of those expressed in this book.

[2] Th. Zielinski, *Horace et la société romaine du temps d'Auguste* (1938) 169ff.

[3] W. Wili, *Horaz und die aug. Kultur* (1948) 184ff., 191.

[4] G. Williams, *Tradition and Originality in Roman Poetry* (1968) 557.

[5] R.G.M. Nisbet and M.E. Hubbard, *Commentary on Horace, Odes Book 1* (1970) xiv.

[6] ibid. 73.

to be, or to do, in order to judge it and to respond to it; we shall in this chapter be concerned chiefly with love-poems, but other related questions arise and are important. For example, were the poets really under pressure to write encomiastic epic on the *res gestae* of Augustus, or was this merely a poetic convention?[7] Was the relationship of Horace and Maecenas one of affection or of interest merely?[8] Are homosexual poems of a different order of unreality from heterosexual ones?[9] It is impossible to maintain an attitude of suave agnosticism to all these questions, without abandoning altogether the attempt to come to grips with the poems. It also seems highly likely that our answers to them will tend not to be unrelated, but that the same general attitude of credulity or scepticism towards poetic claims will characterise all the particular views we find convincing.

That 'Greek' is tantamount to 'literary', and 'literary' to 'unreal', is something of a leitmotif in this criticism. For example: 'A charming blend of the Greek and the Roman, the fanciful and the actual, is a characteristic feature of Horace's *Odes*';[10] 'We must not think of Tyndaris as an actual person ... rather, she is a dream figure, belonging to the world of Alexandrian pastoral.'[11] Sometimes one feels it is carried to an almost fanatical extreme: 'Violent quarrels of jealous lovers are a motif of New Comedy',[12] or 'A realistic picture, eminently suggestive of the comedy',[13] or even 'The poet adopts the time-honoured custom (Tibullus 3.2, Propertius 3.17.1, Horace, *Epode* 9, Ovid, *Rem. Am.* 805, *Heroides* 16.231, *Anth. Pal.* 12.49, Alciphron 1.35, etc.) of drowning his troubles in drink.'[14]

The procedure here adopted in opposition to this view is as follows. First, evidence is summarily assembled to show that Roman life, and

---

[7] Thus Williams, loc. cit., 102: 'A more reasonable explanation of the *recusatio*-poems is, not that Maecenas and Augustus kept nagging at leading poets to write epic', but that this was 'an invention', and that the poets chose the Callimachean form 'to make political statements in verse'. It is clear that we must be very careful as to whose conception of 'reasonableness' is being applied. Ockham's razor may shave the flowing locks of a poet too short. Cf. also n.243, and J. Griffin, '*Caesar qui cogere posset,*' in *Caesar Augustus* ed. Millar and Segal (1984) 189ff.

[8] Contrast Williams, op. cit. 44, who believes in a real friendship: 'The historical evidence of that friendship is sufficient to make its insertion in the picture obligatory,' with Nisbet and Hubbard, op. cit. xxi: 'scholars tend to take too literally Horace's courteous protests (sic) of affection. One cannot detect in the relationship any of the equality required by essayists on *amicitia.*' The implication, that 'essayists on *amicitia*' are better evidence, in an individual case, than Horace's poems or Maecenas' will ('Remember Horace as you remember me'), is a striking one.

[9] e.g. Nisbet-Hubbard 71 (on *Odes* 1.4): 'The homosexual implication has no bearing on Sestius' actual behaviour but is a conventional motif derived from Greek erotic poetry.' Cf. G. Williams in *JRS* 52 (1962) 39; *Tradition and Originality* 556.

[10] Nisbet-Hubbard 109

[11] ibid. 216.

[12] ibid. 226.

[13] K.F. Smith on Tibullus 1.2.93-7.

[14] idem on Tibullus 1.2.1-6.

particularly the life of luxury and pleasure, was so strongly Hellenistic in colouring and material that no simple division into 'Greek' and 'Roman' elements is possible. This necessarily involves reviewing a body of factual evidence, not indeed new,[15] but apparently not sufficiently brought into relation with contemporary poetry. Secondly, it will be argued that another and related distinction is also, in any simple form, unsound: that between 'literature' and 'life'. For not only does literature reflect, at whatever remove and with whatever stylisation, the experiences of life, but also in its turn it affects actual behaviour; and can do so with great force. The existence of a given pattern of conduct influences the conception which people have of the ways in which it is possible to behave or to live. If this were not so, the existence of fashions in these matters would be inexplicable; that, for example, Europe in 1800 was full of Young Werthers, in 1825 of Byrons; while in 1860 virtuous youths and maidens had returned to the forefront of the stage.[16] That 'few people would fall in love if they had not read about it' is an epigram which combines truth and falsehood; but it certainly seems true that the manner of experiencing and expressing the passion varies widely from period to period, and from group to group within a period.

The general influence of a milieu as a whole is clear enough, but it is also certain that particular individuals and particular books can have a mighty impact on the way others feel and live. No long residence in a University town is necessary to verify this for oneself, but a few examples from literature may be suggestive. Thus, when Stendhal entered Italy for the first time, he records: 'I said to myself: I am in Italy, in the country of *Zulietta* whom J.-J. Rousseau met in Venice, and in Piedmont, the country of Mme. Bazile ...'[17] It is no surprise that as soon as he reaches Milan he is caught up in a passionate love affair. A writer on Stendhal's life observes that in attempting the seduction of Melanie Guilbert 'he can never forget the example of Laclos' Valmont'[18] (the hero of *Les Liaisons dangereuses*). Delacroix, to maintain a high level of romantic fervour, reminds himself of passages from Byron.[19] The young Baudelaire

---

[15] See Nisbet-Hubbard xv: 'These of course were Roman institutions as well, but their repeated mention in such poems owes much to the convention of the genre.'

[16] We know from Aristophanes that young contemporaries emulated Euripidean characters; cf. B. Snell in *Gnomon* 19 (1943) 71. Also P. Boyancé and J. Bayet in *Entretiens Hardt* 2 (1956) 41f.

[17] *Vie de Henry Brulard* (Paris, edn. Le Divan 1949) 483. Of his love, Stendhal writes: 'La femme que j'aimais, et dont je me croyais en quelque sorte aimé, avait d'autres amants, mais elle me préférait à rang égal, me disais-je! J'avais d'autres maîtresses ...' It could be Propertius speaking.

[18] W.H. Fineshreiber jr., *Stendhal the Romantic Rationalist* (1932) 27.

[19] E. Delacroix, *Journales* for 11 May 1824: 'Rappelle, pour t'enflammer éternellement, certains passages de Byron; ils me vont bien.' In his *Correspondance générale* 1, 85 (of 20 October 1818) we find him writing of the imitation of Rousseau by some of his friends: 'Ensuite un ami qui écrivait la tête dans ses mains, non pas pour rendre les élans de son cœur, mais pour les rendre d'une certaine manière et pour faire du Rousseau ...'

'read with feverish interest Sainte Beuve's one novel, *Volupté*, published in 1834, and this ... helped to crystallise what had hitherto been vague and undefined in him and scarcely admitted even to himself.'[20] Later Baudelaire wrote a poem about it, in which he tells Sainte Beuve that, reading the book when already

mûri par vos sonnets, préparé par vos stances,

matured by your sonnets, made ready by your lyrics,

he took it into himself:

J'en ai tout absorbé, les miasmes, les parfums,
Le doux chuchotement des souvenirs défunts,
Les longs enlacements des phrases symboliques ...
Livre voluptueux, si jamais il en fut ...[21]

I absorbed it all, the fumes, the aromas,
The sweet murmuring of dead memories,
The leisurely intertwining of phrases heavy with meaning ...
Voluptuous volume, if ever there was one ...

On a larger scale, the Latin Quarter was popularised by Henry Murger. His book *La Vie de Bohème* was published in 1851; by 1855, as a result of its success, there was an American restaurant in the Quarter, and in the same year James Whistler, aged twenty-one, threw up his government job in Washington and went to live there and be an artist.[22] Such things, I think, help to confirm that these 'literary' influences can be vital; what might be written off as 'literature' is inextricable from 'life'.   The second chapter of this book concentrates upon a particular type of historical figure, on the reciprocal relation of such men with scandal and propaganda, and on the existence in Roman life of conspicuous figures who were believed to live a life strikingly similar to that claimed as their own by the love poets. It will be argued there that the importance of all this has been greatly underestimated, and in particular that the life of Mark Antony, as presented in literature, shows one of the most spectacular men in the world living a life which could be depicted, without absurdity, as in important respects akin to that lived in 'literature' by Propertius.

In the context of Latin literature, discussion of Greek influence on

---

[20] E. Starkie, *Baudelaire* (1957) 47.
[21] Baudelaire: *A Sainte-Beuve.*
[22] e.g. A. Moss and E. Marvel, *The Legend of the Latin Quarter* (1964) 142. A further twist is added by the fact that Du Maurier later included a character, recognisably Whistler, as 'Joe Sibley' in the first version of *Trilby*, his novel describing artistic life in Paris; the publishers were made to apologise, and the offending chapters were omitted. The combination of biography and literature in all this is indissoluble. Murger's novel was a romanticised version of his own life ...

Rome tends to be over-weighted towards the intellectual side. For men like Horace and Propertius it was of course important that the Rome they lived in was now full of Greek intellectuals[23] – poets,[24] scholars,[25] philosophers,[26] doctors,[27] scientists,[28] astrologers[29] – and was now even acquiring, on the Alexandrian model, her first public Library.[30] But the Hellenistic refinements which went to make up the life of pleasure were no doubt even more significant, and some of the evidence for this will now be set out. As a preliminary remark it may be said that such a life was evidently felt by Romans, including the poets, as being a definite and recognisable unity, which a man might choose and live, or live part of the time, in preference to other ways of life. Cicero refers to the *delicata iuventus* (luxurious young men) almost as if they constituted a political party,[31] and both he and Sallust[32] talk of such people as

---

[23] Listed by A. Hillscher, 'Hominum literatorum Graecorum ante Tiberii mortem in urbe Roma commoratorum historia critica,' *Jahrb. für klass. Phil.*, Suppl. 18 (1892), 335-40. See also G.W. Bowersock, *Augustus and the Greek World* (1965); R. Heinze, *Die august. Kultur* (1930) 65-76. For example, the historians Diodorus of Sicily, Dionysius of Halicarnassus, Nicolaus of Damascus, Strabo and Timagenes all visited Rome and worked there.

[24] After Parthenius of Nicaea, whose importance is rightly stressed by W.V. Clausen, 'Callimachus and Roman Poetry', *GRBSt.* 5 (1964) 181-96, for example Antipater of Thessalonice and Crinagoras of Mitylene, who lived in the Imperial household.

[25] Strabo 675, Rome is 'full of scholars from Tarsus and Alexandria'. Cf. P.M. Fraser, *Ptolemaic Alexandria* (1972) 1.474.

[26] e.g. Athenodorus the Stoic, influential with Augustus (Strabo 674; see also P. Grimal in *REA* 47 (1945) 261; ibid. 48 (1946) 62); and Areius Didymus, whose *consolatio* to Livia is quoted by Seneca, *ad Marciam* 4.5. Augustus' literary output included *hortationes ad philosophiam* (Suet. *D. Aug.* 85).

[27] C. Allbutt, *Greek Medicine in Rome* (1921); J. Scarborough, *Roman Medicine* (1969) 110ff. on the prevalence of Greek doctors in upper-class households.

[28] Fraser, op. cit. (n.25) 425: 'The migratory movement of Alexandrian scientists and grammarians to Rome, so noticeable in the fields of grammar, medicine, and philosophy ...'.

[29] A. Bouché-Leclercq, *L'Astrologie grecque*, ch. xvi; F.A. Cramer, *Astrology in Roman Law and Politics*, *Mem. Amer. Philos. Soc.* 37 (1954). Cramer remarks, p. 88, on the 'astounding familiarity with astrology among his readers' assumed by Propertius 4.1. I should not share the confidence of some scholars (*Critical Essays on Roman Literature: Elegy and Lyric*, ed. J.P. Sullivan (1962) 191) that the astrologically inclined Leuconoe of Hor. *Odes* 1.11 is 'an imaginary person with a Greek name'.

[30] Suet. *D. Aug.* 29. It is striking how little the poets have to say about the Library.

[31] W. Kroll, *Kultur der ciceronischen Zeit* (1933, repr. 1966) 160ff. Cicero *ad Atticum* 1.19.8 'The dislike of me which was worked up in the minds of the licentious and luxurious young men has been so mitigated by my affability that I am supreme in their attentions' (a typical piece of optimism from 60 B.C.); cf. *Catil.* 2.23. At *de Officiis* 1.106 he contrasts two ways of life: one 'frugal, restrained, moral, sober', the other 'luxurious, soft, full of debauchery'. The contrast was already a stock one by the time of Terence; cf. *Adelphoe* 863ff., Donatus on *Adelphoe* 9. Lucilius fr. 1058M is referred by Housman, *CQ* 1 (1907) 156 = *Collected Papers* 2.693, to 'dissolute young men of fashion'.

[32] Sallust *Cat.* 10-17, 23, 25, etc. Cicero presents such a way of life from a hostile standpoint in the *Philippics* and from an apologetic one in the *Pro Caelio*, a speech exploited in this connection by A. Guillemin, 'L'élément humain dans l'élégie latine', *REL* 18 (1940) 95ff. The standard elements are listed, in connection with Hannibal in Capua, by Livy 23.18.12; *somnus et vinum et epulae et scorta balineaeque et otium*, 'sleeping and feasting and drinking and tarts and baths and idleness'.

numerous and clearly identifiable. The life we glimpse in the poems of Lucilius, and again in those of Catullus and his contemporaries,[33] has precisely this character: a life of *amours*, parties, drinking, jealousy, and (for some) poetry and music. And this is the life, one of sloth and debauchery, *inertia* and *nequitia*, which the Augustan elegists proclaim as their own.[34] And of course from an early date such a life was felt to be Greek: the meaning of *congraecare* and *pergraecari* in Plautus[35] is unambiguous, and Festus says, flatly, 'pergraecari est epulis et potationibus inservire', ' "Greeking it up" means being devoted to dining and drinking'.

First, the city itself. Its layout,[36] its aqueducts,[37] its basilicas[38] for comfortable lounging, its public baths[39] for leisure, the works of art on show,[40] the marble buildings of which Augustus boasted[41] – all this was unthinkable without Eastern influence.[42] Franz Cumont sums up by saying, in connection with the attempts of 20 and 18 B.C. (inevitably unsuccessful) to exclude from Rome the cult of Isis: 'The prestige of Alexandria was irresistible. Alexandria was more beautiful, more cultured, better policed than Rome; it offered the model of a civilised capital city, and in time the Latins strove to raise themselves up to it. They translated its scholars, imitated its writers, summoned its artists, applauded its institutions. How could its religion fail to impose itself on them?'[43]

Outside Rome, the same is true of the villas beloved by the upper class. Both of the two types are influenced by Greek models,[44] and they are well

---

[33] On it, see J. Bayet in *Entretiens Hardt* 2 (1956) 4ff.

[34] cf. p. 43ff. below.

[35] e.g. *Mostellaria* 22: *dies noctesque bibite, pergraecamini, / amicas emite liberate, pascite / parasitos, obsonate pollucibiliter.* 'Drink day and night, live like Greeks, buy mistresses and give them their freedom, keep hangers-on, dine sumptuously'. 'Greeking it up' is the translation of Erich Segal.

[36] M.W. Frederiksen in *The Romans*, ed. J.P.V.D. Balsdon (1965) 160, of the schematic layout of Roman towns: 'Most likely the idea came from the Greeks.' Architects still came regularly from the East to Rome in the time of Trajan: Pliny *Ep.* 10.40.

[37] 'As for the aqueducts, the idea of course was Greek', A. Boethius, *The Golden House of Nero* (1960) 77. He emphasises (p. 30) that once Roman soldiers had seen the Greek cities of the East, they had to be given similar luxuries in the Western military colonies.

[38] Named after the *stoa basilikē* of the Hellenistic city. All four sides of the Forum had been provided with this convenience by 169 B.C. They were good places for picking up girls, in literature (Prop. 2.32.11, Ovid *Ars* 1.67, 492 etc.), and doubtless in life too. So were the theatres: Ovid *Ars* 1.100, *Amores* 2.2.26ff.

[39] The first big ones were built by Agrippa: cf. R. Heinze, *Die aug. Kultur* 69. Cf. Chapter Five.

[40] e.g. in the Porticus Metelli famous Hellenistic statues; Ovid *Ars* 1.70ff., the Porticus Octavia is *externo marmore dives opus*, and the Porticus Liviae is *priscis sparsa tabellis*: rich with marble and paintings.

[41] Suet., *D. Aug.* 28.

[42] 'As regards comfort, beauty, and hygiene, the cities of the Roman Empire, worthy successors to their Hellenistic parents ...', Rostovtzeff, *SEHRE²* 143.

[43] F. Cumont, *Les religions orientales dans le paganisme romain⁴* (1929) 78. The ladies of elegy incline to the cult of Isis, e.g. Prop. 2.33; Tibull. 1.3.23; Ovid *Am.* 1.8.74.

[44] A.G. McKay, *Houses, Villas and Palaces in the Roman World* (1975) 114ff.

called 'real centres of Hellenistic luxury'.[45] We have only to look at the importance of these villas in the letters of Cicero to see how significant this is. And we observe that all this is true of literature as of life: the palaces in the *Aeneid* are akin above all with the buildings of the Greek city of Naples.[46] It is not surprising that hunting was a Hellenistic importation to Rome;[47] more striking is it that the same is true, despite the more hospitable Italian setting, of the art of the garden.[48] Even the luxury fish-ponds, which became such a symbol for Rome of plutocratic inertia, were a Roman adaptation of a diversion first indulged in by Hellenistic kings.[49]

Italy, and above all Rome, was full of Greek works of art, both sculptures and paintings. It was as loot that the visual arts made their entry to Rome, chained to the chariots of triumphant generals,[50] but such was their vogue that by the end of the Republic some Romans were prepared to pay for works of art.[51] Moralists loved to dwell on their demoralising effect. Thus Livy laments, of Marcellus' triumph over Syracuse in 211: 'That was the beginning (*sic*) of the vogue for Greek works of art and of the modern rage for looting sacred and profane objects on a universal scale'.[52] Of Vulso's triumph over Asia in 187 he laments 'The source (*sic*) of Eastern luxuriousness was brought to Rome by the army on this occasion.'[53] With art goes *luxuria*, debauchery: Polybius says the triumph of Aemilius Paullus in 168 turned young men's minds to 'catamites, courtesans, music and drinking'.[54] Roman innocence was still being corrupted by the East as late as 58 B.C. Pliny laments that the spectacular aedileship of M. Scaurus in that year 'perhaps did most to

---

[45] Boethius, op. cit (n.36) 96: 'The villa acquired more and more luxurious features, many of them borrowed from Greece'; J.P.V.D. Balsdon, *Life and Leisure in Ancient Rome* (1969) 206.

[46] C.C. Van Essen, 'L'architecture dans l'Énéide', *Mnem.* 7 (1939), 225-36.

[47] J. Aymard, *Essai sur les chasses romaines* (1951) ch. 2.

[48] P. Grimal, *Les jardins romains*² (1969) 69.

[49] J.H. D'Arms, *Romans on the Bay of Naples* (1970) 41; *RE* s.v. *Piscina*, 1783. On the *piscinarii* of the late Republic, R. Syme, *The Roman Revolution* (1939) 23. Ibid. 410, Vedius Pollio: the type did not die with the Republic.

[50] Cf. G.A. Saalfeld, *Der Hellenismus in Latium* (1882) 105. Even new trees were led in triumph, Pliny *NH* 12.111: *clarumque dictu, a Pompeio Magno in triumpho arbores quoque duximus.* The sources on the visual arts at Rome are collected by O. Vessberg, *Studien zur Kunstgeschichte der röm. Republik* (1941). See also H. Jucker, *Vom Verhältnis der Römer zur bildenden Kunst der Griechen* (1950).

[51] Vessberg gives the evidence for the looting of Syracuse, 211 B.C.; Capua, 210; Tarentum, 209; Eretria, 198; Macedon, 194; Aetolia and Ambracia, 187; Asia, 186; Macedon again, 168; Carthage and Corinth, 146; Athens, 88; etc. Sulla removed everything from Olympia as well as from Delphi, Epidaurus and Athens. Lucullus, after his rich triumph over Mithridates, incurred 'great expenses' (Plut., *Luc.* 39) in collecting Greek art. Other collections, such as that of Verres, continued to be formed on the older, cheaper, method.

[52] Livy 25.40.1.

[53] Livy 39.6.7-9. A cool view of this assertion: A.W. Lintott in *Historia* 21 (1972) 626-38.

[54] Polybius 31.25.4-8.

debauch our morals'.[55]

The importance of this for our purpose is the significance which works of art had for Augustan poets, especially Propertius.[56] It is also highly suggestive that such works were, in principle, regarded as corrupting and un-Roman; for the whole *vita* of love and pleasure extolled by Propertius had the same character. It is worth remembering that Greek art had for a young Roman a resonance far more exciting than a visit to the National Gallery or the British Museum for us.[57] An aesthete lived amid images derived from Greece and its mythology, of which he was sharply conscious that they were Greek, and that many sturdy Romans disliked and disapproved of them.[58]

Greece itself was of course where the Roman tourist, student, and émigré naturally went. To visit mainland Greece was part of the education of the Roman of good family, and of those who, like the young Horace,[59] emulated their betters. As early as 190 B.C. a hotel for Roman citizens existed at Delphi,[60] and in the second century B.C. Romans made very much the same tour of Greece as Hellenophiles today.[61] Eminent exiles[62] and émigrés[63] were numerous enough to make Caesar limit residence abroad to three successive years;[64] no doubt to little effect. In life, Agrippa withdrew to Lesbos[65] and Tiberius to Rhodes;[66] in literature, Horace's friend Bullatius is begged to come home from the charms of the East,[67] and Propertius' friend Tullus is urged to come home from Cyzicus.[68] In Italy itself, 'it was fashionable to spend time in the

[55] Pliny *NH* 36.113. Cicero loves to make the association: *pro Flacco* 71: *Graecorum luxuria*; *pro Murena* 12: *habet Asia suspicionem luxuriae quandam*; *pro Flacco* 5: *Asiae luxuries*; *Verr.* 2.7.

[56] e.g. J.-P. Boucher, *Études sur Properce* (1965) 41ff.; H. Bartholomé, *Ovid und die antike Kunst* (1935); Rothstein's edition of Propertius, index, s.v. 'Kunst, bildende'.

[57] Propertius has an elegant variation on the motif of 'corrupting works of art' at 2.6.27ff.: *obscene* pictures corrupt *girls*.

[58] It is plausibly argued that even the realistic portrait statues of Rome were actually made by Greeks: so e.g. G.M.A. Richter, 'Who made the Roman portrait statues – Greeks or Romans?', in *TAPhA* 95 (1951) 183ff.

[59] V. Pöschl points out, *Entretiens Hardt* 2 (1956) 95, that in Greece Horace will have heard real Greeks singing. That has its implications for his lyric poetry.

[60] *Syll.*[3] 2.609.

[61] e.g. Livy 37.54.20; 45.27; Polyb. 30.10.3-6.

[62] As P. Rutilius Rufus, in exile at Mitylene and Smyrna (Cic. *Rab. Post.* 27). Milo went to Massilia: on the refinements of that city, and its popularity with Roman grandees, Strabo 181.

[63] Like T. Pomponius Atticus.

[64] Suet. *D. Jul.* 42.

[65] Suet. *D. Aug.* 66.

[66] Suet. *Tib.* 11-13. He apparently led a Greek life there, dealing with the natives 'almost on a footing of equality', wearing the Greek dress, going regularly to lectures by the local intellectuals, and appearing at the gymnasium.

[67] Hor. *Epp.* 1.11.21, *Romae laudetur Samos et Chios et Rhodos absens*, 'Stay in Rome and praise Samos and Chios and Rhodes from a distance'.

[68] Prop. 3.22.

remaining Greek cities of Italy.'[69] The terrible Sulla appeared in the Greek *chlamys* at Naples,[70] and its elegance and the freedom it allowed drew to the city many noble youths and senators.[71] Horace speaks of 'otiosa Neapolis';[72] Virgil says he composed the *Georgics* there, 'flourishing in the studies of inglorious leisure.'[73] The bay of Naples altogether was a popular resort. Baiae was redolent of the franker pleasures,[74] but literary men and philosophers could also be found by those with a taste for them.[75] Augustus, who bought Capri in 29 B.C., spent his last days of life at Naples, where he witnessed the *Sebasta*, the Greek games in his honour,[76] and told Romans to wear the Greek dress and speak Greek, Greeks to wear the toga and speak Latin. Tarentum, on the other coast, was in Cicero's view the perfect place for the Epicurean;[77] Virgil set his ideal *Corycius senex* near Tarentum,[78] which is where Propertius envisages the setting of the *Eclogues*;[79] Horace was moved to wish that he might die there.[80]

The more hedonistic is the aspect of life to which we turn, the more Greek it seems to be. Wine, which figures so large in the poets, was raised to an art in Greece. Pliny the Elder tells us that 'until our grandfathers' time' (sc. the Augustan age) 'Greek wines were preferred at Rome'.[81] The frugal Cato gave recipes for making your own 'Greek wine' and 'Coan wine';[82] Italian wines began to be marked with the vintage in 121 B.C.,[83] and it seems that pressure from Greek wines had raised the standard of the local product. But the imported wines still commanded such high prices that the censors of 89 B.C. stepped in to regulate them. We know the authors of five Hellenistic treatises on viticulture,[84] and no doubt here as in agriculture[85] Greek theory and skill were at work in Italy. We

[69] G.W. Bowersock, *Augustus and the Greek World* (1965) 74.

[70] Cic. *Rab. Post.* 26.

[71] Cic. *Pro Planc.* 65; Strabo 246.

[72] Hor. *Epode* 5.43.

[73] Virgil, *Georg.* 4.563-4: *illo Virgilium me tempore dulcis alebat / Parthenope, studiis florentem ignobilis oti.* The wording is a bow – not without irony – to the ultra-Roman view of such matters as poetry as a 'waste of time': cf. below, p. 177.

[74] Baiae in reality: Cicero, *Pro Cael.* 35; *ad Att.*, 1.16.10; D'Arms, *Romans on the Bay of Naples* 119ff. Baiae in poetry: Prop. 1.11; 3.18; Hor., *Odes* 3.4.24; *Epp.* 1.1.83; [Tibull.] 3.5.3; Ovid *Ars* 1.255ff. Cf. below p. 90ff.

[75] D'Arms, op. cit. 56.

[76] Suet. *D. Aug.* 98; Vell. Pat. 2.123.1. The games were Italica Romaea Sebasta Isolympia: Bowersock, 83.

[77] Cic. *ad Fam.* 7.12.1.

[78] Virgil *Georg.* 4.125ff.

[79] Prop. 2.34.67.

[80] Hor. *Odes* 2.6 fin.

[81] Pliny *NH* 14.87.

[82] Cato *RR* 105, 112.

[83] Pliny *NH* 14.94.

[84] Susemihl, *Geschichte der griechischen Literatur* 1.840.

[85] cf. Rostovtzeff, SEHRE² 1.19 on the introduction of Hellenistic methods into Italian husbandry.

read of outstandingly successful growers, who achieved fabulous results in a vineyard 'in Nomentano agro' and sold it at a huge profit to Seneca the philosopher: their names were Acilius Sthenelus and Remmius Palaemon[86] – both Greek.

Luxury clothes tell a similar story, of the West trying to catch up with Eastern refinement and technique. The most highly prized wool, says Pliny, is that of Apulia, 'and what in Italy is called Greek, but elsewhere is called Italian';[87] Milesian wool holds third place, that of Tarentum and Canusium is very good, so is that of Laodicea. Columella, however, thinks that whereas 'our ancestors' thought the best wool was Calabrian, Apulian and Milesian, and the very best of all came from Tarentum: 'nowadays Gallic wool fetches higher prices'.[88] Gallic and Italian wool, it seems, has now caught up with Greek.[89] The more frankly luxury garments were of unambiguously Eastern origin: 'the best clothing, especially for women, seems to have been imported,'[90] and in poetry the favourite stuffs of Cynthia and her sisters were linen, silk, Tyrian purple, and the see-through Coan dresses, *Coae vestes*.[91] Caesar attempted to restrict the wearing of Tyrian garments;[92] no doubt ineffectively. As for fashion, Greek modes made themselves felt dramatically at Rome when men began to shave, a practice deriving from Alexander; more generally, 'since the late Republic, styles both of dress and of coiffure were open to all the Greek artifices.'[93] The Greek words in use in hairdressing and cosmetics show the pervasiveness of this influence.[94] All readers of the Augustan poets are struck by the attention they pay to the hair of the beloved and to its *cultus*;[95] the smart lover also takes great trouble with his own hair.[96] He too must look to his *cultus* – though he should not use cosmetics or dye his hair, as the girls do.[97]

With clothes and cosmetics goes perfume. Horace refers to perfumes eight times in the *Odes*, and Propertius too loves to talk of them.[98] Perfumes, with spices and jewellery, represented conspicuous and extravagant luxury; like them, they came from the East. Plautus talks of 'unguenta exotica';[99] their importation was forbidden, predictably, in 189

[86] Pliny *NH* 14.48-52.
[87] *NH* 8.190.
[88] *RR* 7.2.3.
[89] cf. Tenney Frank, *Economic Survey* 5 (1940) 164.
[90] ibid. 201 n.42.
[91] Prop. 1.2.1-4; 2.1.4; 16.18; 4.5.22; 5.57; Hor. *Sat.* 1.2.101; *Odes* 4.13.3; *Epp.* 1.12.21; Tibull. 1.9.67; 2.3.53; Ov. *Ars* 2.297, etc. *Byssus* came from Cilicia, Egypt and Syria.
[92] Suet. *D. Jul.* 43.
[93] Marquardt, *Röm. Privatleben*[2] 603.
[94] e.g. *corymbion, galerus, galericulum, calliblepharon, psilothra.*
[95] Ovid *Ars.* 3.133-68; Prop 1.2.1; 1.15.5; Hor. *Odes* 1.5.4; *Epode* 11.28, etc.
[96] Hor. *Sat.* 2.7.55; *Odes* 3.19.25; *Epp.* 1.14.32; Prop. 2.4.5; Tibull. 1.8.9; Ovid *Ars* 1.505ff.
[97] Prop. 1.2.19; 2.18.23; 3.24.8; Tibull. 1.8.43; Ov. *Am.* 1.14 etc. Cf. below p. 000.
[98] e.g. Prop. 2.29.17; 3.10.22; Ov. *Am.* 3.1.7; *Her.* 15.76.
[99] *Mostell.* 43; *non omnes possunt olere unguenta exotica*, 'not everyone can smell of foreign perfumes'.

B.C.[100] Hellenistic Queens had been among the most zealous promoters of perfumes.[101] Pliny says, perhaps rather wildly, that the importation of pearls and perfumes from Arabia cost Rome 100,000,000 sesterces a year.[102] Men, too, used perfumes discreetly;[103] it was a regular part of the convivial evening, and Catullus 13 and Horace *Odes* 4.12 show us how highly it was rated. In the poets perfumes altogether loom much larger than the restrained taste of our society would lead us to expect; in this they exactly reflect their own society.[104]

Cookery was another art despised, so their descendants believed, by the good old Romans of the past. There is a pleasing contrast between Livy's complaint, in his jeremiad on the foreign luxury brought into Rome in 187 B.C., that 'Cooks, regarded by our ancestors as the lowest kind of slave, began to be expensive, and what used to be thought a servile craft started to be called an art',[105] and what we read in Athenaeus on the dignity of cooking, a long diatribe with many quotations.[106] Among these, Heraclides and Glaucus of Rhegium said it was not right that a slave should be a cook, 'nor even a free-man, unless he is somebody special.'[107] In Greek, cookery books go back to the fifth century; Susemihl lists twenty-two whose names are known to us, with six specialised works on baking, and even two on the art of buying food.[108] No less a person than Ennius himself based his *Hedyphagetica* upon the work of Archestratus, whose poem on the subject, in the epic style, was known as the 'gourmet's Hesiod'.[109] The luxuries of the table soon engrossed much time and effort and vast expense.[110] Cicero's *in Pisonem* gives an idea of the standard expected of a senator, with his sneers at the sordid hospitality of Piso; while his letters to Papirius Paetus give a glimpse into the gourmet dinners of his time.[111] Horace satirises an over-elaborate meal;[112] it is not in the manner either of the elegists or of Horace's *Odes*

---

[100] Pliny *NH* 13.24.

[101] For Berenice, Callimachus fr. 110; for Arsinoe and Stratonice of Pergamum, cf. Athenaeus 689a.

[102] *NH* 12.84: *tanti nobis deliciae et feminae constant*, 'That's how much luxury and women cost us'. He lists Eastern sources of perfumes, 13.4-8.

[103] cf. J. Colin, 'Luxe oriental et parfums masculins dans la Rome alexandrine', *RBPh* 33 (1955) 5-19.

[104] The stage was perfumed at theatrical performances, Lucret. 2.416, Brandt on Ov. *Ars*. 1.104. Trimalchio had unconventional ways of distributing perfume to his guests, Petron. 60.3; Nero, with what seems even worse taste, could spray perfume on his from the ceilings of the *Domus Aurea* (Suet. *Nero* 31).

[105] Livy 39.6.

[106] Athenaeus 658e ff.

[107] Athenaeus 661e.

[108] *Geschichte der gr. Lit.* 1.879.

[109] Athenaeus 101f.

[110] Still worth reading is L. Friedländer, *Roman Life and Manners* (English translation) 2.146ff.: 'The luxury of the table and the importation of foreign foods.'

[111] Cic. *ad Fam.* 9.20, 25, 26. At the last of these Cicero found the celebrated Cytheris, see below p. 16.

[112] Hor. *Sat.* 2.8. Cf. below p. 82.

to tell us about the menu at the *convivia* which occupy so much of their poetry, but we are not meant to imagine it, if we think of it at all, as having been unsophisticated.

Jewellery, too, is important. The poets have much to say of pearls, in particular,[113] and the girls they write about have a sharp eye for gold. Pearls of course came from the East (Caesar tried vainly to restrict their use),[114] and the jewellers and their styles were Greek.[115] A notable department is that of signet rings; this is especially important because in the late Republic and early Empire 'every Roman of any dignity must have had an individual signet ring, and men took pride in having a distinctive and artistic seal'.[116] Pompey and Caesar were among the first Romans to collect them,[117] and we are well informed about the seals of Maecenas (a frog),[118] and of Augustus, who used successively a sphinx, a portrait of Alexander, and his own portrait carved by Dioscurides.[119] It is striking that here too, for these highly personal treasures, the source was the same;[120] as it was also for the higher class at least of silver-ware for the table,[121] and for the styles of house furniture in general.[122]

The life of pleasure naturally led to the company not only of *meretrices* but also of actors and mimes. Such famous theatrical names as Aesopus, Antipho, Diphilus, Eros, Spinther, show the origin of these unrespectable people.[123] Sulla, a boon companion all his days, after his retirement 'consorted with women who acted in mimes or played the harp, and with theatre people; the people of most influence with him were Roscius the

---

[113] Prop 1.8.39; 14.2; 2.16.17; 3.4.2; Tibull. 2.2.15; 4.30; 3.3.17; Hor. *Odes* 3.24.48; Ovid *Ars* 1.251, etc.

[114] Suet. *D. Jul.* 43.

[115] 'The jewellery of the early Empire may be regarded merely as a continuation of Hellenistic jewellery ... the chief centres of production were probably in the first place the old Hellenistic centres of Alexandria and Antioch, in the second place Rome itself. The Roman craftsmen, as in the other arts and crafts, were doubtless to a large extent immigrants from the East': R.A. Higgins, *Greek and Roman Jewellery* (1961) 178, 181.

[116] Tenney Frank, op. cit. (n.89) 211. Cf. H.M.-L. Vollenweider, 'Verwendung und Bedeutung der Porträtgemmen für das politische Leben der römischen Republik', *Mus. Helv.* 12 (1955) 96-111.

[117] Pliny *NH* 37.11-12.

[118] ibid. 10.

[119] Suet. *D. Aug.* 50.

[120] 'Most of the signatures on gems of the early Roman period are in Greek and with Greek names ... their techniques, materials and subjects ... remained basically Hellenistic Greek': J. Boardman, *Greek Gems and Finger Rings* (1970) 362.

[121] Of the seventeen celebrated *argentarii* and *caelatores* listed by Pliny *NH* 33.154-7, all have Greek names. Cf. Prop. 1.14.2, *Lesbia Mentoreo vina bibas opere.*

[122] G.M.A. Richter, *Ancient Furniture* (1926) 117, 'There were few original contributions' (sc. from Rome). 'The pre-Hellenistic house must have been simply, even sparsely, furnished with basic articles ... However, a revolution in taste and design attended the sudden entry of Rome into the main stream of Hellenistic history ...', A.G. MacKay, *Houses, Villas and Palaces in the Roman World* (1975) 136. The same is true of mosaics: 'Roman pavements in the first two centuries are almost entirely Hellenistic in inspiration.'

[123] *RE*, s.v. *Histrio*, 2120: most names of actors in the first half of the first century B.C. are Greek.

comedian, Sorix the arch-mime, and Metrobius the female imper-
sonator.'[124] Cicero professes to be outraged by the *mima uxor* of Antony
and by his 'troops of mime actors of both sexes'.[125] The most crudely
unromantic of the *Sermones* of Horace[126] takes *mimae* for granted as part
of the life of dissipation; in the more courtly ethos of the *Odes*, of course,
they are not mentioned, as such at least. The most famous dancers of the
time, on whom violent passions centred, were Pylades of Cilicia,
Bathyllus of Alexandria, Nomius of Syria, Hylas the Carian, Pierus of
Tibur – all Greek names.[127] Augustus himself, in a discreet and dignified
manner, was a good friend of actors.[128]

It is worth while to pause here, in order to emphasise that Maecenas
himself, whose importance for the poets it is perhaps impossible to
exaggerate, was notorious for his luxurious taste in every one of these
areas. He was a by-word for effeminate fabrics,[129] and was teased by
Augustus for his interest in jewels;[130] his house was palatial[131] and his
gardens never lost their celebrity.[132] He produced famous wine[133] and was
notorious too for affected epicurism at table,[134] for his affairs with
women,[135] and for his liaison with the actor Bathyllus.[136] We must ask
ourselves what the probability is that his poets really lived a life quite
different, in respects other than those caused by Maecenas' vast wealth
and their comparative poverty, from that of their great patron.

Also common to life[137] and poetry[138] is gambling (*alea*), intensely

---

[124] Plutarch *Sulla* 36; cf. ibid. 2.

[125] Cicero *Philippic* 2.20, 8.26, etc.

[126] Hor. *Sat.* 1.2.2, 56, 58.

[127] *ILS* 5180-276, *tituli pertinentes ad ludos*, is rich in Greek names. On mimes and poetry
cf. J.C. McKeown in *PCPS* 205 (1979).

[128] Suet. *D. Aug.* 45 and 74. Already for Lucilius *cinaedi* and dancers are proverbial: fr. 32
M. *stulte saltatum te inter venisse cinaedos*, 'Like a fool you've come to dance among the
cinaedi'; and the boast of Periplectomenus at Plaut. *Miles* 668, *tum ad saltandum non
cinaedus malacus aequest atque ego*, 'In dancing no *cinaedus* is as supple as I am'. The
Oxford Latin Dictionary glosses *cinaedus* as 'a man of effeminate or luxurious habits'.

[129] Juvenal 12.39: *vestem purpuream, teneris quoque Maecenatibus aptam*, 'a crimson
robe, fit even for the likes of the effeminate Maecenas'; cf. Martial 10.73.

[130] Augustus' letter, ap. Macrob. *Sat.* 2.4.12 = *Epistula* 32, in Imp. Caesar Augustus,
Operum Fragmenta, ed. Malcovati.[5]

[131] Suet. *Nero* 38.2: *turris Maecenatiana*.

[132] e.g. Suet. *D. Aug.* 72.2, *Tib.* 15.1.

[133] *Vina Maecenatiana*, Pliny *NH* 14.67.

[134] Pliny *NH* 8.170 (attempt to introduce a new dainty: young donkey).

[135] Dio Cassius 54.30.5; Plut. *Amat.* 427.

[136] See pp. 22, 25 below.

[137] Of Verres, Cic. *Verr.* 5.33; of Catiline, Cic. *Cat.* 2.23; of Antony, *Phil.* 2.67 etc. Cicero
likes to associate dicing with *mimi* and *lenones* and *adulteri*: e.g. *Verr.* 2.1.33; *Catil.* 2.23;
Phil. 8.26.

[138] Hor. *Odes* 2.7.25; Prop. 2.24.13; 4.8.45; Ovid, *Ars* 2.205. It would not be unfair to say
that the Propertian and Ovidian passages associate dicing with just the same things as
Cicero does; Horace goes no further than drunkenness.

popular, Greek in inspiration,[139] and (of course) forbidden by the law.[140] Augustus himself was fond of dicing,[141] not restricting himself to the permitted period of the *Saturnalia*, nor avoiding publicity, but giving stake-money to his guests to enable them to play. It is interesting here to observe not only that (as usual) the poets are seen to be assuming the background which was real in life, but also that we have here another example of something not ceasing to happen because it was against the law. The importance of this will become clear later.[142]

As important as any of these aspects of luxury and pleasure is, of course, music. We need not here go into the controversial question how far an indigenous music ever existed at Rome, free of Greek influence; but it is clear that in the late Republic and early Empire the music favoured by the upper class was effectively a branch of the international Hellenistic art. G. Wille, whose book *Musica Romana* (1967) is not inclined to exaggerate Greek influence,[143] shows that Roman *Tafelmusik* was in origin a Greek innovation, just as Roman theatrical music was heavily indebted to Hellenistic practice. So of course were dancing and instrumental music, and one need hardly labour the point in connection with the *Carmen Saeculare* of Horace.

Before coming to the *meretrices* and other girls, it may be well to approach the problem of the life of luxury at Rome from another angle. This is provided by the existence of the epitaphs of a large number of servants of the Imperial household; from these we can form an idea of the staff of a wealthy Roman family of the Augustan period. This evidence, while it is terse and limited, has the advantage that it is not open to the charge of being a literary commonplace merely; these people existed.

The reader of these inscriptions[144] is at once struck by what Weaver calls 'the almost absurdly minute differentiation of duties that seems to have been characteristic of the Palatine establishment'.[145] The number of slaves and freedmen is very large, and even so represents only a fraction of the household,[146] and their titles denote clearly defined duties. The great majority of their names are Greek; in the case of these slaves, it

---

[139] 'In all classes of Roman society gambling and gaming (*alea*) were favourite relaxations, borrowed in every one of their many forms from the Greeks', J.P.V.D. Balsdon, *Life and Leisure* 154.

[140] We are not well informed about the laws on gaming: cf. *RE*, s.v. *alea*, 1359; Denniston on Cic., *Phil.* 2.56. Horace in one of his puritanical poems calls it *vetita legibus alea*, *Odes* 3.24.58, 'the dice which are forbidden by law'.

[141] Suet. *D. Aug.* 71. The chapter goes on to quote letters of Augustus on the subject of his gaming.

[142] cf. p. 24f. below.

[143] 'It sets out to redress the imbalance in favour of Greek music, which has tended to eclipse the Roman achievements,' says E.K. Borthwick in his review (*CR* n.s. 19 (1969) 343). Cf. his pp. 413, 105, 190ff., 218.

[144] *CIL* 6.3926-4326, *columbarium* of Livia; 4327-4413, *familia* of the children of Nero Drusus; 4414-4880, *familia* of Marcella; 4881-5178, 5179-5538, 5539-5678, others of Tiberian and Claudian date; 8639-9101, *officiales ex familia Augusta*. Some names also turn up elsewhere.

[145] P.R.C. Weaver, *Familia Caesaris* (1972) 6.

is not necessary to go into the vexed question how far, in the population at large, a Greek name meant an Eastern origin.[147] The point is that such people, whether or not they were of Greek blood, naturally bore Greek names – because the skills and the refinement they practised were felt to be Greek. Moreover we must remember that Augustus claimed to live a modest, old-fashioned domestic life, and that this claim was not thought absurd;[148] it must follow that the state of affairs revealed by these inscriptions cannot be very greatly different from that in other eminent families of the time.[149]

In an appendix to this chapter I list more than a hundred posts which we know to have been held, in the reigns of Augustus and Tiberius, by at least one person with a Greek name. In many cases we know of more than one, e.g. jewellers, *aurifices*. The evidence is not complete.[150] The point of the list is to give an idea of the number of contexts in which an Augustan grandee found himself in constant and intimate contact with Greek or Hellenized servants; for any refined or skilful service, from the wardrobe to the archives and from the cup-bearer to the doctor, this must have been overwhelmingly the rule. Reflection on this fact will suggest its importance for the question of Greek influence on Augustan literature. It is one aspect, which happens to be demonstrable by us, of 'la société tout hellenisée'[151] in which these poets lived. We return now to the life of love and its presentation in poetry. Influential voices say that poetical treatment is quite separate from real life; the argument here advanced is that it is not. Wilhelm Kroll gave a masterly and underrated survey of these matters,[152] emphasising the presence and importance in Rome since at least 160 B.C. of Greek courtesans and boys. Apart from general

---

[146] e.g. Augustus himself is not adequately represented.

[147] In opposition to the view of Tenney Frank and Kajanto (recently in *Latomus* 27 (1968) 517-34), that all Greek *cognomina* show Eastern provenance, L.R. Taylor argued that they showed servile origin only (*AJP* 82 (1961) 127). Probably H. Chantraine is right to take the 'resigned view' that the preponderance of Greek names is an indication of Eastern origin for most of these people, but that for individual cases certainty is impossible (*Freigelassene und Sklaven im Dienst der röm. Kaiser* (1967) 135). But in the cases here dealt with the special skills greatly add to the likelihood of Eastern extraction.

[148] Suet. *D. Aug.* 73 on the *parsimonia* of his furniture; Tacitus *Ann.* 5.1: *sanctitas domus priscum ad morem*, 'the old-fashioned modesty of his household'. This is not all hindsight in the light of later excesses. Augustus' women-folk made his clothes, and his daughter was given an austere upbringing (Suet. *D. Aug.* 64).

[149] Rightly emphasised by G. Boulvert, *Esclaves et affranchis impériaux* (1970) 24; cf. Weaver, op. cit. (n.145) 228.

[150] Thus we have a *praepositus cellariis* but not a *cellarius. Aurifices*: CIL 6.3927 Zeuxis; 3943 Hedys; 3944 Agathopus; 3946 Epythycanus; 3590 Protogenes.

[151] P. Boyancé in *Entretiens Hardt* 2 (1956), 170. This essay on Propertius handles the question of Greek influence with much more subtlety than it sometimes receives. In the same volume p. 250, L.P. Wilkinson: 'Educated Romans lived in a half-Greek social atmosphere.'

[152] W. Kroll, op. cit. (n.31) 160ff.: 'Das Liebesleben.' Also P. Grimal, *L'Amour à Rome* (1963); A. La Penna, *Orazio e la morale mondana europea* (1969) 91ff.: 'Vita galante della capitale.'

statements that this was so,[153] in our fragmentary evidence, Lucilius presents us with Hymnis and Collyra and Cretaea and Lamia and Bitto[154] on the distaff side, and Gentius and Macedo and Agrion[155] among the boys; both heterosexual and homosexual intrigues and scandal bulk large in his fragments,[156] as does the excessive vogue for Greek things, customs and language, one of his commonest subjects of ridicule,[157] although of course Lucilius himself was thoroughly steeped in every form of Greek culture.[158] The youthful Sulla received a useful legacy from Nicopolis;[159] Cicero makes great play in the *Verrines* with Verres' mistress Chelidon;[160] later we cannot doubt the historical reality or the effectiveness of Cytheris, mistress of Antony and of Gallus, with whom Cicero once found himself dining.[161] It is from our point of view interesting that she was a poetical figure too, being the heroine of Gallus' elegies.[162] No doubt Acme, in Catullus 45, is such another freedwoman. 'These relationships form the background for the fully developed love-poetry of the time,' wrote Kroll,[163] and it is hard not to feel that such a view is almost inevitable.

Yet Gordon Williams is sure that 'the erotic themes of these poems have nothing to do with Horace's real life',[164] and Nisbet and Hubbard know that Horace's own love affairs involved only 'compliant *scorta*' who were 'totally unlike' the glamorous ladies of the *Odes*.[165] As for all the poems on homosexual liaisons, these are 'imaginative compositions that have no connection with real life',[166] and a 'conventional motif from Greek erotic poetry', which 'should not be over-literally interpreted',[167] while the pretty Lycidas of Horace *C*.1.4 'suggests the fantasies of Greek symposiastic verse.'[168] Why not also the realities of Graeco-Roman symposiastic life?

[153] cf. e.g. Cichorius, *Untersuchungen zu Lucilius*, 161.

[154] Fr. 888; 894; 940; 1115; 1193; 517; 925; 1065 Marx.

[155] Fr. 272-5 Marx. These were their real names, according to Apuleius, *Apol.* 10.

[156] e.g. fr. 72; 418-20; 730; 851-69; 1058.

[157] e.g. fr. 88ff. (Albucius); 15-6; 184-8.

[158] Cichorius, op. cit. (n.153) 48 speaks of his 'thorough immersion in Hellenic education, scholarship, and attitudes'. The exclusive emphasis on Callimachus as a source, in M. Puelma-Piwonka, *Lucilius und Kallimachos* (1949), seems to me much too one-sided.

[159] Plut. *Sulla* 2. She was 'a harlot, but wealthy'.

[160] Cic. *Verr.* 1.104 etc. According to Cicero, she was the real power during Verres' praetorship. In Sicily he consoled himself with one Tertia, significantly the daughter of a mime-actor named Isidorus, *Verr.* 2.3.78; 5.31.

[161] *ad Fam.* 9.26.

[162] She was said to have recited the sixth Eclogue of Virgil: Serv. in *Buc.* 6.11. G. Wille, *Musica Romana* 226, accepts the story.

[163] *Kultur der ciceronischen Zeit* 2.45.

[164] G. Williams in *JRS* 52 (1962) 42.

[165] op. cit. 73.

[166] Williams, *Tradition and Originality* 556.

[167] Nisbet-Hubbard 15, 71.

[168] *Critical Essays on Roman Literature: Elegy and Lyric*, ed. J.P. Sullivan (1962) 194.

One is reminded by these edifying views of Prosper Mérimée's judgment on Baudelaire. When *Les Fleurs du Mal* was threatened, in 1857, with prosecution for obscenity, Mérimée was asked to use his influence to prevent it. Declining to intervene, he wrote urbanely: 'A book called *Fleurs du Mal*, very second-rate, not at all dangerous, which contains a few sparks of poetry – such as can be found in a poor boy who is ignorant of life, and who is tired of it because a grisette has deceived him. I don't know the author, but I'd bet my bottom dollar that he's still a virgin and quite a decent fellow.'[169] At this time Baudelaire was thirty-six and had been living for fifteen years a life of 'luxury, frivolity, and dissipation;'[170] for fifteen years he had been suffering from a venereal disease.[171] The respectable have learned not to be shocked by erotic poets, but perhaps it is no less of a temptation to believe that 'really' they are good bourgeois all the time. The private life of the Latin love poets will have borne little resemblance to that of a modern scholar.

A cornerstone in the argument is the interpretation of Catullus 16:

Pedicabo ego uos et irrumabo,
Aureli pathice et cinaede Furi,
Qui me ex uersiculis meis putastis,
Quod sunt molliculi, parum pudicum.
Nam castum esse decet pium poetam
Ipsum, uersiculos nihil necesse est,
Qui tum denique habent salem ac leporem,
Si sunt molliculi ac parum pudici,
Et quod pruriat incitare possunt,
Non dico pueris, sed his pilosis
Qui duros nequeunt mouere lumbos.
Vos, quei milia multa basiorum
Legistis, male me marem putatis?
Pedicabo ego uos et irrumabo.

'I'll bugger you and stuff you,
Effeminate Aurelius and Furius the pervert:
You've judged from my verse that I'm immodest –
My verses being rather saucy.
No: a self-respecting poet should be decent
Himself – there's no rule about his verses.
They lack all wit and spice
Unless they're rather saucy and immodest,
And can arouse a bit of a thrill
Not just in boys but in those hairy fellows
Who can barely move their stiff old loins.
You, having read about many thousand kisses,
Think I'm less than a man, do you?
I'll bugger you and stuff you.'

[169] *Correspondance générale* 8.365.
[170] Cf. E. Starkie, *Baudelaire* (1957) 367.
[171] ibid. 108.

Of this poem, our writers say: 'Catullus replies that a poet uses an autobiographical form but that this is poetic license and no evidence for his life. This plea becomes a commonplace with Roman poets, and it will sufficiently protect the conqueror of the Cimbri'[172] (sc. Q. Lutatius Catulus, who composed paederastic epigrams based on – not 'translated from'[173] – Hellenistic models). Is there not a *petitio principii* involved in relying upon one 'poetic commonplace' as truthful and reliable, in order to show up other poetical utterances as conventional and unreal?[174] And in any case Catullus' answer to the slander of which he complains is to threaten drastic homosexual chastisement – which shows that the charge was not homosexual love as such, but effeminacy.[175] To this alone could such a threat, however humorous, be a rebuttal.

The same procedure seems detectable also in the use of Horace, *Satires* 1.2 in order to show that 'in real life' the poet had to do only with 'compliant *scorta*', not with the more glamorous and capricious girls of the *Odes*. For that poem is itself just as literary as the *Odes*; its theme seems to have been handled by Lucilius,[176] and is in any case Hellenistic. In fact, the resemblance between lines 105ff. and Callimachus, *Epigram* 1 GP, and between lines 125ff. and Cercidas 5.31f. is actually closer than is Horace's practice with his models in the *Odes*.

In the case of Catullus, we see the poet evading an irritating charge by means of a deft, handy and humorous literary expedient, which does not seem to lend itself to being treated as the touchstone for his whole poetic output. In that of Horace, the genre of his *Satires* called for the expression of attitudes at once more earthy and more didactic than the *Odes*,[177] and it is as arbitrary to use the *Satires* to undercut the *Odes* as it would be to use the *Odes* to blot out (as used to be done in some quarters) the ugly aspects of the *Satires*. In the *Odes*, experience is stylised in a different mode. There, as in Greek lyric, gods intervene personally; there, following Greek stories, the infancy of Horace is presented as a symbolic

[172] Williams in *JRS* 52 (1962) 40, quoted with approval by Nisbet-Hubbard 71; cf. also *Tradition and Originality* 555.

[173] So Williams, *JRS* 52 (1962) 40, 'the epigram of Callimachus of which this is a translation.' In fact, Catulus, *Epigram* 1 Morel stands to Callimachus 4 Gow-Page, as Catullus 70 stands to Callimachus 11.

[174] 'The poem *Odes* 4.10 to Ligurinus is consequently imaginary', Williams, op. cit. 41.

[175] *male ... marem*. Cf. Tac. *Ann.* 11.2.2, Valerius Asiaticus, accused of effeminacy, retorts to his accuser: 'Ask your sons, Suillius; they will admit that I am a man.' This illustrates the nature of *mollitia* (Catullus vs. 4 *versiculis meis ... quod sunt molliculi*), and also what was, and what was not, felt as really degrading. Boys and girls are offered at the same price in Pompeii – and with Greek names, too: *CIL* 4.4592: *Eutychis Graeca moribus bellis assibus II*; ibid. 4024: *Menander bellis moribus assibus II*. Cf. also nos. 2189, 2191, 2268, 2273, 2278, 2450, 4150, 4441, 5338, 5345.

[176] In *Satire* 29: cf. Cichorius, op. cit. (n.153) 157ff., with the corrections of E. Fraenkel, *Festschrift für R. Reitzenstein* (1931) 121ff.

[177] See U. Knoche, 'Erlebnis und dichterischer Ausdruck in der lateinischen Poesie', *Gymnasium* 65 (1958) 146-65.

statement of his poetical vocation,[178] in contrast with the homely details of his schooling in the *Satires*.[179] But Horace *did* believe in his vocation, certainly no less, perhaps more, than in the importance of the details of his school. And the *vie galante* of Rome is not dissolved into unreality when it is shown that it too contained Greek aspects and elements.[180]

For again we must emphasise that not only does literature imitate life, but also life imitates literature.[181] Young Romans read Menander and Terence, who took for granted the cultivated *meretrix* and the life of pleasure. Those who were poets were impressed by the erotic poetry of Callimachus and Meleager; the myths, at least since Euripides, had more and more taken on an erotic character. They lived surrounded by the apparatus of pleasure, itself Greek or professing to be so;[182] like Naples, Athens[183] and the rest, Rome itself offered unlimited opportunities.[184] The picture which Lucilius and Catullus allow us to glimpse, of a *jeunesse dorée* living in a round of parties, affairs, quarrels, jealousies, with some music and poetry – the whole not incompatible with a political career, as we see from men like Calvus, Cornificius and Helvius Cinna[185] – is just like that which Sallust ascribes to the circle of Catiline, which we find being lived by Sulla, and which Cicero palliates in the case of M. Caelius Rufus, but excoriates in that of Antony. It also is the life which is described in the *Satires* and *Epodes*[186] of Horace, and which in the *Odes* and in the elegies of Propertius is, in two different

---

[178] In *Odes* 3.4. Cf. A. La Penna, op. cit. (n.152) 7ff.: 'Una autobiografia quasi simbolica.'

[179] *Sat.* 2.6.

[180] The contrary view seems to involve saying that the Romans did not understand their own literature. Valerius Maximus 8.1.8 tells of Valerius Valentinus, who lost a law-suit because the jury were disgusted by a poem (quite irrelevant to the case), 'in which with poetic freedom he said he had debauched a boy and a girl of respectable family'. (Cichorius 343 dates the case *c.* 111 B.C.) The plea which must 'sufficiently protect the conqueror of the Cimbri' seems in this case to have been unavailing; and later poets seem not to have taken warning from it. When Ovid, in his exile, harps on the distinction between his poetry and his morals (*Trist.* 1.9.59; 2.353ff.; 3.2.5.; *ex Ponto* 2.7.47; 4.8.19), we detect the pressing motive. Before his disaster, he was proud to call himself *ille ego nequitiae Naso poeta meae*, 'Naso, the poet of my own naughtiness'. (*Am.* 2.1.2): is one more 'real' than the other? If so, which?

[181] The point is not missed by Boyancé, *Entretiens Fondation Hardt* 2 (1956), 169ff., 195.

[182] As London courtesans in the nineteenth century might have French *noms de guerre*, and Swedish ones today.

[183] Where Cicero's son, for example, took to a life of dissipation.

[184] *Tot tibi tamque dabit formosas Roma puellas / 'haec habet' ut dicas 'quidquid in orbe fuit'* ... *Quot caelum stellas, tot habet tua Roma puellas*, Ovid, *Ars* 1.55ff.: a rewarding passage. ('Rome will offer you so many beautiful girls that you'll say it has everything in the world. Girls in Rome are as numerous as the stars in the sky'). The commentators point to the parallel of Alexandria, cf. Herodas 1.26ff. and Headlam ad loc.

[185] D. van Berchem, 'Cynthia ou la carrière contrariée,' *Mus. Helv.* 5 (1948) 148 points this out; and also that Catullus himself, like Propertius' friend Tullus, took at least the first step in such a career by going out to a province in the *cohors* of a governor.

[186] See *Epodes* 8, 11, 12, 13, 14, 15; *Sat.* 1.2, 2.2, 2.3, etc.

modes, stylised and raised to high poetry, removing what would be too specific and particular, and creating a consistent poetic atmosphere.

The seventeenth Ode of Horace's first book can serve here as an example, as it is taken by Nisbet and Hubbard as evidently unreal: 'We must not think of Tyndaris as an actual person ... rather, she is a dream figure, belonging to the world of Alexandrian pastoral.' They cite as an example of the pastoral background the epigram by Nicaenetus, no. 4 GP: another similar passage is [Theocritus] 8.55. But even Hellenistic poetry relates to life, and the same sensibility comes in a story told by Phylarchus of Ptolemy II: old and gouty, he saw through the window some poor Egyptians making their meal by the river, producing the simplest foods and lying at ease on the sand. 'He cried out, "Unlucky devil that I am! To think that I cannot even be one of those fellows!"' [187] Ptolemy was the patron of poets: the picnics which took place in reality appear, stylised and refined, in verse. *Odes* 1.17 opens with a charming picture of Faunus/Pan coming from Arcadia to look after Horace's flocks on his estate. The third stanza gives the name of the addressee, Tyndaris; after a fourth stanza, on his own divine inspiration and protection as a poet, Horace invites her to enjoy the delights of his valley, to drink and sing, free from the violent attentions of Cyrus. What does Tyndaris' name convey? There were real women with the name,[188] but here it surely evokes the mythical daughters of Tyndareus, whom Aphrodite made 'bigamous and adulterous and foresakers of their men' (Stesichorus fr. 223 P): both Helen and Clytemnestra left their men. And this Tyndaris is to leave Cyrus for Horace; hence perhaps the name. She is to drink and to sing: her song will be of two women contending for one man, a sly reversal of the present situation.

Is this musical *fête champêtre* a transparent fiction? I think it is not, and that we can trace it through a less exalted stylisation to reality. In *Odes* 2.11.13ff. the situation recurs:

cur non sub alta vel platano vel hac
pinu iacentes sic temere et rosa
canos odorati capillos
dum licet, Assyriaque nardo

potamus uncti?

'Why not stretch out beneath the tall plane tree or this pine, without fuss, anoint our grey hair with perfume while we can, and drink?' – and fetch Lyde, that choice *scortum*, with her lyre. Here we are less grand: here alone in the *Odes* the low word *scortum* appears, and the country setting is not adorned with gods. Yet the ingredients are all the same: a

[187] Phylarchus *FGrH* 81 F. 40, ap. Athen. 536e: trans. Loeb.
[188] Thus *CIL* 4.5090 (Pompeii): probably no better than she ought to have been.

girl, music, drink, in the country. We come down to realism in Ovid's account of the holiday in honour of Anna Perenna, *Fasti* 3.523ff.: on the banks of the Tiber,

> *plebs venit ac virides passim disiecta per herbas*
> *potat, et accumbit cum pare quisque sua.*

'The common people come and lie about on the grass and drink, each man stretched out with his girl.' They too have their music, 535:

> *illic et cantant quicquid didicere theatris*
> *et iactant faciles ad sua verba manus ...*

'There they sing the songs they have picked up in the theatres, and wave their arms about in time with the words.' This unromantic and plebeian scene is, presumably, 'realistic' enough, and shows that one could have a picnic in Augustan Italy without becoming a poetical fiction. The motif is burlesqued in the *Epodes*, in line with the tough tone of that collection of poems (*Epode* 2.23ff.), developed more sentimentally by Tibullus (2.5.95ff.):

> *tunc operata deo pubes discumbet in herba,*
> *arboris antiquae qua levis umbra cadit*

'Then the young people will make their offerings to the god and lie on the grass, where the shadow falls of an aged tree,' and treated in different ways in the two *Odes*.[189] In 1.17 Virgilian allusions raise the tone and provide the god (Faunus comes from *Georgic* 1.16): Horace invites Tyndaris into a country equipped with Virgilian deities, in which it is natural for him to speak of his own poetic inspiration and protection. The gentle humour of the end ('I am nicer than Cyrus') gives a characteristically Horatian irony to the close. The poem, then, is not a fantasy in no relation to life, a 'dream', but a stylised and refined version of reality.[190]

A second example may be Horace's poems on the theme of the amorous ageing woman. In *Epodes* 8 and 12 it is developed with ferocious obscenity, in accordance with the Archilochian *animi* emulated in the iambic poems; in the *Odes* with urbanity and irony (2.25; 3.15; 4.13), avoiding obscene words. Nisbet and Hubbard, on *Odes* 1.24, say: 'of

---

[189] It is also adjacent to a 'philosophical' theme, that of 'simple food in simple surroundings': e.g. Augustus' boasts of his simple country fare, Suet. *D. Aug.* 76, and Seneca *Epp.* 87, *culcita in terra iacet, ego in culcita ... de prandio nihil detrahi potuit ...* 'the mattress lay on the ground, and I lay on the mattress'.

[190] H.P. Syndikus, *Die Lyrik des Horaz* (1972) 188, who does not deal with the *fête champêtre* theme, yet rightly says of the poem that it rests on reality but, rather than simply representing it, raises it to the level of art.

course, the unreality of the situation is obvious ...' By contrast, A. La Penna inclines to believe that Horace when young and poor had to undergo with wealthy women of a certain age the experiences he evokes so repulsively in the *Epodes*.[191] This would help to explain Horace's obsession with the subject; for after all the discovery of literary parallels is only the beginning, not the end, of an answer to the question.[192] Roman society contained such ladies, and a cruel use is made of the charge by Cicero against Clodia in the speech *pro Caelio* 36. The poems versify and transmute reality.

Williams suggests that 'licentious mixed parties were unusual at Rome';[193] the overwhelming balance of the evidence seems to me to be that on the contrary they were very common. A poem like Horace, *Odes* 1.27, for example, is thus to be seen rather differently from the way it is seen by some recent interpreters. 'The setting is Greek and the element of reality negligible,' writes one;[194] from our present point of view the distinction and the inference both seem misleading. Cicero professes some self-consciousness at dining with so very notorious a woman as Cytheris, but this seems to be only because of his own age and status; and, consoling himself with the stock parallel of Aristippus, he goes on: 'It's the party I enjoy.' There is no reason to suppose that Atticus, who was also present, felt any embarrassment.[195]

As for homosexual relationships in poetry and in life, one of the chief arguments used by those who regard the poems as 'unreal' is that at Rome such practices were 'the object of penal legislation'.[196] I do not find this such an obstacle as do its proponents. We have seen the light-hearted way in which Augustus himself disregarded the laws about dicing; he was not less complaisant about the affair of Maecenas with the actor Bathyllus.[197] The dourness of Augustus' morality can in any case be exaggerated. In the triumviral period he had been both target and author of highly improper lampoons; after Actium, Antony made an appeal to him, 'reminding him of their friendship and kinship ... and recounting all

---

[191] op. cit. (n.152) 17f.

[192] F. Cairns, *Generic Composition* 89 thinks *Odes* 1.25 is a *kōmos* and means 'therefore let me in now, before it's too late': ('since no other hypothesis gives Horace a reason for saying what he says to Lydia, it may be presumed ...'). This will surely be one of the curiosities of scholarship; did anyone ever hope to soften a girl's heart by telling her that soon, tortured by unsatisfied lust, she will be vainly accosting men in the street? The inadequacy of the generic method to answer all questions about these poets is here strikingly apparent ('since no other hypothesis gives Horace a reason ...'). Cf. Chapter Three.

[193] *JRS* 52 (1962) 41.

[194] *Critical Essays on Roman Literature: Elegy and Lyric*, ed. J.P. Sullivan (1962) 188.

[195] Cic., *ad Fam* 10.26.

[196] *JRS* 52 (1962) 40. One notes that the jurors at the trial of Clodius were swayed, according to Cicero, not only by 'nights with certain women', but also by 'introductions to aristocratic youths', (*ad Att.* 1.16.5).

[197] Tac. *Ann* 1.54.3, cf. R. Syme, *Roman Revolution* 342; Dio Cassius 54.17.5.

the amorous adventures and youthful pranks which they had shared together.'[198] The few fragments we have of Augustus' letters show him addressing Maecenas as 'mattress of the adulteresses' and Horace as 'purissimus penis'.[199] The grimness of the end of the reign, when Maecenas was dead and the Julias had disgraced the family, is not to be reflected back to its beginning. As Suetonius puts it (*D. Aug.* 69), 'Not even his friends deny that he was an adulterer.' Moral legislation at Rome was in any case much easier to enact than to enforce. Philosophers and *rhetores* were expelled from Rome in 161, *rhetores latini* in 92: but 'the edict remained ineffectual'.[200] The sad history of the sumptuary laws makes the point only too clear. Aulus Gellius 2.24 and Macrobius, *Sat.* 3.17 list the laws which attempted to outlaw extravagant living at Rome. Lucilius ridiculed that of Fannius,[201] and urged the evasion of that of Licinius;[202] Sulla breached his own laws on the subject;[203] the law of Antius Restio, says Macrobius sadly, was rendered ineffectual by the 'obstinacy of luxury and the concerted resistance of the vicious'; Caesar as dictator had to admit the failure of his own sumptuary laws.[204] Even the matrimonial legislation of Augustus, which so impresses modern writers, was carried with difficulty and enforced without much success.[205] Propertius might well feel that he was quite right to have said (2.7.5) that Augustus had no power over the heart:

'At magnus Caesar.' sed magnus Caesar in armis:
   devictae gentes nil in amore valent.

' "But Caesar is mighty," you will say. 'Yes, but he is mighty in arms: the conquest of nations has no effect on love".' It was easier to conquer the world than to fly in the face of fashion.[206]

---

[198] Suet. *D. Aug.* 69; Martial 11.20 = Augustus, *Carmen* 4 ed. Malcovati. (Martial, no mean judge, is impressed by the *Romana simplicitas* of Augustus' obscene verses); Cassius Dio 51.8.1, trans. Cary (Loeb). It is not easy to see when this would have been invented, if not true.

[199] *Epistulae* fr. 32, ed. Malcovati; ib. fr. 41.

[200] Schanz-Hosius 1.210.

[201] *Fanni centussis misellus*, fr. 1172M.

[202] *legem vitemus Licini*, fr. 1200.

[203] Plut. *Sulla* 35.

[204] Cic. *Att* 13.7.1: Caesar announces his intention to stay in Rome, 'so that his laws should not be disregarded in his absence, as his sumptuary law had been'.

[205] P.A. Brunt, *Italian Manpower* 558ff.: the Lex Julia apparently, although it aroused bitter resentment, did not have the effect intended; and even after the law of A.D. 9, 'the copious testimony to the later prevalence of celibacy and childlessness attests its continuing failure' (565).

[206] Two more examples: the decree of the Senate in A.D. 15 that pantomimes might only be performed publicly, not in private houses. 'This soon became a dead letter,' Friedländer, *Roman Life and Manners* 2.110. And (G. Wille, *Musica Romana* 219): 'the censors of 115 B.C. banned foreign music from Rome; in the following year, M. Junius Silanus and Q. Curtius struck a coin with a cithara on one side ...'. M.H. Crawford (*RRC* no. 285) dates the coin to 116 or 115; the contrast is perhaps not much less striking, even so.

The lack of adequate police or other means of enforcing such laws was no doubt part of the reason for their failure, but it must also have been true that public opinion, whatever moralists might say, did not really want them enforced. When we reflect that the authors of sumptuary legislation included Sulla and Caesar, two men notorious for debt, extravagance and profligacy, and that prominent among the moralists was the plutocratic and shady figure of Sallust, we can perhaps understand that there was a good deal of insincerity about the whole thing. The old Lex Scantinia on homosexuality was indeed invoked 'as a weapon in political manoeuvres between Caelius and Appius Claudius in 50 B.C.',[207] but then the law on high treason, *perduellio*, was invoked against C. Rabirius in 63, and that had been a dead letter for generations;[208] and perusal of the letter in which Caelius describes his own affair to Cicero does not convey a sense of the majesty of the Lex Scantinia, or of its serious application.[209] In the political prosecutions of the end of the Republic, anything went.

We have seen that the poets cheerfully confess to dicing and luxury, laws or no laws, and we have found that in this they were true to their society. The same is, I think, true of their allusions to pederasty. Before proceeding to positive evidence, I draw attention to the tendency in some academic minds to be excessively impressed by codes of law, and to infer that what is forbidden does not happen. This touching belief led, for example, Sydney and Beatrice Webb, writing in 1934, to form a view of Stalin's Russia not entirely in accordance with the facts;[210] it would have led a trusting enquirer into the *Statuta et Decreta* of the University of Oxford (*si parva licet componere magnis*) in recent years to an equally misleading view of affairs in that body.[211]

---

[207] Williams, *Tradition and Originality* 551.

[208] cf. Mommsen, *Staatsrecht* 618. Heitland comments gruffly (edn. of Cic. *pro C. Rabirio* (1884), 9): 'It is clear that this antiquated form of trial was revived simply as a convenient means of securing a triumph for the so-called "popular" party.'

[209] *ad Fam.* 8.12.3, 'The shameless wretches arranged for me to be summoned under the Lex Scantinia at the end of my Circus Games. The moment Pola uttered the words I announced a charge against Appius the Censor under the same law. I never saw anything make such a hit ...'

[210] S. and B. Webb, *Soviet Communism: A New Civilization?* (1935): on the question, Is Stalin a Dictator?: 'First let it be noted that, unlike Mussolini, Hitler, and other modern dictators, Stalin is not invested by law with any authority over his fellow citizens ... He has not even the extensive power which the American Constitution entrusts for four years to every successive president. ... In this pattern individual dictatorship has no place' (431-3). On the purges, 'Every decision regarding a Party member must be concisely "motivated", and the minute has to be accompanied by documentary evidence of the charges. ... There is, from every decision, an effective right of appeal. ... This appeal may be pursued right up to the Central Cleansing Committee in Moscow ...' (381). And: 'the constitution of the USSR provides for the active participation of the people in the work of government in more than one way' (3).

[211] It appears from the *Statuta* for 1963, for example, that in that year members of the University of Oxford could be punished for failing to step out of the path of the holder of a

The evidence collected by Kroll,[212] and indeed by Nisbet and Hubbard,[213] strongly suggests that relations with boys, provided they were not *ingenui*, were both very common and very lightly viewed. Kroll points to the number of jokes and allusions to the subject in Plautus, to the vocabulary of abuse in Catullus, to the regularity of accusations and scandal of this sort in the late Republic, and to the evidence of Pompeian inscriptions. Insufficient consideration has been paid also to his citation of the entry in the excellent Praenestine calendar,[214] of Augustan date, for 25 April: *Festus est puerorum lenoniorum quia proximus superior meretricum est*: that is, boys employed in male prostitution had their own holiday, and this was duly recorded in the State calendar. We have only to try to imagine a public festival, say, for adulterous matrons, to see what the Roman state really thought criminal.[215] The index to Volume 6 of *CIL* lists from the inscriptions of the city of Rome no less than twenty-eight men named Paederos, a statistic hard to reconcile with a public opinion which really condemned such loves. In such a society the poets write sometimes of the love of boys; a society in which Maecenas was the subject of scandal for his relations with Bathyllus, and in which Horace wrote a poem to him introducing that name in a way which must have been meant to be obvious to all those in the know (*Epode* 14).[216] Horace accuses himself of *mille puellarum, puerorum mille furores* 'a thousand crazy passions for boys, a thousand for girls',[217] and in that one of the *Sermones* which is sometimes taken to reveal his 'real' ideas, lumps the two sexes blandly together.[218] As for the final argument,[219] that the homosexual poems are shown to be unreal because they lack 'inner emotional life' and are less passionate than those on

---

higher degree; that 'walking idly in the street' was also a punishable offence; that all undergraduates must be in their Colleges by nine o'clock, and might not enter any building where alcohol or tobacco was sold; that the University officers had power to enter the houses of the citizens at any hour of the day or night, to see if members of the University were there improperly; that *gladiatorum spectacula* might be given in Oxford only with the consent of the Vice-Chancellor, who might imprison *gladiatores* who contravened this; and so on. All this, needless to say, was the merest fantasy.

[212] *Die Kultur der ciceronischen Zeit* 177 ff.

[213] op. cit. 71: after declaring that, in *Odes* 1.4, 'the homosexual implication has no bearing on Sestius' actual behaviour, but is a conventional motif derived from Greek poetry', they go on: 'In fact, the practice was widespread (Cic. *Cael.* 6-9, *RE* 11.905f.), and at least where slave boys were concerned seems to have provoked little censure ...'

[214] *CIL* 1², p. 236 = *Inscriptiones Italiae* 13.2.17, of A.D. 6-9. *Ceteris fastis quos habemus hi Praenestini et magnitudine lapidum quibus inscripti sunt et copia rerum adnotatarum longe praestant*, Degrassi p. 141.

[215] cf. the curious anecdote in Valerius Maximus 8.1.12.

[216] It is notable that his commentators largely ignore this: nothing in Heinze, Lejay, Tescari, Wickham. But cf. H. Hommel, *Horaz* (1950).

[217] *Sat.* 2.3.325. Cf. Cic. *ad Att.* 1.16.5, quoted in n. 196.

[218] *Sat.* 1.2.117. Ovid has a characteristic reason for liking boys 'less' than women: *Ars* 2.683f.

[219] e.g. Williams, *Tradition and Originality* 553.

women, that is just the aspect of such affairs which the poets claim as their great advantage.[220] To sum up, then: the practice was common in society, it was in reality less disapproved of than people pretended, Maecenas was a subject of scandal for it, boys with Greek and Roman names had appeared in Latin poetry at least since Lucilius, these poets write about it: *but* – it is in them exclusively Hellenistic and literary. The last step seems somehow unexpected, does it not?

The object of this discussion has been to suggest that the relation of literature to life has been distorted by inelastic conceptions of 'the Greek' and 'the Roman'. Of course we are not to start writing a diary of Horace's intrigues: the days have passed when we used to wonder whether Chloe came before or after Glycera, or how to fit together the occasional chronological hints in Propertius. But the central question with Augustan poetry remains that of the degree and manner of its removal from reality; and in this we can make out, in our other sources, a world thoroughly permeated with Hellenistic elements of every sort. They are not transposing the reader into a realm of pure fantasy, but making poetical (and that includes making it more universal, less individual)[221] a mode of life familiar to their readers. That conclusion, if accepted, has its importance for other areas of their poetry.

The reluctance to accept it is perhaps partly due to the disappearance in the modern world of the *demi-monde*, a society with its own etiquette, as distinct from marriage as it was from the drabs who were picked up in the street.[222] In the nineteenth century such women as, to take English examples, Harriette Wilson, the mistress of the Duke of Wellington, and Mary Ann Clarke, the mistress of the Duke of York, were treated, within certain limits, as ladies; except of course that they did not meet gentlemen's wives and sisters. The *Memoirs* of Harriette Wilson[223] provide in many respects an illuminating parallel to these poets. She is fluent in French (Greek the language of love at Rome),[224] she is musical,[225] she loves poetry,[226] and each new affair begins with her

---

[220] Propertius 2.4 fin.; Juvenal 6.34-7; perhaps already in Lucilius (Marx on fr. 866: referred to women instead by Cichorius, *Untersuchungen* 162); boys are less trouble and less demanding than women.

[221] 'The ancients were concerned to suppress the excessively personal elements of their experience, in order to give the most universal value to the expression of their feelings', Van Berchem, *Mus. Helv.* 5 (1958) 138. See also H.P. Syndikus, *Die Lyrik des Horaz* (1972) 1.188f.

[222] Harriette Wilson, *Memoirs* 234, describes her horror at getting accidentally into a position where she is treated in this way: cf. the 'common harlots' with whom Propertius contrasts Cynthia (2.23, 2.24), and the *togatae* recommended by Horace *Sat.* 1.2.82ff.

[223] (Shortened) edition by Lesley Blanch, 1964.

[224] Lucretius 4.1166ff.; Martial 10.68; Juvenal 6.185; Boyancé in *RÉL* 34 (1956) 125.

[225] 'Music I always had a natural talent for. I played well upon the pianoforte' (*Memoirs* 29). Cf. also William Hickey's account of Fanny Temple (*Memoirs of William Hickey*, ed. P. Quennell (1960) 54): 'She was a mistress of music, had an enchanting voice, which she managed with the utmost skill, danced elegantly and spoke French *assez bien* ...' Epitaphs of Roman women with musical skills: G. Wille, *Musica Romana* 218 n.91, and ibid. 316-24.

'falling in love', always with a man of wealth, and proceeds through the cycle of happiness, jealousy, infidelity, reproaches, reconciliation, and rupture, which is both familiar in the poets and also inevitable in life, if love-affairs are to be made significant enough to provide an engrossing way of life for those with the *otium* and the money needed to live it.

In earlier societies the disreputable world was as stratified and as class-conscious as the respectable world on which it lived, and to whose tastes it had to cater. It is wrong to suppose that outside the pale of the married home there was nothing but the gutter, while poets and their readers nourished in the solitude of their imaginations fantasies of something more refined and more exciting. The Roman courtesan was as familiar with Menander as her patron; Cytheris was presentable enough in manners to dine with senators, as her Hellenistic predecessors had been fit to dine with kings. They all acted out together the same conception of the life of pleasure.[227]

As for the question, so vehemently discussed, of the social status of the girls in these poems, what are we to say? For some, Cynthia is obviously a *meretrix*;[228] for others, a married woman.[229] Or perhaps she behaved like a *meretrix* without being one.[230] Did she come from a noble family,[231] or was she a *libertina*,[232] or a foreigner?[233] Or is the question not yet decided?[234] Or does it not really matter?[235] Surely the trouble is that the alternatives are too narrowly conceived and too sharply opposed. The

---

[226] 'I know not how to praise the poet as he merits. Yet few, perhaps, among the most learned, have in their hearts done more honour to some of the natural beauties of Shakespeare than I have' (*Memoirs* 57). Cf. 353, her letters to 'poor dear Lord Byron'. This point is worth dwelling upon because it is often assumed that, in the words of Nisbet and Hubbard (p. 15), 'the blonde and musical girls owe more to the conventions of erotic writing than to the realities of *Venus parabilis*.' If you wanted girls who possessed or simulated musical and poetical interests, it is impossible to doubt that they were forthcoming; just as they were in the *Quartier latin* in the 1850s. Cf. G. Wille, *Musica Romana*, 234ff, 'Horaz in der Musik der Antike.' He believes that Horace's poems were sung; and that for instance *Odes* 4.11.34ff., *condisce modos, amanda/voce quos reddas*, 'learn a song to sing with your charming voice', is to be read in the light of the fact that Horace did in fact teach the choir to sing the *Carmen Saeculare*. As for the blondeness, both hair-dye and wigs feature in the poets (e.g. Nisbet-Hubbard on *Odes* 1.5.3), as they did in life.

[227] Cf. P. Grimal, *L'Amour à Rome*, 153.

[228] E. Burck, *Gymn.* 70 (1963) 89 = *Vom Menschenbild in der röm. Lit.* (1966) 238: 'Propertius 1.4 shows unambiguously that she was a *meretrix*.' So too Camps, edn. of Propertius 1 (1966) 6.

[229] G. Williams, *Tradition and Originality* 528ff. 'As if divorce were not allowed at Rome!' is the comment on this of L. Alfonsi, *Studi Calderini-Paribeni* 1 (1956) 200.

[230] G. Luck, *Gnomon* 34 (1962) 156.

[231] G. Luck, ibid., 'We have in 1.16 reliable evidence that Cynthia was of noble birth'.

[232] F.O. Copley, *Exclusus Amator* = *TAPA* Monograph 17 (1956) 103, 'Delia, like all the women of elegy, was a *liberta*.'

[233] F. Cairns, *Generic Composition* 156, 'Foreigners such as elegiac mistresses ...'

[234] *Adhuc sub iudice lis est*, A. Guillemin, *REL* 18 (1940) 100.

[235] L. Alfonsi, op. cit. (n.224) 199. See now the review of the evidence by F. Della Corte in *ANRW* 30.1 (1982) 550f.

demi-monde did not contain only professionals of low extraction, although it did include them.[236] It also contained amateurs like Catullus' Lesbia, and quasi-amateurs like Praecia the influential mistress of Cethegus,[237] and noble debauchées like Sulla's daughter Fausta[238] and (unless she was framed) Augustus' daughter Julia. There will also have been many women of less clear-cut status, the 'camp-followers of marriage'.[239] This was a great age of divorce, and some divorcées will have swelled the ranks of the available. So will widows, and grass-widows, and dowry-less girls who failed to marry,[240] or whose marriages broke down. The illegitimate, too, will sometimes have lived in this way,[241] and women who had once enjoyed the half-way status of *concubina* but later lost it. Between *libertinae* and prostitutes, between actresses and *meretrices*, even between some professionals and some *matronae*, the dividing line cannot have been so easy to draw as in theory, perhaps, it should have been. Propertius follows up one side of the poetry of Catullus[242] (and, no doubt, of Gallus) in depicting the life of love as deeply serious. Such a conception inevitably demands that the poems should be concerned with one woman, and that the emotions, to be deep, must be painful. Horace did not aim to produce that effect, and so he writes of many different women, and his tone is ironical and oblique, making no show of profound passion. But it is the same life which they both, in their different ways, describe; a life of pleasure, in which the important feminine roles could be played satisfactorily only by sophisticated women. And in Rome such women must either have been of Eastern origin, or have had a veneer of Hellenistic culture.

In conclusion, we must observe again that, as we have seen, our interpretation of other aspects of Augustan poetry will not be unaffected by our view of this one. The reality or unreality of pressure from Augustus and Maecenas to write laudatory epic, for example, will affect our view not only of the *Aeneid* but of all the passages where the poets

---

[236] In poetry, for example, Prop. 2.6, *Non ita complebant Ephyraeae Laidos aedes*, 'The house of Lais in Corinth was not so thronged with lovers', and Horace, *Odes* 2.11.21, *quis devium scortum eliciet domo Lyden?* 'Who will fetch out the choice call-girl Lyde?'

[237] Plut. *Lucullus* 6.

[238] Hor. *Sat.* 1.2.64; cf. Münzer in *RE* s.v. *Cornelius*, nr. 436. Also Fulvia: *RE* s.v. *Fulvius*, nr. 112, 'an aristocratic but utterly immoral woman': Sempronia (Sallust *Catiline* 25), etc.

[239] A phrase used in conversation by Sir Ronald Syme.

[240] Harriette Wilson's friend Julia Johnstone came of a distinguished family but ruined herself by an early indiscretion and lived as a kept mistress.

[241] cf. R. Syme, 'Bastards in the Roman Aristocracy,' *PAPhS* 104 (1960) 323-7. He points out that we hear surprisingly little of such people, who must have existed. It seems not to occur to scholars that Cynthia, if descended from the poet Hostius, might be so by the left hand.

[242] *Entretiens Fondation Hardt* 2 (1956) 27ff., 186ff. L. Alfonsi, *L'elegia di Properzio* (1945) 15ff. shows that the *dolorosa vita dell'amore* is for Propertius less violent and more langorous than in Catullus. Propertius himself regarded the 'neoteric' poets as his predecessors, 2.25.4; 34.85ff., where he lists Varro of Atax, Catullus, Calvus and Gallus.

talk of their desire, or their reluctance, to produce epic. Gordon Williams and Margaret Hubbard, for example, take the view that no such pressure existed.[243] This cannot be fully argued here; but the view I have been defending of the love poems goes naturally with a different interpretation of this matter, too. That is, if they are less remote from life and conventional, then it may seem plausible that on epic, too, the poets are stylising real facts rather than inventing pure 'literature'; that the Princeps, in his thirst for *gloria*, not unnaturally expected such poems as had been produced for the military *res gestae* of Marius, Lucullus, and Caesar;[244] that Callimachean *recusatio*, adapting to a new purpose the *Aetia* prologue, had its great vogue for that reason; that the prologue to the third *Georgic* shows Virgil leading Octavian to believe that he will write it;[245] and that it was only as he came to try that he realised decisively that it was impossible, Maecenas all the time acting as infinitely skilled and tactful interpreter and mediator between poets and Emperor.[246]

Appendix: Some Imperial Servants

I list here the posts in the Imperial household for which I have found at least one holder with a Greek name. By 'household' I mean those in domestic contact with the Imperial family, not for example financial agents in the provinces; I have tried to list all and only those which can with reasonable certainty be dated to the reigns of Augustus and Tiberius. Except where noted, the figures refer to *CIL* 6.

[243] *Tradition and Originality* 102, cited in n.7 above. M.E. Hubbard, *Propertius* 99: the poets 'pretend that Maecenas wanted them to celebrate Augustus' exploits ... That was formal and conventional, and everybody knew it'. She means by 'pressure' something more forcible than I think was applied ('Even after Maecenas' fall the progress of suppression of opinion was not swift ... in the twenties poetry was not yet under pressure ...' (p. 100)). The striking fact remains that in Book 1 of Propertius, where we have no Maecenas, there is no question of writing epic about Augustus, and no mention of Callimachus; but in the first poem of Book 2, addressed to Maecenas, both these things appear at once. Thereafter they tend to remain together in Propertius' work (2.10, 34; 3.1, 3, 9), and until Book 4 Callimachus serves exclusively as a device of *recusatio*. If there was no real question of an epic, the pattern seems to remain inexplicable.

[244] cf. Cicero *pro Archia*, passim. Cicero had to write his poem himself in the end. Some such laudatory epics really were produced: *Annales Belli Gallici* by Furius Bibaculus, *Bellum Sequanicum* by Varro of Atax, etc. Cf. Schanz-Hosius 2.281f.

[245] E. Norden points out, *Kleine Schriften* 399ff., that vv. 16ff. seem to promise the reverse of the *Aeneid*, not a poem on Troy with glimpses forward to Augustus, but a poem on Augustus with glimpses back to Troy; and that Propertius 2.34.61ff. seems to envisage the production by Virgil of *that* poem. The curious manner of the Georgic prologue, at once profuse and evasive, is certainly not against the supposition that the poet was conscious of a considerable difficulty.

[246] See J. Griffin, '*Caesar qui cogere posset*', in *Caesar Augustus*, edd. Millar and Segal (1984).

adiutor a commentariis ornamentorum: 8951, Chrysaor; *adiutor a sacris*: 8717, Theophilus; *aedituus*: 3926, Euphro; *ancilla*: 5239, Galatea; *arcarius*: 3931, Amiantus; *architectus*: 5738, Anicetus; *argentarius*: 8727, Seleucus; *ab argento*: 5539, Philetus; *ad argentum potorium*: 8730, Anthus; *atriensis*: 3942, Antiochus; *avium fartor*: 8849, Cinnamus; *aurifex*: 3951, Stephanus; *praepositus ab auro gemmato*: 8734, Philetaerus; *balnearius*: 8742, Colchus; *a bibliotheca*: 8743, Alexio;[247] *calciator*: 3939, Menophilus; *capsarius*: 3952, Eutactus; *praepositus cellariis*: 8747, Trophimus; *cistarius a veste forensi*: 5193, Anteros; *cocus*: 8753, Eros; *coelator*: 4328, Antigonus; *colorator*: 3953, Anteros; *a Corinthiis*: *CIL* 10.692, Anthus; *corporis custos*: 8804, Linus; *cubicularius*: 8781, Cissus; *decurio cubiculariorum*: 3959a, Nicodemus; *supra cubicularios*: 3954, Myrtilus; *custos rationum patrimonii*: 3926, Bromius; *dispensator*: 3970, Calamis;[248] *dispensator ab toris*: 8655a, Thoas; *dissignator*: 8846, Eros; *fistulator*: 4444, Eros; *fullo*: 3970b, Pothinus; *glaber ab cyatho*: 8817, Liarus; *ornator glabrorum*: 8855, Dipantius; *glutinator*: *CIL* 10.735, Stichus; *ex hortis*: 6152, Anteros; *ab imaginibus*: 3972, Syneros; *inaurator*: 3928, Philomusus; *ad insulam*: 3972, Helenus; *praepositus insulariorum*: 8855, Daphnus; *invitator*: 3975, Philippus; *lanipendus*: 3977, Blastus; *lapidarius*: 8871, Astracalus; *lecticarius*: 4349, Olympus; *lector*: 3978, Panaenus;[249] *lictor*: 1871, Chrestus; *a manu*: 3980, Ismarus;[250] *margaritarius*: 3981, Geleuthus; *marmorarius*: 8893, Anteros; *medicus*: 3983, Boethus;[251] *medicus ocularius*: 8909, Thyrsis; *supra medicos*: 3982, Orestes; *mensor*: 3988, Diadumenus; *ministrator*: 5351, Agathemerus; *nauarchus*: 8927, Hilarus; *nomenclator*: 5352, Admetus; *obstetrix*: 4458, Hygia; *opsonator*: 8945, Aphareus; *ab ornamentis*: 3992, Irenio; *a commentariis ornamentorum*: 8955, Cnidus; *ornatrix*: 8880, Dionysia; *ostiarius*: 3995, Amphio; *paedagogus*: 3999, Malchio; *palaestrita*: 5813, Heracla; *pedisequa*: 4003, Thamyris; *pedisequus*: 4001, Anthus; *qui praefuit pedisequis*: 33788, Diognetus; *pictor*: 4008, Heracla; *pistor*: 4010, Philadelphus; *qui praeest pistoribus*: 8998, Telesphorus; *a porticu*: 4461, Onesimus; *ad possessiones*: 4015, Hyperbolus; *praegustator*: 5355, Diadumenus; *procurator*

---

[247] Even the 'Latin library' seems to have been staffed by Greeks; cf. 5189: *Julia Acca mater Callisthenis Ti. Caesar. Aug. a bibliothece Latina Apollinis, et Diopithis f. eius a byblioth. Latina Apollinis*. Also 5884: *Antiochus Ti. Claudi Caesaris a bibliotheca Latina Apollinis*.

[248] Another *dispensator*, Diomedes, showed cowardice when walking with Augustus, Suet. *D. Aug*. 67 – a charming story.

[249] cf. Cicero *ad Att*. 1.12.4: 'I am rather upset as I write. A charming boy, my reader Sositheus, is dead: it has distressed me more than perhaps a slave's death should.'

[250] These secretaries were important. Suet. *D. Aug*. 101, Polybius and Hilarion wrote Augustus' will; ibid. 67, a story of Thallus.

[251] cf. Cic. *ad Att*. 15.1.1: 'What a shame about Alexio! You wouldn't believe how much it has distressed me – and certainly not chiefly for the consideration that most people mention to me: "What doctor will you go to now, then?" It is his affection for me, his goodness and his charm that I miss.'

praegustatorum: 9003, Zosimus; *procurator*: 9006, Atimetus; *procurator a regionibus urbis*: 4018, Merops; *puer de paedagogio*: 33104, Hyllus; *puerorum ornatrix*: 33099, Chloe; a *purpureis*: 4016, Parmeno; a *rationibus*: 33467, Apolaustus; *redemptor operum*: 9034 Onesimus; *sacerdos a Bona Dea*: 4003, Philematio; a *sacrario*: 4027, Aphrodisius; *sarcinatrix*: 3988, Lochias; a *sede Augustae*: 3967, Lydus; *speclariarius*: 8660, Symmachus; *praepositus speclariariorum*: 8659, Epictetus; a *statuis*: 4032, Agrypnus; *strator*: 4033, Atticus; *structor*: 4034, Parthenius; *ab supelectile*: 4035, Anteros; *sutor*: 9050, Epigonus; *symphoniaca*: 33372, Europa; *symphoniacus*: 4472, Syneros; *tabularius*: 4038, Pasicrates; *tesserarius*: 8663, Symphorus;[252] *tonsor*: 4474, Antiochus; *tricliniarchus*: 9083, Hyllus; *trierarchus*: 8928, Caspius; *ad valetudinem*: 9085, Philargyrus; *praepositus velariorum*: 9086, Strato; *ad Venerem*: 4040, Amianthes; a *veste*: 3985, Isochrysus; a *veste regia*: 8551, Corinthus; *vestiarius*: 4044, Pamphilus; *victimarius*: 4362, Castor; *vilicus*: 7528, Isidorus; *unctor*: 4419, Xystus; *unctrix*: 4045, Galene.

---

[252] Apparently not a maker of mosaics but a servant who passed on orders to other servants (Boulvert, p. 34). The existence of such a position underlines the size of the household.

CHAPTER TWO

Propertius and Antony

You shall see in him
The triple pillar of the world, transform'd
Into a strumpet's fool – Shakespeare

In the first chapter it was argued that much recent scholarship has
misjudged the Augustan poets in certain important respects, because it
has been thought in principle possible to separate 'literature' and 'life',
as if they were clearly distinguishable entities; in reality, the two affect
each other in a ceaseless mutual interaction. That argument was
developed as a general treatment of the life of pleasure as presented in
Latin literature, and as lived in reality in a society in which Greek and
Italian elements, poetical motifs and real behaviour, were inextricably
intermingled.

The present chapter applies the same approach to a more particular
enquiry into one poet and one type of historical figure. I argue that
Propertius' presentation of himself in poetry as a lover – romantic,
reckless and obsessed – is closely related to the figure in history of Mark
Antony.[1] That historical figure is itself to be seen in a long tradition of
great lovers of pleasure, in which the actual lives of real men can be seen
to be shaped and coloured by the influence of 'literature'.

Like all the Augustan poets, Propertius of course follows the Augustan
interpretation of Actium, as a war between Octavian with the Senate at
his back, and the degraded hordes of the East: eunuchs, Anubis, and the
incesti meretrix regina Canopi, 'the harlot queen of immoral Canopus'.
He even goes further than Horace and Virgil in expressing spiteful
hostility and loathing for Cleopatra. Not only is she a harlot queen, but
also *famulos inter femina trita suos* 'a woman enjoyed by her own
servants'; when she takes to flight, it is *hoc unum, iusso non moritura die*
'all she achieves is to escape dying on a fixed day' – but she would in any
case have been unworthy to appear in a Roman triumph. The
self-consciously noble manner of Horace, *Odes* 1.37 is far away, let alone
the genuine magnanimity to which Virgil rises at *Aen.* 8.711.[2] Such
hostility to the formidable queen is striking, and there are other features
of Propertius' poetry which make it even more surprising; for his

---

[1] I have called him 'Mark Antony' rather than 'M. Antonius' because I am concerned
with him as much for his literary resonance as for his historical reality.

[2] Some suggest (W. Richter in *WS* 79 (1966) 463) that in 4.6 Propertius deliberately
attacks Horace's restrained treatment of Cleopatra's death, with the simple aim of the

treatment of Antony is much more interesting, more complex, and more sympathetic.

Propertius begins 3.11:

> *Quid mirare, meam si versat femina vitam*
> *et trahit addictum sub sua iura virum?*

'Why be surprised if a woman runs my life and leads my manhood captive like a slave?' This highly typical Propertian opening is developed with a list of dominant women in history, Medea,[3] Omphale,[4] Semiramis,[5] Cleopatra; and then turns, to the reader's surprise, into a lengthy attack on Cleopatra and glorification of Augustus for his victory over her. 'The point of the elegy, which is a passionately developed encomium of the victory at Actium, is only loosely connected with the poet's own love-life', comments Rothstein in his edition,[6] and it may be that Propertius was trying to produce the sort of poem which Horace sometimes succeeds in writing, which combines a public, political theme with an incident of his own life as a lyric poet. *Odes* 3.14 is a good example, where Horace opens with public ceremonies to greet Augustus on his return from Spain, and via a central verse expressing his personal trust in him concludes with a private celebration with Neaera. *Odes* 4.5 and 4.15, and (significantly) 1.37 on Actium, are also in this mould.[7] But the exquisite tact with which, in *Odes* 3.14, Horace refers to his

---

greatest possible praise of Augustus at his enemies' expense. But encomium by Propertius too often fails to rise above the tepid for this to be plausible; cf. 2.1.25: *bellaque resque tui memorarem Caesaris*, 'I should tell of the warlike achievements of your Caesar', in a context where Prop. mentions the Perusine War (29), a piece of history which might perhaps have endeared Antony rather than Octavian to the poet; 2.10.8; and 3.4, a very ironical poem. On 3.4, rightly L.P. Wilkinson in *Studi Castiglioni* 2.1093-1103 and Margaret Hubbard, *Propertius* (1974) 103; by contrast F. Cairns, *Generic Composition* (1972) 186, sees only 'unabashed admiration', while G. Williams, *Tradition and Originality* (1968) 433, thinks it 'may be more pleasingly ironical than he intended'. These careless elegists! After 69 lines of 4.6 Propertius is frankly tired of his subject, and with a disarming *bella satis cecini*, 'I have sung of wars enough', turns to the more congenial topic of a party. See A. La Penna, *Orazio e l'ideologia del principato* (1963) 133; J. Griffin in *Caesar Augustus*, edd. Millar and Segal (1984) 189ff.

[3] Medea in the vocabulary of political abuse: Cic. *Cael.* 18 (of Clodia); *de Lege Manilia* 22 (of Mithridates). See n.79 below.

[4] Omphale in the vocabulary of political abuse: Plutarch, *Pericles* 24; idem, *Comparatio Demetrii et Antonii* 3.2 (of Antony). Some moderns assert that it was applied to Alexander and Roxane (so H. Volkmann, *Kleopatra* (1953) 134), but I have found no source.

[5] Semiramis in the vocabulary of political abuse: Cic. *de Prov. Cons.* 9 (of Gabinius).

[6] L. Alfonsi, *L'elegia di Properzio* (1945) 66f. thinks the two motifs blend better, and even finds 'lo spirito è piuttosto virgiliano'. Contra, Margaret Hubbard, op. cit. (n.2) 89: (in certain poems in Book 3) 'the development of the topics is often derivative and unconvinced, like the Cleopatra episode of 3.11'. See now W.R. Nethercut in *ANRW* 30.3 (1983) 1846ff.

[7] cf. on this point A. La Penna, op. cit. (n.2) 127. Prop. 3.11 is not mentioned in this connection either by him or by F. Solmsen, 'Propertius and Horace', *CP* 43 (1948) 105 = *Kleine Schriften* 2.278.

Republican role – now long over – at Philippi is very different from the
way in which Propertius has allowed the logic of his own poem, if read as
a unity, to push him into the role of Antony; for he says 'No wonder if I
am dominated by a woman – look at Cleopatra'.

Naturally we do not want to force this implication, but perhaps we
should look further for an explanation before accepting 'the laxness of
thought-connection which is characteristic of Roman elegy' (Rothstein
ad 3.11, *init.*). What of Propertius 2.16? In this poem[8] Propertius
complains: 'My venal mistress is excluding me for a richer rival; curses
on wealth! I should be ashamed of this humiliation – but a degrading love
is proverbially deaf. Look at Antony: *infamis amor* was his ruin; glory to
Octavian for his clemency. As for you, may your ill-gotten gains be swept
away; and beware of divine punishment for your treachery'. The Actium
episode here is described by G. Williams[9] as 'the conventional account of
Actium, with its denigration of Antony ... Propertius is lured into the
conventional public contrast of right with wrong, of Augustus with
Antony or Cleopatra ...' But is it so conventional? Again the poet draws a
parallel between Antony and himself; and at the end of the poem he is
still persevering in his 'degrading love', not breaking free. It is perhaps
appropriate to look back with a fresh eye at ll. 19-21:

> *atque utinam Romae nemo esset dives, et ipse*
> *straminea posset dux habitare casa!*
> *numquam venales essent ad munus amicae* ....

'I would that nobody were rich in Rome, and that our leader himself
could live in a cottage. Then our girls would not be venal and greedy.'
The Princeps prided himself upon his unostentatious mode of life;[10] is
not the natural interpretation of these lines, in the context of this curious
poem, an ironical and malicious suggestion that he ought to be *really*
poor – to the end, not of correct moral edification, but of making more
agreeable and less expensive the life of love?[11]

How many swallows make a summer? Twice we have found Propertius
committing the *gaffe* of identifying himself with Antony; will an appeal
to the 'laxness of thought-connection characteristic of Roman elegy'
suffice to cover both? I hope it will seem implausible, when we have
considered some references to Paris. The correct attitude to Paris for an
Augustan poet was surely austere, and Horace treats him in this spirit. In

---

[8] Discussed by Hubbard, op. cit. (n.2) 58f., with different results.
[9] *Tradition and Originality* 559.
[10] Cf. p. 15 above, n.148.
[11] With the technique compare for example 3.14. The poem opens with a straight-faced
announcement that 'there are many things we admire about the Spartan education'; but it
turns out that, instead of the all too familiar praise of Spartan toughness and self-denial, we
find an amusingly unexpected encomium on the unparalleled advantages it offered the
lover for getting close to his girl. Cf. p. 108 below.

Odes 1.15 he will run away like a stag in battle; in *Odes* 3.3 he is the *fatalis incestusque iudex* who ruined his country; in *Epp.* 1.2.10 the paradigm of a fool. In the *Aeneid* it is to Paris that his bitterest enemies compare Aeneas (*Aen.* 4.215). But Propertius anticipates the frivolous Ovid in sympathising with the Trojan seducer.

In 2.3.35 Cynthia is so beautiful that Troy would have done better to fall for her than for Helen:

> *olim mirabar, quod tanti ad Pergama belli*
> *Europae atque Asiae causa puella fuit:*
> *nunc, Pari, tu sapiens et tu, Menelae, fuisti,*
> *tu quia poscebas, tu quia lentus eras,*

'I used to be surprised that Europe and Asia fought a great war at Troy over a girl, but now I find both Paris and Menelaus were sensible – the one to ask for Helen back, the other to be reluctant to part with her.' Paris is a model for Propertius' own erotic tastes at 2.15.13; at 3.8.29f. the poet says that Paris, like him, found his desire keenest amid the alarms of war:

> *dulcior ignis erat Paridi, cum Graia per arma*
> *Tyndaridi poterat gaudia ferre suae:*
> *dum vincunt Danai, dum restat barbarus Hector,*
> *ille Helenae gremio maxima bella gerit.*

'Paris' love was sweeter when he came to Helen's arms through the Greek army. While the enemy won and Hector fought, he waged his greatest battles in her embrace.' (The last two lines, we note, could serve as a perfect summary of the picture given by our sources of the inactivity of Antony during the Perusine War.) Like Antony, the glamorous hedonist Paris, who loses all for a woman, was not an expected subject for Augustan panegyric, however witty. It comes therefore as no surprise both that the moralistic tradition explicitly compared Antony to Paris 'running away from the fighting into Cleopatra's bosom',[12] and also that Propertius' poem 2.15, in which at l. 13 the poet compares himself to Paris, goes on to make the point (l. 41) that 'if only everyone would live the life of love and wine, there would be no Roman corpses floating in the sea at Actium'. W.A. Camps[13] calls this 'an extravagant paradox'; I cannot see why. It seems to be, in fact, a bitter truth, however unexpected such a thing may be in an Augustan poet mentioning Augustus' greatest triumph. 'Had he lived like me – like Antony – the disaster of Actium need never have happened ...'

In order to understand Propertius and Antony, it is necessary to put

---

[12] Plutarch *Comparatio* 3.
[13] Edition of Book 2 ad loc.

the figure of the man of action who lived for pleasure into its full perspective, and in accordance with my argument this must be done both in literature and in life, in their reciprocal relationship. To begin with literature, we must be alive to the fact that Hellenistic literature did not consist only of high-brow poets. Propertius and Virgil boast of certain Hellenistic precursors: Philetas, Callimachus, Theocritus, Euphorion. These were great poets and creditable names, and a Gallus or a Propertius was proud to admit their influence. By contrast, mythological hand-books and short-cuts like Parthenius' little work on the *Sufferings Caused by Love*, perhaps more often looked into by these poets than the works of Philetas,[14] did not receive honourable mention in their poems. No more did they parade their acquaintance with unedifying works of propaganda and scandal, but these too may turn out to be unexpectedly important; more especially when we remind ourselves that the subjects and the attitudes which will be discussed here were even more pervasive in conversation than in written form. The latter is only the one which we now can see and control, and as we do so we must allow for the vast and formless mass of sub-literary and oral material which was taken for granted by men of the time.

Hellenistic literature was rich in scandalous and scurrilous works on the great figures of classical Greece,[15] as well as on contemporaries. An ignoble mentality avenged itself upon the higher pretensions of great men by attaching low or titillating stories to their names. Sexual scandal was assembled about philosophers,[16] some of which has got into Diogenes Laertius; some at least of the epigrams ascribed to Plato seem to come from such a source,[17] and it is significant that Lucilius[18] can be seen to make use of a story of this sort about the Academic philosophers Xenocrates and Polemon. Serious philosophers joined in: Chrysippus for example accused Epicurus of being a disciple of Archestratus in debauchery. Hieronymus of Rhodes and Idomeneus of Lampsacus circulated similar scandal about poets and politicians;[19] in history, the cynical Theopompus ascribed to all comers in his huge *History* unworthy and sordid motives, while sensationalists like Douris added lurid scenes of imaginary indulgence. The base work known as 'Aristippus *On the luxuriousness of the Ancients*' was the source for a great deal of sensational material in the thirteenth book of Athenaeus. Such

---

[14] I am sceptical about Propertius' knowledge of Philetas; even of Callimachus, copies of whom must have been easier to find, what he says in Books 2 and 3 is extraordinarily slight. Outside the *Aetia* prologue, his knowledge of Callimachus before he wrote Book 4 was hardly great. Cf. below p. 201 n.22.

[15] Locus classicus on this: U. von Wilamowitz, *Antigonos von Karystos* (1881) 47f.

[16] Susemihl, *Gesch.d.gr.Lit.* (1891-2) 1.148f. The *Silloi* of Timon are relevant: see fr. 9, 30, 54, 56 and 59.

[17] W. Ludwig in *GRBS* 4 (1963) 59f.

[18] Fr. 755 Marx.

[19] Susemihl, op. cit. (n.16) 1.148.

pre-Hellenistic figures as Alcibiades were thickly encrusted with anecdotes, mostly of salacious or luxurious character,[20] and so were Diadochi such as Demetrius Poliorcetes, and not least Alexander himself. Another relevant genre is that concerned with the doings and sayings of courtesans. Machon[21] versifies a large number of more or less improper stories about the mistresses of the poets and the Hellenistic dynasts, and such women as Laïs, Lamia, Phryne and Thaïs became celebrated, stories multiplying about their behaviour; Lucilius made use of this, too.[22] Plutarch is among the authors who tell us, for example, that Alexander burnt the palace at Persepolis to please Thaïs;[23] his *Life of Demetrius* includes such material in abundance. Monographs were produced on luxurious dinners.[24] The luxury ship of Hieron II was the subject of a special work,[25] whose extant portions still make impressive reading. A more scholarly taste was gratified by such works as those *On the Athenian Courtesans*, identifying those who appeared in literature;[26] for the philosophically inclined, there were treatises *On Pleasure*,[27] with

[20] Its importance for the ancient conception of him is realised by F. Taeger, *Alkibiades* (1943) 86 n.10. The material goes back as far as Lysias 14; [Andocides] 4, *Against Alcibiades*; and Antiphon fr. 67 (Blass). Douris contributed some melodramatic flourishes. Cf. D.A. Russell, *PCPhS* 192 (1966) 37, who points out that material on Alcibiades' life was quite unusually rich, and that he was early a subject for full-scale biographies. 'Public opinion in the 390s was remarkably preoccupied with the memory of Alcibiades', G. Dalmeyda in the Budé edition of Andocides (1960) 109.

[21] Ed. with commentary by A.S.F. Gow, 1965. Stories about Euripides and Sophocles (18), Diphilus (3, 16), Philoxenus (9, 10), and the citharode Stratonicus (11), as well as the dynasts. In Rome, Volumnia Cytheris is found dining with senators, Cic., *ad Fam.* 9, 26; cf. supra p. 16. Cf. G. Luck, 'Women's role in Latin love poetry', in *Perspectives of Roman Poetry* (1974).

[22] Fr. 263M: *Phryne nobilis illa ubi amatorem improbius quem ...*, 'When the notorious Phryne had done something naughty to one of her lovers'.

[23] Plut. *Alexander* 38, from Clitarchus, *FGH* 137 fr. 11. *RE*, s.v. *Thaïs*, gives the efforts of modern historians to tone down, without rejecting, this romantic story. Plutarch, *Alexander* 40 and 67, further examples of his luxuriousness. 'L'exemple de la chasteté d'Alexandre n'a pas tant fait de continents que celui de son ivrognerie a fait d'intempérants', observes Pascal (*Pensées*, edn. de la Pléiade, p. 1134).

[24] Plut. *Demetrius* 27: the dinner made by Lamia for Demetrius 'was so celebrated for its extravagance that Lynceus of Samos wrote it up'. An account of a luxury meal by Hippolochus, Athenaeus 128-31; cf. Susemihl, op. cit. (n.16), 1, 486f. All this is an obvious source for poems like Horace *Sat.* 2.8, and for the conception, and reality, of the luxury of Sulla and Antony.

[25] Athenaeus 206d-209e. Susemihl speaks of 'the fabulous luxury and still unequalled splendour of this ancient "Great Eastern", built with the aid of Archimedes' (1.883). The luxuriousness of Cleopatra's shipping was still a conventional theme centuries later; Pacatus, *Pan. Lat.* 3.33: 'Is there an historian or a poet who has not talked about Cleopatra's ships and the elaboration of their tackle, their crimson sails and ropes of gold?'

[26] We know of works by Ammonius, Antiphanes, Apollodorus, Aristophanes and Gorgias of Athens. Evidently there was a demand.

[27] E. Bignone, *L'Aristotele perduto e la formazione filosofica di Epicuro* 1 (1936) 276f. Speusippus, Xenocrates, Theophrastus, Heraclides Ponticus, Clearchus, Aristoxenus and Strato all wrote on pleasure. The long fragment (50, Wehrli) of Aristoxenus' *Life of*

detailed accounts of the hedonism which the authors took pleasure in condemning. Straightforward pornography was abundant.[28] Deliberate propaganda plays a large part here. Accusations of every kind of wantonness had always been part of the standard material of Greek oratory,[29] and Roman polemic was no less slanderous.[30] Yet even lies, as a constant atmosphere to live in, have an effect on public morale and in the long run influence behaviour. The accusations made against Sulla, Catiline, Caesar,[31] and Antony,[32] to select only the most eminent names – accusations of a life of reckless, profligate debauchery – were calculated to arouse in the audience a prurient envy familiar to anyone who opens one of the more vulgar Sunday newspapers. That it was expected by competent judges to produce an effect emerges clearly from the war of propaganda between Antony on the one hand, and Cicero and Octavian on the other. It emerges from that episode also that it did have an effect. Not only was Antony obliged to write *On my Drunkenness* in self-defence, but his eventual ruin was partly brought about by skilful propaganda against him.[33]

Archytas (= Athenaeus 545b seqq.) deals with luxury and pleasure in different parts of the world; cf. also Clearchus fr. 19 (Wehrli) (from his *Gergithius*), fr. 24, 25, 29, 30 etc. (from his *Eroticus*), and fr. 41-62 (from his *Lives*). Fr. 47 of Clearchus gives an idea of the ostensible morality of such works – 'And so one must avoid what is called luxury', etc. Heraclides Ponticus *On Pleasure* praised pleasure as the highest good (55), said Pericles lived for pleasure (59) – and sometimes gave the 'moral' (fr. 61, 'All this was done by unrestrained luxury'). The philosopher Aristippus was a focus for anecdotes setting out with censorious relish his hedonistic life and philosophy. Cicero invokes him (*ad Fam.* 9.26) after dining with Cytheris; Horace uses him (in *Sat.* 2.3.100 and *Epp.* 1.1.18; 1.17.14) as an emblematic figure, rather than as a philosopher whose works one reads. That is to say, he was a creation of anecdote. His connection with Laïs ('I possess her, she doesn't possess me') was important to this picture.

[28] Sex-manuals etc., mostly published under the name of some famous hetaera: 'Philaenis', cf. *P. Oxy.* 2891, Athenaeus 335b-e, 457; 'Elephantis': Polybius 12.13, Athenaeus 220f., 162b. Improper fiction existed: Sisenna, praetor in 78 B.C., translated into Latin the *Milesian Tales* of Aristides (the Parthians were shocked to find it in the baggage of Crassus' officers at Carrhae, Plut., *Crassus* 32). For the celebrity of these works at Rome, cf. Sueton., *Tib.* 43; *Priapea* 4; Martial 12.43. On 'Philaenis', see K. Tsantsanoglu, 'The memoirs of a lady from Samos', in *ZPE* 12 (1973) 183f.

[29] W. Süss, *Ethos* (1910), 249f.

[30] R.G.M. Nisbet, edition of Cicero, *in Pisonem*, 192f. If a prosecutor did not produce accusations of debauchery in youth, the omission was a striking and telling one: Cic. *Font.* 37.

[31] The Bithynian scandal was played up for all it was worth, Plut. *Caesar* 1; Suet *D. Caes.* 2 and 49. It was versified by Calvus, written up in prose by C. Memmius, ventilated in the *actiones* of Dolabella and the elder Curio, published in edicts by Bibulus, joked of by Cicero, sung of at his triumph – vexing him sufficiently to make him deny it on oath. Other stories were gleefully exploited: M. Actorius Naso told of his enormous presents to Queen Eunoe (Suer. *D. Jul.* 52); 'some Greek writers' are quoted for the assertion that Caesarion really was his son by Cleopatra and resembled him (ibid.).

[32] K. Scott, 'Octavian's propaganda and Antony's *De sua ebrietate*', *CP* 24 (1929) 133f.: idem, 'The political propaganda of 44-30 B.C.', *MAAR* 11 (1933) 7f.

[33] Stähelin in *RE* 11.767. 12f.: 'This imponderable consideration proved to be the heaviest weight in the scale'.

Before treating Antony seriously, it is interesting to observe that the stereotype, of the man of action who lives a life of luxury, goes back a long way. It presents us with a striking example of the interplay of experience and literature. Already with Alcibiades there was doubtless both a spectacular personality and a conscious playing up to the legend which surrounded him; Plutarch shows him performing an outrageous but trivial act 'so that the people should talk about that and not say worse things about him'.[34] Thereafter, the existence of the stereotype must itself have been important for the conception of themselves entertained by Alexander, Demetrius, Sulla, Antony and the rest – and of course it was self-reinforcing. Alexander's own example was an immensely powerful stimulus,[35] while I suspect that Antony, taking the East as his portion and emulating Sulla in marching on the West, will have said to himself not only *Sulla potuit: ego non potero?*[36] but also *Sulla fecit; ego non faciam?* On the other hand, the fact that polemic could present as sunk in debauchery even men of undeniable and spectacular achievements (Alexander, Sulla, Caesar, Antony) meant that the stereotype became constantly more credible and more capable of being used. The belief in the *exemplum* was powerful, and there the *exempla* were for depicting as a voluptuary the powerful adversary, whoever he was, of today; while on the other side his flatterers encouraged him to see himself in the glamorous and congenial role of the man who loves his pleasures but at need is formidable in action. Meanwhile, historians revelled in depicting and exaggerating his excesses.

Thus it is a complex process which creates and repeats the type of which the period from 350 B.C. to A.D. 100 presents so many examples. Sallust depicts Sulla[37] in just this way, and, shifting the emphasis more completely on to his vices, Catiline[38] too. Velleius' characterisation of Maecenas is in the same mould,[39] and Maecenas seems to have played up

---

[34] Plut. *Alcibiades* 9.
[35] cf. O. Wippert, *Alexander – Imitatio und röm. Politik in der rep. Zeit*, Diss. Würzburg (1972).
[36] Said *crebro* by Pompey in the Civil War, Cic., *ad Att.* 9.10.2: 'Sulla could do it: shall I not be able to?' and 'Sulla did it: shall I not do it?'
[37] *BJ* 95: *animo ingenti, cupidus voluptatum sed gloriae cupidior; otio luxuriosus esse, tamen ab negotiis numquam voluptas remorata ...*, 'A great spirit, greedy for pleasure but still more greedy for fame; in his leisure he was debauched, but pleasure never kept him from important business'.
[38] *BC* 5.14-16, 60 (his heroic last fight). Cicero, at need, gives the same picture, *pro Cael.* 12-13: (of Catiline), *flagrabant vitia libidinis apud illum; vigebant etiam studia rei militaris*, etc., 'He was on fire with lust and vice, but also he was a capable soldier'. 'The old Republic knew that vice and energy are not incompatible', R. Syme, *Tacitus* 2.545.
[39] 2.88.2: *ubi res vigiliam exigeret, sane insomnis, providens atque agendi sciens; simul vero aliquid ex negotiis remitti posset, otio et mollitiis paene ultra feminam fluens*, 'When his position demanded vigilance, he could be sleepless, far-sighted, capable of action; but as soon as he could relax from business, there was hardly a woman to match him in his inactivity and his softness'.

to it, appearing in informal attire and unbuttoned even when left in charge of Italy.[40] Tacitus has a notorious affection for the type, discerning it in Sallustius Crispus,[41] L. Vitellius,[42] Otho,[43] Petronius,[44] Licinius Mucianus,[45] and T. Vinius.[46] The Sallustian background is obvious,[47] but the resemblance of the type to Greek models like Alcibiades and Demetrius shows it is older. Plutarch finds the same qualities in Lucullus[48] as well as in Antony,[49] and the pattern was probably influential in convincing him of the general proposition that 'great natures are most exposed to temptations'.[50] Peripatetic influence has been detected.[51] In any case, in the late Republic and early Empire[52] men existed who conformed to the pattern, and who no doubt did so consciously. Sir Ronald Syme, comparing Antony and Petronius, speaks of 'a class of Roman nobles by no means uncommon ... whose unofficial follies did not prevent them from rising, when duty called, to services of conspicuous ability or the most disinterested patriotism. For such men the most austere of historians cannot altogether suppress a timid and perhaps perverse admiration.'[53] And by less punctilious persons the admiration has always been felt less timidly, even when mixed with a not unpleasing *frisson* of disapproval.

Above all, we must allow for the appeal to Antony of the career and character of Caesar. He succeeded, even more completely than Sulla, in uniting the man of pleasure and the man of action; Antony had before his eyes an example of marvellous glamour. Octavian, on the other hand,

---

[40] Seneca, *Epp.* 114.6. The tutor of Nero is never weary of attacking the vices of the friend of Augustus.

[41] Tac., *Ann.* 3.30.4: *per cultum et munditias copiaque et affluentia luxu propior. suberat tamen vigor animi* ... 'His dandyish elegance, his wealth and extravagance made him almost a voluptuary, but underneath there was a powerful will ...'

[42] *Ann.* 6.32.4

[43] *Ann.* 13.46.3; *Hist.* 1.13 and 21.

[44] *Ann.* 16.18.

[45] *Hist.* 1.10.

[46] *Hist.* 1.48.

[47] R. Syme, *Tacitus* 2.538 n.6; F. Krohn, *Personendarstellung bei Tacitus*, Diss. Leipzig (1934) 96. Valerius Asiaticus, too, combined luxury and *in rem publicam officia*. He showed undaunted courage at his death.

[48] *Lucullus* 39-41; *Cimon* 3; *Comparatio* 1.

[49] e.g. *Antony* 17.

[50] *Alcibiades* 2; *Agis* 2; *Coriol.* 1; *Themistocles* 2; *Demetrius* 1; *Moralia* 552b.

[51] A. Dihle, *Studien zur gr. Biographie* (1956) 84f.; D.A. Russell, *Plutarch* (1973) 105, 123.

[52] Surely this kind of life, essentially aristocratic in conception and at the opposite remove from the caution of the good functionary, was a way in which some Roman nobles kept their self-respect under the early Empire, when consistent displays of talent and energy were dangerous. Had Tacitus wished, he might have recognised in it another path than that trodden by the virtuous Agricola and the weighty M. Lepidus, *inter abruptam contumaciam et deforme obsequium* (*Ann.* 4.20). Perhaps he did.

[53] Nor they alone. In fiction, the Scarlet Pimpernel, Rudolf Rassendyll, Bulldog Drummond, Lord Peter Wimsey and James Bond all witness to the appeal of the type to more popular tastes. In life, the success of Churchill as a war leader owed something to his evident love of cigars, brandy and champagne.

2. *Propertius and Antony*

once he had become Augustus, rather hushed up the un-Augustan figure of his adoptive father. Antony served in Egypt under Gabinius, notorious for his perfumes, wine and dandified coiffure (Cic., *post red. in Sen.* 16; *pro Sestio* 18); a dancing man, or rather a dancing girl (*saltatrix*: Cic., *pro Sest.* 18). Antony's liaison with the notorious Volumnia Cytheris, later the mistress and poetical inspiration of Gallus, brings him into pleasingly intimate connection with the elegiac poets; and his life as we see it in the late 40s and 30s is an irregular and gallant one. The scene Cicero so well records at *Philippic* 2.77 – he comes home at night, disguised as a messenger, with a letter to Fulvia, 'written in amorous style', promising to cast off his mistress and be true to her – is precisely in the ethos of elegy; see for example Propertius 1.3 and 2.29a. 'O hominem nequam!' 'Worthless man!' comments Cicero; 'nequitiae caput' was what the virtuous called Propertius (2.24a.6).

It is fortunately not necessary for our purpose to speculate about the precise mixture of truth and invention in the stories of Antony's luxurious life at Alexandria. There was some truth, and there were some pure fantasies.[54] The important thing is the nature of the picture, and the fact that it could be projected as being at least in large part believable. We observe that in the propaganda of both sides orgies played a central role. The blasphemous banquet at which Octavian and his friends impersonated the twelve gods[55] was matched by the one, for example, at which Plancus danced the role of Glaucus, nude, kneeling, painted blue, and dragging a tail[56] – or so they said. The apex of invention was the fleshly delights of extravagance, drunkenness and sexual licence. But Octavian's propaganda went one step further and with brilliant success represented Antony as enslaved and bewitched by Cleopatra; officially, he was reduced to her degraded appendage. Not only was war declared on her, not on him, but his conduct was systematically interpreted as that of an enslaved sensualist throwing away military glory and self-respect for her. Thus, he remained inactive during the Perusine War because she 'carried him off to Alexandria'[57] and 'gave the orders';[58] he threw up the Parthian campaign 'through his own fault, since in his eagerness to return to Cleopatra he would not spend the winter in Armenia';[59] and in the end he flung away everything for her at Actium, 'being dragged along by the woman as if he had become incorporate with her and must go where she did'.[60]

[54] There seems no reason to suspect the evidence of Plutarch's great-grandfather and of Philotas (*Antony* 28, 68). But e.g. Plutarch, *Antony* 59, 'Most of the charges brought by Calvisius were thought to be falsehoods', and some of the stories are too fantastic: cf. I. Becher, *Das Bild der Kleopatra* (1960) 39, 134.
[55] Suet. *D. Aug.* 70.
[56] Vell. Pat. 2.83, perhaps from Pollio; cf. G. Williams, *Tradition and Originality* 85.
[57] Plutarch *Antony* 28.
[58] Appian *BC* 5.9.
[59] Livy *Periocha* 130.
[60] Plut. *Antony* 66.

We turn now to Propertius and observe in his poems a life depicted which bears much more resemblance to the life ascribed to Antony than to that of a good Augustan citizen. Many writers have emphasised the 'anti-Augustan' side of the poet,[61] more nakedly visible in him than in the other Augustans; it remains to show the model to which such a side is related. In contrast with the Roman life of *prudentia*, disciplined action, Propertius claims to live *nullo consilio*, 'from moment to moment';[62] he renounces the Roman marriage – *nos uxor numquam, numquam seducet amica* –[63] as Antony abused and rejected Octavia, that model of Roman matrons. He rejects military and political activity and career[64] at the behest of an imperious woman, his *domina*, who is not even respectable: 'Love is a god of peace,'[65] and he will fight in no campaigns but those of love.[66] Consistently with this, he begs his friend not to leave his love for the army, and curses those who through greed for gain prefer war to love:

si fas est, omnes pariter pereatis avari,
et quisquis fido praetulit arma toro.[67]

'If it is permitted, may all those perish who love money, or who put military service before true love.' Propertius is inspired by works of art; Antony collected for Cleopatra the masterpieces of the East, enabling Octavian to restore them with a virtuous boast.[68] Antony's friends remonstrated with him and tried to cure him of his destructive passion;[69] Propertius' friends took exactly the same line.[70] 'The virtuous and sober disapproved of Antony's whole way of life'[71] as the *senes duri* criticised

[61] D. Van Berchem, 'Cynthia ou la carrière contrariée', *Mus. Helv.* 5 (1948) 137f.; J. Fontenrose, 'Propertius and the Roman career', *Univ. Calif. Publ. in Class. Phil.* 13 no. 11 (1949) 371f.; E. Burck, 'Römische Wesenszüge der aug. Liebeselegie', *Hermes* 80 (1952), 163f. = *Vom Menschenbild*, 191f.; J.-P. Boucher, *Études sur Properce* (1965), ch. 1.
[62] Prop. 1.1.6; cf. 2.12.3: *sine sensu vivere amantes*, 'The life of love is irrational'; Boucher, loc. cit. 17: for Antony, e.g. Plut. *Antony* 37, 62.
[63] Prop. 2.6.41: cf. 2.7. 'Propertius rejects the approved Roman woman', Fontenrose, loc. cit. 378. This is the meaning of Prop. 1.1.5: *donec me docuit castas odisse puellas*, 'until she taught me to reject respectable girls' – despite Allen in *YCS* 11 (1951) 266, Otis in *HSCP* 70 (1965) 40f., and others; no 'nuance of irony' (Otis, 41), either. ' "Irony" last resource of despairing commentators', quips E. Fraenkel, *Horace*, 457 – a lapidary phrase.
[64] cf. Boucher, op. cit. (n.61), 21f., 'Refus de la carrière politique'.
[65] Prop. 3.5.1; cf. 1.6.30; 3.12, 4; Boucher, op. cit. (n.61) 20, 'Refus de la guerre'.
[66] Prop. 1.6.30, *hanc me militiam fata subire volunt.*
[67] Prop. 3.12.5f.
[68] *Res Gestae* 24. Cf. *RE* 11.767. 41f.; supra p. 000.
[69] e.g. Plutarch *Antony* 68, 69.
[70] In the programmatic first poem, 1.1.25: *et vos qui sero lapsum revocatis, amici ...*, 'You friends who are trying to win me back from disgrace', and in the poem in which he finally dismisses Cynthia, 3.24.9: *quod mihi non patrii poterant avertere amici*, 'which my family friends could not avert'. Also in other poems, e.g. 1.4.
[71] Plutarch *Antony* 9. In a careful study of the Perusine War, E. Gabba finds that as early as 41, with stories circulating about his intrigues with women in Cappadocia and Egypt, 'even the Antonians themselves were not certainly satisfied with their leader's conduct', *HSCP* 75 (1971) 149.

that of Propertius,[72] and of Catullus before him. Octavian in 32 said that Antony had lost his self-mastery under the influence of drugs; Propertius says the same thing of himself.[73] Antony identified himself with Dionysus; Bacchus is surprisingly prominent in Propertius, as in the other Augustan poets, and wine is one of his commonest topics.[74] Antony wasted his precious time in immature and luxurious dalliance;[75] it is the shame and the glory of the elegiac poet to do likewise.[76] He cannot go on service, his fate is idleness and ignominy –

me sine, quem semper voluit fortuna iacere,
  hanc animam extremae reddere nequitiae.[77]

'As for me, for whom destiny plans constant subjection, let me breathe my last in utter profligacy.' This is the meaning of his long *servitium*[78] and the *infamia* it has brought him.

Above all, Antony is the slave of the woman. This is meant to be a bitter and cruel taunt, an utter condemnation of a degraded man,[79] but for the elegiac poet it is a boast: his beloved is his mistress, *domina*, and a cruel and arbitrary one. The conception is alien to Greek love poetry until a much later period, and scholars speak of the existence of 'a gap between the Greek and Roman writers, not only of time, but also of

---

[72] e.g. Prop. 2.24, 30.

[73] Plut. *Antony* 60.1. Cf. Propertius 1.5.6, 3.6.25, 4.7.72. Plutarch says of Antony (*Vita* 37): 'He was not master of his own faculties but, as if he were under the influence of certain drugs or of magic rites, was ever looking towards her ...'.

[74] It is hard to feel that we fully understand the role of Bacchus in the work of these poets. P. Boyancé (*Entretiens Fondation Hardt* 2.196f.) argues for the existence of a regular *sodalicium* to which the poets belonged, with Bacchus as its patron. E.T. Silk, *YCS* 21 (1969) 195f., emphasises the element of *recusatio* in Horace's poems to Bacchus, but ignores the poems of the other poets on the theme. A cool view: Margaret Hubbard, *Propertius* 79, 'Probably it all seems more strange and wonderful to us than to a Roman, who saw many such things in the gardens of civilised villas and town houses' (*sc.* as the mystic paraphernalia of Bacchus). Cf. below pp. 70ff.

[75] Plut. *Antony* 28 (during the Perusine War).

[76] cf. also Tibullus 1.1.57. The point is wittily put by Ovid, *Ars.* 1.504: *arbitrio dominae tempora perde tuae*, 'Waste your time at your mistress' whim'.

[77] Prop. 1.6.25.

[78] e.g. F.O. Copley, 'Servitium amoris in the Roman elegists', *TAPA* 78 (1947) 285f.: Oliver Lyne in *CQ* 29 (1979) 117-30.

[79] As when Creon calls Haemon 'slave of a woman' (Sophocles *Antigone* 756), or an historian says of Claudius that he 'was dominated by his slaves and his wives' (Cassius Dio 60.2.4). The disgrace of being dominated by a woman is a common theme of Roman oratory: of Verres, Cic. *Verr.* 2.1.140; 2.3.30; 2.3.77f.; 2.4.136 – quite an array of women to whom the disgusting creature subjected himself and his office. The role is ascribed to Clodia in *pro Caelio*, e.g. 32, 38, 67, 78; to the wicked Sassia in *pro Cluentio* 18; cf. the charge against Antony, *Philipp.* 6.4, and nn.3-5 above for the appearance in political invective of the dominant women Medea, Omphale, Semiramis – who are for Propertius parallels to his mistress. It is tempting to connect this Roman obsession with dominant women, whether dreaded or desired, with the strongly masculine ethos of Rome and the compulsion to manly behaviour.

ideas'.[80] The gap is in part to be filled by the rhetorical and political material in which a man is accused of this relationship; that the poets accept and glory in it is a symptom of their whole attitude towards proper Roman values, of their boasting of a life which the respectable would altogether regard as *nequitia, inertia* and *infamia.*

It was indeed implicit in that attitude that the jeers of the world should become their slogans. Another pleasing example can be found in the only long poem of Gallus about which we really know anything. At the end of the tenth *Eclogue*, Virgil presents Gallus wandering on the mountains of Arcadia, lamenting in mellifluous and sentimental verse his loss of Lycoris: she has left him and will cross the icy Alps (ll. 46f.):

> *tu procul a patria (nec sit mihi credere tantum)*
> *Alpinas, a! dura, nives et frigora Rheni*
> *me sine sola vides. a, te ne frigora laedant!*
> *a, tibi ne teneras glacies secet aspera plantas!*

'Far from home _ oh, let me not believe it! – without me, alone and heartless, you see the Alpine snows and the frozen Rhine. Oh, may the cold not hurt you! – Oh, may the hard ice not cut your soft feet!' It has long been agreed that there lies behind these lines a poem of Gallus himself, as is implied by the famous note of Servius on l. 46 ('All these lines are by Gallus, taken from his actual poems') and this is confirmed[81] by the use of the same motifs in Prop. 1.8; cruelly abandoning me, says Propertius (1. 7):

> *tu pedibus teneris positas fulcire pruinas,*
> *tu potes insolitas, Cynthia, ferre nives?*

'Can your soft feet walk across the ice? Can you bear the unfamiliar snow?' Cicero's speeches against Catiline do not seem the obvious place to look for a parallel, but in the second *Catilinarian* he declaims against the fashionable and vicious young men who will, he hopes, leave Rome and join Catiline: 'But what are the poor creatures thinking of? They won't be taking their trollops with them on campaign, will they? But how can they manage without them, especially in these cold nights? And how can they bear the Appennines and all that ice and snow?' (23). As with 'slavery to a woman', 'tender feet amid the ice' appears from opposite presuppositions as a cutting joke or as a tender lament. For us it is interesting that the most characteristic note of the elegiac temperament can be so closely related to a device of rhetoric by which an orator, in the real world, actually got important things done. Cicero is not trying to

---

[80] Copley, loc. cit. (n.78) 291. It is surely odd to discuss such a theme with no mention of Antony.
[81] P.J. Enk, edition of Propertius 1 (1946) 79. J. Hubaux in *Miscellanea Properziana* (1957) 34.

transport his audience into an ideal realm of exotic fictions, but to present recognisable and real people in a special way, to lead to decisive action.

Even the sensibility of Propertius for death[82] finds far more of an echo in Antony than in Augustus. On his death-bed, we are told, Augustus 'asked his friends whether they thought he had played well the comedy of life, and asked them, in the familiar Greek tag of the actors to "dismiss him with applause" '; he died in the arms of his wife with the words 'Livia, live with the memory of our marriage: farewell'.[83] This death, so exquisitely in harmony with his life, makes him depart with irony and uxoriousness. For Propertius, in dramatic contrast, death is envisaged as romantically tragic.[84] Sometimes the lovers are to crown a life of suffering and devotion by dying together: whether as a threat,

> sed non effugies: mecum moriaris oportet;
> hoc eodem ferro stillet uterque cruor,[85]

'But you shall not escape: you shall die with me; one steel shall drip with the blood of us both,' or as a promise,

> ossa tibi iuro per matris et ossa parentis ...
> me tibi ad extremas mansurum, vita, tenebras;
> ambos una fides auferet, una dies.[86]

'I swear by the bones of my mother and father ... that I shall be true till the shadows of death: one true love until the same day carries us both off.' Sometimes she will survive him, and then her vividly imagined grief will console him for death;[87] beyond the grave they will be together.[88] Tibullus too prays to die in Delia's arms:

> te spectem, suprema mihi cum venerit hora,
> te teneam moriens deficiente manu.[89]

'May I gaze at you, when my last hour comes; may I hold you in my failing arms as I die.' Long before his death Antony had provided in his will that his body should be sent to Alexandria and buried beside Cleopatra's[90] – an instruction which Octavian turned to good account in

---

[82] e.g. Boucher, op. cit. (n.61) ch. 3: 'le sentiment de la mort'.
[83] Suetonius *D. Aug.* 99.
[84] Prop. 1.17.19f.; 19; 2.1.71f.; 24.35f.
[85] Prop. 2.8.25.
[86] Prop. 2.10.17f.; cf. 2.28.39: *una ratis fati nostros portabit amores*, 'One ship of death shall carry both lovers'.
[87] Prop. 1.17.21.
[88] Prop. 1.19.11f.; 4.7.93f. Cf. pp. 142ff. below.
[89] Tibull. 1.1.59f.
[90] Dio 50.3.5, Plutarch *Ant.* 58.8.

propaganda; and in the end we find that, as Alcibiades was accompanied to the last by his faithful mistress Timandra[91] and was buried by her, so in their last few days Antony and Cleopatra dissolved their society of Inimitable Livers 'and founded another, not at all inferior in daintiness and luxury and extravagance, which they called the Partners in Death'.[92] Antony died in her arms, and Plutarch makes her address a passionate prayer to his spirit before she took her own life:[93] '... Hide me there with you and bury me with you, for of all my many sufferings none has been so great and so cruel as this short time that I have lived without you'.

How early was this story of the death of Antony and Cleopatra? We know that her physician Olympus wrote an account of her last days, which Plutarch used,[94] and it is natural to suppose that this was produced when interest was at its height, shortly after the event.[95] Oral sources, particularly important for this _Life_ of Plutarch,[96] will have been copious and fascinating; and of course a version had to exist to explain to Rome her suicide,[97] and the representations of her at the triumph in 29 B.C. If, as seems most likely, Propertius published Book I in 29 B.C., and Book II by 25 B.C.,[98] it seems pretty certain that the _Liebestod_ of this spectacular pair, who after all had attempted to rule the world, will have been immediately present to him. And Antony, in that story, is shown dying a romantic Propertian death, after living, in many respects, the life which Propertius wished to live; while conversely the Roman audience will have found the life Propertius claimed to live all the more plausible, because recent history afforded such a sensational instance of it in Antony.[99]

Of course it is not being claimed that Propertius was inspired to his conception of the life of love only by the career of Antony. In history, satirists had long ago compared Pericles' relationship with Aspasia to that of Heracles with Omphale,[100] and the Successors of Alexander

---

[91] Plut. _Alcib._ 39.6. Scholars give what seems to me rather surprising credence to the vaguely reported story ('they say', says Plutarch) that this Timandra was the mother of one of the courtesans called Laïs: so Göber in _RE_ s.v. _Timandra_ (3), Geyer in _RE_ s.v. _Laïs_ (2). In view of the contradictory reports about these women, such a natural piece of gossipy prosopography is probably worth nothing.

[92] Plut. _Antony_ 71: _sunapothanoumenoi_.

[93] ibid. 84.

[94] ibid. 82.

[95] Jacoby observes, on Socrates of Rhodes (_FGH_ no. 192), that 'very many Greeks' must have written of Antony's career, immediately after Actium, in a sense acceptable to Octavian, to explain to the Eastern world what had happened. D.A. Russell, _Plutarch_ 140, conjectures that Antony's companions at the end, Aristocrates and Lucilius, may have left written accounts (for 'p. 1' read '69.1').

[96] cf. H.J. Rose in _Annals of Arch. and Anthrop._, _Liverpool_ 2 (1924) 25f.

[97] Some (Nisbet-Hubbard 410) doubt the historical reality of Cleopatra's suicide.

[98] So Margaret Hubbard, op. cit. (n.2) 43f.

[99] It is pleasing that Antony's son Jullus Antonius was a close friend of the witty and indiscreet Julia.

[100] Plutarch, _Pericles_ 24. The same image is used by Plutarch of Antony: _Comparatio_ 3.2.

offered plenty of examples of men overcome with the life of pleasure. The late Republic, too, was familiar with the type long before Antony. And quite apart from this sort of source, Propertius draws on other types of model: on contemporary experience, on his Latin predecessors, on Hellenistic poetry. But such a life as that of Antony does, I think, have a particular interest. Antony was no doubt influenced, in pursuing the sort of life he led, by examples both from life and from 'literature', as well as by natural inclination; and in terms of self-interest, even, the role of the dashing and careless soldier was one which made him popular with the troops – for a time.[101] Where his life took a particularly interesting turn was in concentrating at the end on one woman, and also in its tragic conclusion.

Antony, in the latter part of his career, was driven on not only by his own impulses and political calculations, but also by the existence of literary stereotypes, which from the one side lured him into the role of the dashing hedonist, and from the other pilloried him as a typical monster of vice. Such a career is itself a great example of the way life and literature affected each other. It is a further turn of the same spiral when Propertius finds a literary *persona* for himself which so strikingly recalls the career of Antony; and yet another when in poems actually about Antony he expresses an attitude at variance indeed with that proper to an Augustan poet, but in harmony with other elements of his poetry. After all, if Antony had won the Battle of Actium, Propertius would have been an Antonian poet.[102]

---

[101] Plut. *Antony* 6 and 43.
[102] Fergus Millar points out the suggestiveness for Augustan literature of the anecdote in Macrobius, *Sat* 2.4.29-30: a man produced to Octavian after Actium a trained crow, which could say *Ave Caesar victor imperator*, but was forced to reveal that he also had a second, which had been taught to say *Ave victor imperator Antoni*: not only 'Hail to Caesar the victorious' but also 'Hail to Antony the victorious'.

CHAPTER THREE

Genre and Real Life in Latin Poetry

For rhetoric, he could not ope
His mouth but out there flew a trope – Samuel Butler

As long as poetry has existed, men have wondered and argued about its relationship to reality. The Muses, meeting Hesiod beneath Mount Helicon, told him that they knew how to tell many lies that sounded like truth; Solon and Pindar echo the chastening refrain,[1] and Plato and Aristotle are concerned to find new answers to the hoary problem. Poetry is in fact a very slippery stuff, which seems to turn into something else as we try to comprehend it; like Proteus, it can turn under our grasp into a raging fire – the revolutionary Marxist view, perhaps; or a wild beast – the Freudian id, as it might be; or, most commonly, into a stream of water, which flows away to nothing between our hands.[2]

In the time of our grandfathers a popular and respected way of avoiding the difficulty of talking about poetry was to transform it into biography. The lives of poets are much easier to enjoy than their works, as we see from our more pretentious Sunday papers, which are full of speculations about Shakespeare's love life (who is Emilia Lanier, what is she?) and of gossip about the busy childless beds of Bloomsbury, perused with pleasure by a public which does not often open the *Sonnets* or *The Waves*. The biographical method had the specially pleasing feature that it had two modes, the adulatory and the snide, to cater to the two commonest attitudes of posterity towards the mighty dead; sophisticated practitioners can indeed combine the two.

That method is now, among the more knowledgeable, out of favour. We have come to see that it is sadly naive to try to turn the poems of Propertius into a coherent narrative of the life and loves of the poet and a woman who could, if only we knew how, be firmly pinned down, fitted into a prosopography, and provided with a beginning, a middle, and an end. In enlightened quarters, again, the quest to identify Virgil's farm, armed with the first and ninth *Eclogues* and autopsy of the Mantuan region, raises only a weary smile. To such an extreme, indeed, have the enthusiastic carried this abstention, that in some places it is now a dogma that *no* experience of the poet is to be allowed to raise its head in

---

[1] Hesiod *Theogony* 22-8; Solon, fr. 29 West; Pindar, *Ol.* 1.30.
[2] *Omnia transformat sese in miracula rerum, / ignemque horribilemque feram fluviumque liquentem.* Virg., *Georg.* 4.411-2.

the interpretation of his poems; I need only mention Pindar.[3]

If poetry is not, after all, concealed biography, then what can it be? In the discussion of Roman poetry one attractive possibility has seemed to be that it is, in reality, made up of poetical motifs, Greek in origin, which have little or no connection with the real world of Augustan Rome and the real lives of Horace and Propertius; that, for example, 'Horace's erotic poems are set in a world totally removed from the Augustan state'; and that the girl he writes about are 'totally unlike the compliant *scorta* of Horace's own temporary affairs'.[4] It follows that the provision of parallels in other poets, even in poets who wrote centuries later, comes to have great explanatory power; the parallel in Paul the Silentiary or in Anacreon shows that the motif is a current one, existing in a world not just not identical with but 'totally removed from' that of Horace's experience. I have tried in Chapters One and Two to explain why this sort of approach, influential as it is, is false to the reality of poetry, dissociating it from life and setting it down in bookish seclusion. Poetry, although it is not just the same thing as life, is not totally remote from it either; not only is poetry influenced by history, but human behaviour in turn is influenced by poetry. Nor is one necessarily anxious to accept the implication that all poetry is really about other poetry, rather than being about the many and various things which it professes to be about, such as life and love.[5]

It is another and evidently related way of handling poetry which finds the key to it all not in poetical motifs, nor in biography or autobiography, but in rhetorical treatises and the doctrine of rhetorical genres. In an influential and interesting book Francis Cairns argues with great energy for a general view: 'The theory which underlies this book is that the whole of classical poetry is written in accordance with the sets of rules of the various genres, rules which can be discovered by a study of the surviving literature itself and of the ancient rhetorical handbooks dealing with this subject.' Not only are the poems written in accordance with the rules of these genres; in fact, 'the poems of classical antiquity are not internally complete, individual works, but they are members of classes of literature known in antiquity as *genê* or *eidê*, which will be described in this book as genres.' Thus, for example, on this view a poem like Propertius 1.3 is not just like a *kômos*, the revelling arrival of a lover at

[3] E.L. Bundy, *Studia Pindarica* 1 and 2 (1962); and e.g. W.J. Slater, 'Futures in Pindar', *CQ* 19 (1969) 86. A balanced view: H. Lloyd-Jones in *JHS* 93 (1973) 109-37.

[4] G. Williams, *Tradition and Originality in Roman Poetry* (1968) 557; Nisbet-Hubbard 73.

[5] This is a widespread modern notion. We observe that many modern novels are about the writing of novels, and many modern poems about writing poetry; and Leo Steinberg had great success in the 1960s, as a critic of painting, with his dictum that 'Whatever else it may be, all great art is about art' (cf. Tom Wolfe, *The Painted Word* (1975) 81, for a cruel handling). 'Poems do not exist just to show us their relation to other poems': John Bayley in the *TLS* 1982, p. 500.

the house of his beloved, it actually is a *kômos*; and Propertius 1.6 actually is a *propemptikon*, an example of the rhetorical form for which rules are given by Menander Rhetor. It can thus be said that 'pseudo-Dionysius of Halicarnassus and Menander Rhetor are good witnesses to the literary practice of the whole of antiquity.'[6] These rhetoricians, who hitherto have led quiet lives respectively in the second volume of Usener and Radermacher's Teubner edition of the *Opuscula* of Dionysius and in the third volume of Spengel's *Rhetores Graeci*, thus have sudden greatness thrust upon them; they become the key to the understanding of ancient poetry, Greek and Latin, from beginning to end. For there is in effect no change from one generation or period to another, and indeed 'In a very real sense antiquity was in comparison with the nineteenth and twentieth centuries a time-free zone' (p. 32). Such a claim is bold enough to call for a considered reply; for its acceptance carries, as we shall see, momentous implications. What, first, do we find, when we take these authors from the shelf where, perhaps, they have rather seldom been disturbed?

First, we find that all their activity is directed towards one sort of speech. There are three kinds of oratory, says Menander: that of the law-courts, *dikanikê*, that of politics, *politikê*, and that of display, *epideiktikê*. This last is his subject. It has two divisions, reproach or rebuke, *psogos*, and praise, *enkômion*. That is to say, the speaker sets out either to lower something in the eyes of his audience or to raise it in their esteem. In fact – since no doubt there was no call for speeches attacking things and nobody would pay for them – Menander is concerned almost exclusively with praise. The reader learns how to praise the different gods, in various sorts of prose hymns; how to praise cities and countries; how to praise men. A great man is invited to come to our city, in a *klêtikon*; he is praised on his arrival, in an *epibatêrion*; he is praised when he leaves, in a *propemptikon*. Weddings, birthdays, funerals, all are occasions for the orator to show his skill and to lavish praise. Pseudo-Dionysius is exactly the same: nothing but praise from beginning to end of his dreary little work. Obviously, that was what those who paid rhetors, and who wanted occasions embellished by a few jewels of rhetoric, would pay for. But doubts arise in the mind when we remember that these little vade mecum handbooks for orators are no less than 'good witnesses to the literary practice of the whole of antiquity'. Can it really be that the whole of ancient poetry consists of panegyric? Or, to allow for the phenomenon of 'inversion', by which a poem like Horace's tenth *Epode*, in which the poet heaps curses on a departing enemy, is diagnosed as an 'inverse *propemptikon*', of panegyric plus abuse?

There are other objections which can be pressed against this generic approach, which I think have weight but which I cannot develop here. I

[6] F. Cairns, *Generic Composition in Greek and Roman Poetry* (1972) 31, 6, 73.

shall only mention some of them in passing. Thus, although the point of this form of analysis is supposed to be that it conforms to the thinking of antiquity, yet many of the alleged 'genres' do not exist in the ancient texts and have to be invented and named by the contemporary scholar. Nor is it at all certain that in the Augustan period even such genres as the *propemptikon*, as it is treated by Menander, actually existed at all. More importantly, while some of the 'genres' are defined in terms of the occasion on which they are employed – which is on the whole the method of Menander and pseudo-Dionysius – others are defined in quite different ways. Thus, the term 'dithyramb' is defined by its recipient, the god Dionysus; and we observe that there is no hint in the rhetorical writers that this term could apply to a composition in prose – except indeed as a metaphor for bombastic style. Other genres are of a quite different character: 'gloating over fulfilment', the 'genre' to which we find ascribed poems like Horace *Odes* 3.15, 'I said you'd get old and past it, and now you are, ha ha!' is defined by what is said, neither by a regular occasion (a departure, a wedding) nor by the recipient. Again, some of the 'genres' are things for which we can well imagine patrons or clients paying, such as a speech at a wedding, a greeting to a newly arrived governor; but others are not. Who would pay a rhetorician to produce 'gloating over fulfilment', for instance, or the equally unexpected 'genre' of *mandata morituri* – the last words of a dying man? To that unconvincing category is assigned, for instance, Horace *Odes* 2.20.

It is another serious problem that the rhetoricians themselves derived their own material from the existing practice of poets. In a *kateunastikos logos*, or speech uttered while the bride is put to bed, says Menander, 'take what the poets do as your model'; in an epithalamium, 'there is plenty of material in the poets and prose writers ... use the love poetry of Sappho and that of Homer and Hesiod'.[7] If you are called upon for abuse, then Archilochus will help; in general, you need to have in your memory 'Homer, Hesiod, and the lyric poets'. As for a monody, or speech in lamentation for a dead man, 'Homer the divine poet, among all the things he has taught us, has not omitted the genre of monody', giving good examples in the laments he puts into the mouths of Andromache, Priam, and Hecuba. There is at least one form, that of the *apopemptikos hymnos* (valedictory hymn), which is *only* found in the poets. In fact, pseudo-Dionysius feels it necessary to remind his pupil that, while Sappho is a useful source, 'the procedure in poetry is not the same as in prose', so that the speaker needs to change the form of his material, to suit it for oratory. Evidently some aspiring orators stuck too closely to their poetical texts. But a question of principle presents itself with some sharpness: what justifies us in breaking the circle at just this point, and

---

[7] See now the edition of Menander Rhetor by D.A. Russell and N.G. Wilson (1981) 31-5 and D.A. Russell, 'Rhetors at the wedding', *PCPhS* 205 (1979) 104-17.

insisting on the primacy of the rhetoricians over the poets, when they themselves explicitly base their work on that of the poets? Another point, also heavy with consequence, is that this conception of Greek and Latin poetry seems to limit us severely in judging the poems. Poems which we have wanted to say were rather poor turn out, because of their correct relation to the supposed generic framework, to be immune to our censure. Thus Theocritus 12, in which little good has been found by those who have commented upon it at all, has 'merit' revealed by its assignation to the genre of *prosphônêtikon* (public address); of Theocritus 17, another poem in generally low esteem, we read: 'When we have such good evidence of Theocritus' critical approach to the generic pattern and of his careful and judicious selection of material, it is no longer possible to assent to any sweeping condemnation of *Idyll* 17.' If a poem plays the generic game, then it must be a good poem – or at least it cannot be a bad one; and the qualities of neatness, ingenuity, and sophistication become, without our having fully understood how, the framework within which we are to judge ancient poetry. What place is there for passion, sublimity, or truth, if all poems are composed, and to be judged, within a framework of rhetorical genres?[8] Finally, we observe that there is a strong implication that none of the poems will really be about the poet. Rhetors were not commissioned to talk about themselves; if they are the model, then we must not be surprised if poets do not, either.

These are, I think, real and disturbing questions. But having simply drawn attention to them I pass on to one of a different sort: how true is it that the poems of the Augustans, with whom I shall on the whole be concerned, actually do exemplify the rhetorical genres of the rhetorician Menander? How far do they really exist in a time-free zone, without contact with society and life? I propose to take two main examples, both arising from poems in the First Book of Propertius.

One of Propertius' most familiar and memorable poems is 1.3. The poet tells how he stood beside Cynthia's bed as she lay asleep, lit only by the moon. He gazes at her, comparing her to various glamorous ladies of mythology. She is like Ariadne, left fast asleep as Theseus sailed away; like Andromeda, in her first sleep after her delivery from the rocks; like a maenad, exhausted by ranging over the mountains in Bacchic ecstasy.

---

[8] Cairns 25, 112. One is reminded here of ideas that have been powerful at times in French literature, with results that may seem suggestively similar. Thus Chateaubriand in his *Essai sur la littérature anglaise* (Garnier edn., vol. 11, 588ff.), in a section significantly headed 'Shakespeare corrupted taste', pleads: 'Persuadons-nous qu'écrire est un art, que cet art a des genres, chaque genre a des règles. Les genres et les règles ne sont pas arbitraires ...'. The bad thing about Shakespeare is that 'il ne distingue pas les genres', and Chateaubriand triumphantly concludes that Racine is not only a better poet but actually more natural, because he observes them. One sees how readily technicality and classicism go hand in hand. N.M. Horsfall, *Echos du monde classique* 23 (1979) 84, doubts whether many Romans of the Augustan period knew anything about the 'doctrine of the genres'.

Drunk and excited as he is – he has been to a party – the poet is transfixed by the sight. Gently he approaches her, smooths her hair, tries to put on her head the garland he is wearing from the party which has kept him so late, attempts to give her the fruit he is carrying. But when she wakes she deluges him with reproaches and complaints. The poem is a little drama, which contrasts the ideal beauty and tranquillity of Cynthia asleep with the shrewish vehemence which Propertius knows and dreads when she is awake (line 18, *expertae metuens iurgia saevitiae*); the statuesque beginning gives place to an angry end.[9] The opening, in particular, was found striking enough by contemporaries for Ovid to produce a witty and unkind burlesque of it at *Amores* 1.10.1-8. Analysis on generic lines finds, what had not hitherto been suspected, that the poem is a *kômos*.[10] A *kômos* was a more or less noisy, often violent, progress of the lover, with or without companions, to the house of his beloved, by night; once arrived, he could either beg for admittance or attempt to force his way in. Sometimes he succeeded, sometimes he failed; sometimes he spent the night, or part of it, ostentatiously freezing and suffering on the doorstep of the adored object, singing, wheedling, or possibly writing verses on her door.

All this is of course familiar enough. We have read a lot about komasts in the last few years. In fact no less than five of the idylls of Theocritus which are analysed by Cairns turn out to be *kômoi* – 2, 3, 6, 7, 11. What is gained, or lost, by the assertion that Propertius 1.3 is a *kômos*? We observe at once that the fundamental feature is missing: there is no arrival, no pleading, no violence; no decision, even, by Cynthia whether to admit her lover or not. Propertius, it is evident, has (as we should say) a key, and the drama begins with him already in her bedroom. Not only has he a key, she has promised him that for tonight she is his; at line 37 she asks him bitterly 'Where have you spent the night that belonged to me?' As a *kômos*, in fact, the thing is a complete frost, and neither of the pair has made a success of the komastic role. The memory of the lover in his excluded position, clamorous or plaintive at the door, subject to the arbitrary decision of the beloved to make him happy or to make him miserable – all that is in the background only. The poem puts us in a world in which such things happened between lovers and their girls, but this time, he tells us, it was different. To insist that this actually is a *kômos* is surely to force this delightful poem on to a Procrustean bed. It obliges us to put too much weight on what is not there, to the comparative detriment of what is; and it turns out, not much to our surprise (p. 336), that the poem contains no less than four witty points,

[9] On Propertius 1.3 see O. Lyne in *PCPhS* 196 (1970) 60-78; G. Williams, *Figures of Thought in Roman Poetry* (1980) 72. We could construct a 'genre' of 'the rape of the sleeping beauty' (cf. *AP* 5.275; Terence *Eun.* 600ff.; Ovid *Ars* 3.765ff.), and invoke that, too, to help explain the poem ...

[10] F. Cairns, *Emerita* 45 (1977) 336ff.

all based upon the *kômos* assumption. As I suggested earlier, the element of ingenuity and wit is over-valued in a poem which begins with a beautiful and touching tableau, and ends with a picture of the lonely Cynthia spinning and singing and waiting for the lover who does not come, until at last she falls asleep. That shift of emotional tone is a very natural consequence of our adopting this model of analysis of poems; as I said, its consequences are momentous.

I pause here to make a digression on the theme of the excluded lover. There are many Augustan poems on this theme, and I am sure I am not alone in feeling at times that perhaps there are even too many. Parallels are found in the Hellenistic epigram, in Comedy, perhaps even in archaic lyric; but at Rome the motif flourished astonishingly. The discovery of parallels is not, let us say with emphasis, an explanation for such a thing, interesting though it is; in fact the more parallels we find, the more pressing becomes the need to make sense of the phenomenon, in terms both of human nature, which changes very little, and of human society, which changes a great deal. I here offer an explanation which attempts to go beyond the simple collection and categorising of parallel material.

In Rome, as in most early societies, relations between the sexes were organised in a way which left very little room indeed for romance. Marriage, in the upper class, was a family alliance, contracted without courtship and experienced without passion, however devoted spouses often became to each other.[11] Plutarch tells us that the reason why a Roman bridegroom approached his bride for the first time in darkness was so that he should be accustomed to come to his wife with modesty; if she is modest and reserved, he should reflect that he cannot treat the same woman both as a wife and as a hetaera. A Roman bride was very young, too, which must have had its consequences in the attitude towards her of a humane husband.[12] Outside marriage there were spread out for his pleasure, and at his expense, the various temptations of the demi-monde. But the human heart is not always satisfied with a choice between the modest wife who does her wifely duty – *officium faciat nulla puella mihi*, says the hedonist Ovid[13] – and the professional, the *meretrix*, who obliges because she is paid. There is the desire to be loved for oneself, to be chosen; Sir Kenneth Dover has shown how in Greece

---

[11] For instance, the well known story of the betrothal of Tiberius Gracchus to the daughter of Appius Claudius Pulcher: Plut. *Tib. Gracchus* 4.

[12] Plutarch, *Coniug. Praecepta* 29 = *Moralia* 142c; and *Roman Questions* 65 = *Moralia* 279f., on the question why the Roman husband approached his bride for the first time in darkness; R.O.A.M. Lyne, *The Latin Love Poets* (1980) 5ff., and P. Grimal, *L'Amour à Rome* (1963) 105ff. on 'les pudeurs romaines' about marriage. Martial rebukes a modest wife who dislikes having the light on (11.104.5). On the age of Roman brides, K. Hopkins in *Population Studies* 18 (1965) 309-27.

[13] Ovid *Ars* 2.688, 'Let no girl do an act of duty to me.' See also *Ars* 3.585: *hoc est, uxores quod non patiatur amari: conveniunt illas, cum voluere, viri*: 'This is what stops wives being loved: their husbands enjoy them whenever they choose.'

this clamorous desire of the heart led to demanding and extreme conceptions of homosexual love, men behaving, in the pursuit or in the service of a beloved boy, in ways which to us recall the conduct of romantic lovers.[14] The boy was in principle a social equal, possessed of the power of choice, able to say Yes or No to his admirer; that was, perhaps, the most important and exciting thing about him. Such a train of thought is suggestive also for the excluded lover and his well-publicised woes, and indeed goes well beyond it to the whole conception of the cruel mistress, the *dura domina*, of elegiac love poetry.

Neither obliged by wifely status nor simply hired for money, the high-class girl who is taken seriously by Catullus and his successors is exhilarating because she can say No. That is what is important about her, far more than the question, so much debated, whether she is or is not married. Disreputable yet bewitching, she intoxicates her lover by accepting him for himself alone, not (as he is always reminding us) for money. When she says Yes, that has value *because* she can and does say No. The poets themselves are aware of this, and Propertius makes his *lena* advise her girl to promise herself and then refuse; Ovid's *lena* gives the same advice, and so does the poet himself in the third book of the *Ars*.[15] The whole flavour of the relationship, its masochistic overtone, is connected with this fundamental fact, that here at last is an object of love who has power and uses it; and nowhere does she use it more vividly than in refusing to open her door at all. When that happens, the lover feels not only pain at his exclusion, but also a profound pleasure. 'She has admitted me in the past, she will again, and that gift is a true one, as is proved by her ability not to give it; therefore I have been truly loved and can hope to be again ...' Different social customs, the insignificance in Rome of the whole Greek culture of the palaestra and athletics, combined no doubt with other differences in the relation of the sexes, gave a heterosexual turn to a set of feelings which in Greece characteristically took a homosexual one. The importance of this sort of argument, I suggest, is that it tries to explain not merely that a poetical form is recurrent, but why it was attractive to poets: the excluded lover at the closed door of his mistress is a quintessential vision of his whole life of love.

From the *kômos* and love locked out I turn to the other poem which I take as an example, the sixth poem of Propertius' first book. In that poem, addressed to Tullus, Propertius says that while Tullus is going abroad on state service, he himself is kept at home by his fatal love; it is not for him, born as he is to an ignoble life of *nequitia* and suffering, to comply with any of the patriotic functions of his class. The poem is intensely Propertian, full of his characteristic ethos. It is subjected to

[14] K.J. Dover, *Greek Homosexuality* (1978) 52ff.
[15] Prop. 4.5.33ff., Ov. *Amores* 1.8.73, *Ars* 3.580.

generic analysis and appears – it is the first poem dealt with in Professor Cairns' book – to be a 'schetliastic *propemptikon*'. The rhetorical writers, at least in the second century A.D.,[16] were conscious of the *propemptikon* as a rhetorical form: a departing friend or official is given a speech at his send-off, which expresses the grief and disappointment (*schetliasmos*) of those who are left behind. There may appear to be nothing very contentious about connecting Propertius' poem with such speeches, but as we shall see positive identification has serious and unfortunate implications.

First, since Tullus is going on state service as a member of his uncle's staff, the *propemptikon* must be of the type from an inferior to a superior. Roman governors are the top of the social scale. It seems to follow that Tullus is Propertius' patron, and also that anything in the poem which appears not to be complimentary to Tullus must be re-interpreted, for 'In ancient literature it is impossible that a poem addressed to a patron-cum-dedicatee should be uncomplimentary. Despite appearances, therefore, the contrast cannot be uncomplimentary to Tullus. How then can we explain it?' (p. 4). It is time to stop and reflect. Did Propertius, at the time of Book One, have a patron? Miss Hubbard places the dedicatee, Volcacius Tullus, rightly, when she says that he came from 'a family of social status like that of the Propertii, but one that had followed the different road of the Roman official career'.[17] Propertius addresses Tullus in four poems in Book One, including the first and last, clearly the position of honour; but he also addresses four poems to Gallus, who is also, it appears, *nobilis* (1.5.23). In the sixth poem Tullus is off to 'soft Ionia', while in the fourteenth poem he is rich and idle, drinking rare vintages on the banks of the Tiber, *abiectus Tiberina molliter unda*. It might seem a reasonable inference that he is not a patron but a friend, who can be treated with a certain humour; his tastes are not much more Spartan than the poet's own. It comes, on this view, as no surprise that in fact Tullus turned out, once in Asia, anything but Catonian, and Propertius wrote 3.22 to suggest that after all there was something to be said for coming back to face the realities of life in Rome. We contrast the way Propertius addresses Maecenas, once he has come on the scene – *Maecenas nostrae spes invidiosa iuventae* (2.1.73), 'Maecenas, hope of my youth, cause of jealousy in others'. The poet is a gentleman, of an equestrian family,[18] and like Catullus he speaks, in

---

[16] Cf. for instance Gordon Williams in *Oxford Classical Dictionary*[2] s.v. *Propemptikon*: 'The genre as such and its detailed specifications were probably the invention of Menander.' It is in fact striking that the term appears in poetry before it does in rhetoric: the celebrated *Propempticon Pollionis* of Cinna (*Fragmenta Poetarum Latinorum*, ed. Morel (1927) 87).

[17] M. Hubbard, *Propertius* (1974) 24.

[18] ibid. 96ff.; cf. Hanslik in *RE* s.v. *Propertius*, 758.48. Of another elegist, too, Sir Ronald Syme remarks 'The *Amores* enlist no persons of high rank as patrons or protectors' (*History in Ovid* (1978) 76). See also 93-103, on the friends of Propertius, and 180: 'For Ovid as for Propertius, "sodales" are disclosed, of about the same age and class.'

3. Genre and Real Life in Latin Poetry

Book One, to friends and equals. There is, then, no need to suppose that Tullus is a 'patron', and consequently no need to insist that everything said to him must be straightforwardly complimentary.[19]

Finally, we are no longer inhibited from saying that 1.6 is not, in its primary nature, a poem about Tullus at all. It is, of course, really about Propertius and his love, and more than half of the poem is explicitly about that. As with most of the first book, the poet is telling us about his own life, what it is to be the slave of passion and to live for love; the interesting part of 1.6 is the account of Cynthia pleading with him not to leave her, sulking and threatening, prevailing upon her susceptible lover to choose life and death with her rather than the University of Athens or the opulent cities of the East, rather even than the life of glory and duty.[20] Tullus, by contrast, is fairly colourless; we have no clear picture of what he will be doing in Asia,[21] nor are we keenly concerned. The generic analysis thus leads again to an unsatisfactory reading of the poem as a whole, which turns out to be distorted in just the sort of way we anticipated *a priori*: insistence that it is the same kind of thing as what rhetoricians produced was bound to lead to the conclusion that it would be impersonal and encomiastic, like their set speeches of praise. Rhetoricians were not often paid to talk about themselves.

I shall turn to the general question of the significance of the rhetorical genres for poetry after a glance at another poem in Book One; the eighth poem, which, like most recent writers, I shall treat as being one poem.[22] In the first half the poet laments the departure of his beloved, who is leaving him to sail away with another man; in the second he exults that after all his prayers and his love prevailed upon her, and she did not go. This too, we find, is a *propemptikon*. The poet has complied with the rhetorical form in expressing resistance and opposition to her departure, and she has done what such a speaker wants by yielding to his *schetliasmos*. Reflection on this suggests reservations. A rhetor was employed, not to make a departing governor of a province actually change his mind and decide to stay, but to express in formal terms the sadness of his subjects at seeing him go. Rhetoric and Roman constitution alike would be thrown into confusion if the proconsul were to disembark and announce his intention of staying on for another year. Nor would the situation be wholly different in another case which Menander envisages: the departure of a pupil from the rhetor's school. His studies over, the pupil leaves; the occasion is turned to account by the rhetor to

---

[19] Cf. J. Clack in *CW* 71 (1971) 187. On the general question of literary patrons, see P. White, 'Amicitia and the profession of poetry in early Imperial Rome', *JRS* 68 (1978) 74-92. I think this important article is misleading in one significant respect: a poet differed from other *amici* in claiming the power to bestow immortality. That put him into a special category.

[20] Cf. W. Stroh, *Die röm. Liebeselegie als werbende Dichtung* (1971) 41.

[21] F. Cairns in *AJP* 95 (1974) 150.

[22] *Contra*, O. Skutsch in *CP* 58 (1963) 238, J.A. Barsby in *Mnem*. 28 (1975) 31.

show how one speaks on such occasions. But all would become burlesque if pupils were so overcome by the exposition of correct sentiments that they could not bring themselves to depart. It is both important and amusing that Menander actually tells us how a real rhetor behaved: 'You should protest as if you wished to persuade him not to go, and failed to succeed; then you can go on "Since your mind is made up and I have been defeated, come, let us go along with your decision ..." '

The poems at which we have been looking all have in common, I want to say, a setting which is not wholly remote from the sort of genre alleged for them. The ancient world was one in which recurrent events and occasions were signalised by rhetoric and poetry; poems for birthdays, like speeches to mark the departure of grandees, were actually composed. And Romans were tolerant, in fact enthusiastic, about the elegant rehearsal of appropriate and well-turned phrases and motifs, however familiar. But none of this compels or even allows us to make the giant leap of asserting that every poem which plays with such a set piece, or which alludes to it or glances at it, actually is an example of it. I give a couple of examples from English poetry. In 1926 W.B. Yeats wrote:

> It is time that I wrote my will;
> I choose upstanding men
> That climb the streams until
> The fountain leap, and at dawn
> Drop their cast at the side
> Of dripping stone; I declare
> They shall inherit my pride ...

In twentieth-century Ireland the making of a will was a serious matter, overseen by the law, the duty of a prudent man. Instructions for the making of wills were on sale. But of course Yeats is not really writing the kind of will which was deposited with the family lawyer; the point is too obvious to labour. At the death of Yeats, Auden wrote:

> Earth, receive an honoured guest:
> William Yeats is laid to rest.
> Let the Irish vessel lie
> Emptied of its poetry ...

Again, not something of the same stuff and form as the words which were in fact spoken at the funeral. In each case the poet makes use of occasions and ceremonies which recur in the real world, using them as part of his unique creation; the existence of real wills and real funerals is the necessary background to the poems, the starting point of their flight. In a society in which the dead were burned or exposed to vultures, Auden's poem would have little power.

Poets, we are told, can give to airy nothing a local habitation and a name. That, however, is not what they usually do. Very often a poet

needs or delights to have a starting point, something which can be made
to happen. A love poet, for example, cannot write very many poems
simply repeating that 'I love you'; he soon feels the need for things to
occur. Shakespeare's *Sonnets* refer, not always very lucidly, to various
happenings in a complex story of love; Herrick writes of Julia moving in a
silk dress; Ben Jonson makes use of the custom of toasting the beloved
('Drink to me only with thine eyes'); Lovelace leaves his Lucasta for the
wars; and so on. The poet observes in the world certain tremendous facts
which do not change – that there are two sexes, that children are born,
that we all must die. He observes also other facts which are important in
a given society or setting; ceremonies, customs, occasions. All of these
can serve as subjects for his poetry: not only death but also funerals, not
only birth but also birthdays. As the Augustan poet looked at his world
he saw in it such things as the set speech which marked the occasion of
the departure of a high functionary, a show-piece for the rhetorician; he
also observed social customs such as the hopeful lover revelling through
the night to the beloved's door, in which the rhetorician had no part; and
thirdly he saw such universal things as gloating, the pleasure with which
one who has uttered or thought a cruel prophecy for another observes its
fulfilment, which was not only not a matter for the rhetorician but was
not a social custom at all. Like poets of other times and places, he was at
liberty to exploit all this material, and he did so.

In 1.6 Propertius makes use of a setting which might have held a
formal rhetorical speech on the virtues of Tullus and the grief of those he
leaves behind; he uses it to create a work in which Tullus' virtues are
adumbrated but thinly and with less than complete conviction, and in
which the emphasis is all upon himself. So far from his missing the
virtuous Tullus, in fact, his thoughts will be fully occupied with Cynthia;
perhaps *Tullus* will occasionally think of *him* (lines 35f.). If he does, he
can be sure that Propertius' mind is full of Cynthia and her cruelty. In 1.8
the same sort of setting is again not far from Propertius' mind; but since
the poem is not, in fact, a rhetorical set speech but a quasi-dramatic
piece which glances at such things, the impossible can happen, and the
departing Cynthia after all stays at home with him – an occasion of
despair for the rhetor, of delight for the poet. Poets can glance at such
things and then turn to something else; they are not tied to the rhetorical
forms, even if they really are aware of them in detail, as opposed to being
familiar with the sort of occasion on which a speech might well be made.
In the case of Propertius 1.3 any connection which exists between the
poem and the form – itself not rhetorical – of the *kômos* is even more
exiguous. Often lovers arrived by night, made a scene, and pleaded for
admission; this time none of that happened. The languorous opening, so
beautiful and touching, gives place to anger and abuse, but at no point
do we really come close to the *kômos*-situation.

If what I have been saying is right, then we find a simpler explanation for the fact that some poems do seem to stand in a definite relationship to these rhetorical genres, while others do not, and many others come close at one moment or another to one or more of them. We shall not, that is, have to think that a poem like Horace *Odes* 3.27 is 'a *propemptikon* including an inverse *epibaterion*' or that Tibullus 1.7 is 'a *genethliakon* (birthday poem) including a triumph-poem.' We have seen reason to reject the idea that poems are to be regarded as incarnating one 'genre' each; the problems involved in any attempt to treat them as compound entities made up of several 'genres' will be far greater, and all the difficulties of principle will still remain. It will be a welcome consequence that we shall be delivered from the necessity of grappling with such scholastic questions as whether 'independent genres could become topoi of other genres' or conversely whether 'topoi could become independent genres'.

I turn back now to Propertius 1.6. It will prove possible to look at the poem in a way which is not liable to these objections, and which, more importantly, has the positive advantage of showing how a surprisingly large part of Augustan poetry can be seen to be intimately connected and related. This will emerge from an analysis to which the rhetorical genres are essentially irrelevant. The contents of the poem can be summarised thus:

Tullus, you are off on military service; I should like to go, too, but my mistress keeps me at home. No true lover can be unresponsive to the beloved's tears; and so I cannot sail off to the cities of the East. You are serving your country, but I was not born for glory or for arms – my military service is that of love. As you do your duty amid the luxuries of Ionia, think of me suffering for love.

We have seen that a love poet needs things to happen; he cannot for ever descant simply on the greatness of his love. An obvious thing which can happen is that the lovers can be parted, and it has the advantage that unhappiness and suffering make much better material for poetry than conjugal serenity; consider that slimmest of volumes, the poetry of married love. We can avoid the terms 'genre' and 'topoi' at the basic level of our analysis (which will be a considerable gain, as they are by no means free of obscurity and confusion)[23] if we begin from this simple human situation. It has its variations. He can leave her, or she can leave him; he can go willingly or unwillingly; she can go innocently or with another man; they can part for a time or for ever. Having been separated they can be reunited, with many possibilities of manner and motive. They can be finally separated by death – or indeed in death they may be finally united. Both their separation and their union may suggest by contrast other ways of life than that of their mutual devotion. That

---

[23] See for instance M.P. Cunningham in *CP* 72 (1977) 76-8 – a discussion worth pondering.

contrast may be bitter (how humiliating to live like this, when there are such alternatives!) or sweet (how much better to live like this, than the banal alternatives!). In developing this material, which derives from life, and relates intimately to it, the poet can indeed use, among other things, the devices of the rhetoricians.

In Rome at this period the universal situation of lovers parting could be related especially to important aspects of real life. First, the sophisticated courtesan was well aware of the importance of not being always available; thus with elegant brevity Ovid advises her,

> *quod datur ex facili, longum male nutrit amorem:*
> *miscenda est laetis rara repulsa iocis.*[24]

'What is easily given fails to feed a long-lasting love. You should include a few rejections with your enjoyable sports.' Again, travel was easy, both within Italy[25] and overseas.[26] So too Volumnia Cytheris toured Italy with Antony,[27] and later left Gallus in a way which could be represented as going off with another Roman commander over the Alps.[28] The Roman Empire, too, like the British Empire, called men away to duties overseas. The departure of a Roman governor was an occasion for pomp and spectacle,[29] and he expected to take friends with him on his staff. Even Catullus, we remember, went out to Bithynia as a staff officer; an appointment hard to beat for unsuitability, at least until Edgar Allan Poe served as a regimental sergeant-major. The lover can thus travel to duty and to war[30] – or refuse to do so.[31] He can deftly bridge the gap with the idea that love *is* military service.[32] He can travel with a friend – 'a classical commonplace of literature' according to Cairns,[33] but a regular feature also of philosophy[34] and of life.[35]

---

[24] *Ars* 3.579-80; cf. Prop. 4.5.33ff., Ov. *Am.* 1.8.73, Callimachus *Epigram* 31 Pf., Horace *Sat.* 1.2.105.

[25] Cynthia at Baiae, Prop. 1.11; in the country, 2.19; touring Italy, 2.32.

[26] Illyria, Prop. 1.8; Asia, 1.6.

[27] Cic. *Philipp.* 2.58.

[28] Virg. *Buc.* 10; Prop. 1.8.

[29] e.g. Livy 42.49; Kroll, *Die Kultur der ciceronischen Zeit* (1933) 187.

[30] Hor. *Epode* 1.11, Tib. 1.10.3; cf. Tib. 2.6.1 *castra Macer sequitur: tenero quid fiet Amori?* 'Macer is going on campaign: what will become of the gentle Cupid?'

[31] Hor. *Epode* 1.1, Tib. 1.3.1, Prop. 3.4.

[32] Tib. 1.1.75, Hor. *Odes* 3.26, Prop. 4.1.135; Ov. *Am.* 1.9.

[33] *Generic Composition* 4.

[34] cf. J.C. Yardley, *Phoenix* 27 (1973) 287, who cites Aristotle *Nic. Eth.* 9.2, Plut. *Mor.* 491d, 52b-c, 95c-d, 97a; Lucian *Toxaris* 18, 43.

[35] Men even accompanied friends to exile: Cn. Sallustius went with Cicero as far as Brundisium and perhaps further (*ad Fam.* 14.4.6. Münzer in *RE* s.v. *Sallustius*, 1912.44); Cicero awaited Atticus at Dyrrachium and Quintus in Epirus (*ad Att.* 3.7.3; 3.8.1; cf. also *post red. ad Quir.* 8). He promised to accompany Sestius, if he were exiled (*pro Sest.* 146). Tiberius was accompanied by a senator and at least two *equites* on Rhodes (Tac. *Ann* 4.15); one brave soul could claim to have accompanied Seneca to Corsica (Martial 7.44,45).

It seems to me an important point that many of the motifs which can be used of the lover lend themselves with equal facility to another style of life, that of the philosopher. As a man can leave love for war, so he can leave love for philosophy,[36] or again he can leave philosophy for war.[37] As we can say that it is useless to fly from the pains of love,[38] so we can say that travel is no cure for the anxieties which menace philosophical serenity;[39] as the lover is indifferent to military success and patriotic glory, so the philosopher, too, looks down on 'Roman history and kingdoms which must pass away', *res Romanas perituraque regna;*[40] as the desire for wealth is an obstacle to love,[41] so it is to philosophy.[42] And as a poet can say farewell to love,[43] so he can to philosophy, also.[44]

So, too, themes which come in a context of sexual love recur with equal freedom and elegance in a context of friendship. A friend can leave the poet, whether for the wars[45] or for some other reason,[46] and that is an occasion for a poem no less than the departure of the beloved.[47] A friend can be begged to return,[48] and can come home and be greeted with rapture.[49] And so on.

It is not hard to see the threads which lead from this nexus of ideas to other important strands of Roman poetry. The opposition of love to wealth and to war is part of the rejection of the proper career of the Roman gentleman; the separation of lovers looks to the second *Eclogue*, and the fourth book of the *Aeneid*, and the *Heroides*; the motif of 'going away' can take yet further forms, in the flight from the ravaged countryside of *Eclogue* 1.64, the flight from Italy of the sixteenth *Epode*, the flight from Rome of the third satire of Juvenal. The beloved comes back to the poet (Prop. 1.8b, Ov., *Am.* 2.11.42); or she comes, but slowly (Prop. 1.15); or she comes, but not to him ([Virg.], *Catalepton* 1). The absent lover wonders what she is doing (Prop. 2.29, 1.3), or sends a spy (Prop. 3.6), or arrives unannounced (Tib. 1.3.83).[50] She can leave him by death,[51] or he can die and leave her;[52] or they can die together,[53] or in

---

[36] Memorably in [Virg.] *Catalepton* 5; cf. Prop. 3.5.19ff., Horace *Epp.* 1.1.10ff. Reversed: Prop. 2.34b.

[37] Hor. *Odes* 1.29.

[38] Prop. 2.30. Reversed: Ov. *Rem. Am.* 539.

[39] Hor. *Odes* 3.1.40, *Epp.* 1.11.27.

[40] Virg. *Georg.* 2.498.

[41] Lovers are poor, Tib. 1.1.5, Prop. 3.16, Ovid *Ars* 2.165, etc. Reversed (poverty drives out love): Ov. *Rem. Am.* 743.

[42] Hor. *Odes* 2.2.9-16, *Epp.* 1.1.43.

[43] Catull. 8, 11; Prop. 3.24, 25; Ov. *Am.* 3.25.11.

[44] Hor. *Odes* 1.34.

[45] Hor. *Epode* 1, Tibull. 1.3.

[46] Hor. *Odes* 1.3. Reversed (curse on a departing enemy): Hor. *Epode* 10.

[47] Prop. 1.8, Hor. *Odes* 3.27, Ov. *Am.* 2.11.

[48] Prop. 3.22, Hor. *Epp.* 1.11, Hor. *Odes* 4.5.

[49] Catull. 9, Hor. *Odes* 1.34, 2.7.

[50] Or she can spy on him (Prop. 4.8) – or Ovid can recommend, as a cure for love, arriving unannounced, to see how unattractive she really is (*Rem. Am.* 341-8).

[51] Catull. 96, Virgil *Georg.* 4, *Aen.* 2 (Creusa), *Aen.* 6.472, Prop. 2.26.

death they can be finally united,[54] in an erotic Elysium[55] – or, by a final twist, even there one lover can spurn the other.[56] The reader will see how it would be possible to go on extending, varying, and reversing these and cognate ideas, as they run through the poetry of Catullus and the Augustans. If we turn back to the generic analysis with which we started, we find that some of these poems are classified as examples of one or another rhetorical genre: 'inverse *epibatêrion*', 'excusatory *propemptikon*', 'inverse *syntaktikon*', 'inverse *prosphonêtikon*', and so on.[57] Such names, I suggest, have little explanatory power. When she sails away from me (Prop. 1.8), we seem to find a rhetorical situation to hand in the *propemptikon*; but when I sail away from her (1.17) there is none, so that generic analysis has to concentrate, not on my leaving her, but on my arrival somewhere else, and the poem becomes an *epibatêrion*. But that disguises its real nature. And all the poems in which abandoned ladies complain of the men who have left them, from Catullus 64 to the *Heroides*, should be seen simply as the counterpart of the ones in which *she* leaves *me*; a satisfying simplicity which is obscured by calling the latter *propemptika* and leaving the former nameless.

It may be true sometimes that poets glance at rhetorical set pieces, but these are at most only one in their armoury of devices; the material they use is that of the real world of Roman experience, and it falsifies the nature of the poems if we single out the rhetorical genres, give them the centre of the stage, and make them into the single, privileged key. The poets draw upon material which is itself a complex of individual experience, conventional expectations, literary models, propaganda, and fantasy. They mould it in their different individual ways. Propertius 1.6 combines the motif of 'friends parting' with others – 'lovers staying together', 'love rather than duty', 'love is suffering'. The poem he produces is uniquely Propertian. Horace lets his characteristic irony play over all these themes – he cannot be a soldier (*Epode* 1.16; cf. *Carm.* 2.7.9ff.), just as he is no philosopher (*Sat.* 2.2), and no epic poet ('unfortunately I lack the stature', *Sat.* 2.1.13, *Odes*. 1.6.10-12); he is – alas! – less attractive than young men like Calais or Telephus, too (*Odes* 3.9, 4.11). And so she has left me – but she may come back (*Odes* 3.9) – after all, she might do worse (*Odes* 1.13, 4.11). That is a tone which Propertius does not strike; the supple material lends itself with equal readiness to the combinations and the colourings which different poets wish to impose on it.

[52] Prop. 1.17.19, 2.13.17; Tib. 1.1.59.
[53] Prop. 2.8.
[54] Prop. 1.19.11, 4.7.93. Variant: she can recall me from death, Prop. 2.27.
[55] Tib. 1.3.55, Prop. 2.28c. Cf. p. 151 below.
[56] *Aeneid* 6.450ff.
[57] Respectively: Horace *Epode* 1; Tibullus 1.3; Juvenal 3; Prop. 2.16.

Because Rome had an Empire, and that Empire needed the service of the men of the upper class, the universal situation of the parting of lovers is sometimes set against that background. So the life of the lover is contrasted with that of the good citizen, soldier, barrister, and man of *auctoritas*. But there may be no such nuance. Cynthia may go off, not to a province but to the seaside temptations of Baiae;[58] or Propertius may think of leaving her, not for Asia but for the grave.[59] All the varieties and permutations of separation, absence, and reunion were of interest, both in friendship and in love, the supreme themes of these poets. All of them, it seems, actually occur in their work, whether they have an erotic colouring or a philosophical one, a patriotic or a seditious tone, a setting which would or would not suit a performance by a rhetorician. This sort of situation can form the main substance of a whole poem, as when Propertius bases 2.16 on the coming of a rich rival who has displaced him in the favours of the venal Cynthia; or of most of a poem, as when Horace welcomes Augustus back from Spain in *Odes* 3.14 – but even there he turns to his own love life at the end; or they can be no more than a passing allusion in a poem based on other things, as when Tibullus mentions a *dives amator*, a wealthy rival, in the middle of 1.5. This sort of material, the situations of the love poet, is capable of many transformations. It is in fact as various, and as interesting, not as the set-pieces of the rhetoricians, but as life itself.

---

[58] See below Chapter Five.
[59] See below Chapter Seven.

CHAPTER FOUR
Of Wines and Spirits

Verbum hercle hoc verum erit, 'Sine Cerere et Libero friget Venus'

– Terence *Eunuchus* 732

You may find temptations both in wine and women
– Lord Kitchener

The life of pleasure was naturally incomplete without the joys of wine. What the Romans called a *convivium*, a living together, corresponds to what the Greeks called a *symposion*, a drinking together. When Cicero attacks enemies like Piso and Clodius and Antony, we hear a lot about orgies of drinking, along with the loose women, the dancing, and the rest.[1] Comedy automatically includes wine and women in its lists of pleasures.[2] There is no need to labour a point so obvious. What is interesting, however, is the question of the way in which these pleasures can be represented in the more ambitious styles of poetry: stylistic levels, that is, on which it was not appropriate to describe the coarse orgy of a couple of boozy slaves, as in the *Stichus* of Plautus, or men vomiting from excess, as Cicero can do from the rostrum in his attacks on Antony.[3]

Several methods offered themselves for the purpose of raising the level of wine. One was the development of connoisseurship in drinking. In the second century B.C. Italian wines began to be marked with the vintage,[4] and under the pressure of Greek sophistication Romans became keenly aware of the differences between one wine and another. The Elder Cato already thought it worth including in his Farmer's Handbook some instructions about the different vines suitable for different types of soil;[5] two hundred years later the Elder Pliny devoted a book of his great Encyclopaedia to wine, with the zestful question 'Who can doubt that

[1] Cicero, *in Pis.* 22, *post Red. in Sen.* 13, *Philipp.* 2.42, 63, etc.
[2] E.g. Plautus, *Bacchides* 87. Occasionally Plautine wines have titles: *vinis Graecis* at *Rudens* 588, but Chian at *Curculio* 78, and at *Poenulus* 700 Leucadian, Lesbian, Thasian, and Chian. All the names are Greek and presumably come from Plautus' originals: Italian wines hardly had individuality enough for the poet's purpose.
[3] Cicero, *Philippic* 2.63.
[4] Pliny, *NH* 14.94 dates this to 121 B.C. with an accuracy doubtless illusory – this was the year of the consulship of Opimius, a celebrated vintage.
[5] Cato *de Re Rustica* 6-7. The same author tells his reader what to consume *si voles in convivio multum bibere* (156.1). Horace remembers him as a hearty drinker, *Odes* 3.21.11; cf. Cicero, *de Senectute* 46.

some kinds of wine are more agreeable than others? Who does not know that when two wines come from the same vat, one may be better than the other – either because of their different casks, or because of some piece of chance? So that each man will think himself fully empowered to decide which is the best. Livia put down her long life to constant drinking of Pucine wine ... Augustus preferred Setine ...' The book ends with four sentences of shocked disapproval of beer (*heu, mira vitiorum sollertia!*), and the statement that there are 185 kinds (*genera*) of wine: or almost double the number, if one counted varieties (*species*).[6]

Pliny's anecdotes about the favoured vintages of emperors and others show how widely this sort of thing was discussed, as do the constant complaints of Martial and Juvenal about stingy hosts who give their guests wine inferior to what they are drinking themselves. Horace in his least interesting satire presents the picture of a host as tiresomely concerned to explain his wines as his food (*Satires* 2.8.13-17). This wine snobbery was not felt to be appropriate to all levels of poetry. It is above all Horace who makes extensive use of the names of different wines. He refers to Falernian no less than fifteen times, seven times to Caecuban, six times to Chian. In a number of passages he refers to several different ones, saying for instance that he can offer only humble Sabine home-grown to Maecenas: 'you can drink Caecuban, Calenian, Falernian, and Formian, but I have none of them' (*Odes* 1.20.13-16).[7] He knows all about the devices of adulterating one wine with another, and how to strain it and treat it; it is natural for him to compare the insertion of Greek words into a Latin poem with the blending of Chian and Falernian, a Greek and an Italian growth; he takes up the image of the soul retaining its first youthful impressions as a cask retains the savour of the wine stored in it.[8] He speaks of choice vintages which will be brought out on special occasions: *tu vina Torquato move / consule pressa meo*, 'produce the wine laid down in my birth year, the consulship of Torquatus', or 'on this day every year I shall drink a jar of wine laid down in 65 B.C.', or 'until now it would have been wrong to bring out the Caecuban from our ancestral cellars' – before Cleopatra was roundly defeated, that is.[9] He can talk of particularly choice Falernian – *interiore nota Falerni* (*Odes* 2.3.8): the mere name of the distinguished growth was not necessarily sufficient guarantee. Even the wine he offers to a girl, the musical Phyllis of *Odes* 4.11, is a very respectable Alban growth, nine years old; and he can make a nice point by specifying that the wine he will offer the patrician Torquatus comes from the precise area in which

---

[6] Pliny *NH* 14.59 and 14.149-50.
[7] Cf. *Epode* 9.33-5, *Sat.* 2.8.15-17.
[8] *Sat.* 2.4.56 *Surrentina vafer qui miscet faece Falerna / vina; ib.* 51, how to strain wine; *Sat.* 1.10.24 *ut Chio nota si commixta Falerni est; Epp.* 1.2.69 *quo semel est imbuta recens servabit odorem / testa diu.*
[9] *Epode* 13.6; cf. *Odes* 3.21.1 *o nata mecum consule Manlio* ...; *Odes* 3.8.11; *Odes* 1.37.5. Cf. S. Commager, 'The function of wine in Horace's *Odes*'. *TAPA* 88 (1957) 68-80.

his great ancestor, T. Manlius Torquatus, won his memorable victory three hundred years earlier.[10]

Clearly Horace had given a good deal of thought to such matters. It will be recalled that he was a regular diner at the table of Maecenas; that great epicure, as one would expect, had his own taste in drink.[11] The elegists do not share this taste for expertise about wine. The Caecuban which Horace mentions seven times is never named by Propertius or Tibullus; Chian, unmentioned by Propertius, is a wine which Tibullus envisages drinking only on a special occasion, in honour of Messalla (Tib. 2.1.28). Even Horace's beloved Falernian is for the elegists something which might be drunk in honour of a great patron:[12] in their depiction of their own lives it is only an object of fantasy. After vainly expostulating with Cynthia to get her to leave a party, Propertius resigns himself to saying that even if she goes on drinking Falernian and spills it from goblets of silver gilt, she is still irresistible to him:

> *largius effuso madeat tibi mensa Falerno,*
> *spumet et aurato mollius in calice*   (Prop. 2.33.39-40).

Tibullus complains that his faithless boy had promised to remain true despite all offers of bribes, even if he were tempted with the Falernian vineyard (Tibullus 1.9.34). Evidently this sort of gourmet luxury, the consumption of famous wines, was felt by the elegists to be not a part of their own poetical personality, and the idea of drinking them to celebrate the patron's victories was, I imagine, suggested to them by the ninth *Epode* of Horace. Ovid indeed, who might have been thought likely enough to underline his own sophistication to the reader by showing his familiarity with named wines, took from his predecessors the hint that they were not appropriate to elegy. It is noticeable that the Hellenistic epigrammatists observe similar conventions. Asclepiades and Meleager, for instance, who often mention wine, never specify its type; Philodemus twice mentions Chian wine, but only to reject it for himself, or to say that he cannot offer it to a patron (Gow-Page 21, 23).

Virgil is more sparing still. Neither the shepherds of the *Eclogues* nor, in a different way, the ancestral heroes of the *Aeneid* would be at home with this kind of expertise. One allusion to Chian wine –

> *vina novum fundam calathis Ariusia nectar*   (Ecl. 5.71)[13]

---

[10] *Epp.* 1.5.4-5; cf. R.G.M. Nisbet in *CQ* 9 (1959) 74.

[11] *Vina Maecenatiana*, Pliny *NH* 14.67.

[12] Tibullus 2.1.27, Propertius 4.6.73. Tibullus also invites Bacchus himself to come to Messalla's birthday celebrations, 1.7.39; Falernian wine and the epiphany of the god are alternative ways of achieving the same effect, the exaltation of a festive occasion.

[13] It is charming to find Voss arguing that 'Chian wine was cheap enough in Virgil's time to be within the reach of a Mantuan shepherd'. Coleman is nearer the mark: 'this reference breaks the pastoral illusion by its hint of imported luxury.' But surely very little *illusion* can have been there to break, after seventy lines of so curious and complex a poem?

'I will pour fresh nectar, Ariusian wine, from cups' – toys with the breach of the pastoral setting in the same sort of way as the lovesick Corydon's unexpected line

Amphion Dircaeus in Actaeo Aracyntho (*Ecl.* 2.24),

or the elaborately carved cups of *Eclogue* 3.36ff., the work of 'the divine Alcimedon'. The heady mixture which made up the *Eclogues* contains such elements of the startling and the discordant, confident that the style of the whole will carry them off. In the second *Georgic*, largely devoted to the care of vines, Virgil naturally refers to the different types. In fact he gives a catalogue of them, a bravura piece of writing, exuberant in its rhetoric. The poet does not give any practical advice on dealing with the different vines, as even Cato had: rather he runs the glittering names through his fingers – Thasian and Mareotic, Raetic and Falernian, Rhodian and Bumastic (*Georgic* 2.91-108). In the *Aeneid* he is careful to avoid such names. Even Homer had used language which might have served as a precedent, with his mysterious Pramnian wine (in later antiquity nobody knew where it really came from – Caria, Ephesus, Smyrna, Icaros, Lesbos were all suggested – but ' it retained its fame'),[14] and with the super-powerful Maronian wine, to be diluted with water in the ratio of twenty to one, which Odysseus fortunately had about him in the Cyclops' cave (*Odyssey* 9.196-212). Virgil did not follow up such hints. His own feeling that the world of Aeneas would not be a world of named and celebrated vintages may have been strengthened by the sort of writers who drew morals, of a flat and edifying sort, from the cuisine and habits of Homer's heroes, applauding for instance their abstinence from elaborate soups and fancy fish dishes[15] – a matter, they supposed, of moral self-denial rather than poetic stylisation.[16] When Dido holds a feast, the wine is special not in its *appellation d'origine* but in the massy golden bowl, from which the Tyrian kings have always drunk.[17]

The practice of Horace in this matter, and its contrast with that of the other Augustans, deserves a last comment. Horace and the elegists were alike concerned to idealise pleasure (rather perhaps than love),[18] but they approach it in different ways. For the elegists the simple presence of wine and the beloved is enough: life is raised in intensity and approaches a transcendent level of being – for Propertius the erotic myths, for Tibullus

[14] Pliny *NH* 14.54; cf. Sommerstein on Aristophanes *Acharnians* 107: 'It was produced throughout the Eastern Aegean area.'

[15] This literature can be sampled conveniently in Athenaeus Book 1, especially 10aff.

[16] Cf. J. Griffin, *Homer on Life and Death* (1980) 15.

[17] Virgil *Aeneid* 1.728; cf. 7.147. It is quantity which ruins the Rutulians, 9.165, 189, 316ff., and which made Troy helpless to the invader, 2.265. Virgil suppresses all the Odyssean detail about the wine which was used on the Cyclops, preferring to say only *simul expletus dapibus vinoque sepultus / cervicem inflexam posuit*, 'as soon as he was glutted with food and drowned in wine'.

[18] Cf. A. La Penna, *L'Integrazione Difficile* 213.

the pastoral golden age. Love is in principle of one girl – Cynthia; Delia, and then after her Nemesis – and as the poet needs no variety of partner, so he is not concerned with the details of an elaborate wine list. For Horace, who makes a point of the number of his amours, not only naming many different girls but also mentioning more than one in the same poem and referring in general terms to his numerous affairs,[19] love is not a transcendental experience at all. Rather, it is one great element in a life of pleasure. He does not feel impelled to stick to one wine, or to affect indifference to the sort of wine he drinks. It is in keeping with this that he shows a more active interest than they do in perfumes and unguents, another regular and enjoyable element of the sympotic and amorous life.[20] As with the selection of a sexual partner, he is a connoisseur.

The other great way to elevate the status of the pleasures of wine was by invoking Bacchic imagery and mythology. Nothing was commoner than the use of such figures on the paraphernalia of the symposium, the tripods and drinking cups and mixing bowls;[21] the mosaic on the floor, too, and the paintings on the walls were very likely to have Dionysiac themes. Pliny records with a decorous shudder that even the rough-hewn Gaius Marius, 'that ploughman from Arpinum who rose from the ranks to be general', celebrated his victory over the Cimbri by drinking from Bacchic tankards in imitation of the god Liber.[22] Propertius mentions drink surprisingly little in his first book: it is as if he felt, in the first outburst of passion for Cynthia, little need for it (later he had much more to say on the subject). When he does speak of coming to Cynthia's bedside late and drunk, it is natural for him to say

ebria cum multo traherem vestigia Baccho (Prop. 2.3.9),

'as I made my way, my steps inebriated with much Bacchus'. The image is carried on, as he speaks of being impelled to lay hands on his sleeping mistress by drunken desire:

et quamvis duplici correptum ardore iuberent
hac Amor hac Liber, durus uterque deus (Prop. 1.3.13-14).

'Caught in a double fire I was urged on by Amor on one side, by Liber on another, each of them a cruel god.' It was a hackneyed excuse to say that erotic misdemeanours were all the fault of love and wine,[23]

---

[19] *si flava excutitur Chloe / reiectaeque patet ianua Lydiae*, 'If blond Chloe is shaken off and the door is opened again to the rejected Lydia', *Odes* 3.9.19; *vixi puellis nuper idoneus*, 'I have lived the life of a ladies' man', 3.26.1; *age iam meorum / finis amorum*, 'Come on, you who will be the last of my loves', 4.11.31, etc.

[20] Cf. p.10.

[21] 'The most obvious subject for drinking cups was the god of wine, Bacchus, or masks of Bacchus and his followers': M. Henig, *Handbook to Roman Art* (1983) 142; cf. p. 150 (tripods), p. 125 (mosaics).

[22] Pliny *NH* 33.150.

[23] The excuse is offered and rejected at Plautus *Aulularia* 745-51, *Truculentus* 828-31.

irresistible gods; Propertius elegantly declines to appeal to that excuse. The impulsion was indeed very strong, but he resisted it. And the gods are not simply a transparent metaphor for desires, as can be seen from the opening lines of the poem. Asleep, Cynthia resembles Ariadne, the deserted heroine whom the god of wine found and made his consort; or she is like a maenad, lying exhausted on the grass after her dances in honour of the god.[24] One of Cynthia's great effects, we learn from a later poem, was dancing the role of Ariadne (2.3.18).

Another essentially commonplace incident in the life of love is made into a poem by similar means: wandering the streets late and intoxicated, he suddenly feels an irresistible impulse to go to Cynthia. This appears in verse (2.29) as a meeting between the drunken poet and a crowd of naked Amores, who take him in charge and escort him to her door. Propertius composed a regular hymn to Bacchus (3.17), a poem of forty lines, in which he praises the god, gives a summary of the myths which he will versify in his honour, and begs for release from love: the god can grant it if he chooses:

> *per te iunguntur, per te solvuntur amantes:*
> *tu vitium ex animo dilue, Bacche, meo*   (Prop. 3.17.5-6).

'By you lovers are joined, by you they are sundered: do you wash away this weakness from my heart.' Commentators produce poetical parallels for the ideas that Bacchus can both instil and dispel the pains of love, but without pressing the central point: it is at *convivia* that one picks up girls,[25] and on the other hand if one drinks enough one can forget about them.[26] And the *convivium*, that eminently real institution, could be represented as the realm of Bacchus.

The god is powerful not only in love but also in poetry.[27] Propertius claims that it is not surprising that girls adore his poems, since Bacchus and Apollo are his patrons:

> *miremur, nobis et Baccho et Apolline dextro,*
> *turba puellarum si mea verba colit?*   (Prop. 3.2.9-10).

---

[24] Cf. R. Whitaker, *Myth and Personal Experience in Roman Love Elegy* (= *Hypomnemata* 76, 1983) 89ff.

[25] See below, p. 82f.

[26] Epigrams: cf. F. Jacoby, *Kleine philologische Schriften* 2 (1961) 108. Of course, as so often in these matters, the reverse is equally true, and drinking makes love worse: cf. Tibullus 1.5.37, Rohde, *Der gr. Roman*⁴ 171 n.3.

[27] References in I. Troxler-Keller, *Die Dichterlandschaft des Horaz* (Heidelberg 1964) 56 n.103. She, following P. Boyancé in *Entretiens Hardt* 2 (1953) 194ff., sees the link between Dionysus and the Attic theatre as crucial to the emergence of the god as a god of poetry. Evidence for him as a god of non-dramatic poetry before Horace is less conclusive than might be wished, but cf. A. La Penna in *Studi in Onore di V. De Falco* (1971) 229f., V. De Falco in *RFIC* 14 (1936) 371-3.

In an extremely exalted moment he imagines wandering through poetical scenery, mountain peaks and mossy caves, with Cynthia at his side: together they will meet the Muses and hear them singing of the loves of Jupiter. The Muses themselves are no strangers to love. Recognising in Cynthia a spirit like their own, they will welcome her into their company, and Bacchus will be in the centre:

> *hic ubi te prima statuent in parte choreae,*
> *et medius docta cuspide Bacchus erit*   (Prop. 2.30.37-8).[28]

There was a society of poets in Augustan Rome, it appears, who together worshipped Bacchus. From his exile Ovid remembers its meetings with nostalgia.[29] We know very little about this body, but as it appears from Ovid's poem that they met only once a year, it sounds like little more than a plausible excuse for a party – we hear of *pocula* (line 50). It does not in itself seem to provide a reason for the important role of Bacchus in Augustan poetry and his association with verse, which is evidently a cliché by the time of the derivative author of [Tibullus] 3.4. This poet imagines Apollo saying to him

> *Salve, cura deum: casto nam rite poetae*
> *Phoebusque et Bacchus Pieridesque favent*   ([Tibullus] 3.4.43-4).

'Greetings, protégé of the gods. The virtuous poet is favoured by Apollo and Bacchus and the Muses.' This indiscriminate assemblage of divine patrons represents a coarsening of more definite ideas, that Bacchus inclined the mind of the poet for creation, the actual art being under other deities: so Propertius 4.6.76, *Bacche, soles Phoebo fertilis esse tuo*, 'Bacchus, you are often fertile ground for your beloved Apollo'. Horace can say, as if it were an unquestioned truth, that all poets hate the noise and occupation of the city and long for rural seclusion:

> *scriptorum chorus omnis amat nemus et fugit urbem*
> *rite cliens Bacchi somno gaudentis et umbra*   (*Epp.* 2.2.77-8).

'The whole band of poets adores the woods and avoids the city; they are appropriately servants of Bacchus who delights in sleeping in the shade.' Horace here puts the idea with a certain irony,[30] as he does in the opening

---

[28] It is the regular thing for commentators on Propertius to trace back Dionysus' connection with the Muses ('leader of the Muses' is among his titles) to *Iliad* 6.132. That passage has of course nothing to do with the Muses.

[29] Ovid *Tristia* 5.3, and the discussion by G. Luck, *P. Ovidius Naso: Tristia* 2 (1977) 290f., with earlier literature.

[30] Cf. C.O. Brink, *Horace on Poetry* 3 (1982) 309. Nisbet-Hubbard on *Odes* 1.1.30 give parallels. Horace *Epistle* 1.19.3, *ut male sanos / adscripsit Liber Satyris Faunisque poetas*, is frankly humorous: Bacchus assigns poets to the company of Satyrs and Fauns because they are crazy.

ode of the first book, saying of his own poetic aspirations:

> *me gelidum nemus*
> *nympharumque leves cum Satyris chori*
> *secernunt populo* (*Odes* 1.1.30-2).

'It is the unheated grove and the fickle band of nymphs and satyrs which raise me above the crowd;' the retinue and scenery of Bacchus were an over-familiar metaphor for poetic inspiration, going back clearly to the *Ion* of Plato.

Plato, however, in that highly ironic dialogue intends no compliment to the poets in saying that they are like Bacchants, inspired by the god and raving in marvellous utterance which they themselves, once the fit has passed, do not understand and cannot explain.[31] The gullible rhapsode Ion takes all this as a compliment to his art, but for Plato what cannot be rationally expounded and criticised is worthless. Horace sometimes uses the image with an ironic nuance, aiming it at the 'romantic' poets of his own time who thought undisciplined craziness the hallmark of genius. It is consequently surprising to find that it is Horace who goes far beyond the other Augustan poets in claiming, in two striking odes, ecstatic Dionysiac experience for himself. How is this to be explained?

In *Odes* 2.19 Horace tells us that he has seen Bacchus in the remote hills teaching music to the Nymphs and the goat-footed Satyrs, their ears pricked. Let posterity believe! His mind still flutters with that recent terror, his breast is filled with Bacchus, an experience of joyous confusion.[32] It has not proved easy to know how to interpret this. Eduard Fraenkel was for belief: 'I think Horace means what he says. He did see Dionysus ... He had only to close his eyes to see the god before him, not as a dim figure, but lifelike in his beauty and strength ... We see how the visions of an old religion, renewed in the enthusiasm of a poet, obtain a fresh life.'[33] Victor Pöschl says it is 'a mighty monument of this religious phenomenon, a hymn to Dionysus': 'the Dionysiac is seen as the essence of Horace's poetry and of poetry in general.'[34] Nisbet and Hubbard as usual are a good deal cooler. 'Horace's vision seems as literary as those of other Roman poets,' they observe, and the poem does not possess 'the seriousness that some critics suggest'.

This ode cannot be separated from two others: *Odes* 3.25, and a

---

[31] E.g. *Ion* 534a 'they rave and are possessed like Bacchants ...' Other references in Nisbet-Hubbard 2.316; and E.R. Dodds, *The Greeks and the Irrational* (1951) 80-2.

[32] Older literature on this poem is listed by V. Pöschl in *Hermes* 101 (1973) 211 n.7; also A. Henrichs in *HSCP* 82 (1978) 203-11.

[33] E. Fraenkel, *Horace* (1957) 200-1. So too for instance Troxler-Keller (above n.27) 63: 'As the poet feels himself initiated into the mysteries of the god and taken up among his retinue, the ecstasy of the maenads turns to poetic enthusiasm.'

[34] V. Pöschl in *Hermes* 101 (1973) 229.

passage in *Odes* 3.4. In the former Horace speaks as he is rushed away, filled with Bacchic afflatus, among the mountain woods and caves. In some remote cave he will sing of the glory of great Caesar, practising to set it among the stars. His subject is to be new, untouched: he feels, in the distant region of his inspiration, the fearful joy of the maenad out on the snowy Thracian mountains at night, gazing down on the white ridges below. This poem presents the Bacchic ecstasy as the precondition for tackling the arduous and perilous theme of Augustus: only in that inspired and extraordinary frame of mind will the poet do it justice. But that inspiration is forthcoming, and the song will be great, sublime, immortal:

> *nil parvum aut humili modo,*
> *nil mortale loquar. dulce periculum est,*
>   *o Lenaee, sequi deum*
> *cingentem viridi tempora pampino* (*Odes* 3.25.17-20).

'Nothing small or mean in style, nothing mortal will I sing. Sweet is the hazard, O God of the Winepress, of following a divinity who wreathes his temples with fresh vine-leaves.' The connection of inspiration and Augustus recurs in the fourth of the Roman Odes. This time it is the Muse whose inspiration is like madness (*insania*, 6). The Muse transports Horace to a new setting of poetical scenery, as she has protected him throughout his life (6-28), and would protect him still, even if he were to go to the most difficult and unsettled spots on the borders of the empire.[35] It is the Muses who give gentle counsel to Augustus and refresh him in a Pierian (poetical) cave, when he has settled his legions in Italy (37-42).

The poem itself is of course an example of praise of Augustus, aspiring in style, original,[36] ambitious: an example, in fact, of the sort of thing Horace envisages in *Odes* 3.25. Again it has required a courage bordering on madness for him to produce it; and he daringly puts Augustus himself in direct relation with the poet, by imagining him, too, receiving inspiration in a cave. Emperor and poet are not, as they had appeared, worlds apart, one an awesome ruler and the other a humble writer. Akin in status, they are akin also in what they do. Augustus, withdrawn from the prosaic world, receives a divine message, as the poet does; and that message is the *lene consilium*, the counsel of gentleness, which Horace actually gives in the second half of the poem, the triumph of rational and

---

[35] On lines 29-36 cf. *The Third Book of Horace's Odes*, edited by Gordon Williams (1969) 51. The poem deftly praises Augustus as conqueror and bringer of peace, and also as perceptive in appreciation of divine and poetic language. On *Odes* 3.4 cf. N. Rudd in *Cambridge History of Classical Literature* 2.378. Another view of *Odes* 3.25: P.J. Connor in *ANRW* 31.3 (1981) 1620; cf. also E. Doblhofer, ib. 1953ff.

[36] On the relation of the two halves of the poem see the subtle arguments of Gordon Williams, *Figures of Thought in Roman Poetry* (1980) 27.

moderate force over wild and savage violence.

It is time to return to *Odes* 2.19, and to Horace's claim to have seen Bacchus. A point of principle is raised, not for the first time, by the procedure of Nisbet and Hubbard. They give an account of the poem which sums up excellently its range of subject-matter and style: 'Horace has listed the god's multifarious aspects not only with brilliant concentration but with subtle fluctuations of tone.' They then assemble a range of parallels and precedents for the idea that 'in the Augustan age Bacchus was treated by the poets as a source of inspiration': poets, philosophers, 'the currency of the theme in Hellenistic poetry may be inferred from a passage in Lucretius', and so on. Then comes the crucial point: 'all this explains why Horace chose Bacchus as a subject, but it does not give the poem the kind of seriousness that some critics suggest ... in the ancient world form might matter more than self-expression, and a poet could assume a mantle without having a message to preach.' This book has been concerned, among other things, to deny that the existence of precedents and parallels explains why a given subject was chosen on a given occasion. There were after all so many things which had been said already and which therefore might be evoked or varied or imitated, and the question 'Why *this* one?' remains crucial.

Horace was a well-known man, a short plump figure, a man about town (always complaining that he cannot get away to the country, as such men do), a regular diner with Maecenas. His parentage was humble, and it was gleefully remembered against him in society that his father was a freedman.[37] He also was a person of great self-consciousness. Impelled to write panegyric, he makes a poetical virtue of his own daunting awareness of the difficulty of the task. Octavian shrinks from inept and untimely praise; I am anxious not to obtrude my poems on him at the wrong moment; by addressing him at inordinate length I should be guilty of injuring the state; I recommend a friend to you, Tiberius, only because he so overrates my influence with you that I should look selfish if I persisted in refusing.[38] Such are the characteristic tones of Horace, his *irony*, of which many more instances could be given. How, then, is such a man to carry off the role of inspired poet, of poetic greatness? The appeal of the Bacchic ecstasy to Horace was surely that it provided a suitable mask, an undeniably poetical stance. If there was one thing that Horace took seriously, it was his claim to be a great poet. Contemporaries never find this an easy claim to grant, and Horace is eloquent on the theme of the malignity of people to contemporary poets; in the *Epistle to Augustus* he spends seventy lines on the subject. All this reverence for dead poets,

---

[37] Horace *Epistles* 1.20.20-8; Augustus *Epistle* 40 Malcovati; Horace *Satires* 2.6.60; ib. 30-2, 2.7.29-35; ib. 1.6.45-6 *quem rodunt omnes libertino patre natum*, 'Everyone sneers at me as a freedman's son'.

[38] Horace *Satires* 2.1.17-20; *Epistles* 1.13.1-5; ib. 2.1.1-4; ib. 1.9. Bibliography on Horace and Augustus: E. Doblhofer in *ANRW* 31.3 (1981) 1925ff.

he says, is insincere:

> *ingeniis non ille favet plauditque sepultis*
> *nostra sed impugnat, nos nostraque lividus odit* (*Epp.* 2.1.88-9).

'This is not love and admiration for talents dead and buried: it is an attack on our talents, a jealous dislike of us and our work.'[39] The image of inspiration, of inspired madness, is a metaphor, sanctioned by long literary usage, for something which the poet was anxious to say: that he really was a great lyric poet, an Alcaeus, a Pindar. They were venerable figures, classics, read at school. Horace is one of them, and the familiar figure of the freedman's son has another side to him, one of which his dining partners know nothing. '*Credite, posteri*' conveys a certain shadow of irony to the literal words of the poem, but none towards its essential truth, a truth which is neither 'a paranormal psychological experience', not a religious revelation, but the considered yet impassioned claim to supreme literary status. This interpretation is, I think, strongly supported by the next poem, *Odes* 2.20. Here Horace claims immortality: he is being transformed into a swan, with feathers sprouting and the skin of his legs becoming loose and rough. Now he will fly all over the world, and the world will admire his song.

This poem has divided the poet's interpreters. Fraenkel and La Penna, for instance, are severe, regarding the metamorphosis as a fault of taste; Williams, like Nisbet and Hubbard, defends the poem.[40] What is certain is that the details of the transformation into the form of a bird are worked out in a way that Ovid repeatedly enjoys in his *Metamorphoses*,[41] but which Virgil is careful to avoid, whether in an Eclogue (*Ecl.* 6.79-81) or in the *Aeneid* (10.189-93). The latter Virgilian passage indeed reads like a model of the tactful way to treat transformation into a swan.

> *namque ferunt luctu Cycnum Phaethontis amati,*
> *populeas inter frondes umbramque sororum*
> *dum canit et maestum musa solatur amorem,*
> *canentem molli pluma duxisse senectam*
> *linquentem terras et sidera voce sequentem* (*Aeneid* 10.189-93).

The hero Cupavo wears in his helmet the feathers of a swan, an ancestral symbol: 'For Cycnus, they say, when his beloved Phaethon died, sang

---

[39] *Epistles* 2.1.20-90. Cf. also the *invidia* of which Horace complains: *Sat.* 2.6.48, *Odes* 2.20.4, *Odes* 4.3.16, *AP* 56. It will not do simply to put all such allusions down to the precedent of Callimachus: here as elsewhere, a precedent or a parallel is only the raw material of an explanation.

[40] E. Fraenkel, *Horace* 299; A. La Penna, *Orazio e la morale mondana europea* (1968) 73; G. Williams, *Tradition and Originality* 574 ('complex and humorous'); Nisbet-Hubbard ad loc. ('shows an agreeable detachment from a deeply felt aspiration').

[41] See the references assembled by Nisbet-Hubbard 2, p. 334.

and solaced his sad love with music amid the poplar leaves and the shade cast by his sisters' (*sc.* Phaethon's sisters, metamorphosed into poplars) 'until he took on the whiteness of age with soft plumage, leaving the earth and pursuing the stars with his singing.' The themes are all there: the snowy feathers, the flying and the music. But Virgil has preferred to place so fantastic an episode not even in the distant time of the *Aeneid* itself, but as a story told (*ferunt*) of a previous generation; and his language, though full, avoids the details of the growth of the feathers or the change in the skin. Horace has created something akin to the elaborate accounts with which Ovid's poem is studded, and their intention was certainly not very serious.

The explanation must be that Horace has tried to create another powerful image for the superhuman nature of his poetry. The musical bird sacred to Apollo presented itself as a possibility, like the ecstasy of the maenads: violent metaphors for the otherness of inspired creation. It is striking that in this context he insists on the contrast between that inspiration and his ordinary, familiar social image:

> non ego pauperum
> sanguis parentum, non ego quem vocas,
> dilecte Maecenas, obibo
> nec Stygia cohibebor unda   (*Odes* 2.20.5-8).

'I the son of poor parents, I whom you send for, my dear Maecenas: I shall not die, nor shall the waters of Styx prevail over me ...' This is often written down to what Nisbet and Hubbard call 'an undercurrent of self-disparagement: he is aware of his humble origins and inferior social position'. More sense is made of the poem if it is taken in a different way. Constantly aware of his exposure to sneers as the freedman's son and the hanger-on of Maecenas, Horace defiantly asserts his transcendence. These things are true of him, and he does not forget or conceal them even at his most exalted; but they are trivial, and the upstart man-about-town really is inspired and immortal.

That is not to say that the poem is one of his most successful. This interpretation of it makes its humour less of a saving grace, and the poet is seen to have been driven, by the strength of his desire for utterance of a cherished belief, to a bizarre image.[42] By contrast the Dionysiac poems, so much more smoothly harmonised, show the advantages which Horace could get from one which was at once more completely mythical, and also more intimately related to his life; for the *convivium* and the drinking of wine[43] are important for the composition of his poems. His model in his

---

[42] The same desire has given rise to another rather comic picture at *Odes* 4.3.19: the Muse to whom Horace owes everything (*quod spiro et placeo, si placeo, tuum est*) is capable, if she chooses, of granting to mute fishes the sweet song of the swan. These passages reinforce each other.

[43] Wine makes its appearance as early as the nineteenth line of the first poem of *Odes* Book 1.

lyric poetry is Alcaeus, and Alcaeus, says Horace, although a warrior and a man of action, sang constantly of wine.[44] The first book of the *Odes* is concluded with a set of three contrasting poems on the theme of drinking: a lively amorous party; a political celebration; a short poem on simplicity of furnishing and company, as without fuss and luxury the poet sits drinking in the shade of a vine.

That summary of the contents of *Odes* 1.36-8 leads into the cardinal point about the theme of drinking in Horace, which is that he can use it as a framework for poems on any subject. Friendship and hospitality are naturally expressed in terms of drinking together – as we shall see, eating is carefully avoided – but this is true with Horace to a remarkable extent. Catullus, for instance, in his ninth poem welcomes home his friend Veranius. What he looks forward to is embracing him, kissing him, seeing and hearing him. Horace automatically makes the return of a friend the occasion for a drinking session. *Odes* 1.36 greets the return home of Numida with promise of a lively party, dancing and heavy drinking. In *Odes* 2.7 Horace hails the home-coming of Pompeius, a comrade in arms from the old days of the civil wars. He expresses the idea 'we are old friends' by saying 'I have despatched many a day with neat wine in your company'. Pompeius' return is to be the excuse for a really rousing party: 'pour out the Massic wine ... I shall be as mad as the Thracian maenads',

> *non ego sanius*
> *bacchabor Edonis*　(*Odes* 2.7.25-6).

Even the joy expressed at the return of Augustus from the wars immediately turns in the same direction: 'bring out a cask of old wine' (*Odes* 3.14.17). The absence of the motif from Catullus' exuberant poem, by contrast, shows that it was not a necessary part of any poem of welcome.

When the snow is on the ground, that is a reason for drinking. When spring drives out the winter, it is time for a party. The heat of midsummer is naturally a good reason for drinking, too.[45] An invitation to a friend can promise a lively party, or alternatively a modest affair which enables the poet to contrast his own wealth and status with that of his grand guest. In more serious vein, unostentatious but rational and enjoyable hospitality can rebuke the vices of the age: its reverse, the

---

[44] Horace *Odes* 1.32.9 *Liberum et Musas Veneremque et illi / semper haerentem puerum canebat*, 'He sang constantly of Bacchus and the Muses and Venus and the boy who always goes with Venus'; cf. the Alcaic drink-poems *Odes* 1.18, 1.37. A crude estimate of the quantity of bibulous poetry by Alcaeus may be given by the fact that in his extant fragments the word *pono*, 'drink', occurs nine times (not once in those of Sappho), the word *oinos*, 'wine', ten times (not once in Sappho; none of the three instances of *oinochoêmi*, 'pour wine', in Sappho refers to an occasion at which she was present, and two of them refer to the gods). The source of these figures is the index to the edition of Sappho and Alcaeus by E.-M. Voigt (Amsterdam 1971).

[45] Snow: *Odes* 1.9. Spring: *Odes* 1.7, 4.12. Summer: *Odes* 3.29.

frankly immoral orgy, can appear at the climax of the last of the Roman Odes, as the root cause of the disasters inflicted on Rome by a justly irate heaven.[46] Political themes find, through the crucial link with Alcaeus the man of action and laureate of the symposium, a form which has the supreme advantage of combining proper Augustan attitudes with the poetical persona of Horace. As the lyric poet is by definition at home with music and wine, political events can be versified as they impinge on that setting. The defeat of Cleopatra is the occasion of rejoicing, and therefore of drinking, and that gives a welcome framework for the expression of correct sentiments in an apparently spontaneous and hedonistic spirit; the return of Augustus from the wars is celebrated by Horace as if it were the home-coming of a personal friend,[47] and that allows him to express loyal emotion in a way which again looks individual and personal. In the fourth book of the *Odes*, when Augustus no longer takes the field himself, his benevolent guardianship of the world is still proclaimed with the aid of wine. Every man is secure on his own property; every man hails Augustus as divine with the drink that follows dinner:

> *condit quisque diem collibus in suis,*
> *et vitem viduas ducit ad arbores;*
> *hinc ad vina redit laetus et alteris*
>   *te mensis adhibet deum*   (*Odes* 4.5.29-32).

Pouring libations of wine we adore him (*ib.* 33); at the end of the day we pray *uvidi*, over our sun-downers, that he may continue to grant Italy a long vacation from history (*ib.* 37-40).[48] The fourth book ends on the same note. With Caesar in charge we fear no violence; all of us alike, with our views and children, shall sing the praises of his ancestry, *inter iocosi munera Liberi*, 'among the delights of sportive Bacchus'.

The theme of wine can thus provide welcome stage property for the lyric poet in his serious political utterances.[49] On a level close to mundane reality, there is the party; private pleasure merges with public attitudes. At another and more stylised level there is the Dionysiac ecstasy. That too can be linked with the praise of Augustus. But the

---

[46] Party, a lively (*insanire iuvat*) *Odes* 3.19; modest, *Odes* 1.20, *Epistles* 1.5; moral, *Satires* 2.2; disgusting, *Odes* 3.6.25 *mox iuniores quaerit adulteros / inter mariti vina* ... 'Soon she is looking for younger adulterers as her husband drinks'.

[47] Cleopatra: *Epode* 9, *Odes* 1.37; Augustus' home-coming, *Odes* 3.14.

[48] '*Longas o utinam, dux bone, ferias / praestes Hesperiae!*' *dicimus integro / sicci mane die, dicimus uvidi, / cum sol Oceano subest:* ' "May you grant to Italy a long holiday, kindly leader," we say in morning sobriety and again in our cups, when the sun is down.'

[49] Cf. A. La Penna, *Orazio e l'ideologia del principato* (1963) 113. It is no coincidence that both Propertius and Tibullus also wrote poems of encomium in the form, or exploiting the motif, of drinking parties: Prop. 4.6.49-86, Tibullus 2.1.27ff. Cf. Pillinger in *HSCP* 73 (1969) 195ff. For them, too, it offered a way of bridging the gap between personal lyric and public statement.

versatility of the material is by no means exhausted. The *convivium* can also serve Horace for the apparently opposite purpose of contrasting with the life of political activity. It is a simple case when he says to Agrippa that the theme of glorifying so great a man's achievement is not for him: his talent is slender and unaspiring, he must leave grand martial poetry to others and stick to *convivia* (*Odes* 1.6). Such a poem is evidently itself an elegant substitute for the encomium which it disclaims.[50] Something similar is true of certain poems addressed to Maecenas: *Odes* 3.8 and 3.29. These odes are more interesting and convey a greater impression of warmth than the rather disengaged poem to the unpoetical Agrippa. Having already addressed to Maecenas an invitation poem which contrasts his own modest vintages with the noble wines to which Maecenas is accustomed (*Odes* 1.20), an urbane formula for praising without bad taste the difference in status between himself and his exalted patron, in his third book Horace writes two poems which urge the great man to turn his mind from the cares of public life to the quiet relaxation of a congenial party. In *Odes* 3.8 the poet suggests that anxiety on the part of Maecenas about foreign affairs is uncalled for, as all the enemies of Rome are defeated, or fighting each other, or turning to full retreat. Maecenas should therefore sit up all night in an intimate drinking session with him, consuming a hundred cups of wine. In *Odes* 3.29 the nuance, as befits the penultimate poem of the collection, is more universal. In this, the last poem of Books 1-3 to be addressed to a named recipient, Horace takes more philosophical ground. Maecenas is not now told that the particular opponents of Rome are as a matter of fact at the moment harmless: the point now is that all anxiety about the future is of its nature vain, as wise heaven has hidden what is to come from mortal eyes –

prudens futuri temporis exitum
caliginosa nocte premit deus (*Odes* 3.29.29-30).

Instead of torturing himself with useless cares, he should come to share a cask of wine (its type unstated) in the peace and serenity of Horace's Sabine estate. The human mind should content itself with enjoyment of the present pleasure.

These poems do of course glorify Maecenas by emphasising his political importance and conscience. They also foreshadow the odes of the fourth book in expressing confidence that there is no need to worry about anything under the new regime. But they also relate to a side of life which Horace loves to connect with himself, and which we know that public opinion ascribed to Maecenas: the life of Epicurean enjoyment. When Maecenas indulges himself, it is as hard-earned intervals of ease in

[50] Not dissimilar is *Odes* 2.12.13ff.

a life of almost excessive public service; and on the other hand the professedly hedonistic lyric poet can be intimate with such a man without departing from his chosen poetic *persona*, because they meet over the wine bowl.[51]

Horace also addresses poems on similar themes to other men. Manlius Torquatus is urged to put away thoughts of the great lawsuit in which he is a speaker, and to come to a party in the house of Horace (*Epistles* 1.5). Quinctius is told to dismiss anxieties about Spain and Scythia, and to recline in the shade and drink (*Odes* 2.11). Messalla Corvinus is invited to take a rest from philosophy and join the poet in disposing of a jar of good wine (*Odes* 3.21). Of these men the first two seem to have been of no special account: Manlius of high nobility but the last representative of his patrician house and unknown to honours, and Quinctius perhaps 'grandson of a Sullan carpet-bagger' and related by marriage to Pollio.[52] Such men can be exhorted to relax their cares for the state without the offence which such public advice might have caused to a man who really was of a rank to expect to have such cares. Messalla Corvinus is a different matter. Consul in 31 B.C., he had governed Syria and as governor in Gaul won a triumph; before his consulship he had campaigned in Northern Italy, in the Alpine territory of the Salassi. He was given but soon resigned the praefecture of the city of Rome; he patronised poets (his great protégé Tibullus never mentions in his verse the name of Augustus).[53] Not a word of any of this in the poem of Horace, only the witty point that Corvinus, though soaked in Socratic dialogues, will not reject the grape:

non ille, quamquam Socraticis madet
sermonibus, te negleget horridus   (*Odes* 3.21.9-10).

Even his pre-eminence as an orator is unmentioned. It has not been unremarked that Horace in his odes never gives military praise to any grandee unconnected with the family of Augustus: that was now a monopoly. To write a pleasing poem to a man of genuine achievements without making any reference to them was a nice problem. The familiar motif of wine helps the poet out again – Messalla was a hearty drinker,[54] and an arch glance at that suffices to individualise the poem (*madet*, in an innocent sense).

It is time to pass on from these political poems, glancing first at a

---

[51] Even the erotic side of the personality of the lyric poet is brought into relationship with Maecenas in *Epode* 14 and *Odes* 2.12; here the tension between the public man and the life of pleasure is more strongly felt, the gap harder to bridge. Both poems have perplexed interpreters.

[52] See Nisbet-Hubbard 2, p. 168.

[53] R. Syme, *The Roman Revolution* 302-3, 309, 329, 426.

[54] Inferred from the fact that Maecenas in his *Symposium* put into Corvinus' mouth an enthusiastic oration *de vi vini*, on the jolly influence of wine (Serv. in *Aen.* 8.310).

passage which shows the same kind of reversal, the employment of a
motif in both of a pair of opposed senses, as has been seen in the use of
the pleasures of the *convivium*. In *Odes* 3.25 Horace imagined himself in
a distant cave, singing of Caesar's glories. In *Odes* 3.4 he placed Caesar
himself in such a cave, refreshed by the Muse after his military labours.
Those passages, closely related, can be seen in another context to form a
series with a third. The first ode of the second book, addressed to Pollio,
hails the *History* of that independent-minded man: a grim subject in the
civil wars, and a high martial narrative. Suddenly the poet checks
himself. Such sad and weighty themes are not for his Muse.

> *sed ne relictis, Musa procax, iocis*
> *Ceae retractes munera neniae,*
> *mecum Dionaeo sub antro*
> *quaere modos leviore plectro*   (*Odes* 2.1.37-40).

'Wanton Muse, do not leave your frivolities to handle the material of
Simonidean dirge: rather, with me in a cave of Venus work out verses
with a light-weight plectrum.' The divine cave now offers a pure relief
from serious poetry on Rome, while in 3.25 it served as the ideal place to
compose it. Augustus was to be refreshed there, but by strains still
possessing a moral and political content (3.4); now it is the setting for
escapism, the poetry of love.

The last Horatian topic to be briefly handled here is that of the
shortness of life, the approach of death. Like love and friendship and
politics this is a pervasive theme with him, and here too he finds the
motif of wine eminently serviceable. 'Pour out the wine more generously
... while hateful age still holds aloof and you are young.' 'Don't ask how
long you or I have to live; this may be our last winter. Strain the wine' (*sc.*
for immediate consumption). 'Bring wine and unguents and the roses
that die all too soon, while your fortune permits, and youth, and the
black threads spun by the three sisters. You will have to leave your estate
and house ...' 'You must leave your land and house and the wife you
love ... Your heir will drink up your Caecuban wine – he deserves it more
than you – and splash on the floor your hoarded vintages ...' 'While you
still can, make up the log fire; tomorrow treat yourself to a holiday and
strong wine;' 'It's thirsty weather, and I have some good wine. Remember
the dark fires while you can, and come to drink it.'[55] In the face of the
oppressive thought of death, he needs a girl, and music, and wine too,[56] to
blunt the force of black care.

Wine is a constant part of the life of pleasure, in poetry as in life. But a
striking asymmetry makes itself felt when we turn to the question of

[55] Horace *Odes* 1.9.16ff.; 1.11.6 with Nisbet-Hubbard; 2.3.13; 2.14.21; 3.17.15; 4.12.13-28.
[56] *Odes* 4.11.

food. Greek Comedy is much obsessed with eating. Fantasy menus and splendid feasts run right through it, from Aristophanes[57] to New Comedy; the special interests of Athenaeus, who preserves so many of our fragments, admittedly distort the picture, but that lip-smacking discussions of rich food were common is obvious. Plautine Comedy, too, can show the same taste: for instance the luscious spread ordered by the lecherous husband in the *Menaechmi*, or the similar one dreamt of by Olympio in the *Casina*.[58] Scenes with cooks and with the preparation of food were also a stock feature of Roman as of Greek Comedy.[59] Lucilius in his twentieth book described an opulent dinner. Horace in the second book of his *Satires* writes extensively on epicurean dinners, on food snobbery, and on the contrast between rational and foolish cuisine. These topics occur in fact in almost every poem of that collection; they are the main theme of *Satires* 2.2 and 2.8, and they are the subject of the fable of the Town and Country Mice in 2.6.79ff.[60] It is even remarkable that when he writes in the *Epistles* a poem inviting a superior to a meal, he talks of vegetarian food and salads, as well as unpretentious wine; but when he invites Maecenas to a humble meal in the *Odes*, he mentions only wine, saying nothing of the food at all. Evidently the higher genres, not only elegy but also lyric,[61] were happy to accept mention of drinking, but would not allow discussion of food. The omission is a striking one, and serves as an example to show how these poets go about stylising experience.

Ovid is explicit about the reason. Having reached the point in the third book of the *Ars Amatoria* where he brings his female pupil into the *convivium*, the moment she has been waiting for –

sollicite exspectas dum te in convivia ducam   (*Ars* 3.749) –

he is emphatic that she should not eat greedily or eat too much. Why, if Paris were to see Helen tucking in with avidity, he would curse his own folly in carrying her off. On the other hand,

aptius est deceatque magis potare puellas:
    cum Veneris puero non male, Bacche, facis   (*Ars* 3.761-2).

'To drink suits girls and becomes them better. Bacchus goes well with Cupid.' As for the male lover, he is as a matter of course thin, *tenuis*, and without appetite. Propertius can boast that as a result of his love

[57] E.g. *Knights 1162ff.*, *Eccles.* 1167ff.
[58] Plautus *Menaechmi* 208ff., *Casina* 744; Erich Segal, *Roman Laughter* (1968) 47f., 35f.
[59] E.g. Terence, *Adelphoe* 420ff.
[60] Also *Satires* 2.3.226ff., 2.4.11ff., 2.6.63ff., 2.7.29ff.
[61] Cf. *Epistles* 1.6.56f.; 1.7.35, 1.10.11-12; 1.12.21ff.; 1.14.21; 1.15.22f., 31-41; 1.16.1-3; 1.17.13f. Poets, who love wine, are at least contented with cheap food: *Epistles* 2.1.123.

nec iam pallorem totiens mirabere nostrum,
aut cur sim toto corpore nullus ego (Prop. 1.5.21-2).

'Nor will you marvel so repeatedly at my pallor, or wonder why my body is altogether non-existent.'[62] Any display of interest in food would be quite out of keeping with such an image – another reason for the repeated emphasis on wine, a form of the real life of pleasure which was not incompatible with the constraints imposed by being a full-time literary lover. It only remains to conclude the topic by observing that in real life the end of the Republic and the succeeding years were a great period for the gourmet at Rome. After the death of Lucullus the serious study of the arts of the table was keenly pursued by such men as Hirtius and Dolabella, Cicero's 'pupils in speaking, teachers in dining'.[63] Maecenas and the disgusting Vedius Pollio were among the celebrated epicures of the succeeding age.[64] Roman interest in the subject had already expressed itself generations earlier in the characteristic form of moral disapproval and ineffective legislation: boar's meat was denounced by the Elder Cato, the consumption at dinner of such delicacies as shrews and dormice forbidden as early as 115 B.C.[65]

This chapter concludes with the question what parties were like, in life and in verse. The importance of social gatherings for the creation, circulation, criticism and puffing of literature has been emphasised by Kroll.[66] When Cicero entertained Caesar to dinner after the latter had murdered the Republic, their conversation was purely literary. Propertius' character and poetry were discussed at parties in a way that made him shudder. The eminently unpoetical Vitruvius complains of the scandalous way in which inferior architects are puffed into reputation by the *gratia conviviorum*, the influence of convivial circles. Ovid complains, or boasts, that in parties where drinking goes on, his name and his love affairs are the constant topic of conversation:

nequitiam vinosa tuam convivia narrant.

Horace describes a tactless poetaster reciting his own work all through dinner with Octavian.[67] Such a mixed bag of references shows that in

---

[62] Cf. also Prop. 2.21.20; 2.22.21; Ovid, *Amores* 1.6.5; 2.9.14 (on thinness), and Prop. 1.1.22; Horace, *Odes* 3.10.14; Ovid, *Ars* 1.729 *palleat omnis amans: hic est color aptus amanti.* References in the novelists: Rohde, *Der gr. Roman*[4] 167.2. In political polemic and propaganda, too, pallor and weakness go with debauchery: so Catiline was *exsanguis* from vicious living (Sallust *Bell. Cat.* 15.5), and P. Clodius strengthless and without *nervi* (Cic. *Pro Sestio* 15). As so often, the boast of the poets is the reproach of the respectable.
[63] Cicero, *ad Fam.* 9.16.7; cf. 9.18.3; 9.19; 9.20.1-2; 9.26.
[64] Cf. p. 11f.
[65] Pliny *NH* 8.210, 223. Lucilius amused himself at the expense of such laws, fr. 1200 M.
[66] W. Kroll, *Studien zum Verständnis der röm. Lit.* (1924) 120ff.
[67] Cicero *ad Att.* 13.52.2; Prop. 3.25.1 *risus eram positis inter convivia mensis,* 'They laughed at me in the drinking parties'; Vitruv. 3 *praef.* 3; Ovid *Amores* 3.1.17; Hor. *Sat.* 1.3.1.

various ways and at various levels of seriousness poetical and intellectual
work was discussed over food and wine. At the other end of a lengthy
scale come wild orgies, the sort which are ascribed to Gabinius by Cicero,
to C. Antonius by Caelius, to Antony by Cicero and Dellius and others.[68]
The Dionysiac orgies of Messallina, featuring not only wine but regular
maenads and thyrsi, were no doubt only an exaggeration of the sort of
thing that went on elsewhere. That a wild party should take on – in life,
not only in verse – these Dionysiac features is a very interesting fact.
Most of the *convivia* actually described in verse are of a more or less
seemly sort, many of them indeed quiet, relaxing, even mildly
philosophical. It is none the less possible to see what many of them
actually were like or threatened to turn into. The two dangers were that
guests would start carrying on with girls who belonged to other members
of the party, or that drunken brawls might break out. The two were
obviously connected.

The youthful old bachelor Periplectomenus in the *Miles Gloriosus* of
Plautus prides himself on his conduct at a party: 'I never make free with
another man's tart ... I never start a row over my drink':

> *neque ego umquam alienum scortum subigito in convivio ...*
> *neque per vinum umquam ex me oritur discidium in convivio*   (*Miles* 652, 654).

Terence in his *Heautontimoroumenos* gives an example of a young man
who over the wine seemed to provoke a fight by indiscreet dalliance with
another man's girl. Horace presents a lively scene in *Odes* 1.27: at his
arrival the guests are in uproar, shouting and fighting. Variants on the
theme of violence at the party occur. Thus Propertius tells of Cynthia
knocking over the table in jealous fury and throwing cups of wine at him:
this is an episode which the poet professes to have enjoyed, as Cynthia by
this display of temper showed the depth of her passion. Horace warns of
the sort of trouble-maker who in his cups insults the company, even his
host.[69] The kind of party envisaged by Catullus in his twenty-seventh
poem, with the imperious Postumia in charge of the drinking and wine
coming round neat, will not have been a very orderly affair; Horace
elsewhere speaks of the *rixarum metuens Gratia*: the three Graces who
are anxious to avoid violence, and who urge the company at another
lively and noisy gathering not to drink wine above a certain strength,
except for the poet himself, who as a votary of the nine Muses is allowed a
mixture three times as strong.[70] Horace's manner is urbane and his

[68] Gabinius: *in Pis.* 22. C. Antonius: *Oratorum Romanorum Fragmenta*, ed. H.
Malcovati[4], p. 483 (ap. Quintil. 4.2.123). Cf. note 1 above.
[69] Terence *Heauton.* 562-71; Horace *Odes* 1.27.1-8; Propertius 3.8.1-4; Horace, *Satires*
1.4.86ff.
[70] Horace *Odes* 3.19.9-20, with Gordon Williams' commentary. Cf. also *Odes* 2.7.26 *non
ego sanius / bacchabor Edonis*; 3.21.3 *seu rixam et insanos amores ...* 1.13.11 *turparunt
umeros immodicae mero / rixae*.

humour elegant, but the potential violence is visible beneath the surface of his poem.

Tibullus uses the idea of striking one's mistress, but places the shocking scene (no lover should use violence: that is for the military) in no definite setting: Ovid writes a whole poem on the theme, but again with no details of the circumstances.[71] If a girl was in fact to suffer violence, the *convivium* was doubtless a likely place, with wine and the presence of other men to stimulate jealousy. Theocritus gives a naturalistic account of such a scene in his fourteenth *Idyll*: at a drinking party a jealous lover strikes his mistress, who runs off to his rival. The motif seems to have proved unacceptable to the Roman poets in this realistic form. The party and the striking of a blow are separated by them into two distinct subjects for poetry. Ovid comes closest to practical realism in his advice to girls not to drink too much at a *convivium*. A girl who gets really drunk is at the mercy of sexual violence:

> *turpe iacens mulier multo madefacta Lyaeo:*
> *digna est concubitus quoslibet illa pati.*
> *nec somnis posita tutum succumbere mensa:*
> *per somnos fieri multa pudenda solent* (*Ars* 3.765-8).

'A woman lying helpless with drink is an ugly sight: she deserves any sexual assault. Nor is it safe to go to sleep at table – many outrages are committed on sleepers.'[72]

It is to be expected, if the general thesis advanced in this book has merit, that the motif of the rowdy party will be reflected on the mythical level. We find a glimpse of the sort of scandal which was talked about contemporaries in the story reported of Cicero's son, a celebrated toper, that in his cups he threw a goblet at Agrippa (Pliny *NH* 14.147). Personal poetry, as we have seen, transforms such ugly material as the drunken brawl in one way: on the level of myth it appears as the famous fight at the wedding of Hippodamia between the Centaurs and the Lapiths. Inflamed by wine, the centaurs tried to carry off the women by force, and the result was a murderous battle.[73] Sure enough the myth finds mentions in Virgil, Propertius, and Ovid.[74] The *Metamorphoses*, a poem which has often been seen to transpose and develop the material of

---

[71] Tibullus 1.10.53ff.; cf. 1.6.73 *non ego te pulsare velim*; Prop. 2.5.23, perhaps a criticism of Tibullus (F. Solmsen in *Philol.* 105 (1961) 273-5 = *Kleine Schriften* 2.299-311); Ovid *Amores* 1.7.

[72] Conversely, of course, a quiet drinking session might advantageously end in sleep: Hor. *Odes* 3.21.4. That point can be raised in style: Propertius' hymn to Bacchus includes a prayer to the god for sleep, Prop. 3.17.13ff., 42.

[73] On this myth in literature and art, not forgetting the metopes of the Parthenon, see F. Bömer's commentary on Ovid *Metamorphoses* 12-13 (1983) 210-535.

[74] Virgil *Georg.* 2.457; Prop. 2.2.9f., 2.33.31; Ovid *Heroides* 17.246f., *Amores* 1.4.7ff., *Ars* 1.591-4.

contemporary Augustan life in heroic and mythical form, handles the episode at enormous length, and finds a parallel to it in the battle which broke out at the wedding of Perseus and Andromeda. Here too an attempt to carry off the bride leads to a general mêlée, described at a length of 235 lines.[75] Ovidian scholars have struggled to account for the episodes, with their enormous length and fullness of detail, invoking the idea of epic parody, perhaps specifically of the *Aeneid*.[76] Such considerations had their weight, no doubt. But there has been a tendency to overlook the link that such myths had with real life. A brawl at a party, banal in everyday experience, is suitable as a veiled background in a poem by Horace or Propertius; or alternatively it can be raised, with the Centaurs, to mythical status.

Ovid shows in his elegiac poetry how intimate the connection is in his mind.[77] In the *Amores* he imagines himself present at a party to which his mistress is coming with her regular partner, her *vir*. In these circumstances he must restrain his natural impulse to break out in anger at the sight of their intimacies:

> *desine mirari, posito quod candida vino*
> *Atracis ambiguos traxit in arma viros:*
> *nec mihi silva domus, nec equo mea membra cohaerent –*
> *vix a te videor posse tenere manus* (*Amores* 1.4.7-10).

'Do not marvel that the fair Lapith queen dragged the centaurs into fighting over the wine: I do not live in a forest, nor is my body half horse, and still I can hardly keep my hands off you.' In the *Ars*, too, he connects the story with his injunction to avoid involvement in rows caused by wine – that is what killed Eurytion the centaur.[78] Restraint at the *convivium*, even if one's girl is embraced before one's eyes by a rival, is urged as the hardest task the lover can face, one from which Ovid the preceptor of love himself shrinks (*Ars* 2.539-52). Spelled out as a rule for himself (*Amores* 1.4), it finds its mythical counterpart in the Epistle of Paris to Helen, in which he tells her how hard it is to control himself when at table she and Menelaus share conjugal tendernesses (*Heroides* 16.217-62). In the same way the Centaurs and Lapiths exemplify and dignify the failure of that restraint, the *convivium* which breaks up in violence. Ovid has gone so far, in the two passages of the *Metamorphoses*, as to versify all the incidents of such a brawl. The women shriek; the centaurs throw the wine-cups and ladles; in an epic exaggeration, massive wine bowls are

---

[75] Ovid *Metamorphoses* 12.210-535; 5.1-235. 'Tedious as well as repulsive' is the verdict of H. Fränkel, *Ovid* 222.

[76] F. Bömer's commentary on *Metamorphoses* 4-5 (1976) 230.

[77] It is the same in Horace *Odes* 1.18.7 *ac ne quis modici transiliat munera Liberi / Centaurea monet cum Lapithis rixa super mero / debellata*: 'Let no one exceed a moderate intake of wine: the brawl between Centaurs and Lapiths over their drink is a warning'.

[78] Ovid *Ars* 1.591-4.

used to brain adversaries; other guests try to make peace, or are too far gone in wine to join in.[79] All the realistic events are thus transposed into heroic verse, while retaining a certain ironic taint of their prosaic origin.[80] For the very highest level of epic poetry such material was not directly usable. Virgil makes his Trojans an easy prey for the Achaeans in the second book of the *Aeneid* by sending them to bed tipsy after the celebrations which mark the supposed departure of their enemies, and he puts the Rutulians at the mercy of Nisus and Euryalus in the same way in Book Nine. Any hint of actual drunken behaviour, however, is carefully excluded. Only one touch recalls the killing of Ovidian revellers with the crushing weight of wine bowls: the Rutulian Rhoetus, terrified spectator of the slaughter of his sleeping comrades,

magnum metuens se post cratera tegebat (*Aeneid* 9.346).

'In fear he cowered behind the mighty bowl.' Something approaching the realistic use of the furniture of the *convivium* has been raised by the poet's skill to a level at which it could appropriately be allowed to appear in the *Aeneid*.

The aim of this chapter has been to show how every nuance of the drinking and appreciation of wine can enter into the work of the poets. Invitations; simple wine and expensive wine; modest parties, philosophical parties, and wild parties; the actual events of the *convivium* – all could be handled, and on levels of stylisation which vary from something very close to realism, all the way to epic elevation on the one hand, or to Dionysiac splendour on the other. The Roman party admitted women more freely than Greek tradition allowed: that too is reflected in the predominance of heterosexual over homosexual sympotic verse. The poets could use the themes for purposes as different as political encomium on great men, statement of Callimachean aesthetic tastes, passionate love, cynical hedonism. The subject-matter, like the style, is varied with infinite subtlety; and it never quite, even at its most highly stylised, loses its vital contact with Roman life.

---

[79] Women, 12.226; cups, 12.242 *vina dabant animos, et prima pocula pugna / missa volant fragilesque cadi curvique lebetes*; bowls, 5.80-84, 12.235-40; peacemaker, 5.102; drunken sleep, 12.316-26.

[80] This discussion is not of course meant to deny some parodic intention; but to talk of 'an anti-Augustan poem, a mock epic,' and of 'the intent to debunk' (Brooks Otis, *Ovid as an Epic Poet*[2] (1970) 351, 362) seems to me crude and exaggerated. I hope the way the poem is handled here is more sympathetic.

CHAPTER FIVE

The Pleasures of Water and Nakedness

Beauty sat bathing by a spring
Where fairest shades did hide her;
The winds blew calm, the birds did sing,
The cool streams ran beside her – Anthony Munday

Italy is a hot country, and its ancient inhabitants delighted in all the pleasures of water. In Rome, as in every other civilised town, the baths were one of the most important of the amenities of life; outside Rome there were the rivers, the lakes, and the sea.

Every modern visitor to Rome must be impressed by the colossal ruins of the Baths of Caracalla and of Diocletian. Of the earlier baths, which in their time were among the glories of the city, we have far less imposing remains. We are informed[1] that in 33 B.C. no fewer than 170 of these establishments were listed. Agrippa conferred a welcome benefaction on the city by building very large baths on the Campus Martius; to the luxurious Maecenas was ascribed the construction of the first swimming pool of warm water in Rome.[2] The constant mention of *balnea* in Petronius and Martial shows how much time a citizen reckoned to spend in them in the first century A.D., and the letters and speeches of Cicero make it clear that they were highly popular in his time, too. The baths came to contain works of art and to be very splendid buildings.

Like all other pleasures, they were of course heartily denounced. The eighty-sixth Letter of Seneca contains a lengthy diatribe against the luxuriousness of contemporary bathing ('The Scipios bathed only once a week: "How do you think they smelt?" – They smelt of military service, of hard work, of man'). The baths were in fact a principal element in the life of pleasure. *Balnea, vina, Venus* – baths, wine and women – is a set phrase in several poems found inscribed on stone, as in the celebrated

Balnea vina Venus corrumpunt corpora nostra,
sed vitam faciunt balnea vina Venus.[3]

---

[1] Pliny *NH* 36.121.
[2] Dio Cassius 55.7.6; on Roman baths see conveniently E. Brödner, *Die römischen Thermen und das antike Badewesen* (Darmstadt 1983); H. Blümner, *Die römischen Privataltertümer* (1911) 420ff.; J.P.V.D. Balsdon, *Life and Leisure in Ancient Rome* (1969).
[3] *Carmina Epigraphica* 1499; cf. no. 1318 and, in Greek, *Anth. Pal.* 10.112 and Plutarch *Moralia* 128c. *Balnea vina Venus faciunt properantia fata* is the version of *CEL* 1923.

'Baths and wine and love debauch our bodies;
  but our lives are made by baths and wine and love.'

Medical writers would instruct patients to give up 'wine, baths, and sex'.[4] Livy sums up the legendary luxury of Capua, which demoralised Hannibal's army, as 'sleep and wine and feasting and harlots and baths and leisure'.[5] It seems that mixed bathing was never the practice in the main public baths in Rome, but it is clear that it did take place in private installations, of which there were many;[6] certainly women bathed and swam freely. Some scholars have believed that prostitutes were to be picked up at the baths,[7] though positive evidence for this is hard to find; but in any case the poems of Martial (and the denunciations of the Christians) show that an atmosphere of sensuality was often present. Quintilian lists among bad habits that of 'boozing in the baths' (*in balneis perpotare*, 1.6.22).

Outdoor bathing was practised at Rome in the Tiber,[8] and Horace in particular refers repeatedly to the sporting young men who swam there. The handsome athlete Hebrus, champion rider, runner and hunter, dazzles his admiring girl friend when his glistening shoulders are fresh from a swim in the Tiber; the seductive Gyges is the fastest swimmer in the river; it is only for love that Sybaris has abandoned its yellow waters (Horace *Odes* 3.12.7; 3.7.25; 1.8.8). We observe that in every case the nuance is erotic: these are the young men whom girls find attractive. Horace even dreams, so he tells us in Book 4, of swimming after the glamorous Ligurinus (4.1.40). Tibullus, too, tells us that one reason for finding a boy attractive was the sight of his white chest cleaving the smooth water (Tib. 1.4.12). The connection between swimming and sex is made in a much more hostile manner by Cicero in his speech for Caelius. Clodia, he says, has gardens which go down to the Tiber: 'all the young men' go there to swim, and that is how she picks up her paramours.[9] One of the most interesting elements in this enquiry will be the way in which Virgil finds it possible to echo the motifs of ordinary life in an exalted mode which fits them for the purposes of his high style. As the temple-palace of King Latinus recalls the Capitoline temple of Virgil's own time, with its hundred columns and its statues of illustrious men of the past,[10] so the underground cave of Cyrene in the fourth book of the *Georgics*, with its streams of water and echoing water-noise, presents the

---

[4] Celsus 3.22.
[5] Livy 23.18.12.
[6] Blümner 427, Brödner 115, Martial 3.51, 3.72, 7.35, 11.75; and *RE* Supplement 5.8353. Brödner (op. cit. in note 2, p. 114) thinks that in the late Republic and Augustan periods the strict separation of the sexes, even in public baths, was relaxed.
[7] So Friedländer on Martial 3.94.14. See H. Herter in *JAC* 3 (1950) 74 n.77, 87.
[8] See Nisbet-Hubbard on Horace *Odes* 1.8.8.
[9] Cicero *pro Caelio* 36.
[10] *Aeneid* 7.170ff.; cf. W.A. Camps in *CQ* 53 (1959) 54, H. Rowell in *AJP* 62 (1941) 261ff.

highest conceivable elevation of the physical setting of the Roman baths. And in it we find, without surprise, a bevy of beautiful nymphs, their thoughts concerned with stories of love (Virgil *Georg.* 4.333-75). Outside Rome the most notorious pleasure-resort was Baiae. Cicero archly says of Caelius that he is still a man of respectable life, although he has 'seen Baiae'. Propertius hopes against hope that Cynthia has proved capable of resisting the temptations of that insidious watering-place, but he can only finish the poem with a desperate plea that she should leave *corruptas Baias* at once – *litora quae fuerunt castis inimica puellis*, 'a sea-side which menaces the chastity of girls'.[11] One could go out in small boats, and one could swim. Cicero in his attempt to discredit Clodia produces a rhetorical climax which puts these activities surprisingly high, as evidence of unbridled promiscuity: 'Not only her movements but also her style of dress and her company; not only her burning eyes, her immodest speech, but also her embraces, her kisses, her watering-place, her boating, her parties' (*aquis, navigatione, conviviis*) 'mark her not just as a whore but as a particularly brazen whore'.[12] Propertius gives us a voluptuous description of Cynthia in the water at Baiae:

atque utinam mage te remis confisa minutis
parvula Lucrina cumba moretur aqua,
aut teneat clausam tenui Teuthrantis in unda
alternae facilis cedere lympha manu (1.11.9-12).

'Would that you were spending your time on a little boat on the Lucrine water, rowed with toy oars; or safely in the limpid waters of Teuthras, which give way so softly to repeated strokes of the arm.' Some scholars have disliked the passage, like D.O. Ross ('four lines of excessive stylisation devoted lovingly and almost gleefully to Cynthia's paddling'); others have admired them, like A. La Penna, who speaks of 'duttilità, subtlety, expressive concentration'. I agree with La Penna: the reader is encouraged to linger on the brilliant picture of Cynthia in her diminutive boat or swimming in the clear and yielding water.[13] But for our present purposes the point is the way in which the poet has created these delightful vignettes out of the unpromising material of a fashionable

---

[11] Cicero *pro Caelio* 27, Propertius 1.11 *fin.*; cf. Martial 1.62, of a wife who fell there: *Penelope venit, abit Helene* – 'She arrived a Penelope, she left a Helen'.

[12] Cicero *pro Caelio* 49. Boats at Baiae and on the Lucrine Lake: Propertius 1.11.9, Martial 3.20.20, Hollis on Ovid *Ars Amatoria* 1.255, Courtney on Juvenal 12.80. Boating and music meant debauchery in the East, too. Strabo gives a vivid and disapproving picture of Canopus, outside Egyptian Alexandria: day and night the music sounds from small boats, with dancing, 'men and women, with the utmost licentiousness' (17.1.17).

[13] D.O. Ross, *Backgrounds to Augustan Poetry* (1975) 76; A. La Penna, *L'Integrazione Difficile* (1977) 109. Cf. G. Petersmann, *Themenführung und Motiventfaltung in der Monobiblos des Properz = Grazer Beiträge* 1 (1980) 117.

sea-side resort. Cynthia is presented to us as if she were alone there: no hint of crowded beaches, of modern villas, even of the necessary men to row her boat.[14] This is the point to which we shall return.

Parties of pleasure could be held on the shore of the sea. Cicero gives a brilliant account of the infamous Verres, while in command of Sicily as *praetor nequissimus inertissimusque*, spending two whole summer months encamped in tents on the shore outside Syracuse, near the spring of Arethusa.[15] There, Cicero tells us, he spent the time in drinking and music amid a harem of Sicilian beauties: *te illo ipso tempore superioribusque diebus omnibus in litore cum mulierculis perpotasse dico*, 'I accuse you of spending that very time and all the preceding days in boozing on the beach with loose women', is Cicero's downright way of putting it. That was a hostile view. From the point of view of the participants no doubt it presented itself more as resembling those delightful parties of pleasure by the waterside which appear so regularly in the novelists.[16] Indeed, the idea of a simple al fresco picnic by water can be used with a strong nuance of moral superiority to the degenerate luxury of life indoors; a twice repeated passage of Lucretius struck a chord of naïve moralising with his successors.[17] Wealthy men might prefer to dine inside, contemplating the grass and the water from the comfort of the dining room.[18] But the water might lend itself to cruder joys. Martial speaks of sexual intercourse in the water, and prurient fantasy invented strange pleasures for the hated Tiberius as he swam.[19]

All this, then, gives a summary of the role of swimming and bathing, in the city, on the beach, and beside streams. The moral objurgation which followed every aspect of the life of pleasure in Rome did not fail to fasten on the baths and the beach, and that helps us to feel sure that we really are dealing with a full and important part of that life. The interesting question is then: What did the poets do with it? Was it capable of playing

---

[14] To make a different point, Tibullus can say that the attentive lover should himself row his beloved in a boat, accepting the hard work to show his devotion: Tib. 1.4.45-8. Presumably derivative from Propertius is the similar passage [Tibullus] 3.5.29-30.

[15] Cicero *in Verrem* 2.5.63-131. Cf. also Alciphron *Epistles* 1.12, Longus 2.12.

[16] Longus 2.25, 4.3; Heliodorus 8.14; Achilles Tatius 4.18.

[17] Lucretius 2.29-33 = 5.1392f.: *cum tamen inter se prostrati in gramine molli / propter aquae rivum sub ramis arboris altae*, etc. Cf. Horace *Epode* 2.33-8, Nisbet-Hubbard on *Odes* 1.1.22, Ovid *Fasti* 6.775-9, Martial 9.90. In real life, it is worth remarking, Cicero can express the longing for *flumina et solitudines*, rivers and getting away from it all (*ad Atticum* 13.16.1); on that occasion rain kept him indoors. The ambitious Roman politician was of course well advised to stay in all day (Q. Cicero. *Comm. Pet.* 37).

[18] E.g. Martial 10.51.7, Statius *Silvae* 2.2.73ff.

[19] Martial 11.21.11; cf. 4.22 (only a kiss: the water was too transparent for anything more); Suet. *Tib.* 44; cf. *Domit.* 22. At Ovid *Metamorphoses* 8.605ff. there is a voluptuous account of a lover (in this case the river Achelous) fondling the body of a nymph whose angry father has thrown her in: *ipse natantis / pectora tangebam*, etc. Unfortunately it is not clear whether this is by Ovid or an interpolation: see the commentaries *ad loc.* of A.S. Hollis and F. Bömer. *Amores* 3.6.81 might be thought to support it. There is an indecent poem on the theme by Luxorius.

a significant role in verse?

A very simple example opens. We have seen humble literary genres amuse themselves with the idea of intercourse in the water. Ovid raises it in style when he makes his Hero say to Leander

> *At nos diversi medium coeamus in aequor*
> *obviaque in summis oscula demus aquis*   (*Heroides* 19.167f.).

If you have not the strength or the time to swim both ways, 'let us meet, from our two sides, in the midst of the sea, and exchange kisses over the waves'. The sea-side dirty postcard is elevated to tragic status: a pair of doomed mythical lovers think of exchanging kisses (nothing coarser) in the sea that separates them, and the heroine shows her passionate love by offering to swim out to meet her lover. So much is clear. But the popularity in Latin verse of the Hero and Leander story is itself interesting. Greeks could swim as a matter of course – 'he can't swim and he doesn't know his ABC' was a proverbial Greek expression for someone whose education was zero[20] – but classical Greek poetry is strangely uninterested in swimming, and the learned article 'Schwimmen' in Pauly-Wissowa's great Encyclopaedia can find only one substantial passage between Homer and Oppian.[21] Leander appealed to Roman, not to Greek taste.[22] Perhaps it will be right to connect this with the greater role of the sea-side and of water sports in Rome, for it is natural to connect Leander with the handsome young men whose prowess in the water aroused the interest of Clodia in life and of Horace's girls in poetry.

Another myth which pleased in Italy was that of Salmacis and Hermaphroditus. The nymph Salmacis was the eponym of a lake near Halicarnassus. In the story she offered herself to the good-looking young man Hermaphroditus, but was rebuffed by him; she then waited till he dived into her lake, and united herself so closely with him that the double-sexed hermaphrodite came then first into the world. The spicy tale is told with great verve by Ovid in the fourth book of the *Metamorphoses*. Again we find a transposition of the banal reality of seduction at the sea-side; not, this time, to the chaste and touching level of Hero's prayer to Leander, but a full-scale treatment of the nymph's shameless approach ('she did not come up to him, desirous though she was, until she had tidied herself up, adjusted her frock, arranged her face, and deserved to be thought attractive'), his indignant refusal, his gradual attraction to the cool water, his undressing for a bathe ('then Salmacis fancied him indeed and flared up at the sight of his naked beauty ... hardly could she bear to wait ...'), his slapping his sides and

---

[20] *Paroem. Gr.* 1.278, 2.39.

[21] *RE* Supplement 5.848.41ff.

[22] Cf. H. Faerber, *Hero und Leander* (München 1961) 30-91 for the story in ancient literature. T. Gelzer, in the Loeb Musaeus (with the Fragments of Callimachus) 306, does not believe there ever existed a 'great Hellenistic poem' on Leander.

diving in, the nymph throwing her clothes far off and leaping in after him (*Met.* 4.317-57).[23] Leander reflects the sporting young man who swims well, Salmacis the sea-side vamp. She is represented 'bathing her shapely limbs in her fountain', and wearing a transparent dress (*perlucenti circumdata corpus amictu*, 4.313), for all the world like a demi-mondaine of Ovid's own time. It is curious that Martial puts her activities not in Asia Minor but in the Lucrine Lake, the familiar pleasure resort near Baiae (10.30.10); scholars speculate on his source for this innovation, but more interesting is the reflection that she belonged in her new setting: a poet reflecting on the water sports he knew would naturally put her there as the mythical embodiment of a type.

Salmacis and Arethusa are raised stylistically not far above the level of Cynthia herself, swimming in the Lucrine Lake. Further degrees of elevation were possible. Thus when the Argo set sail, the first ship to plough the sea, as the foam whitened round the oars:

Emersere feri candenti e gurgite vultus
aequoreae monstrum Nereides admirantes.
illa atque haud alia viderunt luce marinas
mortales oculis nudato corpore Nymphas
nutricum tenus exstantes e gurgite cano   (Catullus 64.14-18).

'Strange faces emerged from the deep, the Nereids of the waters marvelling at the sight. On that day, and no other, mortal eyes beheld the sea nymphs in their nakedness, rising up as far as their breasts from the white water.'

That marvellous tableau opens Catullus' *Peleus and Thetis*, and it is no surprise that its results are erotic. Peleus on the ship and Thetis in the water fall in love. The motif of the beauty in the water and sea-side love here attains a sort of sublimity. The cortège of the Nereids riding on dragons and hippocamps was a popular subject in art, and in the Roman period the sea-nymphs are usually represented as naked to the waist:[24] again fantasy has been at work on the realities of swimming for pleasure. Finally Virgil attempts a yet higher level of solemnity, when the Trojan ships are rescued from the flames and miraculously transformed into sea nymphs (*Aen.* 9.117ff.) – an episode which perhaps does not wholly succeed in satisfying.

[23] Cf. L.P. Wilkinson, *Ovid Recalled* (1955) 208ff.; C.P. Segal, *Landscape in Ovid's Metamorphoses* (1959) 10, on the significance of 'water, associated from the earliest times with generation and sexuality', in this story.
[24] Scopas' celebrated group was on show in Rome, probably set up by Cn. Domitius Ahenobarbus, Antony's admiral: Pliny *NH* 36.26. A spectacular example from the first century B.C., cf. H. Kähler, *Seethiasos und Census, Die Reliefs aus dem Palazzo Santa Croce in Rom* = *Monumenta Artis Romanae* 6 (1966). Half naked: *RE* s.v. *Nereiden* 21.35ff. Virgil describes such a cortège at *Aeneid* 5.239. For R.F. Thomas, *AJP* 103 (1982) 144-64, the Catullus scene is exclusively literary in inspiration, and 'the spirit is essentially polemical'.

Not only men but also women swam, as we have seen. Propertius gives us a striking picture of Cynthia in the water, happily swimming at Baiae: he also gives us a very different one, a dream in which he saw her drowning, shipwrecked in the middle of the sea (2.26). The poem opens with startling abruptness:

> *Vidi te in somnis fracta, mea vita, carina*
> *Ionio lassas ducere rore manus ...*

'I saw you in my dreams, my darling, shipwrecked, moving weary arms in the Ionian sea ...' Her hair weighs her down, she is at the point of death: naturally (in the poet's dream) her thoughts are all of him, and she confesses her infidelities and calls on his name. She looked, he reflects, like Helle when she fell into the Hellespont; she would have made a lovely mermaid, and the other mermaids would have envied her beauty. Just in time, as Propertius tells us he was 'about to jump in', a dolphin rescues her – doubtless the same one which rescued Arion, five hundred years earlier. I once read this pretty piece[25] with a class of sixth-formers, and one of the girls objected that it was 'an unkind poem'. Why does Propertius have so much leisure to contemplate the picture Cynthia makes, and to weave mythological fantasies about it? The reader is not, in reality, expected to take her peril very seriously. This is another glimpse of Cynthia in the water, and whereas in 1.11 the poet exalted the everyday scene by describing it in an enamel-like miniature, set off from its context by its special style, here he transposes the subject by assimilating it to the world of mythology, where everything is beautiful, and where even if you drown you are not really dead but a sea-goddess. Since the dream is part of Propertius' life, naturally Cynthia is as obsessed with him in it as he is with her; and the humour of the narration, which surely is aimed in part at himself (Propertius shows self-knowledge – that is just the way the *iners amator* would behave in a crisis), plays on his own love of mythological comparisons and connections and on the lovers who exist for each other alone. Propertius was often attracted to the theme of death, his own or that of his mistress, and here he allows himself (since the experience is only a dream) to dwell on it with barely disguised relish. One is reminded, not for the only time, of Edgar Allan Poe, who in his *Philosophy of Composition* proclaims that 'The death, then, of a beautiful woman is, unquestionably, the most poetical topic in the world, and equally it is beyond doubt that the lips best suited for such a topic are those of a bereaved lover'.

Propertius' thoughts often turn to ships: sometimes it is Cynthia who

---

[25] In my view editors are right to print 2.26.1-20 as a separate poem, despite the arguments of C.W. Macleod in *Symb. Osl.* 51 (1976) 131-6, and Gordon Williams, *Figures of Thought in Roman Poetry* (1980) 129-31.

will sail away and leave him, sometimes he is on the point of leaving her (Prop. 1.8, 1.6). Sailing leads naturally to shipwreck: in 1.17 he has sailed away without her – and been shipwrecked and lost in a wilderness. Or he imagines them sailing off together, the world well lost, sleeping on the boards of prow or stern – so long as they can sleep together. Together they will be shipwrecked and cast up naked on the shore: he will be happy to find no burial, so long as she is buried on land. But surely the gods of sea and wind, who are lovers themselves, will spare them ... (2.26b). Such fantasies create gratifyingly extreme situations. Prosaic reality can hardly suggest a reason why Propertius should get himself stranded on an uninhabited coast, with nobody to talk to except the halcyons (1.17.2), nor a rational destination for the two lovers to make for together:

Seu mare per longum mea cogitet ire puella,
hanc sequar et fidos una aget aura duos:

'If my darling were to plan a long sea trip, I shall go with her: the same wind will waft two true lovers,' 2.26.29f. The *navigia* of which Caelius was accused, the little *cumba* which carried Cynthia on the Lucerne Lake: it is easier to imagine Propertius and Cynthia in that sort of boat than on an international voyage.

But such excursions were not easy to make into poetry. Instead Propertius raises the level by writing of perilous voyages – such as serious sea-trips really were (though they might not land the shipwrecked traveller in a wilderness provided with halcyons, those eminently poetical birds).[26] The motif of shipwreck for lovers is a regular one in the Greek Novel,[27] where it serves the eminently practical purposes of bringing them into dangers needed for the plot, and sometimes of drowning characters whose usefulness to the author is at an end; but it is not here developed in a sentimental manner. In the Augustan poets the motifs of shipwreck and drowning are quite common. In myth, Leander is drowned and washed up on the shore before Hero's tower; Ceyx, whose tragic story is one of the longest and most moving in the *Metamorphoses*, is wrecked, drowned, and cast up on the shore at the feet of his loving wife Alcyone; Palinurus is cast into the sea, drifts for days clinging to wreckage, and is murdered as soon as he reaches the shore. He too will lie dead on an empty beach.[28] In life Paetus has been drowned in the Aegean and receives from Propertius an elaborate memorial poem (3.7), which contrasts his luxurious cabin on board with the wreck in which his fingernails were torn to the quick and he drank the bitter sea water.

[26] Cf. Ovid's halcyons, *Alcyones solae, memores Ceycis amati, / nescioquid visae sunt mihi dulce loqui* (*Her.* 18.81-2). 'Only I thought I heard the halcyons, mindful of the beloved Ceyx, utter a sweet lament.'
[27] Achilles Tatius 3 *init.*, Heliodorus 5.27, Petronius 114; cf. also Chariton 3.3.
[28] Virgil *Georg.* 3.258-63; Ovid *Tristia* 3.10.41; *Met.* 11.716; Virg. *Aen.* 5.827-71, 6.357-83.

Neither mythical nor immediate is Horace's long ode on the anonymous drowned mariner who ridicules Pythagorean fantasies of reincarnation and begs for token burial (1.28): here we find philosophical reflection and irony.

What Propertius has done is to turn the theme into an expression of the obsessive character of his love: as the Stoic sage was happy when tortured on the rack or roasted in the bull of Phalaris, the Propertian lover will be happy in shipwreck, if only his beloved is with him (2.26b); or, in an ecstasy of masochistic self-abnegation, Propertius will pray to the gods of the sea to give his unfaithful Cynthia a smooth and safe journey, although she is leaving him for another man.[29] And, of course, if Cynthia is in danger of drowning, her last thoughts will be for him, and his name will be on her lips (2.26a).

The motif of the drowning of the beloved recurs in a fully mythological form in Propertius 1.20. Gallus' pretty boy Hylas may be carried off by nymphs, as the Hylas of myth was dragged into the water, if Gallus is not careful:

> *nympharum semper cupidas defende rapinas*
> *(non minor Ausoniis est amor Adryasin)*   (1.20.11-12).

'Be ever careful to ward off the greedy hands of nymphs: the Adryads of Italy are no less amorous.' The poem [30] toys with the idea that women, too, will start to find Hylas attractive. Gallus may find his boy as lost to him as the pretty Hylas of myth, and the 'nymphs' who will have an eye for him are to be feared at watering-places: in lines 7-10, 'whether you are by some wooded river, or beside the Anio, or strolling on the beach of the Giants' shore'. The Giants' shore is the coast immediately north of Naples: as Butler and Barber observe, 'the suggestion is that of a visit to Baiae'. In fact we are back in the familiar world of sea-side seductions, dressed up, this time, with an elaborate and exquisite account of the mythological fall of Hylas. In such a poem Baiae, too, must be dressed up with some trappings of myth: the story that in the neighbourhood the giants fought with the gods.[31]

Verres enjoyed himself on the beach with his *mulierculae*. Cicero says

---

[29] Prop. 1.8.17ff. This must derive, like Virg. *Buc.* 10.46-9, from Gallus (but not the detail of the sea journey): cf. J. Hubeaux in *Miscellanea Properziana* (1957) 31ff. Horace, in a dryer and more ironic manner, uses the same idea in *Odes* 3.27; cf. Colin Macleod in *CQ* 24 (1974) 88-91 = *Collected Essays* 165-8.

[30] Cf. J.C. Bramble in *Quality and Pleasure in Latin Poetry*, ed. Woodman & West (1974) 81-93; D.O. Ross, *Backgrounds to Augustan Poetry* (1975) 74ff., P. Fedeli, *Il Primo Libro delle Elegie di Properzio* (1980) 455; R. Syme, *History in Ovid* 101ff. For the motif of the pretty boy who will soon be attractive to women, cf. Horace *Odes* 1.4.19-20, and also 3.20.

[31] In the poem on the death of Marcellus, who died at Baiae, the place is dignified by being called the site of the grave of Aeneas' trumpeter Misenus, and of a road built by Hercules (Prop. 3.18.3-4).

that Caelius' accusers charged him with *libidines amores adulteria Baias actas convivia comissationes cantus symphonias navigia*, 'orgies, flirtations, adulteries, trips to Baiae, parties on the beach, dinner parties, singing, concerts, boat-trips'. Of these *actae* Austin observes 'such parties were evidently a feature of social life';[32] they could readily be made to sound like debauched occasions, as doubtless they often were. The nymph Salmacis might represent the elevation of amours in the water; other mythical ladies reflected the commoner practice of love beside the shore. This motif is an ancient one. Thetis was ambushed on a lonely shore by Peleus and there subdued to his will, a struggle often represented on early vases. A hero in the *Iliad* was conceived when his father met a nymph by the banks of the River Satnioeis in the Troad; the beautiful Tyro was possessed by Poseidon at the mouth of the River Enipeus, 'and a dark wave stood round them like a mountain, arched over, concealing the god and the mortal woman'. Even in late antiquity we find a good story about an unscrupulous young man coming upon a girl out of a river and passing himself off as the amorous river god.[33] No doubt the shore of a river or the sea was a place where a girl might be found alone, perhaps doing some laundry like Nausicaa. The motif takes a different turn in Greek bucolic, with the love-lorn Polyphemus gazing out to sea for the elusive Galatea, or with an amorous shepherd wishing to recline with his arm round his beloved and gaze on the blue Sicilian sea[34] – we detect a new sentimentality, exploited in Virgil's second *Eclogue* – or when Galatea lies in Acis' lap in Ovid and listens to the distant waves.[35]

Ovid constantly uses the shore as the setting for his mythological amours. It was on the beach that Cornix was pursued by Neptune, and on the beach that Caenis was enjoyed by him. Thetis met Peleus on the sea-shore, and Aesacus saw Cebrenis drying her hair on the bank of a river; from the beach Europa was carried off; Scylla was seen by Glaucus as she walked and bathed naked on the beach.[36] Propertius writes of the heroine Brimo as possessed by Mercury by the shore of a lake.[37] Polyphemus gazing out to sea is a reversal of a commoner poetical pattern, that of the heroine who gazes out to sea for the sail of her unfaithful lover. Catullus presents his abandoned Ariadne looking for the ship of Theseus, with eyes for him alone, as her garments slip unregarded from her upper body and reveal to us her milk-white breasts, a vividly

---

[32] Cicero *pro Caelio* 35, with R.G. Austin's note; Serv. in *Aen.* 5.613.
[33] *Iliad* 4.445, *Odyssey* 11.242, [Aeschines] *Epistle* 10. on this, see E. Rohde, *Der gr. Roman*[4] 596.
[34] Theocritus 6.11; [Theocritus] 8.55f. See W. Elliger, *Landschaft in gr. Dichtung* (1975) 342f., 394.
[35] *Met.* 13.785.
[36] *Metamorphoses* 2.572, 12.195, 11.237, 11.769, 2.836, 13.900ff.
[37] Prop. 2.2.12.

sensuous passage of his Peleus and Thetis poem. T.P. Wiseman says of
this poem 'Ariadne is Catullus himself with very little disguise'. It is
unfair to take such a remark out of its context, but a passage like this
shows how completely Catullus is separate from his Ariadne, savouring
the spectacle of her distress which is soon to be consoled, as Propertius
savours the sight of Cynthia in the waves:

> *non flavo retinens subtilem vertice mitram,*
> *non contecta levi velatum pectus amictu,*
> *non tereti strophio lactentis vincta papillas,*
> *omnia quae toto delapsa e corpore passim*
> *ipsius ante pedes fluctus salis alludebant.*

'Not keeping her fine scarf on her blond hair, not covering her bosom with
the veil of a light garment, not binding her milk-white breasts with the
smooth stomacher: no, all had fallen clear from her body, and there
before her feet they were the sport of the waves of the sea.'[38]
    It was beside the water that Actaeon came on the sight of Diana
undressed; it was beside the sea that Perseus saw and loved Andromeda.
It was over the indifferent waves that Phyllis and Oenone and Hypsipyle
and Alcyone gazed for their lovers, and through them that the wicked
Scylla, who betrayed her country for love, was dragged behind his ship by
Minos.[39] Over them Europa was carried by the bull, a subject not only for
Ovid but also for Horace, *Odes* 3.27; and a subject, it is worth observing,
which was painted on the walls of the porticus Vespasiae Pollae, built by
Agrippa's sister and often called the porticus Europae. Ovid recommends
the painted porticoes of Rome as good places for picking up girls (*Ars*
1.71f.).
    It may be observed here that women might be offered for sale into
slavery by their captors on the sea-shore. We read in the Elder Seneca of
a woman who was abducted by pirates and sold into a brothel: *nuda in
litore stetit ad fastidium emptoris: omnes partes corporis et inspectae et
contrectatae sunt* (*Contr.* 1.2.3) – 'she stood naked on the beach, exposed
to the scorn of the purchaser. Every part of her body has been looked at
and handled.' Such a passage brings home to us, perhaps with a shock,
the existence of another kind of scene on the beach with a woman: one so
sordid that the higher genres of literature close their eyes to it, as they do
to most aspects of the slave-trade. But to return to Actaeon: his story
might naturally lead to another interesting subject, that of nakedness in
reality and in literature. That discussion will follow, but first it remains
to point out further variants on the theme of love and water. The
glamorous swimmers Salmacis and Hero and Galatea find a sister in

---

[38] Catullus 64.60ff.; cf. T.P. Wiseman, *Cinna the Poet* (1974) 117. On this passage see
Richard Jenkyns, *Three Classical Poets* (1982) 116f.
[39] Ov. *Met.* 3.177, 4.670; *Heroides* 2.5.6; *Met.* 11.710, 8.142; [Virgil] *Ciris* 389.

poetry in the nymph Arethusa, in the Fifth Book of Ovid's
Metamorphoses. Her story (she tells it herself) is the reverse of that of
Hermaphroditus. A huntress, she came to an inviting pool when heated
by the chase. First she dipped a foot, then she went in up to her knees;
finally she undressed, hung her clothes on a tree, and swam,

> *nudaque mergor aquis, quas dum ferioque trahoque*
> *mille modis labens excussaque bracchia iacto,*
> *nescio quid medio sensi sub gurgite murmur.*[40]

'Naked I dived into the water. As I tossed it and buffetted it, striking out
a thousand ways with my arms, I heard a strange voice from the midst of
the stream ...'. Frightened out of the water, she unfortunately gets out on
the opposite side from her clothes; she is pursued by Alpheus, the god of
the stream, like a dove by a hawk, naked through the woods. The episode
is a charming one, thoroughly enjoyable for everybody except poor
Arethusa. L.P. Wilkinson observes, in connection with it, that 'The
Metamorphoses is undoubtedly a poem of escape ... However much at
home Ovid may have felt in the sophisticated society of the Capital, he
must sometimes have longed to escape, like Horace, to the hills and
streams, far from *fumum et opes strepitumque Romae*, 'the smoke and
wealth and bustle of Rome'. It may perhaps be permitted to amend this
account a little. In a way Ovid had left the Capital behind in the
Metamorphoses; we are in a rural and mythical world, true enough. But
it is at least as important that he has brought it all with him.

In the *Ars Amatoria* Ovid writes for an audience with leisure, good
health, good taste, and not much to think about except making love.
Rome is full, if you are a man, of agreeable girls (*Ars* 1.51ff.): all you have
to do is take your choice. If you are a girl, you can find men anywhere who
will rise to take your hook (*Ars* 3.425ff.). The world of the
Metamorphoses is just the same: gods look down and pick out girls,
heroines fall in love and are set upon in the most unlikely spots. And
Ovid is careful to give his mythical lovers not just the general psychology
of men and women in the grip of love, but the particular sensibility of his
own time and class. We see that with special clarity in his constant
emphasis on *cultus*, elegance. In the *Ars* he gives full instructions to both
sexes on this all-important topic. Men should be careful about their teeth
and fingernails, their nostrils should not be hairy, they should be well
shaved and well turned out; but they should not go too far, by curling
their hair, for instance. Women should give even more thought to their
appearance and be mistress of the arts of cosmetics, knowing what

---

[40] Ov. *Met.* 5.594-6. On the episode, cf. L.P. Wilkinson, *Ovid Recalled* 174f. 'Ovid makes
Greek myth vivid from Roman experiences of life', says M. von Albrecht, a formulation I
applaud, in his article 'Mythos und römische Realität in Ovids Metamorphosen', *ANRW*
31.4 (1981) 2341; but his subject is handled very differently from mine.

colours and what positions suit them, but the first thing Ovid mentions is the hair:

munditiis capimur: non sint sine lege capilli.[41]

'Elegance is what catches us: let your hair not be a mess.' We have seen how Salmacis made herself up before approaching Hermaphroditus. The theme runs right through his mythological poems: Byblis, in the grip of an incestuous passion for her brother, adorns herself when she is to see him; Polyphemus makes absurd attempts to prettify himself for Galatea; Mercury, though confident in his own good looks, combs his hair and checks his appearance before appearing to Herse; even a female centaur does what she can to make the best of her looks –

> *cultus quoque, quantus in illis*
> *esse potest membris –*

'elegance, too, as far as it is possible for such a figure'. When Apollo is attracted by Daphne, he cannot help the thought that a good hairdresser would do wonders for her:

spectat inornatos collo pendere capillos
et 'quid, si comantur?' ait.

'He eyed her hair hanging unadorned down her back and reflected "Suppose it were combed!".'[42]

These elegant and leisured lovers are, of course, Ovid's familiar metropolitan men and women, but transposed into a setting remote in time and place, and to some extent raised in level by being given mythical status. Much of the pleasure of the *Metamorphoses*, and some of that of the *Heroides*,[43] comes from seeing how this is done. As for Arethusa, her adventure is intended to give us a glimpse of the familiar pleasures of a contemporary watering-place, the pretty girls bathing, the transient amours, which have been given novelty and dignity by being reflected back into primeval Arcadia.

The theme of pretty girls swimming occurs in Hellenistic Greek poetry,

---

[41] Ovid *Ars* 1.505ff.; 3.101ff. On what follows cf A.H.F. Griffin in *G and R* 24 (1977) 61f.

[42] *Met.* 9.462, 13.764, 2.732, 12.405, 1.498, with which cf. *Amores* 2.4.37 *non est culta: subit quid cultae accedere possit* – 'If a girl is not well groomed, I reflect how much good grooming could do for her.'

[43] Two points, for instance, from the *Heroides*, which the poet has extracted from his favourite theme of *cultus*. Deianira complains of the intrusion into her house of Iole, her husband's captive and concubine: 'and she doesn't arrive with hair dishevelled, like a captive, but she struts in glittering with gold' (*Her.* 9.125). Paris hopes to seduce Helen by telling her that 'Sparta is mean, you deserve riches and elegance ... Now that you see how elegant Trojan men are, you can imagine the luxury enjoyed by Trojan women' (*Her.* 16.191-6).

in an epigram the authorship of which is disputed between Posidippus and Asclepiades, and in the fictitious letters of Aristaenetus, a writer of late imperial date. The epigram simply says that Cleander saw Nico swimming and fell in love on sight, subsequently being made happy by her. One letter, of rather feeble construction, purports to be from a fisherman to a friend, describing a girl who suddenly appears on the beach as he is hard at work, asks him to mind her clothes, strips, and swims in the sea. Needless to say she is exceedingly beautiful, resembling a Nereid when swimming and Aphrodite when emerging from the water. The fisherman tries his luck with her but gets a stinging rebuff. It is clear that these simple productions depict the same tableau as Ovid's episode of Arethusa: the sudden apparition of a glamorous woman in water, with its inevitable effect on the leisured male. It is clear too that by the way he has handled it Ovid has transformed the tone and level of an incident which in principle is possible enough in real life. Finally, another letter of Aristaenetus completes the group. Here a lover writes to a friend, recommending him to take his girl friend for a day to a charming garden with a cool spring of clear water in it. Here the writer has just passed a day 'all devoted to Dionysus and Aphrodite', bathing, drinking, and making love: the spring was fine enough in itself, but far more beautiful with his mistress' sparkling limbs within it, and the water 'was so clear that as we swam, and as we embraced and made love, every one of our limbs was clearly visible'.[44] Here are the aquatic embraces which to Martial are a joke, which to the detractors of Tiberius and Domitian were prurient scandal, which Hero was too modest to offer to Leander, which in the stories of Salmacis and of Arethusa are represented only as fantastic changes of nature, with Alpheus and Arethusa united as one stream of water, and Salmacis and Hermaphroditus metamorphosed into one creature with two sexes. From the banal pleasures of Baiae and from simple day-dreams about beautiful naked women Propertius and Ovid have created poems of ideal elegance.

Other writers show us a half-way development of this sort of raising of the stylistic level. Several provocative passages in Longus' *Daphnis and Chloe* deal with the bathing of the young and innocent pair in each other's presence. Chloe's amorous interest in Daphnis is first aroused when she sees him bathing in a spring; later she bathes before him, with a similar effect. These rather prurient scenes take place in the romantic outdoor setting of idealised pastoral, and are thus differentiated from the crudities of Martial on the topic of voyeurism in the baths, one of his favourite subjects. Similarly the epigrammatist Zonas, who seems to have been active in the generation of Cicero, writes of a lover seeing the boy he loves bathing: but the lover is the god Pan, the beloved is

[44] *Anth. Pal.* 5.209 = Asclepiades 36 Gow-Page; Aristaenetus *Epistles* 1.7, 1.3. Further references: S. Trenkner, *The Greek Novella* (Cambridge 1958) 110 n.7.

Daphnis, and the setting is the sea.[45] It is a particular humour of Ovid's treatment of the myth of Salmacis (above, p. 92) that while the setting is fully mythical, the behaviour of the nymph is crudely modern; Longus, who does not go so far in the direction of distancing his narration from ordinary life, keeps his characters far more chaste.

Somewhere between the motifs of shipwreck and of the enjoyable picnic on the shore come two passages which show us how the material is capable of being handled at every stylistic level. Every trace of the sentimental and the erotic had to be removed when Virgil included in the *Aeneid* the scenes of the storm-tossed Trojans making an al fresco meal on the shore of Africa, and when six books later they eat their first meal on Latin soil and fulfil an omen promising their destiny. Scattered and almost destroyed by Juno's storm, seven of Aeneas' ships struggle to land (1.157ff.). With great effort the Trojans achieve the beach they long for –

> *magno telluris amore*
> *egressi optata potiuntur Troes harena.*

'Yearning for dry land the Trojans reach the sand they crave' (a passage full of irony, the more effective for being so muted: they are reduced to desiring sand, and they feel a great love for the African soil which soon they will be desperate to leave). While his men light a fire and get out their spoilt provisions, Aeneas manages to shoot seven deer, which he offers with the most cheering words he can find, though himself dispirited and sick at heart. The scene is a moving one, which coming so early in the poem bears a programmatic weight: this is how it will always be for the leader, alone with his responsibilities, striving to be *pius* under the unjust blows of heaven. We are closer to the pleasure picnic in Book 7. Here the Trojans disembark at Tiber mouth and eat on the shore. The handsome young Iulus is appropriately singled out, as they recline in the shade of a tall tree and spread out their food on flat loaves of bread:

> *Aeneas primique duces et pulcher Iulus*
> *corpora sub ramis deponunt arboris altae,*
> *instituuntque dapes et adorea liba per herbam*
> *subiciunt epulis: sic Iuppiter ipse monebat* (7.107-110).

'Aeneas and the leaders and handsome Iulus reclined under the branches of a lofty tree and set out the meal, putting flat cakes of wheat under the food: so Jupiter himself suggested.' The point of the episode is that the Trojans will 'eat their tables' and so fulfil the prophecy that only when

---

[45] Longus 1.13-14; 1.32. A tragic love story which begins when a young man sees a girl bathing in preparation for a procession, Plut. *Moralia* 771F. Martial: e.g. 3.51, 72, 87; 9.33; cf. Petronius 92.7-11. The Motif is slightly elevated in Rufinus, *Epigrams* 21 and 27 P, Zonas 8 GP; cf. *Garland of Philip* 2.264.

they had done so would they be able to build their city.[46] The fulfilment of the prophecy appears in the Greek tradition as one of a number of portents which occur at once, and not the climactic one; Virgil has simplified and concentrated. The scene has a 'bucolic' flavour. 'Pulcher Iulus' made no appearance in the scene in Book One, where the point was Aeneas' painful isolation; here his presence, that of a good-looking boy, goes naturally with the delightful spot in the shade of a tree. But in the god-loaded world of the *Aeneid* even a picnic[47] is full of heavy meaning. The supreme god suggests the use of the wheat cakes, and when young Iulus shouts 'Hey, we're eating our tables, too' –

> *'heus, etiam mensas consumimus', inquit Iulus,*
> *nec plura, adludens –*

his father snatches at the omen and conducts a thanksgiving service to the gods.

*

Full nakedness! All joyes are due to thee – Donne

Among the delights of the bath and the sea-shore an important motif has been that of naked beauty. No doubt the thought was commoner than the reality, but the connection is certainly there. But nudity is not a simple matter. The nakedness characteristic of Greek art shocked Romans at first, as did the naked sports of the gymnasium.[48] In Greece, scenes of women undressed at the bath are very common on vases from the fifth century onwards: so are scenes in which the women are shown to be nymphs by the presence with them of molesting satyrs.[49] It is clear enough that both the baths and the satyrs are essentially only devices to justify the representation of naked women, either by giving a setting in which all must undress, or by transposing the scene – in the most superficial manner – on to the plane of mythology. The devices of poets, though sometimes more elaborate, are often very similar in essence.

A respectable Roman woman wore long skirts (the *stola matronarum*) and revealed very little of her person. Poets sometimes complain of this, as when Horace says that, apart from other reasons, the seduction of such

---

[46] On the problem about this prophecy, the discrepancy between the account of it in Book 7 and that in Book 3, see Gordon Williams, *Technique and Ideas in the Aeneid* (1983) 272f. The episode is interestingly discussed by F. Klingner, *Virgil* (1967) 501-4. *Details of the Greek tradition:* Dionysius of Halicarnassus *Rom. Ant.* 1.55, and see now P. Oxy. 3648 (Conon).

[47] *Georg.* 4.146 *iamque ministrantem platanum potantibus umbras*, 'the plane tree grown big enough to make a shade for drinkers', shows how close the *Aeneid* scene is to the ordinary life of pleasure – even for Virgil. See the discussion of picnics in literature and life, above p. 20f.

[48] Cf. W.B. Crowther, 'Nudity and morality: athletics in Italy', *CJ* 76 (1980-1) 119-23.

[49] R. Ginouvès, *Balaneutike* (1962) 114ff., 123.

women was an unsatisfactory business because you could not get a good look at them first:

matronae praeter faciem nil cernere possis
cetera, ni Catia est, demissa veste tegentis (*Sat.* 1.2.94f.).

'With a married woman you can see nothing but her face: she covers up all the rest – unless she's like Catia – with her long dress'. By contrast, says Horace, you can really look a prostitute over (ib. 83-5, 101-3): in her see-through Coan stuff she is as good as naked. In another satire he is even franker on the advantages of the bordello and describes the girl *sub clara nuda lucerna* (*Sat.* 2.7.48), 'naked under a bright light'. It appears that the lowest and cheapest type of whore did actually offer herself naked.[50] Petronius' Encolpius belatedly realises that he is in a brothel when he sees *nudas meretrices* slinking about in it. Outside houses of ill-fame, the Roman people traditionally enjoyed the appearance of naked mime-performers (*mimae*) at certain festivals, notably the Floralia,[51] at which magistrates presided; and slaves offered for sale were looked over by prospective purchasers.[52]

All these occasions had in common a certain sordidness. In poetry, and particularly in Propertius and Ovid, we find a kind of idealising presentation of nakedness, as part of a life of love and pleasure which it is the poet's intention to present as not sordid but splendid. It will be suggested, after an examination of the poetical treatments of this matter, that the realities of social life lay behind them.

As we saw with Greek art, the application to the nude of some trappings of mythology could make a great difference to its respectability. Victorian practice was very similar: Alma Tadema's Roman ladies in the bath, and Lord Leighton's Greek nudes, were acceptable where unclothed representations of contemporaries were not.[53] At this period the Judgment of Paris, having originally been an allegorical choice between ways of life, had come to be thought of as a beauty contest between naked goddesses.[54] That is what it is for Propertius. His Cynthia, he says, is so lovely that all three goddesses should yield place to her:

---

[50] Cf. Courtney on Juvenal 6.121 and 3.135. Apparently the *vestitum scortum*, 'dressed tart', in the latter passage, whose expensiveness daunts her impoverished admirer, is a cut above the *nuda scorta*.
[51] *Cf. RE* s.v. Floralia 2751.
[52] Cf. Propertius 4.7.39 *quae modo per viles inspecta est publica noctes*, and the parallels adduced by the commentators; Martial 6.82, 11.70, and Seneca *Contr.* 1.2.3 (above, p. xxx).
[53] Cf. Richard Jenkyns, *The Victorians and Ancient Greece* (1980) 133ff., 322ff.
[54] T.C.W. Stinton, *Euripides and the Judgment of Paris* (1965) 9: 'the beauty contest is especially favoured in the Roman period, when the goddesses are often naked.'

cedite iam, divae, quas pastor viderat olim
  Idaeis tunicas ponere verticibus (2.2.13f.; cf. 3.13.38).

'Yield now, you goddesses, whom once the shepherd saw undress on Mount Ida.' Ovid draws the frank moral from the story that, as Paris looked the goddesses over thoroughly before making his choice, so his male readers, too, should look carefully before choosing a girl (*Ars* 1.247). The picture of a Roman man about town, running an eye over the girls on offer in some louche establishment, is almost tangibly present: the dignifying effect of mythology is very thin. It is hardly thicker when Ovid presents his own muse, Elegia, in a way which would perfectly describe the girls he pursues and writes of:

forma decens, vestis tenuissima, voltus amantis (*Amores* 3.1.9)

'Pleasing shape, very thin dress, amorous expression'.

Paris also, we read in Propertius, liked full nakedness in Helen, and Endymion and Diana both preferred it, too:

ipse Paris fertur nuda periisse Lacaena,
  cum Menelaeo surgeret e thalamo:
nudus et Endymion Phoebi cepisse sororem
  dicitur et nudae concubuisse deae (2.15.13f.).

– And so do I, the poet insists. That poem of Propertius is uncharacteristic in the frankness with which it describes the joys of a night of love. On the whole elegy, however disreputable, is strikingly chaste in such matters. Wishing to make an unusually explicit utterance, the poet naturally turned to the supreme validating device, that of mythology. For in the world of myth girls wore much less than they do nowadays, just as they were less venal and altogether more simple and straightforward.[55] Ovid's *Metamorphoses* have already shown us a fine bevy of unclothed heroines, to whom we can add for instance the involuntary disrobing of Daphne when chased by Apollo – the winds uncovered her body, *nudabant corpora venti* (1.527), and the undressing of Atalanta for the foot-race which was to decide whether her suitor should get her hand or, if he lost the race, be put to death. On that occasion Hippomenes, her eventual husband, was sitting among the spectators, with no more interest than the casual reflection that men were fools to risk their lives for a bride. But

ut faciem et posito corpus velamine vidit

---

[55] For instance Propertius 1.15.9-25, 3.13.23f., and below, p. 114. Ovid, sitting next to a handsome wench at the Races, finds an excuse to lift her skirts a little. *Invida vestis eras*, he cries, *quae tam bona crura tegebas* – 'Spiteful skirt to hide such pretty legs!' The sight at once calls to his mind the short dress of heroines (*Amores* 3.2.27ff.).

'when he saw her face and her body as she stripped', very different thoughts possessed his mind (10.578).[56] Even Horace, who is so careful to distinguish his frankly worded satires from his modest odes, and who, having spoken so openly of naked *meretrices* in the former, is careful to avoid such coarseness in the latter, tips us a wink in the Europa ode. Having been carried across the sea by a miraculous bull (in reality Jupiter himself), Europa is seized with exaggerated remorse for her imprudent and unmaidenly behaviour. She prays for death to avert inevitable dishonour:

> *impudens liqui patrios penates,*
> *impudens Orcum moror. o deorum*
> *si quis haec audis, utinam inter errem*
> *nuda leones!*

> *antequam turpis macies decentis*
> *occupet malas teneraeque sucus*
> *defluat praedae, speciosa quaero*
> *pascere tigres   (Odes 3.27.49-56).*

'I was shameless to leave my father's house: I am shameless to postpone my death. O, if any god is listening, I wish I might walk naked among lions! Before my pretty cheeks are drawn and unsightly, before I become a withered and unattractive prey, I wish to feed tigers while still beautiful'.

The passage has embarrassed many of Horace's commentators, who are reluctant to allow either flippancy or prurience into the speech of a suicidal heroine. *Nuda* means not 'naked' but 'defenceless', according to Heinze; Arnaldi, who rejects this as 'ruinous', as it surely is, assures his readers that Europa wishes to be naked 'not from immodesty, but as an expression of her desperate suffering as a girl, her emerging self-consciousness as a woman'. Gordon Williams offers the suggestion that she would be 'a greater temptation and an easier prey without clothes', so that the lions would dispose of her more quickly. Horace tells us that Venus heard Europa's lamentations with a malicious smile (*perfidum ridens*): that smile would be broader, perhaps, could the goddess overhear her commentators. The verse cannot be separated from the next one, the prayer to fill the maw of tigers while still in good looks and full of *sucus*, juice. Not all commentators have the self-restraint to say, with Wickham, that 'the point of this stanza is not quite obvious', and the view of most of them is that Europa now hates her own beauty, which has brought her into this scrape, and wishes to punish it at the

---

[56] See the learned commentary of F. Bömer on *Met.* 10.578, beginning 'Nacktheit der Frauen ist ein kulturgeschichtliches Kapitel eigener Ordnung', and remarking on the fact that no literary source earlier than Ovid says that Atalanta ran naked; and I. Weiler, *Agonales in Wettkämpfen der gr. Mythologie* (Innsbruck 1969) 24f.

hands of wild animals. But in reality, I think, it is not possible to avoid admitting that the poet, while deliberately making his heroine look rather absurd in her exaggerated heroics, has also indulged himself and his readers with the perverse pleasure of picturing a beautiful girl among the great beasts who could destroy her. It is for that reason that she is to be *nuda*: it is that much more piquant. And since heroines so often are naked in art no further explanation of her state seemed to be called for. Somewhere in the background lie the sadistic pleasures of watching in the amphitheatre.

Ovid in his *Amores* is, while not quite as chaste as Propertius and Tibullus, none the less generally careful to avoid coarseness of expression and direct allusion to sexual acts. Perhaps the most simply sensual poem in the collection is the fifth in the first book. The poet was stretched out, enjoying his midday siesta, with the blinds half closed. The light, he tells us, was like that in a wood (*quale fere silvae lumen habere solent*): that is the sort of light that modest girls like. Suddenly (*ecce*, 9) Corinna appears, lightly dressed: the poet overcomes her token resistance and removes her clothes; seven lines go to an enumeration of her naked charms as she stood before him, ending with the complacent summary

> *singula quid referam? nil non laudabile vidi*
> *et nudam pressi corpus ad usque meum*   (*Am*. 1.5.23f.).

'Why go into the details? I saw nothing that was not praiseworthy, and I pressed her naked body close to mine.' The episode is presented like an erotic day-dream. A 'poetical' touch of the outdoors is provided by the idea that the light in his bedroom was like that in a wood, as if what follows were to be a seduction in the setting of the *Metamorphoses*, or at least of bucolic. But the list of her unclothed attractions ('shoulders ... arms ... breasts ... belly ... legs ...'), and the whole tone of the inspection, recall the connoisseur who picks out his mercenary partners with discrimination. What, the reader wonders, would have been Corinna's fate if her fastidious lover *had* found some part of her less than satisfactory? And the light in the room is not only silvan, it also is that which the man of experience in these matters knows to be the most successful for affairs. The poem is clearly a good deal closer to the realities of the Roman life of pleasure than many that are discussed in this book, but it is worth observing that it is still far from being an accurate transcription of it. Why does Corinna appear at such a perfect moment? The thirty-second poem of Catullus helps us to answer the question. There Catullus tells Ipsitilla, a very exciting girl but not one with whom one needed to use much ceremony, to give him an assignation that afternoon: she is to stay in, not to take it into her head to go out for a walk, and to prepare for nine successive acts of love (*novem continuas fututiones*) with the lust-tormented poet. Reason suggests that if

Corinna appeared it was because she had been sent for;[57] and if she was the sort of girl who came when she was sent for, she was a professional, like Ipsitilla. Why, then, neither in Catullus nor in Ovid any allusion to payment? It emerges that Catullus, too, despite his frank language, observed certain reticences. The interesting question of payment is one to which we shall return in Chapter Six.

The proximity of water provided one sort of excuse for the presentation of attractive nakedness in a context less squalid than that of the brothel. Another, seized on with hardly less eagerness, was that of athletics. In Greece, since an early date, men had competed nude at the Olympic games and elsewhere, a fact which at least from the fifth century struck the Greeks as worthy of remark and different from the customs of other peoples.[58] It is much less easy to find good evidence for the practice among women; though female athletes appear nude in painting, it is hard to know how far this ever corresponded to reality.[59] But whatever the truth may have been, it was certainly believed outside Sparta that girls there exercised on equal terms with young men, wearing either very revealing dresses ('thigh-showers' is a name that comes down to us) or indeed nothing at all.[60] The idea was a stimulating one, and Propertius was inspired by it to a witty poem (3.14).

The reader who embarks on a poem which opens with the words

multa tuae, Sparte, miramur iura palaestrae

'Many things, O Sparta, do we admire about your wrestling-schools', resigns himself to conventional praise of the exemplary toughness of the Spartan way of life. This time, however, the thought takes an unexpected turn: the great thing about Sparta is that there girls exercise naked with men (4): they throw the discus, run, wrestle and ride; they wear armour like the Amazons, martial women with bare breasts. Spartan Helen wrestled like her brothers, her breasts exposed. In fact, in Sparta the law lays down that pairs of lovers must not be parted: a lover is never shut out, nor do you have to fight your way through her expensive clothes, elaborate make-up, and social obstacles. So, he concludes,

---

[57] Oliver Lyne, *The Latin Love Poets* 251f., thinks the point is that Ovid did not expect Corinna. I take the reference in lines 7-8 to 'the sort of light which modest girls need to be offered', *illa verecundis lux est praebenda puellis*, as showing that the scene is set in advance for her arrival.

[58] Thucydides 1.6.5, Plato *Republic* 452c.

[59] I. Weiler, *Der Sport bei den Völkern der alten Welt* (1981) 90 seems to leave undecided the question whether women in fact competed naked in Greece. Some of the representations of the little girls who were 'Bears' of Artemis at Brauron in Attica show them running nude, others depict them in a short dress: cf. H. Lloyd-Jones in *JHS* 103 (1983) 94.

[60] 'Thigh-showers': *phainomerides*, Plutarch *Life of Lycurgus* 14.3, I. Weiler p. 90. The immorality of Spartan mixed sports is denounced with gusto as early as the fifth century, Eur. *Andromache* 595ff.

quod si iura fores pugnasque imitata Laconum,
   carior hoc esses tu mihi, Roma, bono   (3.14.33-4).

'If Rome had emulated the customs and contests of Sparta, she would be dearer to me than she is.' The point is complex: the humour of praising Sparta, of all places, as the most permissive spot on earth; the straight-faced acceptance, only to turn it into ridicule, of Augustus' official propaganda in favour of manly sports for the young men of Rome;[61] the idea that Propertius, *iners* and *nequam* as he is, would love to spend his life in tough athletics – if only; the delightful fantasy of pretty girls undressed in the essentially familiar masculine setting of the sports field. For young Romans of the upper class did ride and wrestle, very much in the way described here: except for the presence of the undressed girls. It would be surprising if Ovid had failed to exploit the theme. The witty Epistle of Paris to Helen takes it up: Theseus fancied you when you were a girl, says Paris, when he saw you at games:

                              arsit
   more tuae gentis nitida dum nuda palaestra
      ludis et es nudis femina mixta viris   (*Her.* 16.151-2).

'He felt the flame ... when, after the custom of your country, you were at play in the glistening wrestling-school, a naked woman among naked men.'

In Greece the wrestling-school and the gymnasium often had an intense homosexual atmosphere.[62] That can give Roman poets a setting in which to set poems on such loves, viewed on the whole with less tolerance in Rome than in Greece. Tibullus advises the man in love with a boy to join in his sporting activities, and at fencing of course to let him win (Tib. 1.4, especially 51f.); Horace dreams of chasing Ligurinus across the exercise ground of the Campus Martius or through the athletes' swimming place in the Tiber (*Odes* 4.1.39f.). On the level of myth Ovid describes Apollo's devotion to Hyacinthus: on the dreadful day of the latter's death the inseparable pair had stripped and rubbed themselves down with oil, and they were engaged in throwing the discus (*Met.* 10.176ff.). Virgil does what he can to make this into a motif worthy of the dignity of epic, when in the funeral games of the fifth book of the *Aeneid* he introduces a pair of lovers, Nisus and Euryalus (5.294ff.). In Book 9 we shall meet this couple again. There, Nisus offers his life to save that of his beloved, and when he fails to save him dies in avenging his death (9.426-49); in the fifth book he tries to cheat so that Euryalus shall win the foot-race. The comparison of the two episodes is strange and disquieting: the Liebestod of Book 9 is, though radically un-Homeric, a

[61] References in Nisbet and Hubbard on Horace *Odes* 1, p. 109.
[62] K.J. Dover, *Greek Homosexuality* 54ff., Plutarch *Eroticus* 5 = *Moralia* 751F ff.

powerful and pathetic scene, while the episode at the games seems almost like a burlesque of it.

In connection with Sparta Propertius spoke of the Amazons, warrior women with bared breasts; that point is dwelt on with a certain relish:

> *qualis Amazonidum nudatis bellica mammis*
> *Thermodontiacis turba lavatur aquis;*
> *qualis et Eurotae Pollux et Castor harenis,*
> *hic victor pugnis, ille futurus equis,*
> *inter quos Helene nudis capere arma papillis*
> *fertur ...* (Prop. 3.14.13ff.).

(The girls of Sparta are) 'like the troop of Amazons, warrior women with bare breasts, who bathe in the streams of the River Thermodon;[63] or like Castor and Pollux on the sands of the River Eurotas (one a future champion at boxing, the other at riding) – among whom Helen, they say, took up weapons with bosom bare ...' Propertius lingers on the same detail when he finds occasion to mention the Amazons again. 'Arethusa' is writing to 'Lycotas' (the exotic names disguise a young Roman married couple), who is away on military service. After developing various complaints, she bursts out:

> *felix Hippolyte! nuda tulit arma papilla*
> *et texit galea barbara molle caput*   (Prop. 4.3.43f.).

'Hippolyte (the Amazon queen) was lucky! Being a barbarian, she carried arms with breast bare and wore a helmet on her gentle head.'[64] So too the Amazon queen Penthesilea had 'her bosom bared by her torn raiment' (Prop. 4.4.71f.). It will not be over-cynical to see in these repeated passages the transposed reflection of a regular feature of encounters with professionals in Rome. Classical scholars are in the habit of producing explicit evidence to support everything they say, however obvious it may appear: a pleasing piece of supporting evidence here comes in the eighth poem of the fourth book, where Propertius describes his disastrous attempt to divert himself with a couple of tarts while Cynthia is away at Lanuvium. In vain are their charms, his mind can think only of his absent mistress:

---

[63] The recurrence of *bathing* when the poet's mind is dwelling on nudity will not surprise the reader of this chapter; who will perhaps not echo the flat-footed comment made on this line by Butler and Barber, that 'the mention of the bathing of the Amazons is irrelevant, as details in similes so often are'. It is surprising to find Boucher (*Études sur Properce* 249f.) contrasting Prop. 3.14.19-20 with Prop. 2.14.13-14 on the ground that the second is erotic, while the first 'appartient à un élogue de la simplicité des moeurs'. That really is a little naive.

[64] Cf. also Prop. 2.22.8, Ovid *Heroides* 16.259-56. Epic of course puts the point in a chaster manner: Virgil's Camilla is *unum exserta latus pugnae* (*Aen.* 11.649 = 803), 'with one side exposed for the fight'.

cantabant surdo, nudabant pectora caeco:
Lanuvii ad portas, ei mihi, totus eram (solus *codd., em.* Cuypers)
(Prop. 4.8.47-8).

'They sang, but I was deaf; they bared their breasts, but I was blind. My whole soul, alas, was at the gates of Lanuvium.' With such a tableau we come back to real life, to a context in which a Roman found in reality the sensuous exhibition of attractive flesh. The bare breasts of women mourners also made a strong appeal to Propertius and Ovid.[65] The Amazons, the Spartans, the heroines of mythology, the glamorous bathers and swimmers, represent a series of devices for raising, to the level of an idealised art, the realities of Roman life.[66]

---

[65] Cf. the references in Chapter Seven, note 23.

[66] That all this does not simply go without saying of any erotic literature is strikingly confirmed by the Greek Novels. With the exception of Longus, whose prurience has already been observed, they (Chariton, Heliodorus, Xenophon of Ephesus, Achilles Tatius) are consistently modest writers in sexual matters: and even Longus displays an ostentatious false modesty. Though the heroines are regularly shipwrecked, captured by pirates, sold into slavery, and menaced with loss of chastity, they are not exhibited to the reader unclothed.

CHAPTER SIX

Meretrices, Matrimony and Myth

Let the poets pipe of love
In their childish way;
I know every type of love
Better far than they.
Old love – new love –
Every love but true love:
Love for sale! – Cole Porter

Base is the slave that pays! – Shakespeare

It has already been remarked that even an apparently realistic poem like Catullus 32 prefers not to mention paying a girl for love. That is appropriate rather to poems of insult, like Catullus 41: 'Amaena asked me for 10,000 sesterces, that worn-out hideous whore. She must be mad!' or 110: 'Aufillena, respectable women say No; tarts at least go through with it, if they take your money. You say Yes, you take the money, and you don't do it: that's worse than being the lowest kind of whore.' Propertius can talk of the profits Cynthia has made out of her lovers, but only in anger or horror,[1] and of his own *munera* to her only in poems of rejection and despair –

munera quanta dedi vel qualia carmina feci!
illa tamen numquam ferrea dixit 'amo' (Prop. 2.8.11f.).

'What presents I have given her, what poems I have made! Yet her hard heart has never said "I love you".' Or, after listing the toils and humiliations he has gone through,

deinde, ubi pertuleris quos dicit fama labores
Herculis, ut scribat 'muneris ecquid habes?' (Prop. 2.23.7f.).

'Then, when you have endured all the labours that fame ascribes to Hercules, to have her write "Have you got a present for me?".' It is notable that in the first of these poems Propertius plans to kill himself and her, and in the second to give up the attempt to be faithful to her and instead to plunge into indiscriminate profligacy. The elegists constantly

---

[1] E.g. Prop. 2.11.3 (on which cf. Stroh, *Werbende Dichtung* 71-2), 2.16.15.

denounce the venality of the age and the conquest of love by money;[2] but when we actually see them making a present to the beloved, it is of course a different story. Thus when Propertius stands beside her bed as she sleeps, he takes the festive garland from his own head and puts it on hers, and pours out for her the apples and other *munera* he has acquired in an evening of revelry. The scene is a charming one,[3] and its charm would be marred by any hint of substantial cash value in the presents. What we see, in fact, is an elevation to the level of high poetry of the motif of presents to the beloved: not money but fruit, which recalls both a celebrated episode in the *Aetia* of Callimachus and also a pretty vignette in Catullus.[4] Even Ovid, who often plays with the motif of payment, insists that the gift we actually see him send to his girl, a ring, is one of small intrinsic price, to be cherished only as a token of the love and fidelity of the giver:

> *anule formosae digitum vincture puellae,*
> *in quo censendum nil nisi dantis amor ...*
> *... parvum proficiscere munus:*
> *illa datam tecum sentiat esse fidem* (*Amores* 2.15.1-2, 27-8).[5]

'Little ring for my mistress' finger, of no value except for the giver's love ... Go, little gift: may she feel that with you I give her my true love.' The appeal for these poets of the Callimachean story of Acontius and Cydippe may be partly for this very reason. Acontius won the hand of Cydippe by rolling in front of her an apple in whose skin he had written 'By Artemis, I will marry Acontius'. Reading this aloud constituted a valid oath, which the goddess then enforced on Cydippe. This episode more than any other seems to lie behind Callimachus' reputation of being a love poet, and Ovid composed a marvellously amusing pair of verse letters between the two (*Heroides* 20 and 21).[6]

Propertius makes the point wittily explicit, writing in praise of Virgil's *Eclogues*. 'You tell,' he says,

> *utque decem possint corrumpere mala puellas ...*
> *felix, qui vilis pomis mercatur amores!* (Prop. 2.34.69, 71).

'You sing of girls corrupted by the gift of a dozen apples ... Happy the

---

[2] K.F. Smith on Tibullus 1.4.57-60 talks of 'the ever recurring attack on avarice and venality which we find in elegy, epigram, comedy, etc.', and gives references; cf. also Nisbet-Hubbard on Horace *Odes* 2.4.19.

[3] On this poem cf. R.O.A.M. Lyne in *PCPS* (1970) 60-78.

[4] Callimachus frr. 67-75, Acontius and Cydippe; Catullus 65. Cf. D.O. Ross, *Backgrounds to Augustan Poetry* 54ff.

[5] An interesting Pompeian parallel to this epigram is discussed by M. Gigante, *Civiltà delle forme letterarie nell'antica Pompei* (1979) 88-99.

[6] Cf. E.J. Kenney in *Arion* 9 (1970) 388-414.

man who pays for his inexpensive amours with fruit!' The degrading reality of mercenary love receives a pretty pastoral veneer.

Acontius made his first approach to a girl by way of a present: there are few other mythical or poetical models to dignify so extremely mundane a procedure, familiar as it was in life to the love poets of Rome. The golden apples which enabled Hippomenes to win Atalanta provide another, and that theme, too, attracted Ovid, who tells the story at length in *Metamorphoses* 10. Danae, to whom Zeus came in the form of a shower of gold, could be readily seen as succumbing to the precious metal rather than the god; we find the idea in Horace (*Odes* 3.16.1-8), in Ovid (*Amores* 3.8.29-34), and in a Greek epigram by a poet writing in Rome in the Augustan period (*Anth. Pal.* 5.30 = Antipater of Thessalonica 112 GP).[7] That alerts us to the significance of the wording when Ovid describes Atalanta 'picking up the rolling gold' and the 'glittering gold' (*Met.* 10.667, 675). The luxurious presents which Paris promises Helen in Troy (*Heroides* 16.179, 187f., 193f., 337f.) also echo on the level of myth the offer of metropolitan opulence to a girl from a country town; Helen is made to reply that, while she does not really care about the presents he offers, 'They are enough to shake a goddess' (*Her.* 17.65f.). That amounts to a confession of interest. Ovid knew.

Another aspect of the poets' dealings with girls brings out clearly the nice compromise in their work between realism and unreality. That is the complete disappearance of the *leno*, the pimp. That standing figure of the Comedy, who appears in most of the plays of Plautus and whose shadow lies long over those of Terence, is suppressed in Augustan verse in favour of the *lena*, the madam, a much less significant figure in Comedy and, no doubt, in life too. It is noteworthy that Cicero, who is very free with the word *leno* both in its literal and in its metaphorical senses, himself uses *lena* only once; and then in a bold metaphor, of nature recommending herself.[8] *Lenones* appear in the *Catilinarians*, the *Verrines*, the *Philippics*;[9] nowhere does Cicero think it worth accusing anybody of dealings with a *lena*. Yet in verse we find whole poems devoted to this figure: Tibullus 2.6 (and 1.5.47-60), Propertius 4.5, Ovid *Amores* 1.8, while neither Tibullus nor Propertius ever alludes to a *leno* at all, and Ovid does so only in connection with girls who are expressly contrasted with Corinna, poor sluts compelled to be at the mercy of all comers at the orders of a hated *leno*, or in metaphorical senses which

---

[7] Also *Carmina Epigraphica* 938. Christian writers treated the story in this sense; see the references given by H.D. Jocelyn in LCM 9 (1984) 19.

[8] Cicero *Nat. Deor.* 1.77; at *Tusc.* 4.67 he quotes from the comic poet Trabea a line containing it. For the poets the abolition of the *leno* is naturally accompanied by the disappearance of sordid deals involving sharing a girl or exploiting someone else to pay for her, of the realistic sort which we find in comedy: cf. Plautus, *Asinaria* 918; *Truculentus* 867; Terence, *Eunuchus* 1072.

[9] Cicero *Verr.* 2.1.33; 4.83; *Catil.* 4.17; *Philipp.* 2.58; 6.4.

avoid the ugly central meaning.[10]
The *lena*, an old and tipsy woman who advises the poet's girl to be
heartless and mercenary, is a repulsive but at the same time a feeble
creature, whom he can treat with contumely. A *leno* like the formidable
Ballio of the *Pseudolus*, invoked in a striking passage of his defence of
Roscius the actor by Cicero,[11] would have shattered the delicate fabric of
this poetic world. The poets, as has been seen, skirt round the question of
payment: it is evident that the girls have to be paid, but talk of 'presents'
blurs it, and the whole position of the girls is deliberately never made
clear. Who owned the house in which Cynthia lived? Are we to infer from
Propertius 4.7 that her servants, who after her death seem to belong to
Propertius, were his all the time? And if so, how can she have made a
practice of excluding him?[12] But when presents were to be given, they
were given directly to the girl herself. The greedy hand of a *leno* could not
be imagined, even in fantasy, as playing a part in this charade of
transfigured realism. Nor could he be sentimentalised, as the old women
can be who are sometimes mentioned as having helped a poet to the
enjoyment of his love. Delia's mother, that golden-hearted old lady,
'leads you to me by night, waits for me at the door, joins our hands in
furtive trepidation': Tibullus will always love her, and for her sake even
love the faithless Delia (Tibullus 1.6.57-66). Cynthia's old nurse could
have been demanding with Propertius, but she was not; after her
mistress's death she should be looked after in her old age (Propertius
4.7.73-4). Cynthia too, like Delia, can on occasion have a mother, but
only for a moment's pathos. If you try to refuse me, says the poet in
elation after a night of love, *ostendes matri bracchia laesa tuae*, 'You will
have bruised arms to show your mother' (Prop. 2.15.20). Another 'golden
old lady' appears for a moment, complaisant and sympathetic. These
touching vignettes could have no counterpart if a real pimp were allowed
to intrude into the picture. Again it is possible to see in detail how the
poets go about the stylisation of their world.[13]

---

[10] Ovid *Amores* 1.10.23; 2.19.57 (*quid mihi cum facili, quid cum lenone marito?* 'I can't
be bothered with a complaisant husband, the pimp of his own wife'); 3.12.11 (*me lenone
placet*, 'She is attractive because like a pimp I have advertised her charms!').
[11] Cicero *Q. Rosc. Com.* 20.
[12] See W. Stroh, *Die römische Elegie als werbende Dichtung* (1971) 177.16 on this and on
the amusing attempts of scholars to reconcile the poem with what appeared to be the
assumptions of Books 1-3. H. Erbse, *Kleine Schriften* 538 thinks 4.7 shows us what Cynthia
was really like all the time – faithful and wrongly suspected: 'At last the reader of
Propertius learns to know the true, the better Cynthia.'
[13] Oliver Lyne asks whether we can be confident that *lenones* really existed. The law
thought it worth while to subject them to *infamia* (Digest 23.2.43, Mommsen *Strafrecht*
699), and provincial towns listed them on inscriptions among those disqualified for office
(*ILS* 6085.124 = Bruns *Fontes*[7] p. 108). Even more convincingly prosaic is the fact that from
the time of Caligula they were taxed (Suet., *Cal.* 40; *RE* s.v. Lenocinium 1942.35;
Dizionario Epigrafico s.v. lenocinium). The Praenestine fasti which list April 25th as *festus
dies puerorum lenoniorum* add *quia proximus superior meretricum est* ('festival for boys

The lover who can afford to pay is inherently an unpoetic figure. The poets are emphatic that they themselves are poor: Catullus tells us that he made nothing at all in Bithynia, he can't afford a single sturdy slave, his purse contains nothing but cobwebs. Tibullus speaks of 'my poverty'. Propertius was impoverished in the triumviral confiscations and as a matter of course cannot compete with the extravagant presents which others can make to a girl.[14] Ovid, as so often, draws aside the curtain a little when he tells us that

> *non ego divitibus venio praeceptor amandi;*
> *nil opus est illi, qui dabit, arte mea.*
> *secum habet ingenium qui cum libet 'accipe' dicit;*
> *cedimus, inventis plus placet ille meis.*
> *pauperibus vates ego sum, quia pauper amavi*   (*Ars* 2.161-5).

'I don't come forward as a teacher of love to rich men; a man who can pay has no need of my science. He has his own talent, who can say "Here you are" any time he likes; I give him precedence, he finds more favour than my researches do. I am a poet of the poor, since I have been poor and in love.'

Now, of course all these men were in prosaic fact well-to-do. Catullus' father entertained Caesar at his house in Verona; Horace says to Tibullus 'Heaven has given you riches and the skill to use them';[15] Propertius has intimate friends who are senators; Ovid began on a senatorial career, and from exile looked back with longing on his Paelignian estates and the gardens

> *quos ego nesciocui colui, quibus ipse solebam*
> *ad sata fontanas, nec pudet, addere aquas:*
> *sunt ubi, si vivunt, nostra quoque consita quaedam,*
> *sed non et nostra poma legenda manu*   (*ex Ponto* 1.8.45-8),

'which I have cultivated for another to enjoy, to which I am not ashamed to say that I myself used to bring spring water for the plants; there are

---

run by pimps ... because the day before is a festival for prostitutes'), clearly assuming that both boys and girls are controlled by *lenones*. It is true that the word is thrown about in rhetoric – common in Cicero's speeches, it never occurs in his letters; but many references in the *Verrines* and *Philippics* are to professionals, not just to 'debauched persons'. In a satire (not of course in an ode) Horace introduces a *leno* as spokesman for all the luxury traders and the *Tusci turba impia vici*, 'the vicious crew of the Tuscan Road,' who offer their wares to Nomentanus (*S*.2.3.231, *verba facit leno*): the scene is meant to be an exaggerated but recognisable picture of life. In a society like Rome a girl would have been in a very vulnerable position without a man to fight her battles, and to exploit her.

[14] Catullus 10 and 13; Tibullus 1.1.5; Propertius 4.1.127-130; 2.16.

[15] Horace *Epp*. 1.4.7. C. Brink thinks it 'by no means certain' that this poem is addressed to Tibullus (*Horace on Poetry* 3.531); it cannot be proved, but it seems to me highly probable. Cf. R. Syme, *History in Ovid* 178.

fruit-trees, too, if they are still alive, planted by my hand, but I shall not pluck the fruit.'[16] It is possible to find good Greek precedent for the poverty of the poet. Callimachus wrote a couple of epigrams on the theme, one protesting to a mercenary boy that he knows perfectly well that he has no money, and it is very bitter to be constantly told so; the other observing that there are two different cures for love, poetry and hunger, and that he is in the happy position of being able to defy Cupid as he has them both.[17] It is also a commonplace that the lover does not care about making or saving money, and the Plautine lover is constantly in desperate need of cash.[18] But, as usual, we have not explained a regularly recurring motif when we have pointed out a handful of 'sources' for it. The lover is poor for strong and pressing reasons: because he has enrolled in the life of love, which is consciously opposed to the hard-headed life of *frugalitas* and attention to one's *res* which was enjoined and encouraged by correct Roman society; because he is young; because he is loved for himself, not for his money. The resemblances between much of this and Roman Comedy are not all to be seen as borrowings. To a considerable extent it is rather a case of similar causes producing similar effects, and in areas central to the poetry of the life of love.

In Comedy the lover is naturally out to get what he wants without paying for it, while the prudent *meretrix* ensures that he shall have to pay. As the cynical old woman puts it to the credulous young girl in the *Hecyra* of Terence,

nam nemo illorum quisquam, scito, ad te venit
quin ita paret sese abs te ut blanditiis suis
quam minimo pretio suam voluptatem expleat.
hiscin tu, amabo, non contra insidiabere?   (*Hecyra* 67-70).

'You can be sure there is not a single man who comes to you without the intention of getting his pleasure at the least possible expense by making up to you. So surely you'll be equally crafty in your dealings with them?' Just so is the lover's ambition expressed by Ovid:

hoc opus, hic labor est, primo sine munere iungi   (*Ars* 1.453).[19]

---

[16] I single out this poem as an example of one which many readers, victims of the undiscriminating generalisation that Ovid's poems from exile are 'monotonous', would find unexpectedly attractive.

[17] Callimachus *Epigrams* 7 and 3 Gow-Page.

[18] E.G. Plautus *Poenulus* 328 *namque edepol lucrum amare nullum amatorem addecet*, 'Good Heavens, no lover should be in love with money'; *Truc.* 231 *neque umquam erit probu' quisquam amator nisi qui rei inimicust suae*, 'No one has the makings of a real lover unless he declares war on his own property'; *Trinumm.* 230-55.

[19] The echo of *Aeneid* 6.129 *sed revocare gradum superasque evadere ad auras,* / *hoc opus, hic labor est*, 'But to recall one's steps and regain the upper air: that is the task, that is the toil,' is one of Ovid's most feline.

'This is the task, this is the toil, to achieve union without paying in advance.' Propertius has already been seen, in a context of despair, crying 'What presents I have given her!' In a different mood, however, he looks back with complacency on the history of his affair, now seven years old. She has been very kind to him: she has often let him in,

> *nec mihi muneribus nox ulla est empta beatis:*
> *quidquid eram, hoc animi gratia magna tui* (Propertius 2.20.25f.).

'And I have never paid for a night with expensive presents: whatever I got was from the great generosity of your heart.' Not only Cynthia but also Lycinna, the servant girl with whom he first experienced love, cost him nothing, he tells us:

> *illa rudis animos per noctes conscia primas*
> *imbuit, heu nullis capta Lycinna datis* (Propertius 2.15.5f.).

'She was the first to share nights with me and teach my inexperience: poor Lycinna, not won by any gifts from me.' In Comedy one response to the desire of the lover to be loved for himself is the loving *meretrix*, the girl who refuses to act the rapacious and heartless role which belongs to her.[20] The lover can try to impose on a *meretrix* the obligation to be faithful to him alone, perhaps by a written contract,[21] or simply by a mutual commitment;[22] he can hope to be her *summus amator*,[23] chief lover – for a time; he can indeed treat her as being a kind of wife, *pro uxore, in uxoris loco*.[24] Some lovers in Comedy find mercenary doxies; others find benevolent and affectionate *meretrices* who wish to be faithful to them. Such girls may, with the help of fortune, turn out to be marriageable, and actually to marry the hero, as Glycerium does in the *Andria*, after living with him in extra-marital fidelity and bearing his child.

That turn of events has the rare effect of producing a real marriage which is a union of passion. Here we come to a cardinal point about Roman society and Roman poetry, which will repay treatment at some length. Like most societies, ancient Rome did not conceive of marriage as primarily the union of a man and woman who were passionately in love

---

[20] *Asinaria* 3.1; *Cistellaria* 68ff.; *Mercator* 533ff.; *Mostellaria* 1.3; *Pseudolus* 50ff.; Terence *Andria* 131ff.; *Eun.* 197ff.

[21] *Asinaria* 238, 746ff.: cf. F. Leo, *Plautinische Forschungen* 154.4, Demosthenes *Neaera* 26; reff. ap. Herter in *JAC* 3 (1960) 81.194.

[22] *Mercator* 536, *Cistellaria* 241, 460. That Plautus did not really understand the classier forms of Hellenistic *vie d'amour* and presented them as straightforward brothels is convincingly argued by Ed. Fraenkel, *Elementi Plautini in Plauto* 140ff.

[23] *Truculentus* 79.

[24] Terence *Andr.* 146, 271 *quam ego animo egregie caram pro uxore habuerim; Heaut.* 104.

with each other. Crook puts it well when he says 'to the Romans marriage was an honourable estate, for the purpose of concordant life together and the begetting of children;'[25] to which must be added that the marriage of two individuals produced a link between all the members of their families. Many if not most societies have had a conception not dissimilar, and in India (for example) it is still normal; as is its traditional accompaniment, the arranged marriage. Roman girls married surprisingly young – an average age of twelve to fifteen emerges from recent research[26] – and their consent to betrothal and marriage was barely a requirement, such consent being taken as present 'unless she manifestly disagrees'[27] with her father, who betrothes her. A son was indeed allowed to dissent, but in fact the pressure on him to accept his father's choice was very strong. Roman history is full of anecdotes and events which show how completely, in the upper class, the choice of marriage partner was a matter for the parents.[28] And afterwards the husband should be respectful and restrained, the wife modest and decorous, in sexual relations.[29]

All this is often said, and it is true. But it is also true that evidence is there to be seen of a different conception: the hope that the couple will not only be a respectable and virtuous husband and wife, but also that they will be passionate – even the bride. That emerges from the Wedding Song of Catullus for the marriage of Manlius Torquatus, an aristocratic contemporary marrying a real woman.[30]

> *Ac domum dominam voca*
> *coniugis cupidam novi,*
> *mentem amore revinciens*
> *ut tenax hedera huc et huc*
> *arborem implicat errans*   (Catullus 61.31-5).

'And call the mistress home, longing for her new husband, winding about

---

[25] J.A. Crook, *Law and Life of Rome* (1967) 99. See also A. Watson, *Roman Private Law* (1971) 16ff.

[26] M.K. Hopkins in *Population Studies* (1965) 309ff.

[27] Digest 23.1.7-11. Ovid makes his Acontius say to the 'official' fiancé of his Cydippe *haec mihi se pepigit, pater hanc tibi:* 'her father betrothed her to you: she betrothed herself to me' – inadvertently, of course (*Heroid.* 20.157).

[28] For instance those assembled by R.O.A.M. Lyne, *The Latin Love Poets* (1980) 5ff. Philosophers added that since the choice of a wife was 'morally indifferent', it was a thing in which a man should obey his father's will: Gell. 2.7.18.

[29] E.g. Plutarch *Moralia* 139-45 on husbands; and Seneca *fragment* 13.84ff., arguing that passionate love of a wife is a form of adultery. Wives should not move much in the sexual act, unlike *meretrices*: Lucretius 4.1268.

[30] Perhaps T. Manlius Torquatus, praetor in 49 B.C.; his bride, Vibia Aurunculeia, according to R. Syme (Junia according to the manuscripts: adopted into the Junii, thinks G.P. Goold, *Catullus* (1983) 248), is presumably related to Caesar's legate L. Aurunculeius Cotta.

her heart with love as the clinging ivy strays all over the tree and holds it tight.'

> *illi non minus ac tibi*
> *pectore urit in intimo*
> *flamma sed penite magis*   (Catullus 61.169-71).

'His inmost breast is scorched by the flame no less than yours – no, even more deeply' (addressed to the bride). Such language goes with the hope expressed in the same poem, not merely that children will be born to the marriage, but that the couple will enjoy *multa milia ludi*, many thousands of amorous delights, more numerous than the African sands or the stars of the sky (199-203).[31] Suggestive badinage was a regular part of the Roman wedding (*Fescennina iocatio*), as of many others, and these passages give us a transposition of that into a high poetic style: the hope of mutual ardour, mutual delight.

A trace of similar feelings is to be detected in the speeches which were regularly made at weddings during the Empire. 'Rhetoric means respectability', D.A. Russell observes on the rhetoricians' handbooks of instruction for the making of these speeches,[32] and there is no thigh-slapping broad humour about such prescriptions. Yet mythical comparisons form a large part of them, with echoes of the sensual poetry of Sappho: 'on a higher level still, when you refer to the gods, you can tell a story or two about Poseidon marrying Tyro in the estuary of the River Enipeus ...' (say) 'thus Anchises, king of the country round Troy, wedded Aphrodite ...'[33] Such mythical comparisons evoke a world of passion, pleasure, the outdoors: all the things that a high bourgeois marriage was in many ways not meant to be. And in the two examples here singled out from Menander's lavish supply ('Dionysus and Ariadne – Peleus and Thetis – Alpheus and Arethusa ...') the most superficial acquaintance with Greek poetry would have reminded the wedding guests that it was Aphrodite who sought out Anchises for love, and Tyro who fell 'passionately enamoured' of the River, in whose borrowed shape Poseidon possessed her beside those lovely waters.[34] Such stories, like the images of 'groves of Aphrodite' as the imagined setting for the encounter of the happy couple,[35] exalt the occasion from the commonplace to the

---

[31] It is not surprising that the circumspect Statius preferred to go no further, in epithalamium poems, than to speak of the bride's *castissimus ardor*, 'most modest flame' (*Silv.* 5.1.41), or than the use of the verb *tepere* 'be warm' (1.2.139; *tepuisse viro*): also 2.2.153ff. *sanctusque pudicae / servat amicitiae leges amor* – 'respectful love obeys the laws of modest friendship'. The epithalamia of Claudian will be searched in vain for anything so lively.

[32] D.A. Russell, 'Rhetors at the wedding', *PCPS* 205 (197) 105.

[33] Menander Rhetor 2.402.10; ib. 409.7 (translation by Russell and Wilson).

[34] [Homer] *Hymn to Aphrodite*; *Odyssey* 11.235ff.

[35] Himerius *Oration* 9.19.

significant and beautiful, and by means obviously similar to those which the poets use to exalt their lives and loves; and also they colour the restrained reality with the hues of the passionate. 'On a higher level', says Menander, one can talk about the gods. That could serve as a slogan for a considerable part of the poet's arsenal.

*

Endearments, kisses, grunts, and whispered oaths;
But were her thoughts on breakfast, or on clothes? – Robert Graves

A Roman woman, then, married very young, and was under heavy pressure to be a decorous and respectable, rather than a passionate and romantic, partner. Yet evidence of many kinds conspires to show that there was a desire for a different kind of love. Ovid can express it, at times, with jaunty hedonism:

odi, quae praebet, quia sit praebere necesse,
siccaque de lana cogitat usque sua;
quae datur officio, non est mihi grata voluptas:
officium faciat nulla puella mihi (*Ars* 2.685-8).

'I can't stand a woman who allows it only because she must, who stays dry and thinks about her housework; a pleasure that is given out of duty is no pleasure to me – let no girl "do her duty" by me.' Such objections would apply, in a slightly different way, to the professional who obliges for money, no less than to the dutiful wife. Propertius shows us the same demand in a more elevated form in his poem 1.15. He has been in danger, he says, and Cynthia has shown the hardness of her heart by failing to rush to his side, instead spending her time on elaborate coiffure and toilette. 'That was not the way Calypso behaved when Odysseus left her ... Hypsipyle was not like that ... Alphesiboea shed blood ... Evadne threw herself on her husband's funeral pyre':

quarum nulla tuos poterat convertere mores,
tu quoque uti fieres nobilis historia (Prop. 1.15.23-4).

'None of them could change your nature, so that you, too, might become a famous legend.' Despite the differences, the resemblance can be seen between this elaborate outburst and Ovid's simple quest for pleasure. Cynthia said she loved the poet (25 *periuria*, 35 *mentita*); she swore to it and shed tears (40); but her horrible *sang-froid* shows how meaningless it all was. She, too, was not really devoted to passion.

The demand that love should be an obsession runs right through the erotic writers. In Comedy we find it well stated by Terence's Phaedria: when you are forced to be with someone else, he says,

dies noctesque me ames, me desideres,
me somnies, me exspectes, de me cogites,
me speres, me te oblectes, mecum tota sis   (Ter. *Eun.* 192-4).

'Love me night and day, miss me, dream of me, wait for me, think of me, hope for me, delight in me, be totally with me in your thoughts.' Catullus' forty-fifth poem gives a pretty picture of a pair of obsessed lovers for whom the world has ceased to exist: Acme delights Septimius by insisting that her passion is still greater and more fiery than his,

ut multo mihi maior acriorque
ignis mollibus ardet in medullis   (Cat. 45.14-15).[36]

The Greek novelists insist that for their lovers the world is well lost;[37] the elegists hope for the marks of passion in their mistresses, not simply for sexual favours. When Propertius planned to sail away, he tells us, Cynthia carried on in so gratifying a manner, with embraces, pleas, threats, changes of colour, that he had to stay at home:

a pereat, si quis lentus amare potest!   (Prop. 1.6.12).

'Curse on the man who can be unemotional in love!' If she screams at him and throws the crockery, that is a delicious proof of the genuineness of her love (Prop. 3.8),

nam sine amore gravi femina nulla dolet   (Prop. 3.8.10).

'Without serious passion a woman feels no distress.' Tibullus and Ovid agree, Ovid particularly dwelling with complacency on the delights of having a woman show jealousy, anger, loss of colour. That is the real thing (*Ars* 2.447f.; cf. Tibullus 1.10.63, Catullus 82). The ideal is that which Poe expresses so memorably: 'This maiden lived with no other thought / Than to love and be loved by me.'

Ancient literature is, with few exceptions, created by men. It therefore tends to find the mental processes of women mysterious; many parts of it find that mystery fascinating. Obvious indications show whether a man is in the grip of sexual passion. The puzzling question for a woman is that of his long-term intentions and moods, not his immediate mental condition: hence the preponderance in poetry of deserted heroines, who misunderstood their man and found it out too late. For a man there is another galling question, very hard to get rid of once it has entered the mind: what is she thinking of *now*, at this moment? What Ovid does not

---

[36] Cf. Leo, *Plautinische Forschungen* 145; Catullus 76.23; Tibullus 1.2.63.
[37] Thus Xenophon of Ephesus 2.4.1; 5.18 (the story of two runaway lovers from Sparta): in exile 'we lived in poverty, but so much in love that we seemed to be rich in everything because we were together. At length she died ...' Heliodorus 4.18.2 'Rescue two wanderers, who have given up their country and everything for the sake of one thing only – each other's company'.

want, he tells us, is the sort of woman officially esteemed as a good wife: the *lanifica*, the woman whose hands are never idle, making clothes for her family. But even if one gets away from all that, to an officially disreputable woman who is a partner in pleasure: even if she goes through all the motions, as far as the external eye can see, of being the creature of passion, vowing, changing colour, weeping; even so her heart may not be in it, her thoughts may be elsewhere. As the housewife thinks of her practical duties, Cynthia (Propertius imagines in this dark mood) thinks of her practical advantage, the money of her lover.[38] Not every temperament is worried by this kind of thought. Horace in his early works can express serene indifference. Thus in the second satire of the first book he discourages his reader from adulterous liaisons: not worth the expense, anxiety, and risk. Better to avoid all that and settle for a simple tart, as long as she's clean and reasonably good looking. 'In my arms she's as good as Ilia or Egeria (nymphs from Italian myth) ...' Bluff common sense dismisses as absurd the question whether such a girl loves one or not.[39] Like other coarse, no-nonsense attitudes of the *Satires* and *Epodes*, this one cannot appear in the *Odes*, at least not on the surface. In the *Odes* Horace manifests humorous concern for the unpredictable moods of Pyrrha, jealousy of Lydia's preference for another man, desire to be remembered by Galatea even as she abandons him.[40] But the use of so many different women's names, so unlike the practice of Catullus or Propertius, tells its own tale: a girl lasts no longer than a single poem. The homage which Horace pays to the more passionate erotic fashions of the time is always meant to be felt to contain a good deal of irony. That irony is clearly in evidence in the rare allusions to *munera*[41] in the *Odes*.

In *Odes* 2.4 Horace addresses Xanthias, a man who is in love with a slave girl. No need to blush, he says: Achilles loved Briseis, Ajax loved Tecmessa – and besides, no doubt your Phyllis is of noble stock, a princess enslaved. You are welcome to think (*crede*, a deftly non-committal word) that she doesn't come from the villainous plebs: no humble mother could produce a daughter so devoted, so averse from gain.

> *crede non illam tibi de scelesta*
> *plebe dilectam, neque sic fidelem,*
> *sic lucro aversam potuisse nasci*
>   *matre pudenda*   (*Odes* 2.4.17-20).

[38] E.g. Prop. 2.16 *semper amatorum ponderat illa sinus*; Prop. 2.23.8; 2.24.

[39] Aristippus, we read, when told by someone that Lais did not really love him, replied unruffled that he did not imagine the fish and wine he consumed loved him either, but that did not diminish his pleasure: Plut. *Eroticus* 4 = *Moralia* 750d.

[40] Horace *Odes* 1.5; 1.13; 3.27.

[41] Typical of the *Epodes* but unthinkable in the *Odes* is the malicious reversal in *Epode* 12: the love-lorn lady sending presents to the poet, and being rejected.

He leaves no doubt that the disinterestedness of the girl is not to be taken seriously, by extolling it in a verse which follows one declaring that she is 'no doubt a princess'[42]–

> *regium certe genus et penates*
> *maeret iniquos*

'She mourns for her princely family, I'm sure, and her ill-starred birth' – and which precedes a concluding verse in which the poet expresses shocked surprise that anybody could dream of suspecting him of having designs on this pretty girl: why, he is forty years old – as if that were any guarantee. Clearly Xanthias had better watch out.

Not dissimilar is the use of the motif in *Odes* 3.10. Here Horace presents himself as lying outside the door of the disobliging Lyce, and in stormy weather too. She should hurry up and open it:

> *non te Penelopen difficilem procis*
> *Tyrrhenus genuit pater.*
>
> *o quamvis neque te munera nec preces*
> *nec tinctus viola pallor amantium*
> *nec vir Pieria paelice saucius*
> *curvat, supplicibus tuis*
>
> *parcas ...*   (*Odes* 3.10.11-17).

'Your Etruscan father did not beget a Penelope in you, recalcitrant to suitors. Although gifts and prayers alike fail to move you; although you are not moved by the pallor of your lovers, nor by your husband's infidelity in Macedonia, have pity on your suppliants – I shan't stay out here in the rain for ever.' Lyce is no better than she should be, clearly, with her luxurious Etruscan background; this chaste Penelope act is transparent, and the poet deftly undermines the all too familiar motif of the *exclusus amator* who will stay at the beloved's door all night. The irony of all that again colours her rejection of amorous offerings: she is a professional.

In one poem Horace even allows himself to play, most discreetly, with a still more subversive use of the theme. Opening the fourth book of

---

[42] Nisbet and Hubbard might have cited, in their note on this line, the Tacitean passage in which Claudius' freedman Pallas is officially thanked by the obsequious Senate because 'though sprung from the Kings of Arcadia' (*sc.* the Evander of *Aeneid* 8) ' he subordinated his ancient nobility to the interests of Rome' (*Ann.* 12.53). Every slave in Rome must have had such a line to offer, if circumstances ever allowed him – or her – to produce it; like the students nowadays who tell their friends 'In my own country I am a chief'. But it is surely not right to think the point of the poem to be 'a free man with a slave's name is embarrassed by his love for a slave-girl with the name of a princess' (Murgatroyd in *CQ* 30 (1980) 540). There are more than forty women named Phyllis in *CIL* volume 6, many of them freedwomen.

Odes, he deprecates for himself the incursions of Venus. He is fifty, too old for all that. The goddess will find the perfect man in someone very different: Paullus Fabius Maximus (consul in 11 B.C.), about to marry Marcia,[43] a daughter of the imperial house. Noble, handsome, eloquent in the law-courts (a very Roman touch in such a context: Paullus is no mere Greek playboy), he will carry Venus' standards far afield:

> *et, quandoque potentior*
> *largi muneribus riserit aemuli,*
> *Albanos prope te lacus*
> *ponet marmoream sub trabe citrea*   (*Odes* 4.1.17-20).

'And after smiling in triumph as he prevails over the presents offered by a lavish rival, he will offer a statue of Venus in marble in a shrine of citrus-wood near the Alban lakes.' Page quotes the translation of Martin:

> And when he shall with smiles behold
> His native charms eclipse his rival's gold:

that is, Paullus is in himself more powerful than the most lavish presents could be. No doubt that is the meaning the words are meant to convey, though Horace might have made it clearer: 'native charms', 'conquering personality',[44] the phrases of translators and commentators flesh out the poet's omission revealingly. For his words would be compatible with another sense: Paullus can outbid the · most generous offers from potential rivals, thus becoming the only lover to be praised for his wealth. A hint of insipidity, it will be recalled, seems to have attached to this great aristocrat.[45]

The demand that the woman take one's sexual demands seriously, not as a mere occupation as humdrum as any other, issues naturally in two directly contrasted, and indeed apparently opposite, ideas. One is that of rape; the other that of the passionate woman who welcomes the act of love. The idea of rape runs through a lot of ancient literature, in one form and another, from the peremptory and one-sided amours of gods with mortal women in myth, and the scenes of rapine regular at the sack of a city, to the language of public oratorical abuse and the subjects which were found interesting for discussion in the rhetorical schools. Thus no fewer than eight of the themes on which the elder Seneca records the

---

[43] So R. Syme, *History in Ovid* 143ff.; Bradshaw in *CQ* 20 (1970) 142.

[44] 'Die sieghafte Persönlichkeit des Maximus', as opposed to his rival whose personality does not count, is the gloss of Kiessling-Heinze.

[45] Cassius Severus' verdict on Paullus is telling: *quasi disertus es, quasi formosus es, quasi dives es: unum tantum es non quasi, vappa* (Sen. *Controv.* 2.4.11; cf. R. Syme *Roman Revolution* 487): 'You are almost eloquent, almost handsome, almost rich' (the very qualities praised by Horace): 'one thing you are not "almost" – a dud.' Ovid, flattering from exile, referred to his 'Herculean simplicity' (*ex Ponto* 3.3.100).

controversiae of his youth (the generation of Ovid) turn on rape; and it is no surprise that all Cicero's enemies went in for it. Thus the approach of Catiline to Rome would mean 'panic among virgins and young boys, and assaults on the Vestal Virgins'; Antony's creatures carried off 'married women, virgins and boys'; and as for the loathsome L. Piso, who obstructed Cicero's return from exile, his lusts, in his province of Macedonia, were so inordinate that virgins of noble families could evade them only by throwing themselves down wells.[46] On the other hand, it was possible to take a very different view, if circumstances made it necessary. Cicero waves away the accusation that his client Cn. Plancius was a man of bad character. The prosecution had charged him with the forcible abduction of an actress: *raptam esse mimulam ... vetere quodam in scaenicos iure maximeque oppidano*, 'a mere mime-acress was carried off, in accordance with a sort of traditional privilege, highly metropolitan, in dealing with stage people', says Cicero: this is not only untrue of Plancius, but it isn't even against the law anyway (*cum quod licuerit obiciatur, tamen id ipsum falsum reperiatur*).[47] The passage gives food for thought.

De Sade says that to make fornication really interesting it is good to do it with virgins, nuns, and those to whom the act will make a great difference. Otherwise they may not be sufficiently impressed. Don Giovanni, too, had a similar taste, we are told by Leporello:

Sua passion predominante
È la giovin principiante –

'His chief passion is for the young beginner.' Such, perhaps, is a natural result of a career of profligacy, which can threaten to dwindle into a routine like any other. Not least in a society like that of Rome, where respectable and disreputable women were in principle sharply differentiated, and the daughters of the upper class were locked away and difficult to get at.

Rape is a regular event in New Comedy, often serving as a sort of introduction between the young hero and the girl he will in the end marry for love. So it is in Menander's *Samia*: the *jeune premier* tells us how he forced a girl at a night festival: 'I hesitate to tell what happened next, but perhaps I am ashamed where there's no point; still, ashamed I am. She became pregnant ...'[48] Young men who ravish girls in Comedy remain secure in the possession of the audience's sympathy, characters in the plays making such comments as –

---

[46] Seneca *Controv.* 1.5; 2.3; 3.5; 5.6; 7.6; 7.8; 8.6; Cicero *in Catil.* 4.12; *Philipp.* 3.31; *de Prov. Cons.* 6.
[47] Cicero *pro Planc.* 30-1.
[48] *Samia* 43. Cf. also the plot of the *Georgos, Epitrepontes, Heros, ?Kitharistes.*

persuasit nox amor uinum adulescentia:
humanumst ...

and

fecere alii saepe item boni uiri (Ter. *Adelphoe* 470, 688).

'You were egged on by night, passion, drink, youth: it's only human', and 'Many good men have done the same in their time'.[49] It is clear that, by a certain intelligible if not modern scale of values, the violation of a respectable girl is less shocking than her consent to seduction: the one involves only her body, the other changes her mind, too, and makes her into something different from the guarded *filia familias*. But such stories can end happily only with marriage, as in Comedy they do; and the love poets systematically exclude marriage. Comedy and elegy divide the life of love.

Elegy deals with the events of an erotic relationship continuing through time but not ending in marriage; comedy can tell of affairs which end in marriage, but before that ceremony it can tell only of love at a distance or of a single act of force. Lasting intrigues, in Comedy, can be carried on only with professionals – and force would be out of place with them. It is in line with this division that the Augustan love poets treat the motif of sexual violence in much less direct ways. Horace can sing of snatching kisses, or allude ironically to the *inaudax raptor* who attempts a pretty boy but will be put to flight by a passionate woman;[50] he likes to play with the theme of the girl who is still too young for love but will soon be ready for it, and he can develop it with a certain brutality –

nondum subacta ferre iugum valet
cervice, nondum munia comparis
　　aequare nec tauri ruentis
　　　in venerem tolerare pondus.

circa virentis est animus tuae
campos iuvencae ... (Odes 2.5.1-6).[51]

'She can't yet bow her neck and bear the yoke, she can't yet match the duties of a yoke-fellow, nor accept the weight of a bull rushing into the act of sex. Your heifer's heart is still occupied with the flowery meadows ...' But Horace is careful to keep the subject at a slight

---

[49] Cf. also the off-hand narration at *Hecyra* 822ff. *homo se fatetur vi in via nescioquam compressisse ...* 'He admits that he forced a girl in the street'; also *Eunuchus* 601ff (*interea somnus virginem opprimit*, etc.), Plaut. *Aulularia* 794f.
[50] Hor. *Odes* 2.12.28; 3.20.4.
[51] Cf. *Odes* 1.23; 3.11. On this passage Nisbet and Hubbard observe that 'The Romans were no doubt often brutal in their sexual habits'.

distance. Propertius has already been seen developing the theme of forcible abduction as an amusing fantasy of what might happen to a pretty boy named Hylas, with the elegant reversal: *girls* may abduct *him*. It would not suit his poetical personality to talk of using force on Cynthia, and he and Tibullus like to linger on the gentler notions of tearing her clothes, or in extreme cases, of striking her: all to be paid for, by the poet, with bitter repentance and self-abasement.[52]

Ovid, however, is more business-like in these matters. Girls like to have force used on them, he assures his male reader:

> *vim licet appelles: grata est vis ista puellis;*
> *quod iuvat, invitae saepe dedisse volunt*   (*Ars* 1.673f.).

'You may call it violence: girls like that sort of violence. Often they want to be forced to grant what they enjoy.' The passage goes on to develop the theme with relish. The daughters of Hippocoon, abducted forcibly by Castor and Pollux, loved their abductors (*et gratus raptae raptor uterque fuit*); Deidamia was only too pleased to be forced by Achilles – if there was really any force in the matter at all.

> *Viribus illa quidem victa est (ita credere oportet)*
> *sed voluit vinci viribus illa tamen.*
> *saepe 'mane' dixit cum iam properaret Achilles ...*

'She was subdued by force, or so we are to believe, but she desired to be forcibly subdued. Often she said "Stay" when Achilles was hastening off ...' To be sure, he concludes, there are things which one is embarrassed to be the first to start, but which are enjoyable to experience, if the other party takes the initiative (*Ars* 1.705f.).

The world of the *Metamorphoses* is one in which rape runs riot. Jupiter pursues and possesses Io, and forces Callisto:

> *illa quidem pugnat, sed quem superare puella*
> *quisve Iovem poterat?*

'She struggled indeed, but how could a girl overcome a man – and how could anyone overcome Jupiter?' Apollo chases Daphne, Pan chases Syrinx, Boreas carries off Orithyia, Apollo and Mercury both possess Chione, Neptune pursues Cornix and rapes Caenis and Mestra on the sea-shore, Tereus violates Philomela: of the rape of Proserpina the poet says breezily that she was

> *paene simul visa est dilectaque raptaque Diti:*
> *usque adeo est properatus amor –*

---

[52] Tibull. 1.6.73f.; 1.10.53f.; Prop. 2.5.21; Ovid *Am.* 1.7; Horace *Odes* 1.17.28. A drunken lover heaps *maledicta* on his mistress and later regrets it: Tib. 2.5.101ff.

'Loved almost as soon as seen by Dis, and carried off as soon as loved: so precipitate was his passion.'[53] The old mythical pattern by which heroic and regal families descended from gods, the whole point of the divine union being the engendering of the offspring, not the emotions of the mortal mother, is unpacked into a world full of genially lustful deities[54] and of beautiful heroines to whom the act of love makes a fearful difference, turned as they are into trees and birds and fountains on account of it. That is one way of achieving the sensualist's ideal of the truly vulnerable woman, the woman at an opposite extreme both from the hard-boiled doxy and from the unexcited if compliant wife.

Virgil uses the motif, too, and of Jupiter: the serene and philosophical deity we see in the centre of the stage in the *Aeneid* doubles, surprisingly, as an insouciant Ovidian ravisher. The African prince Iarbas, whose appeal to Jupiter starts the divine machinery which drives Aeneas from Carthage and Dido to her death, is a son of the god, *rapta Garamantide nympha* (4.198) – 'by his rape of an African nymph'. And Juturna has been given her thankless immortality *erepta pro virginitate* (12.141), 'in return for the snatching of her virginity' by the same god.

It is hard to imagine the Jupiter whom we see in action in the *Aeneid* behaving in this casual Ovidian manner, or indeed abducting Ganymede (1.28). Virgil has exploited this old motif with consummate skill, to present the purposes of heaven in a dubious and invidious light. The Jupiter who sends Mercury to drive Aeneas from Carthage with the bitter taunt that his behaviour with Dido is 'uxurious' (4.266), is roused to intervene by the offspring of his own act of rape; and the great charter speech of Book Twelve, Jupiter's last words in the poem, which establishes the future of Rome, is followed by a passionate denunciation by Juturna of the brutal injustice of the supreme god.[55] Jupiter concluded his solemn utterance with the extraordinary claim that the Romans shall excel not only men but even gods in *Pietas: supra homines, supra ire deos pietate videbis* (12.839). Commentators have flinched from taking seriously the implications of that remarkable line,[56] but to play down such an utterance at such a climactic point in the poem would be to charge Virgil with gross carelessness. The poet has in fact shown his Jupiter demanding of Aeneas and the Romans a higher morality than that which he himself always observes – as Juturna bitterly points out:

> *nec fallunt iussa superba*
> *magnanimi Iovis. haec pro virginitate reponit?*
> *quo vitam dedit aeternam?*   (*Aeneid* 12.877-9)

---

[53] Ovid *Met.* 1.600, 2.436, 1.503, 1.701, 6.690, 11.309, 12.197, 8.850, 6.523, 5.395.

[54] 'Most of the male deities (in the *Metamorphoses*) tend to act from lust, and most of the females from jaundice': L.P Wilkinson, *Ovid Recalled* 192.

[55] *Aeneid* 12.830-40; ib. 870-84.

[56] '*Supra ire deos pietate* non est urgendum, is not to be pressed', Heyne; 'A rhetorical exaggeration', Conington; no remark at all in the ancient commentators.

'I recognise the lordly command of great-hearted Jupiter. Is this what he gives me in payment for my maidenhead? Why has he given me immortal life?' And her last words are a passionate wish for death. The god-given destiny of Rome is called powerfully into question as it is uttered, even before the culminating episode of the killing of Turnus ends the poem with an act of impassioned rage and destruction, forced on the hero yet accepted by him. Together the whole series of scenes (the last one is too often discussed and interpreted in isolation) gives a matchless image of the moral complexity of rule and conquest. That was the supreme purpose to which the 'Ovidian' motif of philandering deities could be turned: to serve the most serious central purpose of Rome's greatest poem.

A last related aspect of love in the poems is the youth of the partners. In Comedy, marriage is the goal of young lovers, who are united at the end of the play; the married persons who appear do not give a very enticing picture of matrimony, between nagging wives and grumpy husbands. Indeed, 'acid remarks by old men at the expense of their wives are traditional in comedy'.[57] We are in the world of the old-fashioned Music Hall and comic postcard, where people – and especially women – divide clearly into the young and the old; and where on marriage toothsome girls turn overnight into appalling battleaxes. One's first love affair, perhaps always the most memorable, is in such a society all the more so. The young man before marriage was expected to have a few wild oats to sow. Cicero says with confidence that he could name plenty of men who settled down as *summi homines et clarissimi cives*, 'great men and splendid citizens,' who in youth were notorious for their love affairs (*libidines*), extravagance, and debt: he will not name names, but the jury can think of them for themselves. Two generations earlier Lucilius named a name: that of Q. Opimius, consul in 154 B.C.[58]In Comedy as in life, it could be said that marriage makes a man change his ways: so for instance Terence *Andria* 560, *Hecyra* 164ff. It is touching that Cicero expressed the same hope about the impossible Dolabella, when that unsatisfactory young man was about to marry Tullia. Her good qualities, says the optimistic father, will soon make him behave better.[59]

A Roman boy put on the toga of manhood in his middle teens. In a slave-owning society, and one which was far from having anything like Christian notions about the sinfulness of sexuality, he would not remain inexperienced for long.[60] It is a reflection of this fundamental fact that

[57] Gomme-Sandbach on Menander *Kitharistes* 58-61; cf. Duckworth, *The Nature of Roman Comedy* (1952) 282.

[58] Cicero *pro Caelio* 43, Lucilius 418 Marx. Q. Fabius Maximus Allobrogicus, cos. 121 B.C., had a similar reputation: Valerius Maximus 6.9.4.

[59] Cicero *ad Fam.* 8.13.1; 8.15.2 = 94 and 96 SB.

[60] See for instance A.D. Nock, *Essays* 1.480. That young men should start with *meretrices* was expected: not only such passages of Comedy as Plaut. *Curculio* 36ff., Terence *Andria*

the poet-lover imagines himself as young. Catullus defines himself and Lesbia in opposition to the kill-joy old men, the *senes seueriores*, who surround them and comment on them. Propertius in his second book can still say to himself

> *sic igitur prima moriere aetate, Properti?*
> *sed morere: interitu gaudeat illa tuo*   (Prop. 2.8.17).

'Shall you then die so, Propertius, in your first youth? Die then, and let her take pleasure in your death.' He introduces himself to his reader as suffering in the grip of his very first love:

> *Cynthia prima suis miserum me cepit ocellis*
> *contactum nullis ante cupidinibus*   (Prop. 1.1.1).

'Cynthia was the first to enslave me with her eyes: I was still untouched by any desires.' Tibullus speaks repeatedly of the incongruity of love and advanced years, and in his first poem declares that amours, violence, and quarrels are appropriate to him now when he is still young:

> *nunc levis est tractanda venus, nunc frangere postes*
> *non pudet et rixas inseruisse iuvat*   (Tib. 1.1.73f.).

When Propertius wants to write about another flame, he notoriously tells us that she, too, was 'the first': even before Cynthia, the maid-servant Lycinna taught him to love (Prop. 3.15).[61] Not, that is to say, an autobiographical utterance, in principle true or false to historical facts,[62] but rather an implication that she, too, was important to the poet: the relationship was a significant one, it 'made a difference'.[63] The ironical stance of Horace is marked yet again by his insistence, in the *Odes*, that he is at best a middle-aged lover. Even in the *Epodes*, in an erotic context, he mentions his youth (*Epode* 12.3) only to deny its implications: 'I am no vigorous youth', *non firmo iuueni*. Horace likes to contemplate with middle-aged irony the amorous scrapes of youth: the

---

560ff., but for instance Seneca *Controv.* 2.12.11 *nihil peccaverat; amat meretricem, solet fieri: adulescens est, exspecta, emendabitur, ducet uxorem*: 'He'd done nothing wrong. He loves a tart: that's quite usual. He's young; just wait. He'll change, he'll get married.' Martial puts the point with inimitable crudity, 11.78.11: *Heu quantos aestus, quantos patiere labores, / si fuerit cunnus res peregrina tibi*. It is these adolescent encounters that the poets like to sentimentalise in verse.

   [61] Very interesting on this poem is P. Veyne, *L'Élégie érotique romaine* (1983) 17ff.

   [62] E.g. L. Alfonsi, *L'Elegia di Properzio* (1945) 14: 'Che altre donne abbia prima amato non è escluso', etc.

   [63] The motif so popular in poetry and novels of the Proud Beauty who has always scorned love only to fall at last (Call. fr. 67; Rohde, *d. gr. Roman* 156) is another way of giving significance to a love story.

word *puer* is one he fancies for his very young men in love (*Odes* 1.5.1, 1.9.16, 1.13.11, 1.27.20, 3.9.16, etc.), and girls like Chloe in *Odes* 1.23 and the unnamed 'heifer' of *Odes* 2.5 are at the very threshold of first love. The exigent *meretrices* of Comedy stand behind the glamorous women of Augustan poetry. In Comedy their lovers are young men of fashion, kept short of money by strict fathers. Sometimes a father himself is entangled with a *meretrix*, but only to be humiliated and ridiculed:

> *tun, homo putide, amator istac fieri aetate audes?*   (Plaut. *Bacchides* 1163).

'You dirty old man, you're setting up as a lover at your age, are you?' or

> *tun cano capite amas, senex nequissime?*   (*Mercator* 305).

'You're in love, you grey-haired old wretch?' or

> *sapere istac aetate oportet qui sunt capite candido*   (*Mostellaria* 1148).

'You should have more sense at your age, with white hair' – these are the responses which, in Comedy, the middle-aged lover can expect to get.[64] 'The young always win in Comedy,' remark MacCary and Willcock in their edition of the *Casina*.[65]

The hostility invariably shown in Comedy to the old lover is a favourite theme of Tibullus. The humiliation of being forced to whisper sweet nothings when one's hair is white; combing one's white hair and standing outside a girl's house, the butt of the scorn of the young; the repulsiveness of senile embraces to a pretty girl; all these are dwelt on with gusto.[66] And in yet another poem Tibullus makes the crucial connection of old age and payment:

> *munera ne poscas: det munera canus amator*
> *ut foveat molli frigida membra sinu.*
> *carior est auro iuvenis, cui levia fulgent*
> *ora nec amplexus aspera barba terit*   (Tib. 1.8.29-32).

'Don't ask him for gifts: let a grey-haired lover give them, to get his cold limbs warmed in your soft bosom. A young man is better than gold, with his smooth shining face and no rough beard to spoil his embraces.'[67]

---

[64] Cf. Plautus *Casina* 517ff.: 'Cut out all that about "white hair", "wrong time of life", and so on' – the plea of an infatuated *senex*. The *senex amator* figures prominently in *Asinaria, Bacchides, Casina, Menaechmi, Mercator*; and significantly in *Aulularia, Cistellaria, Rudens, Stichus, Vidularia*. See E. Segal, *Roman Laughter* 27; E. Fraenkel, *Elementi Plautini in Plauto* 226ff. 'Middle-aged': cf. Guy Lee's translation of Tibullus 2.1.74.

[65] Plautus *Casina*, ed. MacCary and Willcock (1976) 20. Already in Menander fr. 442: 'Nothing can be more miserable than an old man in love – except another old man in love ...'

[66] Tibull. 1.1.72 *cano blanditias capite*; 1.2.89-96 ... *manibus canas fingere velle comas*; 1.9.74 *senis amplexus culta puella fugit*. Also 2.1.74 *Amor ... dicere iussit /limen ad iratae verba pudenda senem*; Ovid *Amores* 1.9.4 *turpe senilis amor*.

[67] In comedy, from a slightly different point of view, Plaut. *Persa* 266: It is right to exploit the old skinflints in sexual matters, *nam id demum lepidumst, triparcos homines vetulos, ardos, / bene admordere ...*

The lover, then, is young. The elegists do not tell us how old their girls are (except of course to say that they are 'young and beautiful', 'in the season for love', and so on).[68] The novelists are more explicit. Ninos in the Ninos-Romance is seventeen when he asks for the hand of Semiramis, and she apparently is even younger; in Xenophon of Ephesus, Habrocomes is sixteen and Anthia fourteen. Clitophon is nineteen in Achilles Tatius; the other heroes of the novels are described as 'youths', words which denote an age under twenty, and the heroines are invariably young girls, whose very first awakening this is to love. The extreme youth of Daphnis and Chloe is a main theme of Longus' work.[69] The style of Ovid's *Metamorphoses* admits of numerals, and he likes to tell the age of his lovers. Thus Acis is sixteen, as are Narcissus and Athis; Hermaphroditus is fifteen, Iphis thirteen; Picus is 'under twenty'. Hippomenes and Iphis are both still in possession of an ambiguous beauty, still almost feminine; conversely, the beauty of Atalanta was 'what you might call girlish in a boy, boyish in a girl'.[70] The beautiful Chione is fourteen; Proserpina, in her *puerilibus annis*, is so childlike that when she is abducted by Dis she sheds tears at dropping the flowers she had picked; Pyramus and Thisbe were both very young;[71] and so on. The girls are virgins. The adulteress is an extremely rare figure in the *Metamorphoses*, where even incest is commoner (Byblis, Myrrha) – a fact which shows that the rarity of such a person as the voluptuous vamp Circe[72] is not due to moral considerations but to aesthetic ones. Ovid, who likes to make explicit what his predecessors left implicit, lets his incestuous Byblis plead that her youth makes a shocking love affair quite right and proper:

conveniens annis Venus est temeraria nostris   (*Met*. 9.553)

'A daring love is appropriate to our youth.' Love is too young to know what conscience is, as Shakespeare was to put it. The amours and ardours of such a woman as Circe were not a right subject for the poem, and when *adulterae* are mentioned their emotions are not lovingly unpacked and displayed like those of the young heroines.

But though the heroines are young and in love for the first time, they are capable of great passion. That is, indeed, the regular alternative to rape: either a violent onslaught to which their consent is irrelevant, which issues in the drastic transformations of pregnancy and

---

[68] E.g. Prop. 2.15.21.

[69] Ninos-Romance: F. Zimmermann, *Griechische Roman-Papyri* (1936) 18. Clitophon, Achilles Tatius 1.3; Xen. Ephes. 1.2. 'Youth' and 'ephebe' are the words for the hero, 'maiden' that for the heroine, in novels; Musaeus' Hero and Leander are 'maiden' and 'youth'. *Dionysiaca* 1.525 will serve as an example of Nonnus: 'A tender youth in love with a girl of his own age ...'

[70] Ovid *Met*. 13.753, 3.351, 5.50, 9.714, 14.324, 10.579 8.322.

[71] *Met*. 11.302, 5.400, 4.55. Cf. note 60 on the bearing of this point.

[72] *Met*. 14.25ff.; 14.349ff. Pasiphae and Phaedra get only parenthetical mention, 8.155, 15.500.

metamorphosis, or else the fires of love. The tortured monologues of a Byblis, a Scylla, a Medea,[73] have always been among the high points of the poem. Myrrha is driven to crime by her uncontrollable love; Clytie pines away for love and allows herself to die for it. A couple of times we find the one motif merging with the other. The sun-god comes suddenly upon Leuconoe: at first she is terrified, but then she submits without complaint to his violence:

> *at virgo quamvis inopino territa visu*
> *victa nitore dei posita vim passa querella est*   (*Met.* 4.232-3).

'But the maiden, though terrified by the sudden apparition, was overcome by the splendour of the god and submitted to violence without complaint.' The god Vertumnus courts Pomona in various shapes without success. At last he resumes his proper form and prepares to use force:

> *vimque parat, sed vi non est opus, inque figura*
> *capta dei nympha est et mutua vulnera sensit*   (*Met.* 14.770-1).

'He prepares for rape, but of rape there is no need. The nymph was enchanted by the god's beauty and felt love's wound no less than he.' These episodes, in which the male reader can enjoy both fantasies at once, reflect the view expressed (as we have seen) by Ovid in his non-mythological poems: that women really enjoy being subjected by erotic violence. Of Leuconoe the poet has just observed that, as the god approached, *ipse timor decuit*, 'even her fear was becoming to her'.[74] That idea recurs: when Europa is being carried off by the Jupiter bull over the sea,

> *et timor ipse novi causa decoris erat*   (*Fasti* 5.608).

'Her fear, too, gave her a new appeal,' as the beauty of Daphne is enhanced in the eyes of Apollo as she runs away from him.[75] Like passion or jealousy, fear is a strong emotion, a breach of the serene unconcern which is the most objectionable response a woman can offer to these lovers. So it is that grief can add to a woman's charms (*dolor ipse decebat, Met.* 7.733). So it is that the wicked Tarquin is inflamed by the sight of the wifely tears Lucretia sheds for her absent husband:

> *hoc ipsum decuit; lacrimae decuere pudicam*   (*Fasti* 2.757).

'Her modest tears became her well.' But his hope that she will pass from that emotion to its opposite, and, like Leuconoe, accept violence without

---

[73] *Met.* 9.474ff., 8.44ff., 7.11ff.
[74] *Met.* 4.230.
[75] *auctaque forma fuga est, Met.* 1.530.

complaint, proves vain.

The combination of force and consent in these stories finds its perfection in the Rape of the Sabine women. The story is told by Livy and by Dionysius of Halicarnassus, it appears twice in Propertius and on the shield of Aeneas; and it is a favourite with Ovid. The forcibly abducted Sabines, it is to be observed, are all virgins, not married women: those who believed that Hersilia, wife of Romulus, was among them (already a widow), pleaded that it was an oversight.[76] It is virgins who are the appropriate prey in such a tale, whether in prose or verse. Scholars busied themselves with the spicy theme in their own way, arguing for instance over the number of women involved. Some said only thirty, but Valerius Antias reckoned five hundred and twenty-seven, while Juba put the total at 'six hundred and eighty-three, all maidens'.[77] Livy tries hard to play down any lustful motive on the part of the Romans in his chaste pages, insisting that the action was forced on them by the refusal of inter-marriage on the part of neighbouring states; but even he finds himself admitting that the best-looking girls were carried off and reserved for the leading senators. Propertius puts the theme to frivolous purposes. In Book 2 he accuses Romulus (of all people) of ultimate responsibility for the sexual licence of Rome:

> *tu rapere intactas docuisti impune Sabinas:*
> *per te nunc Romae quidlibet audet amor*   (Prop. 2.6.21-2).

'You showed the way, ordering the rape of the Sabine virgins: thanks to you, love now sticks at nothing in Rome.' In Book Four the treacherous girl Tarpeia, planning to betray Rome to the Sabine Titus Tatius for love, reflects that it will be only fair if the Sabines carry her off in exchange for the celebrated rape:

> *si minus, at raptae ne sint impune Sabinae*
> *me rape et alterna lege repende vices*   (Prop. 4.4.57-8).

'Let not the Rape of the Sabines go unavenged: rape me and pay them out in the same coin.' Both passages are characterised by a certain levity.

Ovid goes further. Two long passages[78] tell the story: that in the *Fasti* is more restrained, that in the *Ars* is less cautious. The theatres have always been good places for picking up girls – ever since Romulus carried off the Sabines there. The Romans laid lustful hands (*cupidas manus*) on the girls, who fled like doves from eagles or lambs from wolves; we learn without surprise that their fright was provocative,

[76] Plutarch *Romulus* 14.6.
[77] Juba is quoted by Plutarch: see footnote 76.
[78] Ovid *Ars* 1.101-34, *Fasti* 3.195-228.

et potuit multas ipse decere timor   (*Ars* 1.126).

'Many of them were made more attractive by their fright. That was the
way to pay soldiers: if the army were paid in Romulus' style nowadays, I
too should enlist. And ever since the theatre has presented dangers for
pretty girls ...' For cheeky elegiac poets part of the appeal of the story is
that it presents Father Romulus in so naughty a light, as a forerunner
and paradigm for their own hedonistic way of life. The virtuous Livy, like
the cautious Ovid of the *Fasti*, shows perhaps a deeper level. Having
carried off these women and married them, the Roman husbands 'used
endearments, *blanditiae*, pleading that they had acted from desire and
from love – the sort of prayers most effective on the hearts of women.
Now the abducted women had altogether come to terms ...' (*iam
admodum mitigati animi raptis erant*).[79] The Roman marriage ceremony
continued to be, to a considerable extent, the representation of marriage
by capture.[80] The story of the Sabine women was an *aition* not only for
such a marriage, but also for its success – the wife so carried off really
would come round and love her abductor. The tale catered to the
anxieties of the respectable, and also to the fantasies of the louche,
assuring them that it was possible to combine the pleasures of violating
the innocent and also of enjoying the woman's love. Like the Sabine
women, like Ovid's Deidameia and Leuconoe and Pomona, one's own
more or less casual pick-ups might fall in love with one.[81]

It may be thought that this line of thought has been pursued far
enough. One further example will none the less be given. One of the most
memorable stories in the *Metamorphoses* is that of Pygmalion, who
makes an ivory statue of a beautiful girl and falls obsessively in love with
it.[82] Venus grants his prayer by making the image turn into a living
woman in his arms:

> *oraque tandem*
> *ore suo non falsa premit dataque oscula virgo*
> *sensit et erubuit timidumque ad lumina lumen*
> *attollens pariter cum caelo vidit amantem*   (*Met.* 10.291-4).

'At last it was a real mouth that he pressed with his: the maiden felt his
kisses and blushed, and raising her modest eyes to his she saw the sky
and her lover at once.' Scholars have felt that some meaning underlies
this haunting tale. Many have found in it the story of 'the creative artist

---

[79] Livy 1.9.16-1.10.1.

[80] The bride's hair parted with a spear, her being carried over the threshold, etc.

[81] Above, pp. 117ff. The same fantasy can take a cognate form in a comedy: thus in the
Cistellaria a young man casually forced a girl at a festival: years later, his first wife having
died, by the workings of chance he finds that his second wife is the same woman. Observe
also Propertius 2.26.51 *crudelem et Borean rapta Orithyia negavit*: 'Orithyia had no
criticism of Boreas' act of carrying her off.'

[82] 'The finest among the many fables he has told,' H. Fränkel, *Ovid: a Poet between two
Worlds* (1945) 93.

par excellence,[83] the artist rewarded; others that the story is one 'of wish-fulfilment', the statue being 'the perfect woman'.[84] But artists do not become obsessed with their own artefacts in this way, which sounds if anything more like a parable on collecting than creating.[85] Perhaps it reflects more the ideal course of a specifically Roman marriage, with the virginal and frozen young bride thawing into life and love, under the affectionate and gentle hands of her husband. It would be appropriate that Ovid, the master of feminine psychology among Roman poets, with his particular concern that the woman should enjoy the sexual relationship as much as the man, should find so sympathetic an image. It would be no less appropriate that Horace, who is capable of considerable coarseness on this subject,[86] should have written several poems on the related theme of 'she isn't ready for it yet, but she soon will be', in which the image is drawn not from a living work of art but from the sexual behaviour of animals.

It is not without deliberate intention that such extensive use has been made here of the *Metamorphoses*. The implication is that Ovid's mythical narratives are in important ways illustrative of the poems which are set closer to contemporary life. The mythical element in elegy allows the poets to juxtapose a freer world to the restricted one of Rome; the *Metamorphoses* permit the unhampered exposition of that world, and so let the reader see some patterns which are present in the elegiac poems, but which emerge with greater clarity and freedom from restraint in a universe created to the poet's own tastes.

It is easy to see that the myths offered an inexhaustible supply of passionate and suffering heroines. Horace made a very modest use of them, giving only two heroines substantial laments in the whole collection of the *Odes*: Hypermestra in 3.11, and Europa in 3.27.[87] This

[83] G.K. Galinsky, *Ovid's Metamorphoses* (1975) 79; so too Brooks Otis, *Ovid as an Epic Poet*[2] (1978) 193.

[84] A.H.F. Griffin in *G and R* 24 (1977) 60. H. Dörrie, *Pygmalion* (1974) 15ff. takes a more directly Freudian view: the statue is a 'substitution' on the part of Pygmalion, 'der in schroffer Weise Misogyn ist'.

[85] 'Eine Parabel vom Künstlertum,' H. Eberle, *Stunden mit Ovid* (1959) 47f.

[86] Ovid *Ars* 2.681ff. 'On ne voit guère qu'il soit question du plaisir féminin ailleurs dans la littérature latine,' observes P. Veyne, *L'Elégie érotique romaine* (1983) 229 n.74. Horace: on *Odes* 2.5 see above p. 127; also 3.11.5-8. Coarseness: e.g. *Satires* 1.2.117 *tument tibi cum inguina, num si / ancilla aut verna est praesto puer, impetus in quem / continuo fiat, malis tentigine rumpi?*

[87] T. Oksala, *Religion und Mythologie bei Horaz* (1973) 178 lists 27 heroines who occur in Horace, as against 43 in Propertius, but remarks that most of them are mentioned only incidentally. The Europa myth has already been brought into relation with real life, the pleasures of the seaside (above, p. 96); a parallel to the story of Hypermestra in *Odes* 3.11, who saves her husband's life at the risk of her own, might be found in the heroic behaviour of Roman wives in the proscriptions – cf. J.P.V.D. Balsdon, *Roman Woman* 204: in the proscriptions 'many wives of rich and important men in Rome risked death in order to save their husbands' lives'. The well-known epitaph of 'Turia' is an example (see now N.M. Horsfall in *BICS* 30 (1983) 85-98); see also Appian *BC* 4.163-70, 189-92, and Velleius 2.89. Seneca *Controv.* 10.3 is precisely on the theme of a father threatening his daughter with death for taking the other side in a civil war.

restraint doubtless goes with the other ways in which Horace shows himself anxious to avoid the stock furniture, and the regular emotions, of the elegists, from the Laudamia of Catullus 68 (and the Ariadne of Catullus 64) to the *Heroides* of Ovid, by way of the amorous heroines of Propertius.

This part of the subject can be despatched with welcome briskness. It has been seen that one way of raising the status of the life of love is by assimilation of its constituent episodes to mythical status. Leander and Hylas and Europa could help to glorify the mundane pleasures of the watering-place; Danae and Atalanta could cast a glamour over the purchase of love; the Judgment of Paris could exalt the parade of unclothed *scorta*; maenads were available to raise the tone of an evening's mixed drinking. More generally, mythology provided an alternative to the prosaic world of Rome: a world of simple motives, freedom from venality, life lived in accordance with the emotions. The beautiful ladies of myth were thus the perfect objects for Propertian love, showing two crucially important things. First, that women really could be passionate and straightforward, living for love and dying for it, carried by it into ecstatic joy or utter despair. Second, that the life of love could be something very much more dignified and splendid than the mere insignificant frivolity (*nequitia*) which Roman orthodoxy thought it.

Greek poetry had status. Respectable persons at Rome esteemed the poets, read them at school, and decorated their houses with scenes and figures from their work. Catullus can be seen, in his sixty-eighth poem, using the prestige of Troy and the Trojan War to glorify an affair which the virtuous would find merely disreputable. At the other end of the period Ovid can be seen amusing himself and his readers by representing unmistakable contemporaries in the dress, and undress, of Paris and Helen.[88] Heartbroken Hypsipyle, heartbroken Oenone and Ariadne; passionate Calypso and Helen and Scylla; even heroines driven by passion to crime, like Medea, or to incest, like Myrrha, or to bestiality, like Pasiphae: the thought of every one of them was at least in one way comforting, as showing the overmastering supremacy of love. That is why Pasiphae had so much appeal, appearing among the dead heroines (*sunt apud infernos tot milia formosarum* – there are so many lovely women among the dead) both in Propertius and in Virgil, as well as her star role in the sixth *Eclogue* and on the gates of the Cumaean temple, the first thing Aeneas sees in Italy.[89]

---

[88] E.J. Kenney in *Philol.* 111 (1967) 214: '*Heroides* 16 and 17 are at bottom a couple of contemporary poems. Paris and Helen are the masks for a fashionable pair of lovers, and the mythical dress serves the purpose of a completely modern depiction of wit, elegance, and irresponsibility.'

[89] Prop. 2.28.48-52, Virgil *Aen.* 6.447, *Buc.* 6.45-60, *Aen.* 6.24ff.

Propertius spells it out:

obicitur totiens a te mihi nostra libido:
crede mihi, vobis imperat ista magis   (Prop. 3.19.1-2).

'You have reproached me so often with men's lustfulness: believe me, you
women are more at its command.' He goes on at once to produce
Pasiphae and what lust made her do; and Tyro who loved a river-god,
and Myrrha the incestuous, and Medea, and Clytemnestra, and Scylla ...
Myth provides six juicy examples of the power of feminine libido, and
that concludes the poem. In another poem, Cynthia is leaving Rome –
avoiding the poet and going off after unsavoury liaisons. 'But,' he
reflects, 'pretty girls have always behaved like that: look at Helen, or
even at Venus herself and her passion for Mars, or Oenone making love
among the herds ... We can hardly expect a glamorous girl to be chaste.
Pasiphae, so they say, fell in love with a bull.'[90] In between the Greek
mythological examples comes modern Rome. 'Are people to enquire,
amid our general debauchery, about the intrigues of a single girl? It will
be an extraordinary fluke if even one defies the Roman trend and behaves
well:

o nimium nostro felicem tempore Romam,
si contra mores una puella facit!   (Prop. 2.32.43-4).

So nobody should enquire where she got her money, or who gave it to her.'
The contrast is precisely in line with the argument of this chapter. As the
amorous heroines of myth could serve to make the comforting point that
women really do feel desire, so too they can cast a glittering sheen over a
contemporary courtesan who makes profits from other men. After a
central glance at Roman realities, the poem concludes by returning to the
myths. The queen of so great a king as Minos did something far more
outrageous; and as for Danae,

nec minus aerato Danae circumdata muro
non potuit magno casta negare Iovi   (59-60).

'And so too Danae, though shut up inside a wall of bronze, could not
remain chaste and say No to mighty Jupiter.' Danae and her shower of
gold serve again as a cover for the stark reality of a woman taking money.
By a deft sleight of hand Propertius exploits our knowledge of that,
avoids explicitly mentioning it, and lets the venal Danae pass as an
example of passionate love. The reader is allowed to see the reality of the
demi-monde, but at the same time it is transformed by myth. The double
vision, in this poem, is unusually complete.

[90] Prop. 2.32.29-40, 57-60. Cf. Ovid, *Ars* 1.269ff.

It is time to turn from the power of myth to glorify irregular passions, and in conclusion to see how it can serve real marriage. What is interesting is not that the myths could point to good stable marriages like those, for instance, of Alcinous and Arete in the *Odyssey* or Philemon and Baucis in the *Metamorphoses*. Such edifying unions do not attract much of the attention of these poets. Much more to the fore are those mythical marriages which can be represented as passionate. The inconsolable desire of Laudamia for her dead husband, which in the end brought him back for a short time from the grave; the similar passion of Orpheus for his dead wife Eurydice; the jealousy and devotion of Procris and Cephalus, and of Ceyx and Alcyone, tragic tales of passion and death: those are the stories which are told at loving length.[91] They go to show that respectable wives could still be dominated by love. Propertius goes as far as he can to produce a Roman wife who is like them, in the epistle of 'Arethusa' to 'Lycotas' (4.3), Greek names behind which are hidden a contemporary couple, the husband away at the wars.[92] She cannot sleep without him, she kisses his weapons – she behaves like Laudamia, in fact; she wishes she could join the army to be with him; she dreads that he may be unfaithful and hopes that he is pale from yearning for her. The climax of her prayers:

> *incorrupta mei conserva foedera lecti!*
> *hac ego te sola lege redisse velim*   (Prop. 4.3.69-70).

'Preserve undefiled your truth to my bed: only on that condition should I want you to come back.' The good Roman wife is made to write with the frankness and passion of a mythological heroine in the *Heroides*, soon to be composed by Ovid; but it could only be done by assuming a Greek veil. The contrast is striking with Propertius' earlier poem in which he sympathises with Aelia Galla for the absence of her husband Postumus.[93] Real names, and probably connections of Propertius: and so Galla does not speak in her own person, and the erotic colour is played down into a respectable emphasis on her *pudicitia* and *fides* (3.12.15, 22, 37-8). The two poems let us see with great clarity the limits of what could be said about a Roman matron; and also how much was left unsaid, what impulses were left unsatisfied, by that austere regimen. That is an example of the reasons why the poets had to invent such elaborate and ingenious ways of expressing it.

The upper class of Roman society, in the two generations of Cicero and of Horace, notoriously played fast and loose with marriage. Political

---

[91] Catullus 68, Ov. *Heroides* 13; Virg. *Georgic* 4.454-527, Ov. *Met.* 10.1-105, 11.1-66; *Met.* 7.690-865, *Met.* 11.410-750.
[92] Which wars? Propertius is indifferent to the question of geography: cf. Kroll, *Studien zum Verständnis der röm. Lit.* 296, R. Syme, *History in Ovid* 187.
[93] Propertius 3.12. On the identity of these people see R. Syme, *History in Ovid* 102.

alliances and frivolous divorces succeeded each other with bewildering speed. Even such moral persons as Cato and Cicero and Augustus went through divorce and variously scandalous remarriage.[94] It was in that society that the poets moved and wrote. Amid their praise of free love they sometimes praise true Roman conjugal union.[95] Those poems are unmistakable testimony to the continuing power of an ideal, unforgotten if unfashionable. It is among the intentions of this chapter to suggest that the magnetic pull of the idea of true marriage can be detected in many other places, too: in the loving depiction of the power of women's love, and of heroines who, on being abandoned, did not just turn easily to a new union with another man but preferred to languish and even to die. Written by men, these poems celebrate an idea of the nature of women which denied the sophistication assumed by the habits of society: insisting that they were not cool creatures who could marry and divorce at will, but emotional and passionate. Augustus, too, wanted to reform Roman marriage, for reasons of statecraft. Starting from opposite assumptions,[96] the poets could agree with him; it is not to be assumed that their utterances in that vein are insincere.

[94] The human cost of such transactions is usually concealed by the nature of our sources, but the suffering of Tiberius when forced to give up his beloved Vipsania (Suet. *Tib.* 7.2-3) will serve as a striking example. There must have been much more.

[95] Catullus 61; Horace *Odes* 3.6.33ff., *Carmen Saeculare*: Propertius 4.11; Tibullus 1.5.19ff.; Ovid's poems from exile about his devoted wife.

[96] It would be amusing to have the comment of Propertius or Tibullus on the defence which Augustus' friends gave of his adulterous affairs, that they were committed not out of lust but calculation (*non libidine sed ratione commissa*), to extract political secrets about their husbands (Suet. *D. Aug.* 69).

CHAPTER SEVEN

Love and Death

Aye, in the very Temple of Delight
Veiled Melancholy hath her sovran shrine – Keats

Traicit et fati litora magnus amor – Propertius

Men have died from time to time, and worms have eaten them; but not for love – Shakespeare

If love is to be glorified in significance, no comparison is more obvious than that with death. Whatever lacks importance and finality, death possesses them. The English expression 'to be dying for' something or somebody finds its exact equivalent in the use of the word *depereo*.[1] The extreme banality of the idea in antiquity is clear for instance from the first letter of the second book of Aristaenetus, where a girl is urged to show pity on a young man: 'His life hangs by a thread, he'll be dead if you don't grant him speedy aid. For God's sake don't let people accuse your beauty of murder ... And,' the writer goes on, 'you *are* an *hetaira*, you will not be attractive for ever: a woman is like a meadow, with a beauty which must fade.' Clearly this 'death' is not to be taken seriously, even by her. Horace gives his reader a characteristically urbane wink in *Odes* 3.9, a charming poem. A man and a woman tease each other: they might come back together, but each has a partner, far more attractive, already.

> *me nunc Thraessa Chloe regit*
> *dulcis docta modos et citharae sciens,*
> *pro qua non metuam mori,*
> *si parcent animae fata superstiti* (*Odes* 3.9.9-12).

'Chloe the Thracian governs me now, sweet singer and skilful on the lyre: I should not fear to die, if the fates would let her live.' But the girl knows how to overtrump that claim:

---

[1] Mori *persaepe per quandam exaggerationem sententiae dicuntur amantes cum affectum aliquem nimia violentia sentiunt, seu absentium desiderium*: R. Pichon, *Index Verborum Amatoriorum* (1902) 207, 'Lovers are very often said to "die", in an exaggerated manner of speech, when they feel some emotion, or the absence of the beloved, with very great force.'

me torret face mutua
Thurini Calais filius Ornyti,
pro quo bis patiar mori,
si parcent puero fata superstiti   (ib. 13-16).

'I am in love with Calais, Ornytus' son, and he with me: I should die for him twice, if the fates would let the boy live.' To die twice: the hyperbole which deflates the cliché.

The novelists are of course lavish with the threat of suicide and the longing for death. Chariton's hero demands death from the Syracusans when he thinks he has killed the heroine, tries to drown himself, tries to stab himself, wishes he were dead; his darling wish is only that she visit his grave.[2] In this he is the true predecessor of the heroes and heroines of Achilles Tatius,[3] Xenophon of Ephesus,[4] Heliodorus.[5] These attempts are rarely made without a monologue of passionate lamentation, to express despairing love. Doubtless this death-wish was true also of the Hellenistic love elegies of which so little has come down to us,[6] drawing especially on the myths which appealed to Euripides.[7] In a world in which, provided certain absolute prohibitions were respected, love affairs were taken lightly, the lover needed strong images to produce an impression: on the beloved, on the reader, on himself.

The aim of this chapter is to explore various forms of the connection of love and death in the poets, and in particular to show how closely they are related to ideas and rituals of their society. The material is Protean, and it is striking that it is equally at home in what seem to be opposite expressions. Propertius toys with the thought of killing Cynthia, but more often he imagines his own death, with the voluptuous torment of wondering how she will behave at his bedside and his funeral: will she beat her breasts in passionate grief, or will she show a galling indifference? It is a final reversal here that in the end it is he who fails to honour her funeral. The unsatisfied lover can say he is dying; but making love can itself be spoken of as dying, or conversely amorous pleasure can make the lover immortal. Love can be said to be an urgent necessity because death is the end of delight; no less powerful is the idea that love outlasts death, and an erotic Elysium awaits the lovers beyond the grave.

At the level of rhetoric all this gives the lover and the poet a great range of strong images which transcend the prosaic regularity of ordinary existence, whether by killing, by dying, or by immortality; and which

---

[2] Chariton 1.5, 3.5, 5.10, 6.2, 7.1, 5.10.
[3] 3.5, 3.10, 3.16 (he plans to kill himself on her grave).
[4] 2.1, 2.4 *fin.*, 3.4, 3.5, 3.10.
[5] 2.5.1, 4.6, 10.22. The motif is repeatedly burlesqued by Petronius: 82.1, 94.8ff., 108.10-13.
[6] E. Rohde, *Der griechische Roman* 84f.; Theocritus 23; many of the stories in Parthenius' *Sufferings of Love*; La Penna, *L'Integrazione difficile* 165.
[7] E.g. Euripides' *Aeolus* (Canace), *Hippolytus* (Phaedra).

thus exalt and dignify the life of passion. But it would be cynical to talk as if there were no deeper roots to the link between love and death. Mortal creatures find their immortality in procreation. The guarantee of the reality and worth of love is the idea 'until death', both in the tranquil companionship of marriage and in the violent tragedy of heroes and heroines, from Laudamia and Alcestis to Romeo and Juliet. The supreme moments of love, youth, beauty, evoke by a natural contrast the thoughts of death, extinction, darkness. Every creature feels sadness after sexual union. The connection of ideas is much more than merely decorative. As Empson says, discussing such pairs as pain and pleasure, and as death and the sexual act: 'Evidently these pairs of opposites, stated in the right way, make a direct appeal to the normal habits of the mind' (*Seven Types of Ambiguity* 215).

Catullus' longest meditation on his own passion for Lesbia centres on Laudamia and her tragic love for Protesilaus, the bridegroom who died at Troy. Propertius writes constantly of his own death, and sometimes of the death of Cynthia: he will die of love, he will die young, he does not care about dying if only she will mourn him at his funeral. Tibullus hopes to die in Delia's arms; he will die and be wafted to an erotic Elysium.[8] It was hoped that a respectable Roman would die surrounded by his family, and that his last breath, with which his soul was thought to pass, would be received by his closest relative.[9] Tibullus, a Roman knight, mentally abolishes all that: all he cares for is

> *te spectem, suprema mihi cum venerit hora,*
> *te teneam moriens deficiente manu:*
> *flebis et arsuro positum me, Delia, lecto*
> *tristibus et lacrimis oscula mixta dabis*   (Tib. 1.1.59-62).

'May I gaze at you when my last hour shall come: may I hold you in my dying embrace. You will weep when I am placed on the pyre to burn, and give me kisses mingled with sad tears.'[10]

Propertius thinks of dying on the same day, of killing her and himself; if she dies, he will die too, and Charon's boat shall carry them both together.[11] He hopes to die of love:

> *me sine, quem semper voluit fortuna iacere,*
> *hanc animam extremae reddere nequitiae*   (Prop. 1.6.24-6).

---

[8] Catull. 68; Prop. 1.6.27, 2.1.56 and 75ff., 2.8.17, 1.19.1; Tib. 1.1.59ff., 1.3 fin.

[9] J.M.C. Toynbee, *Death and Burial in the Roman World* (1971) 35; H. Blümner, *Römische Privataltertümer* (1911) 482ff.

[10] Such language could be used with less impropriety of a beloved slave dying with his eyes on his master (Stat. *Silv.* 2.1.148), or of heroines like Procris or Thisbe, dying in the woods with only the beloved near (Ov. *Met.* 7.859, 4.143).

[11] Prop. 2.20.18, 2.8.25, 2.28.39-42. On Propertius' sensibility to death see Oliver Lyne, *The Latin Love Poets* 141ff.

'Fortune has always resolved that I should fail to rise: let me breathe my last in extremity of desire.' In other passages he invokes as a curse on his successful rivals that they should not survive the sexual act itself: may one 'turn to stone amid his love-making', another kill himself by his exertions.[12] Ovid lights on the middle point which the older elegists one way or another preferred to avoid – the wish to die himself in the act of love:[13] a heroic death, in keeping with his life. Tibullus preferred the decent wish to die in Delia's arms: Propertius produces every possible variation on the theme, itself perhaps too frank for his style. But he has created a marvellous image with it: not for himself but on the plane of mythology. Speaking of the amorous raptures of his friend Gallus and his mistress, he tells us that

> *non sic Haemonio Salmonida mixtus Enipeo*
> *Taenarius facili pressit amore deus,*
> *nec sic caelestem flagrans amor Herculis Heben*
> *sensit in Oetaeis gaudia prima iugis* (Prop. 1.13.21-4).

'Not so much did Neptune in the form of the river embrace Tyro in unresisted love: not so much did the fiery passion of Hercules enjoy heavenly Hebe when he possessed her first on Oeta's peak.' The second couplet is the interesting one. Hercules was burned on the pyre on Mount Oeta and became a god and the husband of Hebe. Propertius compresses the myth so that it ceases to be two separate incidents and becomes one: the love of Hercules was 'fiery' in part because it was actually there, on the site of the fire, that he first enjoyed the divine bride who was given to him as a god. Death and love and deification through pleasure: a marvellous creation, and one made by the use of very characteristic Propertian material. The passage is his single most intense crystallisation of it – a warning to those who deplore his mythological passages or find them peripheral to his poetry.

The theme of immortality through pleasure claims a moment's attention. 'To be in heaven', 'to live the life of the gods': these were commonplace expressions of felicity.[14] In Comedy lovers go further.

---

[12] Prop. 2.9.48 *in medio fiat amore lapis*; 2.16.14 *rumpat ut assiduis membra libidinibus*.

[13] Ovid *Am.* 2.10.29-37. Oliver Lyne discusses some of these passages to good effect: *The Latin Love Poets* (1980) 273f. The 'mort de Faure' was evidently a favoured topic in scandal. Comedy alleged it appropriately of Lais and more surprisingly of the Athenian politician Phormisius (Philetaerus frs. 6 and 9 Kock, vol. 2 p. 232); Romans associated such stories with knights, as Cornelius Gallus and T. Haterius (Val. Max. 9.12.8). Two other members of that order perished in the embraces of the same pantomime dancer, the enchanting Mysticus, we are told by the Elder Pliny (*NH* 7.184). The themes of poetry are as so often intimately akin to the themes of scandal. Already burlesqued in Comedy: Com. Adesp. 224, Kock, *CAF* 3 p. 451 'to die in his embrace and get an epitaph'.

[14] *In caelo sum*, Cic. *ad Att.* 2.9.1; *deorum profecto vitam homines viverent*, Cic. *de Legg.* fr. 1 etc.: cf. A. Otto, *Die Sprichwörter und sprichwörtlichen Redensarten der Römer* 62, 109.

di immortales omnipotentes, quid est apud vos pulcrius?
quid habetis qui mage immortales vos credam esse quam ego siem,
qui haec tanta oculis bona concipio? (Plaut. *Poen.* 278-80).[15]

'O immortal and almighty gods, what have you got more splendid? Why should I think you are more immortal than I am, when my eyes give me such delight?'

ego deorum vitam propterea sempiternam esse arbitror
quod voluptates eorum propriae sunt: nam mihi immortalitas
partast, si nulla aegritudo huic gaudio intercesserit (Ter. *Andria* 959-61).

'I believe the reason why the gods live for ever is because pleasures belong to them; for I have won immortality, if no sorrow comes to spoil this delight.' These expressions of erotic exuberance, the attempt to convey an overflowing sense of joy in love, lie behind the two passages in which alone Propertius uses the word *immortalis*. After a triumphant night of love he bursts out with four couplets of mythological comparison, first two heroes and then (climactically) two heroines: none of them, in their supreme moments of happiness, enjoyed such delight as he last night.

Immortalis ero, si altera talis erit (Prop. 2.14.10).[16]

'If I have such another night, I shall be immortal.' In the next poem he is still exultant. In life or death he will be hers; if she grants many such nights, he will be immortal: one night is enough to make a man into a god:

si dabit haec multas, fiam immortalis in illis:
nocte una quivis vel deus esse potest (Prop. 2.15.39-40).

It is also notable that Propertius once addresses his readers and the world, in Lucretian style, as 'mortales':

et vos incertam, mortales, funeris horam
quaeritis, et qua sit mors aditura via (Prop. 2.27.1-2).

'O mortals, you seek to know the hidden hour of your death, and how it will come.' The poem goes on to say that only the lover can know that; moreover, even if he is sitting in Charon's boat, the voice of his mistress

[15] Cf. Ed. Fraenkel, *Elementi Plautini in Plauto* (1960) 208f.; and Plaut. *Curc.* 167, *Merc.* 603; Ter. *Hec.* 843, *Eun.* 550, 693 *deorum vitam apti sumus*, irresistibly glossed by A. Otto (see last note) p. 109 as 'Wir leben wie Gott in Frankreich'. Also Catullus 51 *ille mi par esse deo videtur*, and Sappho; G. Lieberg, *Puella Divina* (1962) 36; D. Roloff, *Gottähnlichkeit* (1970) 58; *CEL* 1867.6.

[16] G. Lieberg in *Rh. Mus.* 112 (1969) 335 anxiously insists that 'what is meant is surely not immortality in the literal, temporal sense (im wörtlich-zeitlichen Sinne) but an existence transcending ordinary human life'.

can still call him back to life. Again, true love is the one thing over which death shall have no dominion. Immortality and love are intimately linked.

Of course these assertions are not statements of philosophical or religious dogma. They have a resemblance to Epicurean ideas of the supremacy of pleasure and of pleasure as the special mark of the existence of the gods,[17] but the vehement pleasures of Propertius (*hostibus eveniat lenta puella meis!*)[18] are very different from the tranquil 'catastematic' delights of Epicurus' heaven. Propertius no more expected to avoid death than Cicero, when he said he was 'in heaven', imagined he was above the clouds; the delight of love could be expressed by the feeling of immortality, but equally (a paradox only to common sense) by the metaphor of dying –

> *cum te complexa morientem, Galle, puella*
> *vidimus et longa ducere verba mora ...* (Prop. 1.10.5-6).

'When I saw you dying in the embrace of your mistress, Gallus, uttering slow and isolated words ...'[19] Equally ready to hand is the Platonic idea (really an anti-Platonic idea: Plato's treatment of it in the *Symposium* is that of an enemy) of the unending embrace. It is in fact developed in the same poem as the other: since youth and beauty are transient, and the everlasting night comes on,

> *dum nos fata sinunt, oculos satiemus amore:*
> *nox tibi longa venit, nec reditura dies.*
> *atque utinam haerentis sic nos vincire catena*
> *velles, ut numquam solveret ulla dies!* (Prop. 2.15.23-6).

'While yet the fates allow, let us sate our eyes with love: a long night is coming, and your day will not return. And I wish you would bind us together as we cling like this, so that no time should ever release us!'[20]

To die transcends life, as immortality does. Love can make you die, it can make you immortal: it can annihilate the distinction between life and death. In Propertian language,

> *traicit et fati litora magnus amor* (Prop. 1.19.12).

'A mighty love crosses the shores of fate.' Protesilaus indeed offers an example of a dead man who came back to his wife because of the greatness of her love; the example is considered, but Propertius prefers to

---

[17] So Donatus on Terence *Andria* 959: an Epicurean dogma, borrowed by Terence from Menander.
[18] 'May my enemies get unemotional girls!', Prop. 3.8.20.
[19] Cf. also Prop. 1.4.12 *sunt maiora quibus, Basse, perire iuvat*, 'There are greater charms in her of which it is a pleasure to die'; Prop. 1.6.27, 1.15.41, etc.
[20] Cf. L. Alfonsi, *L'Elegia di Properzio* (1945) 44.

say that, although he did indeed long for her, it was only a revenant, an *umbra* ('shade') which came back to Laudamia to embrace her in 'unreal arms'.[21] More often it is in that other world that the poets envisage their love continuing.

Before the poet can reach that world, he imagines his funeral. The exequies of a love poet are, as might be expected, based upon the normal funeral customs of his society but given a characteristic twist. Toynbee lists the sequence of ritual events.[22] The closest relative present gave the last kiss to catch the soul which passed with the final breath: it has been seen that Tibullus imagines Delia doing this (1.1.62); Propertius too imagines Cynthia giving him the last kiss (2.13.29). All the relatives called on the dead by name: for Propertius it is Cynthia alone who will do that (1.17.23, 2.13.28). The corpse was washed and dressed, and a wreath laid on its head; Propertius imagines Cynthia giving him tresses of her hair and roses, evidently also from her head to his (1.17.22); it is she who will bring unguents (3.16.23). Hired female mourners (*praeficae*) beat their breasts with hair dishevelled: Propertius, who in 2.13 insists throughout that his funeral should be simple and inexpensive, without procession or musicians –

adsint
plebei parvae funeris exsequiae   (Prop. 2.13.23-4)

'Let me have the small trappings of a plebeian funeral' – rather than the fitting ceremony of his class, delights in the thought that Cynthia will accompany him beating her bare breasts (2.24.52), or even tearing them (2.13.27). The gentler spirits of Tibullus and his imitator Lygdamus shrank from this last detail:[23] Lygdamus wishes Neaera to escort his corpse *longos incompta capillos*, 'her long hair dishevelled' ([Tib.] 3.2.11), Tibullus expressly asks Delia not to tear her hair or cheeks (1.1.67).

Propertius' funeral procession will set out (*exsequiae, pompa*) not from the family home but from Cynthia's house (2.1.56); she would manage it all (1.17.19ff.), even to the collecting of his ashes from the pyre (2.24.35: cf. Lygdamus, [Tib.] 3.2.17ff.) and the decision where they should finally rest (3.16.25ff.). At an orthodox funeral the dead man was the subject of a laudatory address, or even of two: 'the private *laudatio* at the graveside

[21] Prop. 1.19.9-10; cf. O. Lyne, *The Latin Love Poets* (1980) 100f.

[22] J.M.C. Toynbee, *Death and Burial in the Roman World* (1971) 43ff.

[23] The bare breasts of mourning women had an appeal for Propertius; with their combination of the gloomy and the sexy, they became a cliché with Ovid. Dwelt on with gusto in the *Metamorphoses* (2.584, 3.178, 4.590, 8.530, 9.636, 10.723, 11.681, 13.688) and *Heroides* (5.71, 6.27, 10.15, 12.153, 15.123), they come in the *Amores* (3.6.5, 3.9.10), the *Ars* (1.535, 3.707), and the *Fasti* (3.864, 4,454). It is almost shocking that Ovid exploits the motif to describe a real scene of woe: his own last departure from his home to exile (*Tristia* 1.3.78).

(and) the praises of the dead by the *praefica*', a woman with a good voice singled out for the purpose.[24] Propertius hopes that Cynthia will speak a sentence in his praise: 'Alas, after all you were true to me, Propertius, although you were neither nobly born nor very rich' (Prop. 2.24.35-8). On his modest grave his epitaph, too, will record nothing but his love:

> *qui nunc iacet horrida pulvis,*
> *unius hic quondam servus amoris erat*   (2.13.35-6).

'He who now lies dust, was once the slave of one love.' If Propertius needs, in another poem, to be buried by a road in normal Roman fashion, it is in the context of Maecenas, so that the millionaire can rein in his smart chariot and shed a tear for the poet's ashes, saying

> *huic misero fatum dura puella fuit*   (2.1.78).

'A heartless girl was the poor fellow's death.' Every item of this catalogue shows how the poet has exploited the normal ceremony, and how he has defied its purpose. At each stage the ritual act is to be carried out, or something very like it, but the regular social setting, the family of a respectable Roman, is replaced by the irregular woman who has engrossed his life.[25] Even after his death he will have, not the proper epitaph which should safeguard the fame of a man and record his achievements for posterity, but the proud statement that his life contained only one thing: his unofficial love.[26]

*

Laodameia died; Helen died; Leda, the beloved of Jupiter, went before – Landor

Dear dead women, and such hair too – Browning

Poets could find poetic power in the idea that death is the end of delight. When our brief sun has set, we must sleep out an endless night (Catullus 5, Propertius 2.15.24); after death no parties or love affairs, you must

---

[24] J.A. North in *JRS* 73 (1983) 169.
[25] One might say that the poet's family are as invisible as the professionals, the *libitinarii, ustores, vespillones*, who in real life would have had to do the hard work of burial. Cf. La Penna, *L'Integrazione difficile* 161.
[26] Q. Varius Geminus, 'the first of all the Paeligni to become a senator', the man who was what Ovid might have been (cf. R. Syme, *Roman Revolution* 363) has a splendid inscription of the sort which Propertius ought to have wanted: legate of Augustus for the second time, proconsul, praetor, tribune of the plebs, quaestor, quaesitor iudiciarius, praefectus frumenti dandi, decemvir stlitibus iudicandis, curator of the temples and public monuments: that was the record of a life well spent (ILS 932). A successful rhetor, he knew how to turn a pretty compliment to Augustus (Seneca *Contr.* 6.8).

leave behind your agreeable wife, we are dust and a shadow (Horace *Odes* 1.4 *fin.*, 2.14.21, 4.7.15). Tibullus, too, can at times exploit it: after death there is only a bleak lower world peopled with bloodless phantoms:

> *illic pertusisque genis ustoque capillo*
> *errat ad obscuros pallida turba lacus*   (Tib. 1.10.35-6).

'There a death-pale people with pierced faces and scorched hair wanders by the dark waters.' That is in the context of choosing peace rather than war. 'Why hasten on the inevitable approach of death with all its horrors? Far better choose peace, prosperity, and the campaigns of Venus.' The motif is used with greater power in an erotic context by Propertius, in that poem which tells of Cynthia's return to him from the dead, her dress burned on to her body, her ring eaten away by the flames of her pyre, her hands skeletal. She awaits him, to press her bones against his. After all his fears that she would slight his funeral, it was he, she tells us, who slighted hers: he failed to carry out any of the ritual acts which he loved to imagine her performing for him (Prop. 4.7.23ff.). The poem is true to the exclusively erotic conception which dominates the poet's day-dreams of his own funeral, and so it follows that since Propertius failed there was nobody to call her name.

> *At mihi non oculos quisquam inclamavit euntis:*
> *unum impetrassem te revocante diem*   (Prop. 4.7.23-4).

'Nobody called my name as my eyes were failing: if you had called, I should have won another day of life.' Her funeral was of the cheapest: no flowers, no wine, no perfumes, and her head not on a pillow but on a broken pot. No epitaph commemorates her. All this is Propertius' fault. She has in fact virtually suffered the fate dreaded by the poor of Rome.

That dread was extensive and well founded.[27] The poor were often buried in nameless graves, in amphorae, even thrown *en masse* into great ditches: an estimated 24,000 corpses came to light in a moat near the Esquiline cemeteries. To avoid 'the shameful anonymity of a mass grave' men and women joined in burial clubs whose aim was to ensure that dead members were properly buried in an orderly *columbarium*, their names duly affixed and preserved for ever. Propertius hopes for a modest funeral, but not for oblivion: his simple tomb will bear a short epitaph, Cynthia will sit by it, adorn it, guard it (Prop. 2.13.35; 3.16.23). Cynthia comes closer to the real horrors. Her funeral as she describes it is not a matter of an elegant Callimachean preference for simplicity, like his, but realistically sordid;[28] and unless Propertius provides it she will have no

---

[27] I am indebted here to Keith Hopkins, *Death and Renewal in the Roman World* (1983) 207ff.

[28] Cf. Prop. 4.5.65-76 for the vivid account of the wretched death and squalid burial of the old *lena*, and J.P. Boucher, *Études sur Properce* (1965) 78. She is to be buried in an amphora (vs. 75): the realistic end of a poor old woman.

epitaph to preserve her name from oblivion. In reality that was doubtless the normal fate of the woman with no family and no husband to record his conjugal devotion and decorous sense of loss.

After the funeral Roman religion offered little in the way of posthumous existence. Impersonal *manes*, a name on an inscription: dusty answers indeed to the ardent spirit. The desire for an expression of the transcendent significance of love could make something out of hints from Greek and Roman sources combined. In the *Odyssey* Odysseus is made to call up the ghosts of the dead. Among them come the celebrated heroines who were beloved by gods and bore them children: Tyro and Antiope and Alcmene and Leda and the rest. They pass before him and tell the story of their loves; the hero makes no reply. Elsewhere in the *Odyssey* comes another suggestive passage. Menelaus is to be exempted from death and translated to the Elysian Plain 'because he is married to Helen'. When Pindar sings to Theron of the delights of the blessed beyond the grave, he names two heroes who are prominent there, Peleus and Cadmus. What this pair have in common is marriage to a goddess. In second place Pindar adds that Achilles is there, too: his mother Thetis softened Zeus' heart.[29] Like Menelaus all three heroes, it seems, enjoy these posthumous joys through their connection with glamorous goddesses and heroines. Those joys are indeed not described in erotic terms by early poets; but the connecting pattern was surely there for later poets to find. The long line of heroines in the eleventh book of the *Odyssey* derives from the Hesiodic poem called the *Catalogue of Women*, of which extensive fragments survive,[30] some of them overlapping the *Odyssey* passage; other poems were organised on the catalogue principle in later Greek literature, such as the *Leontion* of Hermesianax, in which he listed heroines who had been unhappy in love, and the *Erotes* of Phanocles, which strung in a sequence tales of paederastic amours.

Elysium attained through feminine connections, and lists of amorous heroines: here was a basis on which an erotic Elysium might be constructed. The fourth *Georgic* comes close to it, with the close juxtaposition of Cyrene and her lovely nymphs under the water, and a world of the dead under the earth, which can yield to the power of love.[31] Tibullus took the last step. After his death

> sed me, quod facilis tenero sum semper Amori,
> ipsa Venus campos ducet in Elysios.
> hic choreae cantusque vigent ...
> ac iuvenum series teneris immixta puellis
> ludit, et adsidue proelia miscet amor.
> illic est cuicumque rapax Mors venit amanti ... (Tib. 1.3.57ff.).[32]

[29] Homer *Od.* 11.225-329, 4.561-9, Pindar *Ol.* 2.61ff.
[30] *Fragmenta Hesiodea*, edd. Merkelbach and West (Oxford 1967) nos. 30-2.
[31] Virgil *Georg.* 4.333ff., 467ff.
[32] F. Cairns, *Tibullus* (1979) 51. Some of his connections are hard to accept, as is his view that 'It is to parallel and balance this special hell for sinners against love that Tibullus

'As for me, because I have always been susceptible to the charms of love, Venus herself will lead me to the Elysian Fields. There abound dancing and singing ... Young men play with pretty girls, and love stirs up constant skirmishes. There is everyone who was in love when greedy Death came for him ...' In such an underworld the sinners, too, are as far as possible those guilty of erotic offences: Ixion, Tityos, the Danaids 'because they offended the power of Venus'. Tibullus prays that all the enemies of his own love may share their punishment (Tib. 1.3.73-82).

Propertius also develops similar ideas. Imagining his death, he imagines his arrival among the dead:

> *illic formosae veniant chorus heroinae*
> *quas dedit Argivis Dardana praeda viris,*
> *quarum nulla tua fuerit mihi, Cynthia, forma*
> *gratior* (Prop. 1.19. 13-16).

'There may the heroines come, a lovely group, the girls whom the Argive men got from the sack of Troy; not one of them all will be dearer to me than your beauty, Cynthia.' Here the beautiful women beyond the grave are mythological heroines, in line with the greater interest which Propertius takes in myth, and evidently they come to meet the poet because he is a lover. The myth they come from is the opposite of recherché, being the most familiar of all – another indication that great erudition was not at the root of all this. Propertius and Tibullus were at work on their first published collections at the same time, and influence between the two, in either direction, is a possibility.[33] In Book 2 the idea is more detailed. Cynthia is ill: if she dies, she will be among the heroines of Homer, and she will exchange with Semele the stories of their sufferings for love. But the gods of the dead should spare the life of his sick mistress:

> *sunt apud infernos tot milia formosarum:*
> *pulchra sit in superis, si licet, una locis!*
> *vobiscum est Iope, vobiscum candida Tyro,*
> *vobiscum Europe nec proba Pasiphae* (Prop. 2.28.49-52).

'There are so many thousands of lovely women among the dead: let one

creates before it a heaven specially for lovers'. That seems a perverse way of looking at it; and I very much doubt that 'Tibullus' Elysium for lovers may derive in its entirety from a Hellenistic original' (ib. 52). No great 'learning' (54) was needed for this creation, whose poetic merits are essentially of a straightforward sort.

[33] Ed. Norden, who assumed Hellenistic sources, thought the catalogue of heroines was 'already pretty hackneyed for Propertius' (edition of *Aeneid* 6, 4th edn., p. 247). That seems to me false to the poetry, true only to a reconstructed literary genealogy. W. Wimmel, *Tibull und Delia = Hermes* Einzelschriften 37 (Wiesbaden 1976) 58 thinks Propertius perhaps influenced Tibullus 1.3.

beauty please remain on earth! Iope is with you, with you is the fair Tyro, and Europa, and the wicked Pasiphae' – and all the belles of old Troy and Achaea, and all the pretty girls of Rome: the greedy fire has possessed them all. Dear dead women: the theme is developed in the direction of a voluptuous melancholy.

That character still clings to it in the *Aeneid*, when Virgil brings his hero to the *lugentes campi*. The happy Elysium which Tibullus gave his lovers is far away:

> hic quos durus amor crudeli tabe peredit
> secreti celant colles et myrtea circum
> silva tegit: curae non ipsa in morte relinquunt   (*Aen.* 6.442-4).

'Here are they whom unhappy love consumed with cruel disease. The lone hills hide them and the myrtle woods conceal: even in death their pain does not leave them.' The heroines are an unexpected collection. The wicked Phaedra, the unlucky Procris, the criminal (here called, with striking euphemism, *maestam*, 'sad') Eriphyle, the virtuous Evadne, the lustful Pasiphae; Caenis, once a man, now turned back into a woman; and Dido. The complete absence of moral arrangement leaps to the eye. At line 540 Aeneas will come to the point where the road divides, the wicked being punished in Tartarus, but the killers Phaedra and Eriphyle are not there. Apparently subjection to love overrides everything else, or simply being a pretty girl (for Eriphyle was generally thought to have caused her husband's death not in a *crime passionel* but to get a precious necklace) quite as it does in elegy. It is curious that these lovelorn ladies are the last women Aeneas will meet in the lower world. All the ancestors of Rome whom he meets with Anchises are men,[34] a remarkable fact, and it is only here that the lower world offers female figures. The division is clear: patriotism and self-sacrifice for men, dangerous passion for women. It is one of the great tours-de-force of the *Aeneid* that this piece of decadent verse (these women have no children to tell of, as the *Odyssey* heroines have; their perverse careers put the reader for a moment in the world of the Sixth *Eclogue*, even of the *Ciris*) is made to serve the serious purposes of the poem, when Dido brings home to Aeneas with unavoidable force that he has destroyed her, and that the destiny of the imperialist is guilty as well as splendid. Virgil has exploited the

---

[34] Epecially *Aen.* 6.649 *virum*; 661 *sacerdotes casti* (chaste women like Claudia Quinta could easily have appeared here); 682-3 *nepotes ... virum*; 712 *viri*; 757 *nepotes*. This goes far beyond the simple inclusive use of the masculine gender. Odysseus meets only men after his encounter with the women in *Odyssey* 11, but he is not being shown his descendants, the representatives of a great historical people. A heroine of Roman history like Cloelia can appear on the Shield (8.651) but cannot interrupt the great men in Book 6. On the other hand the inhabitants of the *lugentes campi*, introduced with a masculine pronoun (*quos*, 442), seem in fact to be all women: Dido's first husband Sychaeus did not die for love and is only there for Dido.

material of the elegiac poets with even more spectacular success here than in the Tenth *Eclogue.*

Virgil's indifference to the morality of the dead heroines was not emulated by Propertius in his last haunting use of the motif. In the seventh poem of the fourth book Cynthia tells Propertius of her existence after death. Wicked heroines, Clytemnestra and Pasiphae, are in another part of the underworld: only good ones go to the Elysian Fields. There the good wives Hypermestra and Andromeda tell the story of their sufferings for love (4.7.63ff.; cf. 2.28.27), and Cynthia too tells of hers.

sic mortis lacrimis vitae sancimus amores:

'So as we weep among the dead we sanctify the loves of our lives.'[35]

These last passages have carried the idea of the beautiful dead heroines as far as it can be carried in Latin poetry. That it is largely Greek in ancestry is clear. But Virgil's parade of heroes (*Aeneid* 6.756ff.) will provide a parallel. That too does not derive only from the scene in *Iliad* 3 where Priam and Helen see and identify the Achaean heroes,[36] but also has roots in Rome. One of Rome's most imposing ceremonies was the funeral of a nobleman who had held office. His dead ancestors paraded through the streets to accompany his corpse, being represented by living men wearing masks; Polybius was impressed.[37] No doubt, as has been suggested, Virgil had both that custom in mind and also the commemorative statues of Roman commanders which Augustus set up in the Forum Augustum, each with a *titulus* recording his name and achievements. Augustus meant them to have a moral effect, exactly as Virgil means his parade to have – Anchises cries impatiently

et dubitamus adhuc virtutem extendere factis?   (6.806).

'And do we still flinch from enlarging our worth by action?'[38] The use at Rome of *exempla* of great men, a regular feature of speeches and rhetorical training, must also have been important: the Roman heroes who parade are those whose achievements were in most constant use by the rhetoricians. These aspects of Roman life were hardly less important than the sources in Greek literature for the invention and appreciation of such a scene.

In the case of the heroines in Elysium, Roman sources are perhaps less

---

[35] After that exquisite Propertian passage it goes against the grain to mention anywhere but in a footnote the feebleness of [Virgil] *Culex* 261ff., the heroines on parade to meet the soul of the gnat: again only virtuous ones, Alcestis, Penelope, Eurydice. Even Ausonius' *Cupido Crucifixus* is better than that.

[36] Norden, *Kommentar*[4] 312 thinks in terms of *Iliad* 3 and Lycophron's Cassandra, plus the *exempla* used in the rhetorical schools. The *Ahnenparade*: E. Skard in *Symb. Osl.* 40 (1965) 53-65 and Austin's commentary p. 233.

[37] Polyb. 6.53.

[38] The extant *elogia* are in *Inscriptiones Italiae* 13.3 init. Cf. Suet. *D. Aug.* 31, Degrassi in *Epigraphica* 7 (1945) 88ff., H.T. Rowell in *AJP* 62 (1941) 261ff.

plentiful; but the loving youths and maidens of Tibullus' conception, flirting to music in the open air, are clearly akin to the musical picnics which are mentioned so frequently among the pleasures of real life,[39] while the *sine fraude maritae*, the virtuous wives Hypermestra and Andromeda of Propertius, perhaps owe something to the occasions at Rome, not as uncommon as is sometimes supposed, when the *matronae* assembled. They had a clear role, often expressly mentioned,[40] at the *supplicationes* which were decreed so frequently in the Ciceronian and Augustan periods; Augustus claimed (*Res Gestae* 1) to have had a total of 890 days of *supplicatio* granted to him in 55 separate celebrations. We know from the inscription[41] that at Augustus' Secular Games, in 17 B.C., 110 matrons had special seats of honour. They had a *conventus*, about which we are ill informed.[42] We know so little about the *matronae* that it can hardly be doubted that such occasions were more numerous than we can prove. Another contributing source must have been the enormously widespread works of art which represented mythical heroines, often in idyllic settings:[43] the presence on one's walls and in public porticoes of these paintings cannot have failed to have an effect in suggesting the subject and in making it one for reveries. Originally Greek, this art had become a completely indigenous part of Roman life, exotic, yet very familiar.

The theme of paintings leads directly into the last contributory source of the erotic Elysium of the poets. For centuries there had been a tradition which declared that certain of the myths represented the triumph over death. Plato in the *Symposium* lets Phaedrus say that Alcestis, who gave her life for her husband, was allowed by the gods to return from the dead: 'the gods too give supreme honour to noble actions springing from love.'[44] In a very Platonic work, the *Eroticus*, Plutarch says that to lovers alone Hades ceases to be inflexible and implacable: 'and I observe that those who are initiated into the mysteries of Love and

---

[39] E.g the festival of Anna Perenna, Ovid *Fasti* 3.525, 677ff., and the barely mythologised picnics at *Fasti* 1.397, 6.323 (on them see now E. Fantham in *HSCP* 87 (1983) 185-216); Lucretius 2.29-33, Horace *Epode* 2.23ff., *Odes* 1.1.21; 1.17; 2.3.6; 2.11.13; 3.17.11, *Epistles* 1.14.35; Longus 2.26; 2.31; 3.2-3; 4.38; Heliodorus 8.14; Achilles Tatius 4.18; Martial 9.90; 10.51.7-10. And H. Herter in *JAC* 3 (1960) 101.

[40] 'The participation of the *matronae* is particularly emphasised', Wissowa in *RE* s.v. *Supplicationes* 943.51.

[41] *CIL* 6.32323.101.

[42] Evidence in *TLL* s.v. *matrona* 484.84-485.4. One good story: Agrippina slapped at a meeting of matrons for her indecorous advances to the future Emperor Galba, Suet. *Galba* 5.

[43] On the popularity of erotic legends in Roman art e.g. G.M.A. Hanfmann, *Roman Art* (1964), on Plates xxix-xxxi; D. Strong, *Roman Art* (1970) 34, 53; K. Schefold, 'Origins of Roman landscape painting', in *Art Bulletin* 42 (1960) 92 'the beholder is confronted by realms of fancy, by dreams of fair and pious old Greece, so different from the troubled contemporaneous world ...'.

[44] *Symp.* 179d1, 180a7.

celebrate them have a better place in Hades. It is not that I believe the myths, nor that I altogether disbelieve them; they are right to say, in fact some divine chance has let them touch on the truth, that lovers can come back even from the underworld.'[45] In the immediate context Plutarch speaks of Alcestis, Protesilaus, Eurydice. These myths, along with certain others such as those of the rape of Proserpina, appear constantly on the sarcophagi of which we have such huge numbers from about 100 A.D. onwards. They embody a hope about the life of the soul in the next world: like the protagonists of these erotic myths, the soul is to have the power to transcend the gulf between this world and the next.[46] Alcestis, Eurydice, Persephone could go and return; Ganymede, Ariadne and Endymion were abducted by amorous gods and so succeeded in avoiding death. The Augustan poets are writing at a late and developed stage of ancient society, and many factors bear on them at once. It is from the blending of them all that important features of Augustan poetry arise. Students of ancient poetry, constantly studying what remains of the texts, are tempted to explain it too much in terms of itself: of literary genres and poetical precedents. There is in reality no single source or explanation of a work of literature, and customs and ideas of an unliterary sort must often be invoked if we are to understand.

This chapter has developed some ideas about love and death. It has not been exhaustive. Two further aspects will conclude it: some thoughts on epitaphs, and love among the tombs.

Balsdon remarks that on inscriptions 'women were praised in conventional terms for the same domestic virtues': old-fashioned life (*antiqua vita*), staying at home (*domiseda*), chastity, obedience, agreeableness, economy, restraint in dress, weaving (*pudicitia, obsequium, comitas, frugalitas, ornatus non conspiciendus, lanificium*). Lyne contrasts the praise given to wives with the ideal of 'whole love' which is to be found in the poets.[47] It is certainly true that we find many epitaphs which place heavy emphasis on the household virtues of dead wives. 'Chaste, scrupulous, indefatigable, efficient, watchful, anxious, a woman of one man and one bedroom, a perfect matron in hard work and loyalty'; 'she neglected her person and adorned herself with her virtues'; 'outstanding glory was hers for her weaving, she was brought up in family duty, the fame of her old-fashioned chastity was exceptional'; 'scrupulous towards her husband, chaste in herself, a mother to her

[45] Plutarch *Eroticus* 761e.

[46] F. Cumont, *Le Symbolisme funéraire* (1942) 30f.; J. Engemann, *Untersuchungen zur Sepulkralsymbolik* (1973) 24-8. *CLE* 1109, a poem apparently of Augustan date, describes a dream in which the dead young man Nepos appears to a mourner in a dream, declaring that he is now a god: it was Venus (1.27) who took him to his happy lot, we observe.

[47] J.P.V.D. Balsdon, *Roman Women* (1962) 207; R.O.A.M. Lyne, *The Latin Love Poets* (1980) 7. Bibliography on the merits ascribed to women in epitaphs: H. Krummrey in *Klio* 63 (1981) 538 n.31.

household, she knew not how to lose her temper or attack anyone.'[48] The many epitaphs of which these are representative do suggest something very different from the romantic passion of Propertius.[49]

But it is fair to remember certain things. One is that an epitaph may combine such conventional phraseology with touches of a different sort. 'Euphrosyne was well-born, charming, a pretty girl, cultured, wealthy, dutiful, chaste, modest, respectable' –

> *nobilis Euphrosyne facilis formosa puella*
> *docta opulenta pia casta pudica proba* –

but the stodgy couplet with its overstuffed list of virtues follows the line 'Here my wife has united her bones with mine',

> *ossibus hic uxor miscuit ossa meis* (*Carm. Epigr.* 1136)

– a verse which can stand without shame beside one of the greatest lines of Propertius:

> *nunc te possideant aliae: mox sola tenebo.*
> *mecum eris et mixtis ossibus ossa teram* (Prop. 4.7.93-4).

'Other women may possess you now, soon I shall have you to myself. You shall be with me and I shall grind my bones on yours.' Such a comparison allows a glimpse of the way Propertius has proceeded: he has taken an idea which recurs in real epitaphs, even to the mention of the bones, and raised its intensity. Several Roman epitaphs record the placing together of the bones of a loving couple: thus 'Philemon and Charis, whose bones rest here together', or 'Here lie the bones of my dear wife, waiting for me to bring mine to them'.[50] The ethos of such inscriptions is calm and

---

[48] *Pudica religiosa laboriosa frugi efficaxs vigilans sollicita univira unicuba, totius industriae et fidei matrona; cultu neglecto corporis moribus se ornabat suis; lanificii praeclara fides, pietatis alumna, priscae praecipue fama pudicitiae; in virum religiosa, in se pudica, in familia mater fuit, irasci numquam aut insilire quemquam noverat.* ILS 8444, CIL 8.646, CEL 1123. On the number of Latin verse inscriptions now known, and the difficulty of working with them, see G. Sanders in *L'Ant. Class.* 50 (1981) 707-20.

[49] We sometimes find terrible faults of taste. The well-known epitaph of Allia Potestas, CEL 1988 (bibliography: Lattimore 298, n.274) combines praise of her tireless housekeeping ('She was first up and last in bed ... she never was without her wool in her hands, unless there was a reason') with intimate details of her person ('What of her legs? Atalanta's figure would be comic beside hers ... she didn't allow a hair on her body ...'). The husband, whom Kroll called 'an Italian Candaules' (*Philol.* 73 (1914) 281), claims to wish for death, now she is gone. On a less grandiose scale, Apelles ends the epitaph for his wife by repeating a formulaic couplet which ends *et tenerae aetati ne gravis esse velis*, 'May her tombstone be light on her tender years'; but since apparently she was not young, he frankly writes *et mediae aetati ne gravis esse velis* – 'May the stone be light on her middle age'. A widower records that his wife was *sobria non moecha* (*CE* 548), another that his was 'free from the filthy weakness of women', *nescia delicti spurci quo femina peccet* (*CE* 552).

[50] CIL 6.24085 *quorum ossa quoque una quiescunt; CE* 1027 *his foribus carae recubant mihi coniugis ossa, /exspectantque suis ut mea contribuam.*

serene, and indeed the two people need not be sexual lovers at all.[51] The
same is true of the many epitaphs which declare that a dead spouse
awaits the coming of the survivor. So for instance 'Oppius, my husband,
do not grieve for me because I have gone before you. I await your coming
in a timeless bed', or 'This shall be our shared dwelling when the hour of
my death comes'.[52] Spouses drew comfort from the thought that their
union would continue beyond the grave. 'Julius lived happily with Trebia
for many years; here too he waits in eternal wedlock.'[53]

It is these familiar ideas and practices which Virgil develops into one of
his most powerful conceptions.[54] Dido stabs herself on a pyre she has
built for herself: her solitary act brings out her isolation by its contrast
with the normal. Anna reproaches her for her secrecy, and hopes to be in
time to catch her last breath. The lamentations which greet her act are
not like those of a proper funeral but like the shrieks that accompany the
sack of a city. Anna calls her name: not in the ritual farewell but in
passionate reproach at being cruelly deceived. And Dido's dying wish for
her faithless husband (*coniugium* 4.172, *coniunx* 4.324) is not that he
should show restraint in mourning her death, or that he should tend her
grave: a blasting curse is her last utterance. Above all, the idea of spouses
reunited gave Virgil the key to transform a fine Homeric scene into
something still greater, a supreme moment of the *Aeneid*.

Among the dead, Odysseus met the shade of Ajax, who had killed
himself after being defeated in the contest for the armour of Achilles.
Odysseus addresses him with winning words, but the unforgiving ghost
turns away in silence.[55] The episode is touching, but the *Odyssey* goes on
with the all too prosaic words 'yet he would have addressed me, or I him;
but my heart was eager to see the rest of the ghosts of the dead ...' These
lines were indeed rejected from the text by some scholars in antiquity,
but they remained in the accepted version. Virgil builds on the basis of
that Homeric hint the tremendous encounter of Aeneas with the spirit of
Dido, a scene which T.S. Eliot called 'the most civilised in European
literature'.[56] Her angry ghost recalls that of Ajax, but has far greater
power. The truant husband meets his dead wife, but there is no serene
and affectionate encounter of the kind the epitaphs speaks of. Her bitter
anger is unmollified by time, by death, by his impotent speech of
well-meaning: she turns away and flees from him through the dark wood,

[51] *CIL* 6.9290 Hilara asked for her bones to be put in the urn of her dead mistress Mida.
[52] *CIL* 6.11252 *domine Oppi marite, ne doleas mei quod praecessi: sustineo in aeterno toro adventum tuum; CE* 1982 *(sedes) quae communes erunt cum leti venerit hora; CE* 1559.
[53] *CE* 1325 *Iulius cum Trebia bene vixit multosque per annos: / coniugio aeterno hic quoque nunc remanet.* On the theme see R. Lattimore, *Themes in Greek and Latin Epitaphs* (1942) 247ff.
[54] Virgil *Aeneid* 4.663-93.
[55] Homer *Odyssey* 11.543-67.
[56] Virgil *Aeneid* 6.450-75; T.S. Eliot, *On Poetry and Poets* (1952).

pursued by his tearful gaze.

The whole passage can serve as a paradigm of Virgil's creative procedures. He has a basic framework from Homer. He adorns it with a striking piece of Hellenistic poetry, a simile from Apollonius. He had applied the image of a man seeing or thinking he sees the new moon to the Argonauts catching a distant glimpse of Heracles across the Libyan desert: Virgil finds a far better use for it, as Aeneas describes the form of the ghostly queen through the shades of the lower world. The encounter of the two (enriched by a splendid reminiscence of Catullus, and by a striking echo in reverse of the scene in *Aeneid* 4 where it was Dido who begged Aeneas to stay) ends with her turning away like the Homeric Ajax, but producing on Aeneas the profound effect which Ajax failed to produce on Odysseus.[57] Then, when it seems that the episode is over, Virgil adds a last twist of the knife: Dido is consoled in death by the love of Sychaeus, her first husband:

> *tandem corripuit sese atque inimica refugit*
> *in nemus umbriferum, coniunx ubi pristinus illi*
> *respondet curis aequatque Sychaeus amorem*   (*Aeneid* 6.472-4).

'At length she tore herself away and with looks of hate fled back into the shadowy wood, where her former husband Sychaeus answered her emotion and equalled her love.' The complexity of the construction of the scene is matched by its significance for the poem. Aeneas is brought face to face with what his coming has done to Dido, the knowledge which he tried to avoid as he fled from Carthage (5.4-5, 6.456): the destructive cost of imperial destiny, both for the vanquished and still more for the victor. Unable to undo the evil he did not intend, he is left weeping and alone. The victim is happier than he, finding in the grave what so many ordinary Romans hoped for, the true marriage which is denied, in life and beyond it, to Aeneas; for the ingénue Lavinia will not be to him what Penelope is to Odysseus, or what Sychaeus is to Dido. The characteristically Roman idea of the reunited couple is a vital element for Virgil in creating this symbolic scene. Earlier literature – Homer, Hellenistic poetry, Latin predecessors – is incomplete without the Roman reality.

Propertius too develops the motif in his great poem 4.7, with a new fullness. An angry and eloquent Cynthia awaits him, filled with grievances as she was in life (the end of 1.3 shows programmatically that their relationship was always to be like that). Their union will differ from

---

[57] *Aeneid* 6.453-4, Apollonius Rhodius 4.1477; *Aeneid* 6.460, Catullus 66.39 (the last word has not yet been said on this echo: cf. D.A. Russell in *Creative Imitation in Latin Literature*, edd. West and Woodman (1979) 13, R.O.A.M. Lyne in *CR* 23 (1973) 169 n.4, with further literature); *Aeneid* 6.466 *quem fugis?* with 4.314 *mene fugis?* *Aeneid* 6.469 with 4.331.

that of the model married couple in death, exactly as it differed in life.
Not a submissive wife who 'knew not how to lose her temper' but a
passionate virago; and matched not with a reliable Roman husband who
closes his dying wife's eyes[58] and is proud to adorn and tend her tomb,
but with a fickle creature who did not even go to her funeral, and who
now seems to have forgotten her in the arms of others. On real epitaphs
the dead often ask the survivor to visit and care for the grave,[59] and to
strew flowers on it:[60] these are the omitted duties, of which Propertius
allows her angry ghost to accuse him (4.7.33-4, 79-80), and which in
earlier days he had imagined her performing for him (3.16.22-3).

Conversely his poem on the death of Cornelia does not reverse the
formulae and attitudes of the epitaph but shares and exploits them,[61]
from the opening motif that excessive mourning by the survivor is wrong
and distresses the dead, to the final conclusion that she herself accepts
her death as the culmination of a fortunate and happy life (4.11.1ff.,
97ff.).[62]

> *et bene habet: numquam mater lugubria sumpsi:*
> *venit in exsequiis tota caterva meis.*

'I am content. As a mother I never had to put on mourning: all my family
came to my burial.' Real epitaphs say extremely similar things. 'The
gods granted her prayers: she saw her two children grow up, and she was
buried, as she particularly wished, by the hands of her husband.' 'My
prayer was granted. Many children survive me; as I wished, I was buried
by my husband.' The elevation and compression of the style is what
Propertius has added.

The Elysian Fields, where Cynthia talks with old lovers' ghosts, appear
constantly on tombstones as the imagined place of the dead, as the
reward of the virtuous;[63] they are painted on a tomb of Augustan date,
with trees and birds.[64] Here again, not only in 4.7 but in his other
moments of vision of the next life, Propertius has developed an idea
already present in many minds: the contribution of the poets is to extend
into that vaguely conceived place the passionate love interest of their
poetry.

Of course the claims of the epitaphs must not be pressed too far.
'Literary merit is rare enough in Latin epitaphs,' Lattimore reminds his

---

[58] Giving the last embrace, closing the eyes, receiving the last breath: e.g. *CE* 386, 1030,
452.

[59] *CE* 966 *ne grave sit tumulum visere saepe meum*; 1290 *assidue celebra.*

[60] *CE* 1036.9 *ut sint qui cineres nostros bene floribus sertis / saepe ornent* ... 476.5.

[61] 'Chiara è l'affinità della 4.11 con i carmi funerari', says P. Fedeli: *Properzio, Elegie
libro iv* ... a cura di P.F. (Bari 1965) 244.

[62] Cf. Lattimore, *Themes* 213ff.

[63] Twenty-five occurrences of *Elysium* and *Elysii campi* in the indices to
Bücheler-Lommatzsch, *Carmina Epigraphica.*

[64] Cf. B. Andreas, *Studien zur röm. Grabkunst* (1973) 63.

readers,[65] and all too many unmetrical or uncouth or banal inscriptions must be perused for one of real quality. 'Nowhere is there more genuine feeling, and nowhere worse taste, than in a churchyard': the sad dictum of Benjamin Jowett is true of the burial-grounds of Rome. Yet a last point is worth making about them, both for itself and in connection with the poets. A very large number deal with married couples: 'records of devotion between husband and wife are enormously frequent in Latin inscriptions', notably more so than in Greek ones,[66] and it can be added that many of them attempt to express strong feelings. 'I am tormented by love, but you have peace from care'; 'The water of Lethe cannot drown my grief, my sorrow endures fixed in my breast even by the River Styx'; 'Even now I see you – the love of a lover is not sated'; 'I cannot live without so good a wife'; such phrases could be multiplied. A wife has a statue made of her husband, 'so that she may glut her heart and eyes longer on his dear form'.[67] A husband rises to a single couplet of something like classic stature:

invide, quid gaudes? illa hic mihi mortua vivet:
illa meis oculis aurea semper erit   (CE 1928).

'Why exult, envious one? She will still be alive here to me though dead: to my eyes she will be golden for ever.' The striking epithet recalls the epitaph which Cynthia's ghost demands for herself:

hic Tiburtina iacet aurea Cynthia terra:
accessit ripae laus, Aniene, tuae   (Prop. 4.7.84-5).

'Here in the soil of Tibur lies golden Cynthia. Glory has come to your shore, River Anio.' We have only the chance survivors, mostly from a later period, of a harvest of inscriptional verse which must have been very great, and which surely contained many pieces of a standard above the average of the second and third centuries A.D. from which so many have reached modern times. Great poets, among them Callimachus, wrote epitaphs. Among the things they could have seen in real epitaphs – often underestimated – was the earnest attempt to express powerful love.

A short coda concludes this study of love and death. A connection between them which existed in Rome was the use for erotic purposes of tombs. Prostitutes of a low kind carried on their business in that gloomy environment: Juvenal and Martial both refer to the practice.[68]

---

[65] Lattimore 271.
[66] Lattimore 275-7.
[67] CE 1301, 1305, 424 *nunc quoque te video nec amor satiatur amantis*, 516 *nulla spes mihi vivendi sine coniuge tali*, 480 *oculos animumque / longius ut kara posset saturare figura.*
[68] Juvenal 6.365 0 16 *flava ruinosi lupa sepulchri*, and Courtney's note; Martial 1.34.8, 3.93.15. He refers to *bustuariae moechae*. A burial-ground was a good place for other low sorts of women; cf. Catullus 59.

Inscriptions on the walls of graves sometimes show that the seclusion of such spots was exploited by other sorts of lovers in search of privacy.[69] Petronius' celebrated story of the Widow of Ephesus, who shut herself in her husband's tomb to grieve and in the end made love there with a soldier, shows the motif promoted half-way to the dignity of literature proper. It would be inept to press this as a source for the intimate connection of love and death in the poets,[70] but the idea of making love in such a place must have been a haunting one.

---

[69] Cf. W. Crönert in *Rhein. Mus.* 64 (1909) 447f.
[70] Though it may underlie the occasional scene with a hint of necrophily, such as the discovery by robbers of the beautiful Callirrhoe alive in her grave (Chariton 1.8-9).

CHAPTER EIGHT

The Fourth *Georgic*, Virgil and Rome

So work the honey-bees,
Creatures that by a rule in nature teach
The act of order to a peopled kingdom – Shakespeare

'The last word has not yet been spoken on the relation of the second half to the first half, and to the *Georgics* as a whole,' said the sage Friedrich Klingner.[1] Never were more prophetic words penned. Many and various have been the interpretations put forth since then, and some of them have been very strange indeed. The reader who has duly confronted Coleman, Otis, Segal, Bradley, Wender, Wilkinson, Wankenne, Coleiro, Hardie, Joudoux, Wormell, Otis again, Parry, Putnam, Cova, Chomarat, Stehle, Crabbe, and Nadeau,[2] feels dismay; perhaps despair. For some, the point of the Aristaeus and Orpheus episodes is political propaganda (so Coleiro: Gallus could have survived had he humbled himself like Aristaeus, the moral being the duty of subordination to the Princeps; so rather differently, Joudoux: the poem is propaganda for the supremacy of Octavian, in terms of the threefold Indo-European structure of Dumézil). For others, it is moral (so, for instance, Wender: Orpheus turned away from the hard and morally ambiguous farmer's life, as lived by Aristaeus; Aristaeus gets bugonia as his reward, while Orpheus is dismembered and scattered in order to fertilize the earth); or religious (so Chomarat: the experience of Aristaeus is presented under the schema of initiation into a mystery religion);[3] or political and moral (so Wormell and Otis: Aristaeus 'stands for the sinful self-destruction, atonement and revival of the Roman people'; life emerges from death, 'in political terms, the

---

[1] F. Klingner, *Virgils Georgica* (Zürich 1963) 161 = *Virgil* (Zürich 1967) 298.

[2] R. Coleman, *AJP* 83 (1962) 55-71; Brooks Otis, *Virgil: A Study in Civilized Poetry* (1963); C. Segal, *AJP* 87 (1966) 307-25; A. Bradley, *Arion* 8 (1969) 347-58; D.S. Wender, *AJP* 90 (1969) 424-36; L.P. Wilkinson, *The Georgics of Virgil* (1969); A. Wankenne, S.J., *LEC* 38 (1970) 18-29; E. Coleiro in *Vergiliana*, ed. Bardon and Verdière (Leiden 1971) 113-23; Colin Hardie, *The Georgics: A Transitional Poem* (3rd Jackson Knight Memorial Lecture, 1971); R. Joudoux, *Bull. Ass. G. Budé* (1971) 67-82; D.E.W. Wormell in *Vergiliana* (1971) 429-35; Brooks Otis, *Phoenix* 26 (1972) 40-62; Adam Parry, *Arethusa* 5 (1972) 35-52; M.C.J. Putnam, ib. 53-70; P.V. Cova, *Bull. Stud. Lat.* 3 (1973) 281-303; J. Chomarat, *REL* 52 (1974), 185-207; E.M. Stehle, *TAPA* 104 (1974) 347-69; A.M. Crabbe, *CQ* 27 (1977) 342-51; Y. Nadeau in *Poetry and Politics in the Age of Augustus*, edd. Woodman and West (1984) 59-82.

[3] See already P. Scazzoso, *Paideia* 11 (1956) 25-8.

Augustan restoration from the anarchy of civil war'; 'Aristaeus, it is to be presumed [*sic*], was induced to heed the lesson').

Some find very general solutions indeed: perhaps Virgil 'posits existence as made up of this strange mixture of tragic and comic, human and divine, of death and birth ... serving as complements and inextricably intertwined' (Putnam); Castiglioni[4] and Klingner give accounts not dissimilar. For others, the answer is more specific, one might almost say more specifically modern. Thus for Bradley, 'the myth of Orpheus provides an alternative view of culture'; while Aristaeus stands for 'the work culture',[5] the control of Orpheus is exerted through play, not work, 'not productivity but creativity', and so the work culture inevitably destroys Orpheus because his existence is an intolerable affront to it; he is doomed 'at the hands of a repressive civilisation' – represented, rather to our surprise, by the Maenads of Thrace. Others have taken the episode as being primarily concerned with poetry. The eloquent paper of Adam Parry shows us Orpheus' grief for Eurydice becoming eternal song, and 'the song in turn becomes the condition for the recreation of life': the cruel and dark sides of nature, revealed in the rest of the *Georgics*, can be faced and comprehended only in song, in art. In a more specific way, Hardie sees the poem as about Virgil's own quest for the inspiration and poetic power to write epic. Having killed Orpheus within himself, Virgil as Aristaeus goes down to consult his own *anima*, makes the sacrifice of his excess of ambition, and regains the honey of poetic inspiration. Nor, finally, are those lacking who argue that the episode may be virtually, or entirely, unconnected with the rest of the *Georgics*,[6] added either as a lament for Gallus (Coleman), or simply following the fashion for epyllia (Richter). The last word of this whirlwind doxography[7] shall be the magisterial *non liquet* of Wilkinson:

> To sum up, I believe that Virgil would have thought an *aition* for 'Bugonia' a suitable ending for a book on bees, Aristaeus a suitable hero for this *aition*,

[4] L. Castiglioni, *Lezioni intorno alle Georgiche* (Milan 1947) 185.

[5] So for S.P. Bovie, *AJP* 77 (1956) 355, Aristaeus is 'a silhouette of the Roman practical man' – whose characteristic utterance, it seems, is in the plangent tones of 321ff.: '*mater, Cyrene mater ...*'

[6] This old view still has its supporters. W.Y. Sellar, *Virgil*[3] 251: 'It must be difficult for anyone who is penetrated by the prevailing sentiment of the *Georgics* to reach this point in the poem (sc. 4.315) without a strong feeling of regret that the jealousy of Augustus had interfered with its original conclusion.' R.S. Conway, *Proc. Class. Ass.* 25 (1928) 31: 'Yet no one who approaches the Fourth Book of the *Georgics* with an open mind, after reading the others, can possibly doubt that there must be some reason for the startling break in the middle of the Book.' Magdalena Schmidt, *Die Komposition von Vergils Georgica* (Paderborn 1930) 173-7 found the Aristaeus – epyllion a 'disturbing and tasteless intrusion'. Not many scholars now actually deplore the insertion of this uniquely beautiful piece of poetry; but Coleiro (see note 1) apologises for its feebleness with the argument that Virgil naturally found it distasteful to have to suppress his *laudes Galli* and replace them with an apologia for his disgrace and death.

[7] A fuller one: Cova 290ff.

and epyllion a suitable form for it. He would have looked for a contrasting story to insert in his epyllion. Why he chose Orpheus for this is more a matter of speculation, and also to what extent either the Orpheus passage or (more plausibly) the Aristaeus epyllion has a symbolic meaning for the interpretation of the *Georgics* as a whole.[8]

We have been warned: *parcite, oves, nimium procedere; non bene ripae / creditur*, 'Do not go too far, my flocks: the bank is not to be trusted' (Virgil, *Eclogue* 3.94). And yet the attempt is worth making. After all, this is one of the most beautiful things in ancient poetry, and here as strongly as anywhere in Virgil's work we must feel that more is meant than meets the ear. He will not lightly have put at the end of a long poem a strikingly melodious and pathetic conclusion, whose connection with what precedes, and whose position in his work as a whole, he has made merely mysterious. We are entitled to expect that the poet would not end his poem with so complex and unexpected an episode, and one whose interpretation has proved so difficult, if he had not had something complex to say; but also something to which he attached importance. *Itur*, therefore, *in antiquam silvam*.

Virgil treats his bees, in the fourth *Georgic*, as if they formed a sort of human society.[9] They have *domus, lar, sedes, statio, tectum; fores, limina, portae; aula, oppidum, patria, penates, sedes augusta, urbs.* They have divine reason and practise high-minded communism. Their patriotism is absolute. They will work themselves to death (204) or give their lives in battle (218). Their devotion to their ruler is incomparable (210). They are thrifty (156, 177), orderly (158), indefatigable (185); they all move and rest as one (184, *omnibus una quies operum, labor omnibus unus*. At 201 Virgil calls them Romans, *Quirites*, and scholars have pointed out that the characteristic Roman virtues of *labor* and *fortitudo* ('Those are Roman virtues *par excellence*', Dahlmann, p. 11), and also *concordia*, are their leading qualities.[10] There are clear resemblances with the praise of the Italian countryman and his virtuous life at the end of the second *Georgic* (work, justice, concord, and defence of home, children, and *penates*). All this is clear enough, but disagreement begins when we come to interpret these facts.

At one extreme, especially in Germany, some have felt confident that Virgil means his bees to represent an absolute model for human society. Dahlmann goes so far as to say that this separates Virgil from other

---

[8] Wilkinson 120.

[9] See Dahlmann 6 (but Klingner was right to reject Dahlmann's idea that the bees are expounded in the regular form of an ethnographical *ecphrasis*: *Virgil* 310 n.1); W.S. Maguinness, *Bull. Ass. G. Budé* (1962) 443; Servius in *G.* 4.219; *RE* s.v. *Biene*, 446.19ff. The general point is an obvious one, and I have not laboured it. *Haec ut hominum civitates, quod hic est et rex et imperium et societas*, Varro *RR* 3.16.5.

[10] See H. Oppermann, *Wege zu Vergil* (Darmstadt 1963) 123: 'In the society of the bees is reflected the Roman *res publica*.'

ancient writers: 'We are dealing with a framework which is simply and absolutely paradigmatic, which corresponds to the absolutely valid, rational, and right.'[11] Schadewaldt speaks of 'a charming model of a charmingly ordered natural ideal state'.[12] In English, Wormell implies a similar view, ending his account of the bees' nature by saying that 'this description constitutes a challenge to contemporary human standards and attitudes'.[13] Reservations of several sorts arise, if we try to imagine Virgil recommending to his contemporaries as an absolute model a society like this: impersonal, collective, Stakhanovite, without art. Did the author of the sixth *Eclogue* and the fourth *Aeneid* really think that is what the ideal society would be like – a place with no comprehension or sympathy for Corydon, for Nisus and Euryalus, for Virgil himself?[14]

Fortunately we are not left with no other counter-argument than this general one. Virgil deals with his bees in a tone which does not exclude irony. The epic battle of bees, (*ingentes animos angusto in pectore versalt*, 'Mighty passions rage in their tiny breasts'), ends with these two lines:

> *hi motus animorum atque haec certamina tanta*
> *pulveris exigui iactu compressa quiescent.*   (86-7)

'These mighty passions and these great battles will lie still, put down by casting a little dust.' With consummate skill, Virgil combines a grave humour (the warriors are after all only tiny insects), with a deep and poignant undertone: human battles, too, end with a handful of dust.[16] Such a phrase as that he uses of the aftermath – *melior vacua sine regnet in aula* (90) – has a similar irony, 'Let the better rule in a palace without a rival'; so has, for instance, 106,

> *nec magnus prohibere labor; tu regibus alas*
> *eripe ...*

'It is not hard to prevent them: pluck out the wings of the kings.' Nor can the choice of Cyclopes (170ff.) as a comparison for bees be without its

---

[11] 'Es handelt sich um ein Gefüge schlechthinniger, absoluter Vorbildlichkeit, das dem absolut Gültigen, Vernünftigen, Richtigen entspricht' (p. 13).

[12] '... Das zierliche Musterbild eines zierlich geordneten natürlichen Idealstaats', *Hellas und Hesperien*[2] (Zürich 1974) 716.

[13] In *Vergiliana*, 429.

[14] 'Aspiration towards a society of rules and of work under a beloved chief, that is Virgil's conclusion after ten years of toil,' J. Bayet, *RPh* 4 (1930) 247 = *Mélanges de littérature latine* (Rome 1967) 241.

[16] The technical writers know of this dust as only one of a number of ways of settling bees: Varro *RR* 3.16.30, Pliny *NH* 11.58. Virgil's phrasing is designedly pregnant; compare Lucan on the impromptu burial of Pompey, 8.867: pulveris exigui *sparget non longa vetustas / congeriem, bustumque cadet* ..., 'A short space of time will disperse that little pile of dust; the tomb will disappear ...'

humour.[16] One could labour the point; but it is clear that Virgil presents the bees and their community in a way which combines admiration (*ingentes animos*) with a cool sense of proportion (*angusto in pectore*). Adam Parry was right to pick out this complexity,[17] which surely rules out any straightforward paradigmatic purpose on Virgil's part. From another point of view, it seems to me incredible that the poet could have expected, or even hoped, that his audience (in 29 B.C.!) would accept as their own ideal future a society in which the king is treated with more than Oriental devotion:

> *praeterea regem non sic Aegyptus et ingens*
> *Lydia nec populi Parthorum aut Medus Hydaspes*
> *observant ...* (210-12)

'They honour their king yet more than the Egyptians, Lydians, Parthians, or Medes.' What, then, did he mean by his treatment of the bees? A clue is given by a remarkable omission. Bees and honey in antiquity were constantly associated with poetry and poets. The connection is indeed so familiar that I relegate to a footnote[18] an anthology of evidence, stressing merely that even Varro, a source of Virgil and by no means an excessively poetical writer, in his treatment of apiculture, says of the bees: 'Rightly are they called the winged creatures of the Muses' (*RR* 3.16.7). But Virgil does not make any such connection, and by choosing to suppress it he makes us realise that the society represented by the bees is one from which the arts are consciously excluded. Instead of singing, his bees make mere noise – *fit sonitus, mussantque oras et limina circum* (188), or in time of war they 'imitate the trumpet' (72).[19] Their honey is never brought by Virgil into connection with poetry or the Muses, although it is *aërii mellis caelestia dona*, 'the divine gift of aerial honey' (1), and although in the second half of the poem he will be dealing with the song of Orpheus, son of a Muse.

---

[16] Klingner, *Virgil* 314.

[17] *Arethusa* 5 (1972) 43. See also Otis, *Phoenix* 24 (1972) 58: 'The co-operative state is of course one aspect of reality – Roman and human as well as animal and natural reality – but it is not the whole.'

[18] *Musaeo melle*, Lucr. 4.22; *ego apis Matinae more modoque* ..., Hor. *Odes* 4.2.27; *poetica mella*, Hor. *Epp.* 1.19.44; Plato *Ion* 534b; *RE* s.v. *Biene*, 447.40; poets, orators and philosophers were brought into connection with bees; A.B. Cook, *JHS* 15 (1958) 7, and *Zeus* (1914) 443; Artemidorus *Oneir.* 5.83; Theocr. 1.146, and Gow ad loc.; H. Usener, *RM* 57 (1902) 177ff. = *Kleine Schriften* (Leipzig and Berlin 1912) 4.398ff., esp. 400f.

[19] Contrast the beautiful line, admired by G.K. Chesterton, in the description of bees in *King Henry V* 1.2:

> Others like soldiers, armed in their stings,
> Make boot upon the summer's velvet buds;
> Which pillage they with merry march bring home
> To the tent-royal of their emperor;
> Who, busied in his majesty, surveys
> *The singing masons building roofs of gold ...*

When is it permitted to argue from silence? This silence, it seems to me, is striking enough for us to feel that it has a significance. I venture on to speculative ground in trying to say what it signified. Virgil did not want to connect his bees, inspired though they are, with poetry or song. They exhibit many great virtues, but they are not poetical, and they are free from the bitter-sweet pains and pleasures of love (*Buc*. 3.110; *G*. 4.198ff.). In both they contrast clearly with Orpheus, the fabulous singer who dies for love (and who in this poem is never shown as doing any work or having any other function than song).[20] The virtues they exhibit are indeed the virtues of the old Roman people; but so are their deficiencies. Rome, great in *mores antiqui*, was not a home of the arts, in the view of the Augustans, until

Graecia capta ferum victorem cepit et artes
intulit agresti Latio,[21]

'Captive Greece led her rude conqueror captive and brought the arts to uncouth Latium.' At *Ars Poetica* 323ff., in a famous passage, Horace laments that the traditional Roman education unfitted the Roman for the arts. It is from this point of view that we must, I think, handle the problem. When Virgil was still at work on the *Georgics* he had already in mind the Roman epic which he hoped to be able to produce. The prologue to the third *Georgic* shows him grappling with it, and already keenly aware of the difficulties which such a poem would offer. At that time he apparently was thinking, or wished to give the impression that he was thinking, in terms of a poem on Octavian, with glances back to Troy – the reverse of the *Aeneid* (a poem on Aeneas with glances forward to Augustus).[22] Difficulties of style (was Octavian to be handled like a Homeric hero? What of the gods?), difficulties of material (Horace, *Odes* 2.1 warns Pollio of the risks involved in writing of recent history), the immense difficulty of making recent politics in any way poetic: all these, and others, must have been weighing on Virgil's mind. But not least of his problems, I think, was the nature of imperialism itself, and of Virgil's attitude to Rome.

It is not my intention to depict Virgil as 'anti-Augustan';[23] the term is a

---

[20] Those who, like Wankenne, *LEC* 38 (1970), 25f., talk of Aristaeus and Orpheus as 'two shepherds', are on the wrong track.

[21] This view is already implicit in Porcius Licinus, fr. 1 Morel, *Poenico bello secundo ...* Cf. now H. Funke, *RM* 120 (1977) 168.

[22] See E. Norden, *Kleine Schriften* 400ff., and e.g., U. Fleischer, *Hermes* 88 (1960) 327, Wilkinson 172.

[23] Some salubrious reservations on this word are expressed by G. Karl Galinsky, *Ovid's Metamorphoses* (1975) 210-17. Also W.M. Clarke in *CJ* 72 (1977) 322: 'One of the most amazing trends in recent literary criticism of ancient literature – the attempt to describe Vergil and Ovid as anti-Augustan, anti-establishment radicals, ideologically opposed to a proto-fascist dictator ... there is virtually no hard evidence to support it ...'

crudity. But justified revulsion against its excesses must not conceal the central fact about the *Aeneid*; that it is a poem of loss, defeat, and pathos, as much as it is of triumphant destiny.[24] Aeneas loses his country, his wife, Dido, Pallas; he must kill Lausus and meet among the dead the mistress who killed herself when he left her. To console him he has the vast impersonal gifts of destiny. But not only Aeneas must sacrifice all the wishes of his heart in the service of his fate; the imperial people, too, must pay a high price for its imperial calling. Nowhere does that emerge more poignantly than in the famous passage, *Aen.* 6.847-53:

> *excudent alii spirantia mollius aera*
> *(credo equidem), vivos ducent de marmore vultus,*
> *orabunt causas melius, caelique meatus*
> *describent radio et surgentia sidera dicent:*
> *tu regero imperio populos, Romane, memento*
> *(hae tibi erunt artes), pacique imponere morem,*[25]
> *parcere subiectis et debellare superbos.*

'Let others better mould the running mass
Of metals, and inform the breathing brass,
And soften into flesh a marble face;
Plead better at the bar; describe the skies,
And when the stars descend, and when they rise.
But Rome! 'tis thine alone with awful sway
To rule mankind and make the world obey:
To tame the proud, the fettered slave to free,
These are imperial arts, and worthy thee.' (trans. Dryden)

This unrivalled speech is at once a boast and a lament, a proud claim by a conqueror and a sigh of regret for the cost. Virgil, poet, philosopher, and aesthete, in the middle of his great poem, in which the Latin language and the Roman destiny alike were carried to a beauty which must have seemed impossible, yet must surrender to the Greeks (*alii* – he cannot bring himself to name them) the arts and the sciences. The traditional claim of the Roman patriot, that native morals outshone Greek accomplishments (*ut virtutis a nostris sic doctrinae ab illis* ‹sc. *Graecis*› *exempla petenda sunt*, Cic. *de Or.* 3.137 'Examples of good practice are to be drawn from us: of good theory from the Greeks'), is given a pregnancy and a pathos which transform it. *Hae tibi erunt artes:* these

---

[24] See the masterly article by Wendell Clausen, *HSCP* 68 (1964) 139-47, reprinted in *Virgil: A Collection of Critical Essays,* ed. S. Commager (1966). Suggestive but more vulnerable is Adam Parry's 'The two voices of Virgil's Aeneid', reprinted in the same volume from *Arion* 2 (1963); see also, in the same book, R.A. Brooks, *Discolor aura,* from *AJP* 74 (1953) 260-80.

[25] The discussion of the passage by Otis, 313ff., is flawed by his adoption of the bad reading *pacisque,* 'the habit of peace'. See Eduard Fraenkel, *Mus. Helv.* 19 (1962) 133 = *Kleine Beiträge* (Rome 1964) 2.143.

are your arts, man of Rome – not the seductive beauties of Greece, which meant so much to Virgil as a man, and without which his poems could not have come into existence, but the hard and self-denying 'arts' of conquest and dominion. It is the price of empire that the Roman must abandon for this imperial destiny, splendid and yet bitter, so many forms of beauty.

Virgil embodies this cruel cost again in an episode of his own invention, much criticized in antiquity, from Probus onwards:[26] the shooting of the stag of Silvia in the seventh book. The beautiful tame creature (*forma praestanti*, 483) is shot by Ascanius, without malicious intention on his part. 'Ascanius does not mean any harm: he yields to a young man's keenness to excel in sport, *eximiae laudis succensus amore* and thus, by wounding poor Silvia's pet, becomes a tool in the hands of Allecto.'[27] The Italian rustics flock up with improvised weapons, 506:

improvisi adsunt, hic torre armatus obusto,
stipitis hic gravidi nodis; quod cuique repertum
rimanti telum ira facit.

'Hastily they come up, one armed with a fire-sharpened stick, one with a heavy knotted club – anger makes a weapon of what each one finds.' Then the Trojans come rushing from their stronghold (521), and the fighting becomes a regular battle in full armour (523ff.).

Such a beginning to the great war, the *maius opus* of the second half of the *Aeneid*, has not unnaturally distressed or perplexed some scholarly readers.[28] As a *casus belli*, says Macrobius, all this is 'slight and all too childish'. Why did Virgil put such an unexpected scene in so important a position? R. Heinze suggested that he was concerned to make the responsibility of the Trojans for the war as venial and as slight as

---

[26] Macrob. *Sat.* 5.17.1-2: 'How much Virgil owed to Homer is very clear from the fact that when he is obliged to describe the way a war began, which Homer did not include ... he found the gestation of this new subject difficult. He has made the chance wounding of a deer the cause of the fighting; but seeing that this was light-weight and all too childish, he worked up the indignation of the country people ...' Probus as the likely source: Norden, *Ennius und Vergilius* (Leipzig and Belin 1915) 4ff. With Macrobius' *cervum fortuito saucium*, compare J.D. Denniston and D. Page, *Aeschylus, Agamemnon* (1957) xxv on the portent at Aulis: 'The poet tells us in plain language [sic] that Artemis was enraged *because eagles, sent by Zeus to be an encouraging portent, happened* [sic] *to devour a hare together with its unborn young* ...'. The ways of poets do not change. Nor do those of commentators ...

[27] Fraenkel, *JRS* 35 (1945) = *Kleine Beiträge* 2.153.

[28] Klingner, *Virgil* 511. Heyne was gravely dissatisfied with Virgil here, (*Nolo defendere poetam*), as were many earlier scholars. Conington gives a strikingly tepid defence: 'Some have objected to the incident of the stag as too trivial, as if there were anything unnatural in a small spark causing a large train to explode, or as if the contrast itself were not an element of greatness.' The first point – a mere naturalistic defence of plausibility – is flat; the second, I confess, I can make nothing of.

possible; a mere accident while hunting.[29] Klingner drew the distressingly flat moral[30] that 'if one looks more closely, it is not the death of the tame stag which creates the danger, but the presence of a population of shepherds, half civilized and easily aroused by a triviality' – almost as if he were making an official report to King Latinus on a regrettable incident in a country district. Wimmel sees here a device for making the war 'pastoral' and 'unheroic', one of Virgil's many 'anti-epic procedures'.[31] None of these suggestions seems to do justice to the emotional weight and force of the passage. The stag is tame and beautiful: shot by the incomers, it flees home to its loving mistress, like a human creature:

> *successitque gemens stabulis, questuque cruentus*
> *atque imploranti similis tectum omne replebat*   (7.501-2).

'Moaning it returned home, bleeding and plaintive; it filled the house with cries that seemed to beg for help.' One surely need invoke no hypothetical lost poem to explain the grief it causes. It remains true that Ascanius did not know what he was doing; he meant no harm – but the harm is done. Aeneas has no wish to fight the Italians, and he does all he can to avoid war, but he must fight and kill his future allies. He tries hard to avoid killing Lausus (10.809ff.), but he must kill him. He does not even want to kill Turnus (12.938) … Above all, he had no desire to cause the death of Dido, and yet she, who would have been 'all too happy, if only the Trojan ships had never touched my shores' (4.657), who was so splendid, attractive, and noble when they arrived, is driven to disgrace and suicide when the destiny of Aeneas takes him to Carthage. And Dido, in the first frenzy of her love, is compared to a deer, shot by a shepherd, who does not even know that he has hit her:

> *uritur infelix Dido totaque vagatur*
> *urbe furens, qualis coniecta cerva sagitta,*
> *quam procul incautam nemora inter Cresia fixit*
> *pastor agens telis liquitque volatile ferrum*
> *nescius: illa fuga silvas saltusque peragrat*
> *Dictaeos; haeret lateri letalis harundo*   (4.68-73).

'Poor Dido burns and roams in madness through the town, like a doe shot

---

Virgils epische Technik[3] (Leipzig 1914) 190. Heinze was sufficiently in the grip of the hostile tradition about the episode to say that Silvia's distress over the death of her stag can only be understood in the light of an hypothetical Hellenistic poem about Cuparissus – surely a severe criticism of Virgil. But his main point, that nobody is to blame, is, of course, an important one.
[30] *Virgil* 513.
[31] W. Wimmel, *Hirtenkrieg und arkadisches Rom* (Munich 1973) 48 and 118ff.: 'a bucolic outbreak of war'.

with an arrow, whom from afar a herdsman has shot and left the steel in her side, unawares. The doe flees through the woods, the deadly dart sticking in her side.' The recurrence of the image deserves more attention than it receives.[32] The climax of the three stages in which Juno and Allecto stir up the war is given a form that recalls the suffering of Dido; she too was beautiful, destroyed by the Trojans not by their will (*liquitque volatile ferrum nescius – invitus, regina, tuo de litore cessi*, 'He left the steel in her side, unawares' – 'It was against my will, o queen, that I left your country'). Like the archer in the simile, Aeneas does not know what he has done: *nec credere quivi / hunc tantum tibi me discessu ferre dolorem*, 'I could not believe my going would cause you such distress' (6.463). But that is the effect of the Trojan destiny; to cause suffering without willing it, to cause the destruction of so many beautiful things, from Silvia's stag to the singer Cretheus, slain by Turnus:

> ... *et Clytium Aeoliden et amicum Crethea Musis,*
> *Crethea Musarum comitem, cui carmina semper*
> *et citharae cordi numerosque intendere nervis,*
> *semper equos atque arma virum pugnasque canebat*   (9.774-7).

'And Clytius he slew, and Cretheus dear to the Muses, Cretheus the Muses' friend, who loved to sing and play the lyre ...' the singer Cretheus, to whom Virgil gives so moving a farewell. And with the poet go the lovers – Dido, and Nisus and Euryalus, and Cydon, lover of boys:

> *tu quoque, flaventem prima lanugine malas*
> *dum sequeris Clytium infelix, nova gaudia, Cydon,*
> *Dardania stratus dextra, securus amorum*
> *qui iuvenum tibi semper erant ...* (10.324-7).

'You too, luckless Cydon, as you followed Clytius, your latest darling, whose cheeks were golden with his first down, you were laid low: you forgot your constant love for boys ...' At the end of the *Aeneid* Aeneas is left only a bride he has never met.

In the *Aeneid* Virgil has succeeded in devising ways of bringing out this complex of ideas, central to his vision of Rome and of history: of Roman destiny as an austere and self-denying one, restraining *furor* and *superbia*, and imposing peace and civilisation on the world; at the cost of turning away, with tears but with unshakable resolution, from the life of pleasure, of art, and of love. *Mens immota manet, lacrimae volvuntur inanes*, 'The will is fixed; in vain the idle tears.' In the *Georgics* he was

---

[32] 'Some personal experience must lie behind both this passage and 7.483ff.' is Austin's not very helpful comment. Viktor Pöschl surprisingly does not mention the stag of Silvia in his treatment of 4.68ff. (*Die Dichtkunst Virgils* (Wiesbaden 1950) 131ff. = *The Art of Vergil* (1962) 80ff.). The discussion in H. Raabe, *Plurima Mortis Imago*, Zetemata 59 (Munich 1974) 56, ignores this question.

already confronting the same problem,[33] and not finding it easy.[34] The bees presented him with a powerful image for the traditional Roman state, in its impersonal and collective character. To avoid cluttering the argument, and to enable those who need no evidence for this description of Roman society to proceed more lightly, I have put some support for it into an Appendix to this chapter.

No wider contrast can be imagined than that between the exquisite and sensuous beauty of the evocation of Pasiphae in the sixth *Eclogue*, or the self-indulgent and lyrical passion of Gallus in the tenth, or the love-lorn singer Orpheus, living and dying entirely for art and love, and, on the other side, the old Roman, *non sibi sed patriae natus*, 'Born not for himself but for his country', whose subordination of his own emotions to the state goes so far that for patriotic reasons he will put his own sons to death.[35] Virgil does show us how, in his own style and ethos, he can deal with this traditional Roman figure; Anchises points out to Aeneas the unborn shade of L. Brutus, first consul, who killed his sons for conspiring with the Tarquins:

> *vis et Tarquinios reges animamque superbam*
> *ultoris Bruti, fascisque videre receptos?*
> *consulis imperium hic primus saevasque securis*
> *accipiet, natosque pater nova bella moventis*
> *ad poenam pulchra pro libertate vocabit,*
> *infelix, utcumque ferent ea facta minores:*
> *vincet amor patriae laudumque immensa cupido* (6.817-23).

'Would you see the Tarquin kings and the proud soul of Brutus the avenger, with the fasces he restored? He shall be the first to hold the office of consul and the cruel axes: he shall summon his own sons to execution, to defend liberty against their treason. Unhappy man! however posterity will judge his deed; love of country will prevail, and boundless desire for glory.' I cannot do better than repeat the judgment of Eduard Norden (ad v. 822): 'The lines are a noble monument for the poet who succeeded in combining without disharmony his tender sensibility with his admiration for the rigid grandeur of the old *fortia*

---

[33] It is a commonplace of Virgilian criticism to say that he was working his way towards the solutions eventually found in his epic. See, e.g., Dahlmann 13, Hardie 27ff., Segal 321: 'In the Fourth *Georgic* Virgil is already dealing with some of the issues of the Aeneid.' The end of Segal's article (I am unable to agree with most of it) seems to me to be nearer the truth than most recent work which I have read.

[34] The well-known problem of the apparently contradictory attitudes expressed at the end of the second *Georgic* towards the greatness of Rome and rustic life (contrast the philosophical *ataraxia* of 490-9 with the patriotism of 535-5), is surely connected with this uncertainty. See most recently J.S. Clay, *Philologus* 120 (1976) 232ff.

[35] Polybius was impressed by this extremely Roman habit, 6.65.5: he accepts this as part of the 'zeal for the constitution' of the Roman citizen; no hint of moral ambiguity.

facta.'[36] In such passages of his epic Virgil has succeeded in bringing together two attitudes and doing full justice to them both. The axes of Republican authority are cruel, and Brutus must be an unhappy man; and yet political liberty is a thing of beauty, and his motive was glorious. Unhappy, he is also proud, with all the moral complexity of that word and that quality, and of the very ambiguous 'boundless desire for glory'. Anchises, legendary founder, both extols and grieves for the work of his people. His history of Rome begins as a glorification (756). It ends with the pathetic lament for Marcellus: *o nate, ingentem luctum ne quaere tuorum ... heu miserande puer ...* 'My son, ask not the dread sorrow of your people ... Alas, unhappy boy ...' Not only in detail but also as a whole, the utterance of Anchises juxtaposes the two aspects and leaves them unresolved. In the *Georgics* Virgil has not yet mastered this tremendous technique of compression. The bees and Orpheus do not approach each other in so small a compass, and Virgil indulges himself with a long episode in the plangent and exquisite style which he has learned and improved from Catullus and the Neoterics. It is a style which in most of his writing he denied himself.

The bees, then, with their collective virtues and their lack of individuality and art, serve as a counterpart to the old Roman character. Their patriotism and self-denial (and devotion to their 'king' is only devotion to the state and to authority, not an encouragement to emperor-worship) are admirable. If Rome had only retained more of such qualities, then the tragedies and disasters of the Civil Wars, and of the end of the first *Georgic*, would never have occurred. Hence a real, not a feigned or insincere, admiration and nostalgia for them – and for their human form, the old Italian way of life:

> *hanc olim veteres vitam coluere Sabini,*
> *hanc Remus et frater.* (*Georg.* 2.532-3)

'This was the life lived by the Sabines of old, this was the life of Romulus and Remus.' In the *Aeneid* this strand of thought and feeling will be fully represented: the austere life of Euander (especially 8.364f.), the speech of Numanus Remulus (9.598ff.), the tempering of Trojan luxury with Italian toughness (*sit Romana potens Itala virtute propago*, 12.827).[37]

---

[36] 'So verstanden sind die Verse ein schönes Monument für den Dichter, der sein weiches Empfinden mit der Bewunderung für die starre Grossartigkeit der alten "fortia facta" harmonisch zu vereinigen wusste.'

[37] In the *Aeneid*, bees appear as the subject-matter of two similes. At 1.430-6 Aeneas sees the Carthaginians hard at work on the construction of their new city, like bees busy with the care of their home and their young – a poignant contrast with the homeless Trojans and their enforced idleness. At 6.707-9 he sees the unborn souls of all nations, 'like bees in a flowery meadow on a fine summer day, busy with their pursuits and humming cheerfully' (Austin ad loc.); he marvels that they can wish to be born into the human world of pain – *quae lucis miseris tam dira cupido?* In both passages Virgil finds it natural to compare bees with men, and his picture of them as industrious, and also as oblivious of the sorrows of human life, certainly does not conflict with my interpretation of them in the fourth *Georgic*.

But as the *Aeneid* does justice also to the sacrifice demanded of the Imperial people, so too in the *Georgics* we see the human incompleteness of such a collective state.

In the first *Georgic* Virgil depicted with passion the disasters which lack of order has brought on the word: *fas versum atque nefas, tot bella per orbem, / tam multae scelerum facies.* Only Caesar can rescue a world turned upside down, and Virgil prays desperately for his success. The reconstruction longed for in the first *Georgic* is, we may feel, under way by the fourth; order is being restored, and the poet becomes aware of the cost – a society efficient and admirable, but impersonal and dispassionate.

The deficiency hinted at in the actual account of the bees emerges with great emotional force when they are juxtaposed with Orpheus and Eurydice. The bee-master Aristaeus has inadvertently caused the death of the beautiful Eurydice – we are reminded of the archer in the simile in *Aeneid* 4, and of Ascanius in *Aeneid* 7. Like Aeneas, he does not even know what he has done. Like Aeneas, too, he has a divine mother who helps and advises; like him, he is a founder. He has bequeathed us an art (*artem, G.* 4.315), but the practical one of regaining lost *parvos Quirites*, not the art of song.[38] It is, in fact, an *ars* like that promised to the Roman by Anchises – *hae tibi erunt artes.* And it is a harsh one, whose cruel side is not glossed over: *huic geminae nares et spiritus oris / multa reluctanti obstruitur* (300f.): *sacrum iugulis demitte cruorem* (542) 'Block up the nose and mouth of the ox, for all its struggles', and 'Let the consecrated blood flow from the throat.'

The bees, patriotic, rational, and impersonal, are brought back from death by the device of bugonia. In the fullest sense, *genus immortale manet (G.* 4.208):

> ... *multosque per annos*
> *stat fortuna domus, et avi numerantur avorum.*

'The race survives eternal, the house stands through long years, and generation follows generation.' So too will Rome stand for ever: *his ego nec metas rerum nec tempora pono*, says Jupiter (*Aen.* 1.278). As Rome is upheld by his will, the bees too derive their nature from him (*G.* 4.149). But what of the singer and his love? And how is the poem as a whole to be understood?[39]

The sweet singer Orpheus, robbed of his love through Aristaeus' fault, is shown in poignant endless lamentation. The emotional style and the

---

[38] Cf. V. Buchheit, *Vergil über die Sendung Roms* (Heidelberg 1963) 151ff., G.K. Galinsky, *Aeneas, Sicily and Rome* (1969) 98 n.4.

[39] Adam Parry was therefore misleading to say that 'the song becomes the condition for the recreation of life' (p. 52). Not Orpheus but Aristaeus recreates the bees; song does not set free the half-regained Eurydice. This central fact seems to me to rule out his interpretation of the poem, seductive and powerful as it is.

verbal beauty of Proteus' account of his suffering and song make it a unity, and it is here that the emotional emphasis surely falls, not on the episode of Aristaeus:

te, dulcis coniunx, te solo in litore secum,
te veniente die, te decedente canebat ...

'On thee, dear wife, in deserts all alone
He called, sighed, sung: his griefs with day begun,
Nor were they finished with the setting sun' (trans. Dryden).

The narrative is given a 'neoteric' structure; the scene in which the gods of the dead give back Eurydice and impose the prohibition on looking at her is compressed to nothing (487, a mere parenthesis – *namque hanc dederat Proserpina legem*, 'for Proserpina had given this command-ment'), as in the *Ciris* the decisive actions of the wicked heroine, her crime, her appeal to Minos, and her rejection, are compressed into five lines (386-90). But what was a mannerism in such a poem, or even in Catullus 64, is here put to emotional use: after Orpheus' long lament (464ff.) and the pathetic description of the dead (471ff.), no explicit passage of hope and optimism is allowed to break the mood; already at 488, *subita incautum dementia cepit amantem*, 'sudden madness seized the careless lover'. The whole is plangent, mellifluous, pathetic.[40] No work of art, no human love, can prevail over the power of death; Eurydice is gone for ever, and Orpheus, still singing, has been sent by the cruel maenads to join her.

The account of the first bugonia, 528-58, forms in style a remarkable contrast. A dry and matter-of-fact tone succeeds to the languorous beauty of Orpheus and Eurydice, emphasised by the exact repetitions of lines (538, 540, 544, with 550-62, as if to say: This is what he was told to do, and this is what he did). The bees are reborn. Some readers are content to regard this as a happy ending: 'Catastrophe reigns over the conclusion of the Third Book, confident elevation is restored at the end of the Fourth';[41] 'Books 1 and 3 are gloomy or pessimistic; 2 and 4 are cheerful and optimistic.'[42] For my part I cannot feel that the restoration of bees outweighs the suffering and death of Orpheus and Eurydice, especially in view of the way Virgil has handled the story. An exquisite ambivalence surely prevails. Life goes on, and the virtuous bees will for ever practise their virtuous collectivity; but the artist and his love must die, leaving nothing but the song. For love and art go hand in hand with *furor* and *dementia*, with subordinating reason and interest to emotion. We think of Corydon, who accuses himself of *dementia*, and neglects his

[40] Cf. Norden, *Kleine Schriften* 509.
[41] S.P. Bovie, *AJP* 77 (1956) 347.
[42] Otis, *Phoenix* 26 (1972) 45.

work to sing (*Buc.* 2.69-72), of the erotic myths of which Silenus sang all day (*Buc.* 6), of the ingenuous Meliboeus, who neglects his work to listen to singing, and confesses, *posthabui tamen illorum mea seria ludo* (*Buc.* 7.17), 'I put their play ahead of my serious work', of the suicidal passion of Nysa's lover (*Buc.* 8), of Gallus abandoning himself to love and song and idleness (*Buc.* 10), of the ravages of passion in the third *Georgic*. And yet the song outlasts the singer: still in death Orpheus' voice proclaims his love, and his song fills the air –

> *Eurydicen toto referebant flumine ripae.*

' "Eurydice!" resounded all along the shore.'

It would be an optimistic writer who should hope for universal assent, at this time of day, to an unprovable account of the fourth *Georgic*. The theory here proposed, that this poem bears upon Rome and poetry, upon imperialism and individual sensibility, perhaps finds some support in the poem's very last words:

> *haec super arvorum cultu pecorumque canebam*
> *et super arboribus, Caesar dum magnus ad altum*
> *fulminat Euphraten bello victorque volentis*
> *per populos dat iura viamque adfectat Olympo.*
> *illo Vergilium me tempore dulcis alebat*
> *Parthenope studiis florentem ignobilis oti,*
> *carmina qui lusi pastorum audaxque iuventa,*
> *Tityre, te patulae cecini sub tegmine fagi*   (559-66).

'This ends my song on the care of fields and crops and trees, composed as mighty Caesar thunders on the Euphrates in war, gives law in triumph to willing peoples, and forges a path to godhead. Meanwhile I Virgil have been living in sweet Parthenope, flourishing in the pursuits of ignoble ease: I who played with the shepherds' songs and in my presumptious youth sang of Tityrus lying under the spreading beech.' These eight lines divide naturally into two juxtaposed halves; while Caesar is thundering on the Euphrates, civilising a welcoming world, and winning immortality, Virgil for his part, the frivolous (*lusi*) author of the *Eclogues*, has been writing the *Georgics* at Naples, flourishing in the studies of inglorious ease. The urbanity of this exquisite signature, a Virgilian combination of pride and humility, is easily missed.[43] The *Eclogues* were not serious and the *Georgics* are not glorious, he says; he has been taking it easy in a cultured resort with a Greek name. Caesar, on the other hand, has been working wonders ... And yet of course we remember that the poem is 'your hard command, Maecenas', and that *in tenui labor, at tenuis non gloria*, 'the theme is humble but not so the

---

[43] I think it is much underestimated by V. Buchheit, *Der Anspruch des Dichters* (Darmstadt 1972).

glory'. These two memorable lines alone, casting as they do so ironical a light on *otium* and *ignobile*, suffice to indicate the complexity of the tone. By good old Roman standards, Caesar's actions are glorious, Virgil's are not; Virgil bows gravely to those standards. But the shape of the period puts the poet, not the ruler, in the climactic position, and Virgil overshadows Octavian. Here too Virgil is concerned with the relationship of poetry and the traditional Roman values, as, on the view here put forward, he has been all through the poem. Is poetry less glorious than imperialism? In the *sphragis* to the *Georgics* Virgil has found a way of agreeing that it is, which at the same time, with equal force, implies that it is not. To generalise that *tour de force* through a whole epic – an impossible task! And yet the story of the bees and of Orpheus showed, perhaps, a way in which it might be done.

In this poem, then, the poet is saying something which will be said on a greater scale and with greater mastery in the *Aeneid*. Here the link between the suffering of Orpheus and Eurydice, and the rebirth of the civically virtuous bees, is not as convincing as Virgil makes the link between the triumph of Roman *fata* and the suffering of Dido, of Pallas, and of Aeneas himself. In the *Aeneid* the establishment of empire, which will be the justification and the lasting meaning of history, inevitably involves defeat and sacrifice. In the *Georgic* the role of Aristaeus has something of the arbitrariness of purely Hellenistic mythological combination, the same man appearing both as inventor of an art, and as seducer, a combination by no means inevitable. In the same way, the balance which Virgil keeps so beautifully in his epic is here less certain; the separate elements have not been fused as completely as they might have been, and the pathos of Orpheus is in grave danger of running away completely from the rest. The 'neoteric' use of mythology reminds us of links like those in Callimachus' *Hecale*, or in Catullus 64; the fullness of passionate lamentation and pathos recalls Catullus' Ariadne or Attis, or the Zmyrna of Cinna. In the *Aeneid* Virgil has out-grown and mastered for his own style these youthful models; the fourth *Georgic*, in addition to its own beauties, shows us a vital stage in that development.

Appendix 1: Rome as a collective state

The *locus classicus* on the collective nature of early Rome is the sixth book of Polybius, who at 2.41.9 contrasts the concord of Romans with the 'quarrelsome and ill-conditioned' politics of Greeks. The refusal of Cato to name individual Roman generals in the last four books of his *Origines*, because he regarded their achievements as *populi Romani gesta* (fr. 1 Peter), appeals to the same sentiment; cf. D. Kienast, *Cato der Zensor* (Heidelberg 1954) 109f. Cicero cites him (*de Rep.* 2.2.3) as saying that the Roman constitution was better than any Greek one because it was not

the work of a single legislator but created *multorum ingenio*, by many minds.
   Concordia is the positive name for this quality: see E. Skard, *Concordia* in *Römische Wertbegriffe* (Wege der Forschung 34, 1967, ed. H. Oppermann) 177ff. In the old days there was *concordia maxima* among Romans, says Sallust, *Bell. Cat* 9; his meaning is illuminated by *Bell. Cat.* 52.23, the opposite: 'When each of you takes thought individually for himself ...'

Ancient Roman society may perhaps fitly be compared to life in one of the monastic orders in the middle ages. Both systems display the same methodical combination of example and precept, of mutual vigilance and unremitting discipline. Both show us a community in which the individual is entirely at the mercy of the feelings and opinions of his fellows, and where it is impossible for him to become emancipated from the tyranny of the group. (G. Ferrero, *The Greatness and Decline of Rome* (1907) 1.5).

As far back as we can trace the beginnings of Roman life into the darkness of the remote past, we find the citizen no individualist. He is already living in a well organised community, in which the exercise of personal rights is rigorously subordinated to public opinion and to public jurisdiction ... (E.T. Merrill, *CP 2* (1907) 374)

[In early Rome] an unusually high level of uniformity in thought and action is taken for granted – in direct contrast with, say, Athens ... (R. Heinze, *Von den Ursachen der Grösse Roms* (Leipzig, 1921), 9 = *Vom Geist des Römertums*[3] 12)

Rome was never to emancipate herself entirely from the collective ideal whereby the individual is completely in the hands of the state ... The fundamental idea of the old Roman education was respect for the old customs – *mos maiorum*; the principal task of the teacher was to explain them to the young, and to get them respected as an idea beyond discussion, as the standard to judge every action and thought ... (H.I. Marrou, *Histoire de l' éducation dans l' antiquité*[6] (Paris, 1965) pp. 229, 342)

Until the third century no one even had a memorial tombstone. Cumulative pride in the family and in the community were the rewards of life. And even down to the beginning of the second century the Romans are of interest to us for what they were collectively, indeed for the degree to which they succeeded in repressing individuality. (L.P. Wilkinson, *The Roman Experience* (1975) 26)

C. Nicolet, *Le Métier de citoyen dans la Rome républicaine* (Paris 1976) 521, summarises Polybius 6:

Rome is altogether saturated in a discipline which is collective but also freely accepted, which strongly reinforces social cohesion. This discipline is not merely repressive; it has a happy combination of encouragement and prevention, rewards and punishments. Hence the normal patriotism of the Romans.

Cf. also pp. 27 (on *consensus*), 514-16.

The expression *non sibi sed patriae natus*, which of course has just this meaning, is a favourite one of Cicero's (*pro Murena* 83, *pro Sestio* 138, *Philipp.* 14.32, *de Fin.* 2.45).

I have not found anything on Rome as penetrating as the essay by Hermann Strasburger, 'Der Einzelne und die Gemeinschaft im Denken der Griechen', *HZ* 177 (1954) 227-48. By contrast, it sheds much light on Rome.

Appendix 2: *The alleged change to the end of the fourth* Georgic

One of the most celebrated statements of Servius (in *Buc* 10.1, and in *G.* 4.1) is to the effect that originally the fourth Book of the *Georgics*, 'from the middle right down to the end', contained the praises of Cornelius Gallus, 'which afterwards at the bidding of Augustus he changed to the story of Aristaeus'. Wilkinson deals judiciously with the story in his excellent book on the *Georgics*, pp. 108ff., concluding, with Norden[44] and W.B. Anderson,[45] that it is untrue, deriving originally perhaps from a confusion between 'the end of the *Bucolics*' and 'the end of the *Georgics*'.

I am sure that this verdict is correct, and my purpose is to add another argument to those pressed by others, of artistic coherence[46] and of personal tact (how would Octavian have enjoyed a long recital in praise of a subordinate?).[47] Chronological grounds, it seems to me, rule out the story. Virgil at the end of the fourth *Georgic* says he wrote the poem 'while mighty Caesar was thundering on the Euphrates' (560), which doubtless means before Octavian's return to Rome from the East in August 29 B.C. In a circumstantial story which there is no reason to doubt,[48] coming to us from Suetonius through Donatus, we are told that 'when Augustus was on his way home after his victory at Actium and was staying at Atella to get over a relaxed throat, Virgil read the *Georgics* to him for four days on end, Maecenas taking over whenever his voice failed and he had to stop'. Now, Gallus came to grief in Egypt and felt himself driven to suicide either in 27 B.C. (Jerome) or 26 B.C. (Dio).[49] For at least two years, then, a version of the *Georgics* must have been in circulation containing a different ending, which was then replaced 'at the bidding of Augustus'; and replaced so effectively that not a word of it was preserved.

[44] Norden in *SB Berlin* (1934) = *Kleine Schriften*, 468-532.

[45] *CQ* 27 (1933) 36-45.

[46] Otis, *Virgil: A Study in Civilized Poetry* 408ff.

[47] 'The over-riding objection', according to Anderson and Wilkinson. The story of Orpheus 'undoubtedly' replaces a panegyric of Gallus, according to J. Gagé in *ANRW* 30.1 (1982) 612.

[48] Wilkinson 69.

[49] R. Syme, *The Roman Revolution* (1939) 309 n.2.

Now this sequence of events is, surely, inconceivable. Rome in the early twenties was not like Stalin's Russia, with an efficient and ubiquitous police which could have enforced such a decree throughout the private houses of readers of poetry, even if Augustus had wanted to do so. Even under the grimmer and more frankly autocratic rule of his successors, attempts to suppress books were a failure. We need only recall Tacitus' comment on the affair of Cremutius Cordus, under Tiberius (*Annals* 4.35):

> His books, so the Senate decreed, were to be burnt by the aediles; but they remained in existence, concealed and afterwards published. And so one is all the more inclined to laugh at the stupidity of men who suppose that the despotism of the present can actually efface the remembrances of the next generation. On the contrary, the persecution of talented writers fosters their influence ...

We know that soon after Virgil's death there was a hunger for more Virgilian poetry, which was fed with so mediocre a composition as the *Culex*;[50] in such an atmosphere, could somebody have failed to unearth a copy of such a gem as a suppressed version of a great poem?

I have no doubt that we can name one man, at least, who would have kept a copy – Asinius Pollio, a patron of poets, including Virgil at the time of the *Eclogues*, a friend of Gallus,[51] and a man who under the Principate 'defended his ideals in the only fashion he could, by freedom of speech. Too eminent to be muzzled without scandal, too recalcitrant to be won by flattery, Pollio had acquired for himself a privileged position.'[52] An episode with Timagenes, about which we happen to be informed, gives the flavour of his relationship with Augustus.[53]

The waspish historian Timagenes, who had won the friendship of Augustus, could not refrain from offensive jokes at the expense of the Princeps and his family; in the end, Augustus forbade him the palace.

> After this, Timagenes lived to old age in the house of Asinius Pollio and was lionised by the whole city. Although the Emperor had banned him from the palace, no other door was closed to him. He gave public readings of the histories which he had written after the incident, and he burnt the books dealing with the achievements of Augustus Caesar. He conducted a feud with the Emperor, and nobody was afraid to be his friend ... The Emperor made no complaint to the man who was maintaining his enemy. All he said to Asinius Pollio was, 'Are you keeping a zoo?' Then, when Pollio began to excuse himself, he cut him short, saying 'Make the most of him, Pollio, make the most of him!' 'If you tell me to, Caesar, I shall bar my house to him at once,'

---

[50] Fraenkel, *JRS* 42 (1952) 7 = *Kleine Beiträge* 2.193.
[51] Pollio to Cicero, *ad Fam.* 10.32.5: *Gallum Cornelium, familiarem meum ...*
[52] Quoted from Syme, op. cit. 482; cf. ibid. 320, 'Pollio ... was preserved as a kind of privileged nuisance'.
[53] Seneca, *de Ira* 3.23.4-8 = 88 *FGH* T3. On Timagenes: M. Sordi in *ANRW* 30.1.775ff.

said Pollio. The Emperor replied, 'Do you think I would? Why, it was I who made you friends again.' The fact was that Pollio had at one time been at enmity with Timagenes, and his only reason for ceasing was that the Emperor had begun ...

This story is highly instructive. We see how urbanely, how moderately, Augustus saw fit to treat a writer who personally angered him; and we see how provocative was the attitude of Pollio. Augustus, we are told, publicly lamented the death of Gallus.[54] It is hard to reconcile all this with the Princeps ordering the universal suppression of a poem praising him; it is perhaps even harder to imagine Pollio failing to seize the opportunity to keep a copy of a poem by a former protégé of his own, praising one of his friends, and suppressed in circumstances discreditable to Augustus. The compromise favoured by some scholars,[55] of supposing that Virgil wrote and suppressed not half the poem but a few lines only, seems to me to founder on the same considerations.

[54] Suet. *Aug.* 66.2.
[55] Otis 412f.; Wilkinson 111f.

CHAPTER NINE

The Creation of Characters in the *Aeneid*

We see, therefore that there is nothing irrational in the contention that even
an Epic may serve the purpose of the most fervid poet and soothe deep-rooted
and vital yearning – Keble

The machinations of ambiguity are among the very roots of poetry – Empson

Recent writers on the *Aeneid* have made us more than ever aware of the
complexity of the poem. Virgil's sources are numerous and belong to
more than one category. Homeric epic, Attic tragedy, Hellenistic poetry,
Roman myths, Naevius and Ennius and Catullus, learned aetiologies
and contemporary politics – all are blended into the great unity which
attempts to sum up and to include the whole of the mythical and
historical past and to show it as forming a pattern which will forever
shape and dominate the future. In this chapter I shall examine one
aspect of that complexity, attempting to convey not only what the poet is
doing in his creation and combination of characters, but what his
purpose is and the importance of this side of the poem for the
understanding of the whole.

Already in antiquity there were scholars who sought to explain actions
of Aeneas by reference to Augustus and events of the poet's own time.
The boys who take part in the Troy game at the funeral games of
Anchises wear helmets and carry two spears; we read in Servius that 'it is
agreed that Virgil is here alluding to the presents which Augustus gave to
the boys who took part in his games' – that is, the *lusus Troiae* on which
he was so enthusiastic (*Aen.* 5.556). When Aeneas celebrates games and
offers sacrifices at Actium, Servius observes that Augustus founded the
ludi Actiaci and that Virgil 'in honour of Augustus ascribes his actions to
his ancestor' (*Aen.* 3.274). It is right to point out at once that the ancient
commentators sometimes give examples of this method which startle us
by their crudity; few modern scholars for example would want to accept
the view that when at *Aeneid* 1.292 Virgil speaks of *Remo cum fratre
Quirinus* ('Quirinus with his brother Remus') 'the true explanation is
that Quirinus is Augustus, while Remus is put for Agrippa, who married
Augustus' daughter and waged his wars together with him' (Servius ad
loc.). We remember that this same method was applied to the *Eclogues*
with unfortunate results, tending to turn them into a disguised
autobiography of the poet. Thus Servius says of *Eclogue* 1.1 with a

desperate note:'In this passage we should accept Virgil under the mask of Tityrus: but not everywhere, only where reason demands it.' This sort of interpretation is no less subjective than others, and tact and common sense will be as vital here as anywhere else. I give a couple of modern examples.

Every reader remembers the touching complaint of Dido, that Aeneas is sailing away and leaving her without even the comfort of a child by him:

> *si quis mihi parvulus aula*
> *luderet Aeneas, qui te tamen ore referret,*
> *non equidem omnino capta ac deserta viderer*   (4.328-30).

'If a baby Aeneas were playing in my house, who might resemble you in face at least, I should not seem so completely taken and left.' In 1927, D.L. Drew thought that Sidonia Dido stood for Scribonia, the tiresome wife whom Octavian divorced after she had borne him a daughter; if only she had had a son she might not have been left, as Dido was left. This was, said Drew, 'a decidedly daring move on Virgil's part.'[1] In 1973 A.A. Barrett said the passage was contemporary in reference but in a very different way: it was aimed at those who believed that Julius Caesar had fathered a child by Cleopatra.[2] The intrigue of Aeneas with Dido stands for that of Caesar with Cleopatra; Octavian's line was to deny that his adoptive father had offspring by her, and Virgil obliges by making Dido also explicitly childless.

A second and last example. In Book 5 Aeneas opens the funeral games with a boat race. Drew believed that this stands for the boat race in Augustus' Actian games,[3] although unfortunately the sources describe this in a way which makes clear that it was not a race at all but a mock sea battle; Kraggerud on the other hand maintains that it 'will have reminded the reader of the triumphs of Roman fleets in Sicilian waters'.[4] At least one reader is reminded that of the four craft which enter for the race one runs on the rocks, while the helmsman of a second is thrown overboard by his enraged skipper; the triumphs of Roman fleets seem but hollowly recalled by all this. These examples suggest that we have not left the Middle Ages; they contradict each other and cannot all be true – and yet they cannot be refuted.

The method of finding modern parallels to events and figures in the *Aeneid* has recently been revived, and with a particular twist, that of typology. It is at this that I want to look particularly in view of its vogue; it has been accepted for instance in the last fifteen years by Binder,

---

[1] D.L. Drew, *The Allegory of the Aeneid* 83.
[2] A.A. Barrett, 'Dido's child: a note on *Aeneid* 4.327-30,' *Maia* 25 (1973) 51-3.
[3] Drew 53.
[4] E. Kraggerud, *Aeneisstudien, Symb. Oslo.* Suppl. 22, 128.

Buchheit, Gransden, Knauer, Perret, von Albrecht, and Zinn.[5]
It is I think clear enough that Virgil is not simply telling a story about
Aeneas interesting for its own sake, but that at least some of the episodes
of the poem are to be understood as referring forward through time to
contemporary affairs. I shall not enlarge upon this obvious point beyond
one clear example: the otherwise unmotivated detail that Aeneas' son
Ascanius was particularly fond of a boy called Atys, 'from whom the
Latin Atii derive their descent' (5.568). Ever since antiquity it has been
seen that this is a compliment to the family of the Atii, to which
Augustus' mother Atia belonged; the patrician Julii were already linked
by affection with that not very distinguished clan in the mythical period.
What we need to do is to inquire what is meant by applying the
theological idea of typology to the relationships in the *Aeneid* and
whether it is illuminating.

Typology is the process of 'seeking correspondences between persons
and events not (as allegory does) in meanings hidden in language, but
actually in the course of history, and looking not to the fulfilment of a
prediction, but to the recurrence of a pattern'.[6] Before the birth of Christ
this method was used by some rabbis in interpreting Old Testament
utterances about the Messiah,[7] and it was given a decisive impetus by St.
Paul, above all in I Corinthians 10: the wanderings of the Israelites in the
desert 'happened to them by way of figure (or example), and they are
written for our admonition, upon whom the ends of the world are come'.
Thus the rock which produced water to feed them in the desert was
Christ, the spiritual rock. It is only the same road which is being followed
when Gregory of Nyssa, for example, tells us that the manna on which
the Israelites fed in the desert was the word of God, and that the rod with
which Moses smote the bitter water and sweetened it was the cross,
which makes spiritually palatable what before was bitter with sin.[8]
Eusebius actually goes so far as to deny that Moses and the prophets
were really concerned with their own contemporary history at all, 'for
they were not concerned with predicting matters which were transient
and of interest only for the immediate future', but with Christology and

---

[5] G. Binder, *Aeneas und Augustus: Interpretationen zum 8. Buch der Aeneis*; V.
Buchheit, *Der Anspruch des Dichters in Vergils Georgika* 85; K.W. Gransden, *Aeneid Book
VIII* 14ff.; G.N. Knauer, *Die Aeneis und Homer* 354ff and *ANRW* 31.2 (1981) 889; J. Perret,
'Du nouveau sur Homère et Virgile', Review of G.N. Knauer, *Die Aeneis und Homer, REL*
43 (1965) 128; M. von Albrecht, 'Die Kunst der Spiegelung in Vergils *Aeneis*', *Hermes* 93
(1965) 55; E. Zinn, 'Nachwort zu V's *Aeneis*', in *Vergil-Horaz*, trans. R.A. Schröder 5.320.
Programmatically, von Albrecht, 'Vergils Geschichtsauffassung in der "Heldenschau",'
WS 80 (1967) 182: 'Vergils Weg durch die römische Geschichte steht im Zeichen
typologischer Zusammenschau ...' Cf. now R. Rieks in *ANRW* 31.2 (1981) 813-6.
[6] See N. Nakagawa, 'Typologie im NT', in: *Die Religion in Geschichte und Gegenwart* 6
(1962) 1095.
[7] Ibid.
[8] Gregory of Nyssa *Vita Moysis* 140 and 131.

the destiny of the whole human race;[9] while it is common to find such characters as Jacob, Isaac, Aaron, and Joshua interpreted as types of Christ.[10]

It is now being argued that the *Aeneid* is to be interpreted in this way. Thus Troy becomes a sort of Old Testament type of Rome, and so also do the scenes which Virgil adapts from Greek epic, for new Rome transcends and replaces old Troy and also prevails over and replaces Greece, just as the career and significance of Christ transcend, exceed, and replace the typological models in the Old Testament. This is for instance the argument of G.N. Knauer,[11] who goes on to explain that this is also the reason why Virgil makes his Aeneas resemble both Odysseus and Achilles: he is to sum up and outdo the whole of the heroism of Greece. It is even being suggested that Virgil actually derived this conception from contemporary Jewish writers.[12] I shall argue that while Virgil does intend the reader to see the characters of one time in the light of those of another, yet in important respects the typological analogy is misleading; that there is no need or plausibility in invoking Jewish sources; and above all that in the creation of characters, as with other features of the *Aeneid*, complexity serves a deeper and more poetically interesting purpose than this sort of analysis suggests.

I begin by making the obvious point that Virgil was no stranger to suggestive and multi-layered writing even before the *Aeneid*. The *Eclogues* are among the hardest poems to pin down ever written; nobody can read them without being aware that at times there is a second and more contemporary reference behind the surface meaning. We no longer fancy that we can pinpoint Virgil's farm on a map by careful study of *Eclogues* 1 and 9, but it remains unavoidable that in a disguised way the poet is glancing at recent political events. As if aware in advance that we should try to turn his poems into history, he has been careful to make his Tityrus both old and a slave and not therefore Virgil himself, just as he gives the farm lost by Menalcas topographical features incompatible with the realities of Mantua.[13] In *Eclogue* 5 his Daphnis both does and does not recall Caesar the murdered dictator; Gallus in *Eclogue* 10 is presented as a cross between a character out of Theocritus and the personification of the unhappy lover in his own poetry. As a pastoral figure he is set in Arcadia carving on the trees the name of his cruel mistress; in reality C. Cornelius Gallus was doubtless far away, and it was not a happy idea of the great Friedrich Leo to suppose that he was

[9] Eus. *Dem. Evang.* 5, *Praef.* 20-4.

[10] *Patristic Greek Lexicon*, ed. Lampe, s.v. *tupos*, D.

[11] Knauer, *Die Aeneis und Homer* 352. Cf. Buchheit, *Der Anspruch des Dichters* 85, on Octavian as 'Steigerung und Endpunkt'.

[12] D. Thompson, 'Allegory and typology in the Aeneid', *Arethusa* 3 (1971) 151.

[13] See Conington's remark on *Ecl.* 9.7: 'There are no hills or beeches in the Mantuan territory' (J. Conington and H. Nettleship, *The Works of Virgil* 1.106).

visiting Arcadia on leave from the army.[14] In *Eclogue* 4 Virgil has made his meaning so complex and suggestive that we shall never be able to unravel it all.

In all this I think we can be sure of one thing: Virgil took a crucial hint from Theocritus' *Idyll* 7. That poem baffles the interpreters because it presents a real experience – the poet walks across the island of Cos with two perfectly real friends to a harvest festival given by another perfectly real person – in a disguised form: not Theocritus but Simichidas is the name of the narrator, and the encounter with the goatherd Lycidas is described in a way which recalls meetings with gods, and which obviously meant to its original audience something which it cannot convey to us who are not in the know. This is coterie poetry; reality is represented in a disguised and ironic form. Virgil, who has no equal in literature for deftness in seizing and exploiting the hints offered by his literary models, saw in this fascinating poem an indication of the way in which he could maintain the perfection of Hellenistic literary form and polish, with the remoteness from contemporary Rome which that seemed to entail, but at the same time introduce real life into his poetry. He could thus bring together the two sides that figure in the two different types of poetry written by Catullus and his friends: the contemporary political poetry, and the longer, more polished Hellenistic pieces in the style of Euphorion. This amalgamation of contemporary life and Hellenistic artistry and transformation of contemporary figures into poetic form had already been hinted at by Theocritus.

Hellenistic poetry then was a source for Virgil's allusive style of narration, and in particular for his creation of characters. Tityrus and Menalcas cannot be resolved into separate historical constituents: Menalcas is and is not Virgil, as Daphnis is and is not Caesar, and Dido is and is not Cleopatra. Other Hellenistic models offered themselves for the presentation of present reality in a mythological form. Callimachus in his *Hymn to Zeus* assimilates King Ptolemy to the god, and explains with curious fullness that Zeus' elder brothers were happy to let him be supreme although he was the youngest; we see here an allusion to the circumstances in which Ptolemy II Philadelphus succeeded his father in preference to his older half-brothers.[15] Theocritus at 17.128-34 assimilates the marriage of that Ptolemy with his full sister, repugnant to Greek sentiment, to the union of Zeus with his sister Hera. Virgil could find some partial models in Hellenistic poetry, where another myth was used so as to make us interpret the main myth in a certain complex way. Thus Apollonius of Rhodes makes his Jason, inducing Medea to help him against her own father, tell her about Ariadne, who helped Theseus

[14] F. Leo, 'Virgil und die Ciris', *Hermes* 37 (1902) 18.
[15] See W. Meincke, *Untersuchungen zu den enkomiastischen Gedichten Theokrits* 175ff., rather than the commentary by G.R. McLennan, *Callimachus. Hymn to Zeus: Introduction and Commentary* 99.

against her father (3.998ff., 1074ff., 1096ff.); he does not tell her what the poet tells us in case we do not know, that Theseus deserted Ariadne when she had served his turn (4.433ff.). We see events in the light of the ironic parallel: in the same way Jason will abandon Medea when she has made the sacrifice for him, and although that does not actually happen by the end of the poem it casts its shadow over the union of the pair from its beginning.

But there were many other kinds of parallelism and identification which were available to influence the inquiring mind of Virgil within the Graeco-Roman tradition. I shall list in a necessarily summary way a number of forms which he could have found suggestive. First, because with *Eclogue* 4 we have touched on it already, oracular utterances. The world was full of oracles in Virgil's time – Augustus collected and burned great numbers of them. Characteristically the oracles preserved as Sibylline pretend to have been composed in the remote past; they 'predict' in a cryptic style events which have in fact already happened. They also have a certain vagueness and suggestiveness: they abound in such designations as 'a king of Egypt' or 'a man wearing a purple cloak upon his shoulders, fierce and unrighteous and fiery' (3.389). The audience had to try to work out a particular application for such terms by looking at history, past and present, and seeing an appropriate person whom they were meant to fit. *Eclogue* 4 is explicitly oracular, and Anchises strikes the same note at the end of Book 6 (the address *Romane* translates the *Romaie* of the Greek oracles). The oracular technique of hinting at more than is said, and of referring to people in a way which is ambiguous among several possibilities, was evidently of interest to Virgil.

Another set of ideas is closely related – that of time returning, with the corollary that events and even persons repeat themselves. This conception, which appears both in Pythagorean and in Stoic forms, was so generally familiar that we find, for instance, Virgil's contemporary Dionysius of Halicarnassus opening his work *On the Ancient Orators* by speculating whether the revival of taste for classical Attic oratory should be ascribed to 'the natural cycle bringing the old order round again.'[16] In *Eclogue* 4 Virgil imagined a second Trojan War and 'another Tiphys' to steer the Argonauts again; here we have found another way in which great figures of the past could be seen in the actions of the present. *Redeunt Saturnia regna*, said the oracular *Eclogue*: Augustus shall establish the golden age again in the land where Saturn ruled, says Anchises (6.792f.).

Such conceptions lead us to the interpretation of history in the light of models from the past. This is a fascinating subject which I can do no more than glance at. We know for instance that Alexander of Macedon

<hr />

[16] Dion. Hal. 1.2.2.

compared himself to Achilles, and many historians regard this as central to him. Victor Ehrenberg speaks of 'the sensation of mythical analogy so characteristic of Alexander'. His tutor Lysimachus gave him the nickname Achilles in youth and called himself Phoenix after Achilles' tutor; he once even endangered the king's life by insisting upon going on a dangerous mission with him, claiming that he was no older than ⸱Phoenix when he went to Troy. Alexander also compared himself with Heracles and wore a lion's-head helmet, a symbol of that hero. There is some evidence that he even emulated Dionysus.[17] Alexander himself had an enormous impact upon the imagination of those who came after him. Many of the successor kings claimed descent from him, modelled their portraits on him, and tried to get for themselves as much as they could of the aura which came to surround him, of being the quintessence of royal splendour, glamour, and power.[18] Romans too felt the power of his spell, starting with Scipio Africanus and going on to Pompey and Antony; Cicero, writing a memorandum on government for Caesar, was 'intentionally following the example of similar works written by Aristotle and Theopompus for Alexander'.[19] Augustus in turn was anxious to assimilate himself to the great Macedonian. He used his portrait as his signet, he made a great show of touching his body at Alexandria,[20] and he seems to have encouraged the story that like Alexander he was conceived by his mother after a visit from a divine snake.[21] Augustan poets took hints from the panegyrics upon Alexander for their praise of Augustus.[22] He was also compared or identified with Romulus; the poets, not least Horace, associated him with Hercules.[23]All this is different from

---

[17] V. Ehrenberg, *Alexander and the Greeks* 55. 'The figure which had become central in his experience was Achilles': F. Taeger, *Charisma: Studien zur Geschichte des antiken Herrscherkultes* 2.185. Lysimachus: R. Lane Fox, *Alexander the Great* 59. Cf. Arrian 7.14.4. Heracles: F. Schachermeyr, *Alexander der Grosse: Das Problem seiner Persönlichkeit und seines Wirkens* 408: 'Alexander believed quite seriously that he was becoming – in fact, that he was – a second Hercules.' The helmet: Lane Fox 443. Dionysus: Schachermeyr 411, Lane Fox 399, U. Wilcken, *Alexander der Grosse* 167ff., but cf. A.D. Nock, 'Notes on Ruler-Cult, I-V', *JHS* 48 (1928) 20ff. See also J. Perret, *Les Origines de la légende troyenne de Rome* 419-30.

[18] E.g. A. Heuss, 'Alexander der Grosse und die politische Ideologie des Altertums', *A & A* 4 (1954) 65-104, D. Michel, *Alexander als Vorbild für Pompeius, Caesar und M. Antonius*, O. Wippert, *Alexander-Imitatio und röm. Politik in der rep. Zeit.* Sallust *H.* 3.88M: *Pompeius a prima adulescentia sermone fautorum similem fore se credens Alexandro regi, facta consultaque eius quidem aemulatus erat,* 'From earliest youth Pompey, encouraged by flatterers, believed he would be like King Alexander, and he emulated his deeds and plans.' See now Peter Green, 'Caesar and Alexander: *aemulatio, imitatio, comparatio*', *AJAH* 3 (1978) 1-26.

[19] S. Weinstock, *Divus Julius* 188.

[20] 'Octavian could not have presented himself more clearly as the successor of Alexander than by this gesture', D. Kienast, 'Augustus und Alexander', *Gymn.* 76 (1969) 451.

[21] F. Blumenthal, 'Autobiographie des Augustus', *WS* 35 (1913) 122.

[22] E. Norden, *Kleine Schriften zum klassischen Altertum*, ed. B. Kytzler, 422ff.

[23] K. Scott, 'The identification of Augustus with Romulus-Quirinus', *TAPA* 56 (1925) 82-105; G.K. Galinsky, *The Herakles Theme* 138-41.

rabbinical or Christian typology because it does not imply that the later figure of each pair outstrips and replaces the former, as the Messiah or the Christ fulfilled and replaced the Biblical models, nor that the whole of history is one story with a single pattern and meaning.

Closely related are the themes of propaganda and of family history. Great Roman families encouraged their young members to emulate the virtues of their ancestors, whose images were kept in the atrium and paraded through the streets at funerals. Augustus' funeral went beyond the normal practice and featured the images not only of his kinsmen but 'of other Romans who had been prominent in any way, beginning with Romulus'; all were in a symbolic sense his ancestors.[24] Laudatory speeches also marked these occasions. And we observe that the more eminent *gentes* came to possess a definite character, so that a Gnaeus Piso was expected to be hard and proud, a Lucius Piso to be cultured and civilised, a Domitius Ahenobarbus to be ferocious – and Marcus Brutus was in great part forced to kill Caesar by the success of his own family's propaganda about Lucius Brutus the scourge of the kings. The Latin verb *patrissare*, to act like one's father, suggests by its form a Greek origin, but *patrizein* is never found in extant Greek. This is an area especially Roman.[25]

Propaganda had long used the device of assimilating or identifying contemporary figures with those of myth, and the visual arts had cooperated. Already in Attic art of the sixth century B.C. the tyrant Pisistratus had sought to identify himself with Heracles, while the democracy immediately after the overthrow of the Pisistratid dynasty encouraged a great boom in representations of Theseus. The Parthenon frieze offered a vision of recent history transposed into myth: Greeks fought against Trojans, Amazons, and centaurs, while the gods fought the giants, a reflection of the struggle of Greece against Persia which made it symbolic, as part of a universal victory of civilisation and order over barbarism and chaos.[26] The same sort of conception could be powerful in literature too – Isocrates urged Philip of Macedon to the conquest of Persia by urging on him the example of King Agamemnon, leader of all Greece against the barbarian (e.g. *Panathenaicus* 76ff.). We have seen that his son Alexander preferred, when the conquest came, the less statesmanlike but more glamorous role of Achilles. For Romans, we find that the imagination of the educated class thought naturally of contemporary events in Homeric terms already in the second century

---

[24] Dio Cass. 56.34.2; H.T. Rowell, 'The Forum and funeral images of Augustus', *MAAR* 17 (1940) 132ff.

[25] E. Bethe, *Ahnenbild und Familiengeschichte bei Römern und Griechen* 39ff., 85.

[26] J. Boardman, 'Herakles, Peisistratos and Sons', *RA* (1972) 59, and 'Herakles, Peisistratos and Eleusis', *JHS* 95 (1975) 1-12; cf. also C. Sourvinou-Inwood, 'Theseus lifting the rock and a cup near the Pithos Painter', *JHS* 91 (1971) 98ff., and references there; K. Schefold, 'Antwort klassischer Sagenbilder auf politisches Geschehen', *GB* 4 (1975) 231-42.

B.C., when Cato told Polybius that if he ventured to face the Senate again he would be like Odysseus going back into the Cyclops' cave to fetch his cap and belt, and when Scipio Aemilianus, walking on the ruined site of Carthage, quoted the Homeric lines 'There will be a day when Troy will fall', seeing in the doom of Carthage a warning of the fate of Rome.[27] Romans thought of history as a whole, not merely of their own family trees, as full of *exempla*,[28] and the parade of heroes in the sixth book of the *Aeneid* finds its three-dimensional counterpart in the statues of Roman worthies with which Augustus adorned his Forum, declaring in a public edict that they were to be an exemplar by which he himself and later *principes* could be judged.[29] Cicero repeatedly places himself in a sequence of noble defenders of Rome against the demagogues and the assassins: Scipio Nasica, L. Opimius, Metellus Numidicus. At moments he goes so far as to compare himself with the Decii (*Dom.* 64) or even with Romulus (*Cat.* 3.2). Against him he saw his antagonist of the moment as in another succession, that of the villains: the Gracchi, Saturninus, Sulpicius, Catiline, Clodius, Antony.[30] It is natural to him to call Clodius 'a lucky Catiline', Apronius 'another Verres', L. Piso 'that Semiramis' and 'a barbarian Epicurus'; Calpurnius Bestia is 'another Caesar Vopiscus', while Antony is called 'you new Hannibal' and Verres 'another Cyclops'. Cicero himself by contrast will be 'an immortal example of *fides publica*'.[31] No wonder he emphasises that the orator must have in his mind 'the whole force of old times and of historical examples', so that, for instance, he can discredit an opponent by saying something like 'When I looked at Considius, I thought I was seeing the Blossii and the Vibellii of old',[32] the proud leaders of a Campania hostile to Rome. All this shows how natural Romans found it to 'see through history'[33] and to recognise one event or person in another. We see it again in the quickness of theatre audiences in the late republic at picking up and exploiting any allusion in a play which could be made to apply to an unpopular figure of the time. Cicero gives us many examples, and in the speech in defence of Sestius he says that the audience never failed to catch a possible allusion (118).

It is not a long step from here to the 'canons' in which it was natural for Roman poets to arrange themselves. Ovid clearly puts himself in a

---

[27] Cato: Polyb. 35.6.4. Scipio: Polyb. 38.22.2.

[28] For instance, E. Skard, 'Zu Horaz, *Ep.* 1.11', *Symb. Oslo.* 40 (1965) 57ff., V. Buchheit, 'Vergilische Geschichtsdeutung', *GB* 1 (1973) 38, Cic. *de Or.* 1.201, *Orat.* 120, *Mur.* 66, *Sest.* 130, *Prov. Cons.* 21, *Rab. Post.* 2, *Phil.* 2.26.

[29] Suet. *Aug.* 31; A. Degrassi, 'Virgilio e il foro di Augusto', *Epigrafica* 7 (1945) 88-103.

[30] Cf. Cic. *Sest.* 37 with the note of H.A. Holden; *Har. Resp.* 41 with the note of J.O. Lenaghan; V. Buchheit, 'Ciceros Triumph des Geistes', *Gymn.* 76 (1969) 232 and 245.

[31] Cic. *Dom.* 72, *Verr.*3.31, *Prov. Cons.* 9, *Pis.* 20, *Phil.* 11.11, *Phil.* 13.24, *Verr.* 5.146, *Sest.* 50.

[32] Cic. *Leg. Agr.* 2.93.

[33] A phrase of Gregory of Nyssa, *Vita Moysis* 14b.

succession of elegiac poets, number four after Gallus, Tibullus and Propertius, while Propertius was proud to present himself as a Roman version of a Greek poet, *Romanus Callimachus*.[34] These poets find a form for their own aesthetic ideas and experiences by putting themselves in the position of a predecessor. Thus Virgil, Propertius, and the rest borrow a scene (the poet instructed by Apollo) from the opening of the *Aitia* of Callimachus, who in his turn was producing a variant on a celebrated experience of Hesiod. This blends easily with such things as Mark Antony, after his defeat at Actium, sulking on Pharos and saying that he would 'live the life of Timon the Misanthrope, since his experiences had been the same' (Plut. *Ant*. 69.4).

In religion, identifying women and men with goddesses and gods had by this date a long history. Again a few examples must suffice. Pericles was called 'Zeus'; Ptolemy II liked to be identified with Zeus by his poets; Ptolemy III had himself depicted on his coins with the attributes of Zeus, Poseidon, and Helios; Mithridates Eupator was greeted by the Greeks of Asia as Dionysus; Antony called himself 'New Dionysus'. Lunatics claimed to be gods, and sometimes succeeded in attracting a following. Characters in Plautus freely call themselves and others by such names as Jupiter, Juno, Mars, Venus, Achilles, and so on: 'O my Juno, you shouldn't be so cross with your Jupiter' (Plaut. *Cas*. 230). Proverbial expressions abounded, such as 'This is another Heracles', 'Another Phrynondas' (of scoundrels), 'The man is a Theramenes', 'Agamemnon's feast', 'Ajax' laughter'. At a deeper level some religious activities were conceived as reenactments of mythical events. That is clearly true, for instance, of maenadism, where the worshipper acts out afresh the events of the mythical past.[35] Akin to this but more poetical is the practice of Propertius, making the myths 'visible symbols of a secret reality, a concealed truth, to which his own experience had given him the key'.[36] The amorous and enchanting heroines of his myths present for Propertius a world not only more attractive but also in a way more real than the unsatisfactory and matter-of-fact world of Augustan Rome; he sees himself in the role of Paris or Odysseus to the Helen or Calypso of his beloved. In the novel, both Greek and Latin, characters similarly 'see' their own experiences in the light of mythical models. For instance,

---

[34] Ov. *Tr*. 4.10.51-4; Prop. 4.1.64.

[35] Pericles: cf. O. Weinreich, *Menekrates Zeus und Salmoneus* 82; Ptolemy II; cf. Callim. *H*.1, Theoc. 17; Ptolemy III: F. Taeger, *Charisma*, 2.300; Mithridates Eupator: Cic. *Flac*. 60; Antony: e.g., L.R. Taylor, *Divinity of the Roman Emperor* 109; Lunatics: Weinreich, op. cit.; Plautus: E. Fraenkel, *Elementi Plautini in Plauto* 89ff.; maenadism: A. Henrichs, 'Greek maenadism from Olympias to Messalina', *HSCP* 82 (1978) 121-60; p. 144, 'The Greeks understood maenadism as a reenactment of myth'. Ovidian passages where *Iuppiter* stands for Augustus are listed by P. Riewald, *De imperatorum Romanorum cum certis dis ... aequatione* 274ff.

[36] P. Grimal, *L'Amour à Rome* 194; cf. also J.-P. Boucher, *Études sur Properce*, 227. C.W. Macleod, 'A use of myth in ancient poetry', *CQ* 24 (1974) 82-93.

Chariton 5.10.1: 'What Protesilaus is this who has come back to life in my time?'; Achill. Tat. 2.23.3: 'There is your Cyclops asleep – be a bold Odysseus'; Petron. 9: 'If you are a Lucretia, you have found your Tarquin'; and so on.

The last of this kaleidoscopic series shall be the self-conscious classicism of Augustus and Augustan Rome. The emperor, who claimed to have turned a city of brick into a city of marble, aimed both in architecture and in other arts at the classic style of the fifth century B.C., and in such a work as the Ara Pacis his artists succeeded in creating something distinctively Augustan by combining in one masterpiece the imperial family with Mars and Aeneas and with the symbolic female figures of Rome and Italy.[37] Augustus boasted that he never made innovations, and he liked to present anything new as a revival of the past and himself as an old-fashioned Roman. We can see in this a reflection of the nostalgia for the past which pervades the *Eclogues* and *Georgics*, and which Livy expresses so memorably in the *praefatio* to his history. Messages for the present and feelings about it are in such a time naturally expressed in terms of the past.

The purpose of my long catalogue has been to suggest that there is no need to look outside perfectly familiar features of Graeco-Roman thought and invoke the practice of Jewish rabbis in order to find the background to Virgil's practice. What he does is not in reality closer to the typological exegesis of the Old Testament than it is to these other practices. For Virgil there is not simply one present story in the light of which the past is reinterpreted: past history is itself multi-layered. The voyage of Aeneas to Italy has echoes of the voyage of Odysseus, but it also recalls in a more distant past the exile of Dardanus, an Italian before he went to Troy, and it places the hero in relation to the wanderings of Hercules, which are themselves outdone by the labours and journeys of Augustus (*Aen.* 6.801). Nor is it only the case that we see different times and various events, all of which mutually illuminate and explain each other. Virgil also uses the device to bring out and to do justice to the complexity of our attitude to his story and to Rome itself.

In the first half of the *Aeneid* the main model for the experiences of Aeneas is of course the Odysseus of the *Odyssey*; in the second half he bears a general resemblance to the Achilles of the *Iliad*, culminating in his slaying of Turnus in a scene evocative of the slaying of Hector. But the picture is far more complex. His relationship to Dido and Lavinia causes his enemies to see him as Paris, the foreigner who seduces or abducts local queens (4.215; cf. 9.592ff.). From another point of view he plays the role of Menelaus, demanding the wife who is kept from him in a foreign city. Indeed, the scene in Book 12 where he is wounded in a

---

[37] See, for instance, E. Simon, *Ara Pacis Augustae* 22-9, A Boëthius, *The Golden House of Nero: Some Aspects of Roman Architecture*, 89.

breach of the truce puts him in the role of the Menelaus of *Iliad* 4. With Dido, Aeneas is not only Odysseus (telling his adventures to the Phaeacians and having to disentangle himself from Calypso), but he also plays the role of Apollonius' Jason. Jason both abandons Hypsipyle (Book 1) and beds with Medea in a cave (Book 4), so that we have echoes of two relationships of Apollonius' hero, not one. When he comes to visit Evander, we see him take on some of the colouring of Telemachus visiting Nestor and Menelaus; when he celebrates games at Actium, as we have seen, he foreshadows Augustus, while as for Heràcles, 'Virgil assimilates Aeneas to Heracles from the very beginning.'[38] He is a Trojan patriot, an Italian (descended from the Italian Dardanus), a Roman, an Augustan.

The other important characters are no less complex. Turnus, who dies the death of Hector, was predicted by the Sibyl to become an Achilles, and was born of a goddess as Achilles was (6.89f.). The champion of Italy against the invader, he traces his descent back to Agamemnon's city of Mycenae (7.372). Dido at her first appearance is seen in the light of Nausicaa; then she entertains Aeneas just as Arete and Alcinous, queen and king of the Phaeacians, entertained Odysseus. She attempts to hold on to him, like Calypso; she is united with him in a cave, like Medea; when she is abandoned she echoes the abandoned Ariadne of Catullus 64 (4.316). But she also incarnates the national enemy in Carthage, she is a founder of a city like Aeneas himself, and when she comes to review her own career before her suicide she speaks in the style of the Roman general in his *elogium*, his epitaph for himself (4.655f.).[39] Through the figure of the foreign queen who tries to seduce the Roman from his destiny and his home we feel a certain vibration of the unforgettable Cleopatra.

All this is perhaps obvious enough, but the important thing is what Virgil does with all this learning and all these parallels. As we saw, those who believe in typological explanations see this matter as essentially simple: according to Knauer, for example, Virgil shows how greater Rome exceeds and eclipses lesser Troy,[40] and, according to Perret, Virgil presents in Aeneas a hero who assumes the qualities of earlier heroes such as Odysseus and Achilles, but who supersedes them.[41] The reality is more complex and more interesting. When Dido appears in the light of the young Nausicaa or the touching Ariadne, part of our response to her derives from our response to those models and to the emotional resonance which they bring with them. When she turns to magic like Medea or

[38] Galinsky, *The Herakles Theme* 132; cf. his article 'Vergil's *Romanitas* and his Adaptation of Greek Heroes', in *ANRW* 31.2 (1981) 985ff.

[39] *Urbem praeclaram statui, mea moenia vidi, / ulta virum poenas inimico a fratre recepi.* On this passage see E. Fraenkel, *Kleine Beiträge zur klassischen Philologie* 2.73, 141, 223. I regard as too flimsy the associations of Dido with Scribonia (Drew, *Allegory of the Aeneid* 82) and with Pasiphaë (Kraggerud, *Aeneisstudien* 60).

[40] Knauer, *Die Aeneis und Homer.*

[41] Perret, 'Du nouveau sur Homère et Virgile', (above, n.5).

Circe, we experience a different emotion: the pity appropriate to a young girl is overlaid by the horror and revulsion we feel for a witch. When she struggles to retain her dignity while at the same time asking him to stay, memories of our attitude towards Calypso in *Odyssey* 5 are aroused; when she curses the hero and Rome and invokes the idea of Hannibal as her avenger, we are meant to feel the chill of fear which that terrible memory always had for a Roman.

Even more, the hero of the poem himself, as he appears in different roles and different lights, calls forth different responses. It is wrong to say, as scholars are prone to do, that Aeneas 'is' or 'is not' Achilles.[42] We respond to him in many different ways in the course of his adventures and experiences, and all of those ways contribute to the total sum of our attitudes and judgment on him. In his affair with Dido he puts himself in the line of the seducers of mythology who sail away and leave the weeping heroine behind; our response to him in that role, coloured as it is by our response to Jason and to Theseus, must be at least in part negative. In this pattern the heroine is the one who must win our sympathy. When Aeneas in the footsteps of Achilles slays Turnus, our response is coloured by our emotions when we see Achilles kill Hector; although Achilles is the great hero, Hector is humanly an attractive figure, and his death is tragic. So too we feel that the death of Turnus is tragic. On the one side Virgil has given full justification for his slaying and he must die; on the other he has used our emotional memory of Hector to cause us a certain reluctance to see his death. In the same way we feel a certain unease when Aeneas, urged on by heaven and the bidding of manifest destiny, sails away from a deserted heroine who has recalled some attractive and glamorous literary models.

All this might of course be a mere chaos of contradictory directives and muddled purposes on Virgil's part. It is in reality more than that, because this complexity of response is a vital part of the poet's intention and of the greatness of his poem. I shall not argue here the case for believing that the *Aeneid* is more than the straightforward glorification of Augustus, Rome, and imperialism which no doubt Augustus himself hoped to get. The Roman hero is forced by his hard destiny to turn away from the attractions of philosophy and art: others, Anchises tells Aeneas, will excel in the arts, while for the Roman there remains the self-denying role of the conqueror and legislator (6.847-53).[43] The triumph of Aeneas

---

[42] Thus, for instance, W.S. Anderson, 'Vergil's Second *Iliad*', *TAPA* 88 (1957) 27, calls Aeneas 'the true Achilles of this *Iliad*', whereas V. Pöschl, *The Art of Vergil: Image and Symbol in the Aeneid* 115, believes that 'all that is significant about (Turnus) comes from Achilles'; cf. also p. 127, where he insists 'it is not Hector ... who is the real model for Turnus, as has always been assumed, but Achilles.' The flatness of such a contradiction – and arguments can be offered on both sides – ought to suggest that something is seriously amiss with the procedures that produce it.

[43] Cf. above Chapter Eight, pp. 169ff.

and of Rome is willed by heaven, it is the end and meaning of history; and yet Aeneas must lose home and wife, Dido and Pallas, while L. Brutus must slay his own sons for the republic, and Rome must be deprived of the most wonderful Roman of them all, Marcellus. The heavy cost of imperialism is not underrated by Virgil, and that is not the least of the reasons why his epic is so great. Whereas other Roman writers, even of the rank of Horace, were content to assert in separate places both that Roman conquest was splendid and admirable, and also that aggressive war was wrong and greedy and that only pleasure and beauty mattered, Virgil alone faced the real problems and attempted to solve them. The *Aeneid* was to show both the greatness of Rome and also its human cost, not denying or minimising either of them nor separating them off into compartments in which each one could be developed without mentioning the other, but doing full justice to both and looking both steadily in the eye. Not the least powerful of Virgil's devices for achieving this is the way he exploits our familiarity with his literary predecessors and our emotional response to them.

Because we have felt for Dido a complex of emotions evoked by Nausicaa and Calypso and Medea and Cleopatra, our response to her destruction must also be complex. The opponent of destiny and the enemy of Rome must yield to the inevitable, and must indeed have brought her ruin on herself, but the beautiful and loving heroine must win our sympathy in her suffering and death. The complex harmony is not to be resolved into its simple elements. The doom of Dido is fundamentally complex and meant to be felt as such. This was the price of Rome: the hero does right to sail away and let her die, but he does so in the wake of too many mythological seducers for us not to feel that his hands, like theirs, are dirty. The death of Turnus, dashing and brave yet wrongheaded and impossible, repeats the same bitter lesson. As Achilles standing over the dying Hector rejects his prayer for burial and kills him without mercy, so Aeneas standing over the helpless Turnus rejects his prayer for life and kills him when he might have let him live. The belt of Pallas on Turnus' armour justifies his killing, but our sympathy for Hector helps Virgil to force on us the tragedy of Turnus' death. That too was part of the price. Aeneas would have preferred to avoid paying it and to let him live, and we too in a way would have preferred to see him spared, but empire is not won without such tragedies.

In conclusion, I should like to make three points in a form necessarily summary. First, if what I have been saying makes sense then the idea of typology is fundamentally inapplicable to the *Aeneid*. No typological exegesis sets out to show that events in the Old Testament place events in the New Testament in a morally dubious or complex light, and conversely the *Aeneid* does not represent Rome as simply the triumph and justification of Troy. Rome remains a morally complex phenomenon, and the devices we have been considering help to make it so. Rather than talk in the language of Biblical exposition it will be better to stick to such cautious terms as those of Sir Ronald Syme: 'The poem is not an allegory, but no contemporary could fail to detect in Aeneas a foreshadowing of Augustus.'[44] There is a relationship, a foreshadowing, but it is not to be reduced to an identity, even a typological one.

Secondly, we see again from another angle the vital importance to Virgil of his learning. What might have been a mere burden of decorative or insignificant *doctrina* is put to work in the service of the central purposes of the poem. We do not simply enjoy the pleasure of recognition of a source, but we are guided in our emotional response by Virgil's use of that recognition. He does so in a way that helps him with the task, which must have seemed almost impossible, of developing throughout the poem both sides of the Roman destiny of imperialism.

Thirdly and finally, we see again that even the most highly poetical devices of Roman poetry do not exist in isolation from the realities of ordinary life. The poetry of love is intimately linked with the facts of the life of pleasure and does not exist in a separate world of literary genres and conventions.[45] Virgil, too, in his brilliant exploitation of the device of presenting characters in the light of other characters, of seeing through his Aeneas at one moment Achilles, at another Menelaus, at another Augustus, was following up not an exotic and special borrowing from Judaea but a habit familiar in the law courts, in proverbs, in religion, in politics. Even when he looks through complex vistas of history and mythology, Virgil still belongs to his own world. That was what gave him the power to be its truest interpreter.

---

[44] R. Syme, *The Roman Revolution* 463.
[45] Cf. Chapter One above.

CHAPTER TEN

The Influence of Drama

O Jesu! He doth it as like one of those harlotry
players as ever I see!

– Shakespeare

One element in the creation of the world of Augustan poetry, part
realistic and part fantasy, has received little attention from scholars, and
that is the drama. It is normally to Hellenistic poetry that eyes are
turned in the search for origins and contributors. Thus Richard Heinze,
in his classic article on Ovid's narrative technique,[1] insists on the
primacy of Greek models, especially 'the elegy in the Hellenistic period':
to the learning and urbanity of these works the Roman elegists added a
passionate internal participation[2] which was of course alien to
Callimachus and Philetas. The gulf between the ironic style of
Callimachus' treatment of Acontius ('Acontius' monologue', as Heinze
calls it) and the Roman poets' depiction of Tarpeia or Ariadne, of which
it was said to be the source, remained unbridged; and what might have
seemed the obvious link of Roman tragedy was disregarded.[3] As for
Roman comedy, Friedrich Leo declared that 'there can be no doubt that
the last thing that Tibullus, Propertius and Ovid would read was the
comedies of Plautus, and no doubt either that resemblances between the
love poets and Plautus can only go back to their common source ...
Propertius and Ovid, and doubtless Tibullus too, did know the Attic
comedy ...'[4] The thesis stated with great panache by Felix Jacoby, that
'to put it in a definite form, the Roman elegy developed out of the
(Greek) erotic epigram', continues to find advocates,[5] and generally it
seems that these magisterial pronouncements of the great scholars have
sufficed to suppress, in most quarters, serious thought of Roman

[1] R. Heinze, 'Ovids elegische Erzählung', Berichte d. sächs. Ak. 71.7 (1919) 87-94.

[2] 'Innere Anteilnahme', Heinze 94.

[3] The same is true, to take a couple of recent instances, of D.O. Ross, Style and Tradition
in Catullus (1969), and R. Whitaker, Myth and Personal Experience (1969).

[4] F. Leo, Plautinische Forschungen (Berlin 1912²) 143-4. So for instance E. Fantham,
Republican Imagery (1972) 82: 'since Leo's discussion scholars have agreed that the
affinities of subject-matter and treatment between, say, the Elegists and Plautus and
Terence can only derive from the Greek sources.' Greater openness is shown by J.C.
Yardley, 'Comic influences in Propertius', in Phoenix 26 (1972) 134-9, concluding 'comedy
as a direct influence on elegy cannot, on the basis of the examples here cited, be ruled out
completely'. That is a revealingly hesitant formulation, after the evidence set out in his
article.

[5] F. Jacoby, 'Zur Entstehung der römischen Elegie', Rh. Mus. 60 (1905) 82 = Kleine
Philologische Schriften 2.102; P. Veyne, L'Elégie érotique romaine (1983) 37.

predecessors apart from Catullus.

That is of course in line with what the Augustan poets say themselves, or goes beyond it. It is Theocritus, Hesiod and Homer whom Virgil claims as models. Propertius derives his own work from Callimachus and Philetas, and there were people who professed to write in the manner of Euphorion. Horace admits the influence of Lucilius on his hexameter poems, but in more ambitious mood he claims kin with 'Eupolis and Cratinus and Aristophanes, the masters of the Old Comedy', and his criticisms of Lucilius are damaging,[6] this Roman forerunner appearing almost as much a butt as a model. In his lyric verse Horace will not even admit Hellenistic masters, much as he was indebted to them, and insists that he is the successor of Alcaeus. We tend to be unduly impressed by these explicit claims to literary position. McKeown, for example, in an interesting article on the influence of the Mime on Augustan poetry,[7] observes of the elegists that material from Comedy is undeniably present in their poems, but that 'since they never acknowledge such a debt' the connection is probably an indirect one.

Such a conception imagines these poets as being like modern scholars, conscientiously recording their obligations to their predecessors. In fact such statements, when they make them, are claims about the poets themselves: they declare that they are worthy disciples of the most fashionable and distinguished masters. The absence of Roman comedy and tragedy from the influences which the poets like to name proves only that they were not creditable, not in fashion,[8] not that they had made no contribution. From one point of view the contemporary Greek poet Parthenius, whose influence was in reality considerable,[9] did not rate mention by name, no doubt because a living Greek was not grand enough to count as an authority (it is amusing that Horace is so eloquent on the subject of injustice to contemporary authors);[10] from another, Catullus and the neoterics of the last generation were too close, represented too much the taste of these poets in their own adolescence, afterwards rejected, to be acceptable for mention as models;[11] and the old poets

---

[6] Horace *Sat.* 1.4.1-2; *Sat.* 1.4, 1.10.

[7] *PCPS* 205 (1979) 78. Some delightfully credulous examples of scholars taking such claims literally are assembled by E.A. McDermott in *ANRW* 31.3 (1981) 1650f.

[8] See W. Stroh, *Die werbende Dichtung* 212. The plain man Vitruvius, writing far from the fashionable vie-de-cénacle in which (as he complains) reputations were made among the sophisticated (Vitruv. 3 *praef.* 3), assumes that 'those whose minds are enthusiastic for poetry' will carry in their hearts the image of Ennius and Accius (9 *praef.* 16). Vitruvius is naïve enough to mention Cicero (ib. 17). On such cénacles, cf. Domitius Marsus fr. 11 **Fogazza**.

[9] W.V. Clausen, 'Virgil and Parthenius', in *HSCP* 80 (1976) 179: 'Virgil would hardly look round for Philitas with Parthenius at hand,' and id. in *GRBS* 5 (1964) 190-3.

[10] *Epistles* 2.1.28-101.

[11] One unfriendly mention of Catullus in Horace (*Sat.* 1.10.9). In Propertius two mentions, both in the context of saying 'my erotic verse will be as famous as that of Catullus (2.34.87), or even more (2.25.4)'. Bibliography on the influence of Catullus on Horace: *ANRW* 31.3 (1981) 1655 n.47.

whom one had read at school were passé, old-fashioned, and crude. Horace shows his familiarity with Roman comedy freely in his hexameter poems, but he is careful never to admit being influenced by it. The most impressive evidence we have for the continuing popularity and familiarity of Roman drama in the middle of the second century is of course that of Cicero. He has preserved for us by his quotations 178 lines of Ennius' tragedies in 53 fragments, and fragments of 8 of the 12 known plays of Pacuvius.[12] 'The philosophical works of Cicero are a mosaic of citations of the Roman tragedians' says J.P. Boucher,[13] and Cicero uses them to illuminate every kind of point, from types of madness to rhetorical figures or styles of delivery.[14] The plays of Ennius, Pacuvius and Accius were constantly being revived in the theatre, and their success there emerges repeatedly from Cicero's letters and speeches.[15] 'Who is so hostile to the very name of Rome that he scorns the *Medea* of Ennius or the *Antiopa* of Pacuvius?' he asks (*de Finibus* 1.4), appealing to their celebrity as a justification for his own undertaking of writing works of philosophy not in Greek but in Latin. They had shown that it could be done with distinction. Cicero also possesses a wide knowledge of Roman comedy, and a keen taste for it.[16] He compares a hostile witness to Terence's Phormio; he compares others to Plautus' Ballio, the unforgettable *leno* of the *Pseudolus*. He quotes the *Aulularia* and the *Trinummus*; he exploits a scene from the *Eunuchus* in his defence of Vatinius, and one from the *Heautontimorumenos* in a work of philosophy; he wrote a short poem about Terence.[17] And so on.

Now, when Cicero died Virgil was 27 and Horace was 22, while Gallus was probably about the same age as Virgil. In their schooldays the tragedians were part of the regular education given to young gentlemen (Horace indeed complains that even the poems of Livius Andronicus were still beaten into him by Orbilius). When they were grown up, these plays continued to be popular. Horace complains sourly that despite the crudities of the second century tragedians and comedians,

hos ediscit et hos arto stipata theatro
spectat Roma potens   (Epistles 2.1.60-1).

[12] E. Malcovati, *Cicerone e i poeti* (Pavia 1943) 102.
[13] *Études sur Properce* (Paris 1965) 230. The passage is an interesting one on tragedy as a source for mythology.
[14] Cicero *Tusc.* 3.11; *Orator* 93; *de Oratore* 3.217ff.
[15] Cf. Malcovati (n.12) 95-150; F. Leo, *Geschichte d. röm. Lit.* 196: 'For Cicero and his sort, who were after all familiar with Greek poetry, they were classics of the theatre, thoroughly familiar on the stage and in reading.' In the 50s even a smart young man like Caelius was happy to quote Pacuvius in a letter, it is worth remarking (Cic. *ad Fam.* 8.2). He was not yet démodé.
[16] Malcovati (n.12) 152ff.; C.O. Brink, *Horace on Poetry* 2.307.
[17] *Pro Caec.* 27; *Q. Rosc. Com.* 20, *Philipp.* 2.15; *Divin.* 1.65, *in Pis.* 61, *ad M. Brut.* 1.2.5; *ad Fam.* 1.9.19; *de Fin.* 2.14; *Poetarum Latinorum Fragmenta*, ed. W. Morel, 66.

'These are the poets whom mighty Rome learns by heart and packs the theatre to watch.' Augustus himself had a taste for the old Roman comedy and often put it on.[18] That is to say, in their boyhood the poets cannot have evaded these dramatists, and in later life they moved in a world which was highly conscious of them. They do not talk about them; but it is notable that they do not talk about Cicero, either.[19] The absence of that name from the poems of Tibullus and Propertius is not surprising, but the silence of Virgil and Horace is another matter. The latter might so easily have found it natural to allude in the *Satires* or *Epistles* to the greatest literary man of the last generation; the former goes so far as to juxtapose Catiline, on the Shield of Aeneas, not with Cicero but with Cato. Even his greatest achievement is thus implicitly credited to his rival.[20]

The absence of Cicero from Augustan poetry is not to be ascribed simply to hostility felt to his memory by the Emperor who had betrayed and proscribed him. The rhetorical schools seized on Cicero at once as a favourable subject for encomium; Livy recommended him to his son as the first author to read in Latin; Augustus himself, we are credibly told, found a formula of urbane praise for the dead orator, when a grandson was embarrassed at being found reading one of his works.[21] Conversely, the liking of the Princeps for the old Roman comedy did not stop Horace expressing severe criticisms of Plautus. The reason for the silence must rather be the feeling that Cicero was out of fashion, a man of the last generation – always the least interesting of all generations – and, to the sophisticated, a bore. It was much better to talk about Philetas or Euphorion or Pindar: to be familiar with Cicero's work won no credit, while the names of fashionable Greek poets reflected on those who dropped them the glory of recherché and glamorous knowledge.[22]

Horace in his hexameter poems refers to the *Iliona* of Pacuvius and to

---

[18] Suet. *D. Aug.* 89.1; cf. E. Fraenkel, *Horace* 396 n.1.

[19] S. Treggiari in *Phoenix* 27 (1973) 246 makes the interesting point that not only must Cicero's philosophical works have had an influence on Horace, but also the two men had many acquaintances in common: Trebatius, Plancus, Pollio, Messalla Corvinus, and others. Cf. also E.T. Silk in *YCS* 13 (1952) 145-58; J.P. Boucher, *Études sur Properce* 230; Leo, *Geschichte d. röm.* Lit. 194.

[20] *Aeneid* 8.668-70. Cf. G. Binder, *Aeneas und Augustus* 208; E. Lefèvre in *Gymn.* 90 (1983) 30f. The conception may owe something to Sallust's *Catiline*, in which Cicero is upstaged by Caesar and Cato.

[21] T. Zielinski, *Cicero im Wandel der Jahrhunderte* (1912) 278ff.; Livy quoted in Quintilian 10.1.39; Augustus: Plutarch *Cicero* 69, 'A man of great talent, my boy, and a patriot'. I do not think Drances in *Aeneid* 11.336ff. is a hostile portrait of Cicero (Zielinski 279f.; and, less cautiously, G. Highet, *Speeches in Virgil* (1972) 141; Quinn, *Virgil's Aeneid* 240).

[22] However little they may really have known of them. It is not easy to believe that Propertius and Ovid knew much about Philetas: cf. for instance R.L. Hunter, *A Study of Daphnis and Chloe* (1983) 79. And could they have gone on referring to Callimachus as a love poet, if they had really read much of his work?

the contrasting brothers in the same poet's celebrated *Antiopa*; he recasts into his own metre a snatch of dialogue from Terence's *Eunuchus*.[23] Other phrases and sentiments might well reveal an origin in comedy.[24] That is interesting, because Horace is less consistently on guard in those poems against admitting things which conflict with a high general stylistic level than he is in the *Odes*, or than the elegists are. It is reasonable to suppose that knowledge of these plays is in the background in these higher genres, more often than our inadequate knowledge of Roman tragedy allows us to know. Surely the fifteenth poem of the third book of Propertius, in which the story of Antiope is told at length and in an allusive style, must be composed with consciousness of Pacuvius' play – one of the two tragedies which Cicero singled out as glories of Latin literature.[25] The play also lies behind the rather self-indulgent passage of the second *Eclogue* where the lovelorn shepherd claims to be able to sing like Amphion, Antiope's son:

> *canto quae solitus, si quando armenta▪vocabat,*
> *Amphion Dircaeus in Actaeo Aracyntho*　　(Virgil *Eclogue* 2.23-4).[26]

'I sing as Dircean Amphion used to, when he called the cattle home on Aracynthus the Actaean mountain.' 'Beautiful nonsense of the most precious Alexandrian sort' is the comment of W.V. Clausen;[27] but there is the extra point that the jewelled manner of Alexandria is here applied to material familiar in a very different style – the old-fashioned and

---

[23] Hor. *Sat.* 2.3.60; cf. *Epp.* 2.1.183ff.; *Epp.* 1.18.39; *Sat.* 2.3.259ff.; cf. R. Kassel in ZPE 42 (1981) 17.

[24] Thus *Epp.* 1.4.14 *grata superveniet quae non sperabitur hora*; cf. Ter. *Phormio* 241-51, where the sentiment is burlesqued. It is interesting that the idea of teaching a son to profit by observing the failings of others, put forward by Horace with great apparent earnestness at *Sat.* 1.4.105ff. as a reminiscence of his own father, is an idea not only familiar to comedy but parodied in it: Terence *Adelphoe* 415-16. See also, in this connection, the disconcerting parallel to *Odes* 3.5.2 *praesens divus habebitur / Augustus, adiectis Britannis / imperio gravibusque Persis*, 'Augustus will be thought a manifest god, when the Britons and the dangerous Persians are added to the Empire', at *Phormio* 345: the parasite, speaking of free food and drink, says *Ea qui praebet, non tu hunc habeas paene praesentem deum?*, 'The man who provides them – wouldn't you think him virtually a manifest god?' It is perhaps significant that Horace is happy to use, in an important context, the idea of the Callimachean warning god who discourages from the wrong kind of poetry, even after burlesquing it himself: *Sat.* 1.10.31ff., and *Odes* 4.15.1 *Phoebus volentem proelia me loqui* ... 'Phoebus checked me as I planned to sing of war ...' Such a startling procedure makes one suspect that Horace was well aware of the comic parallels to the other passages in this note. With the phenomenon cf. E. Fantham, *Republican Imagery* 76 on the use by Cicero of images which he claims to reject.

[25] *de Finibus* 1.4. The idea has been suggested, cf. L. Alfonsi in *Dioniso* 34 (1961) 5ff., but prudent commentators point out that it cannot be proved. The 'catalogue-elegy' is the strongest influence on Propertius 3.15, according to R. Whitaker, *Myth and Personal Experience in Roman Elegy* (1983) 27.

[26] Cf. I. le M. Du Quesnay in *Creative Imitation in Latin Lit.*, edd. Woodman and West (1979); M. Geymonat in *Mus. Crit.* 13-14 (1979) 371-6.

[27] In *Cambridge History of Classical Literature* 2.307.

straightforward pathos of Roman tragedy. The way in which Propertius tells the story, concentrating on the isolated figure of Antiope and on her emotions, still recalls the tragic original.[28]

That in fact seems to me to be the crucial contribution of tragedy. The manner of Hellenistic narrative elegy, it appears from what we now know of poets like Callimachus, Hermesianax and Phanocles, or from the erotic mythological poems in hexameters of Euphorion and Parthenius, was consciously aloof, even when narrating pathetic events: combining plangency and dryness in a mixture which is genuinely exquisite in Callimachus, less so in the work of the others. A rather precious literary fashion at Rome dictated, from about 65 to 25 B.C., an exaggerated respect and a one-sided interest in poetry of that sort.[29] Other literary influences were played down by *les jeunes,* among them the tragedies they had read at school. But the two poems of Catullus which most look forward to Augustan poetry draw heavily upon tragedy. Catullus 64 opens with a passage which echoes the famous first lines of Ennius' *Medea Exul.* It goes on to the desertion of Ariadne. That theme goes back to Euripides and the *Minos* of Accius; as Ribbeck put it, 'the rather sentimental conception of Ariadne in later classical literature' is derived from this tragic original, and the retrospective account which Ariadne gives of her rapid love affair doubtless reflects the unfolding of events in it. It is a pity that so very little can be known of Accius' play. Catullus' poem then goes on to the predictions of the Parcae about the career of Achilles, culminating in the horror of Polyxena's sacrifice at his tomb. That too was a Euripidean theme, and from his *Troades* it was represented also in Roman tragedy.[30] In his sixty-eighth poem Catullus told of the tragic love of Laudamia. That again (though the evidence is tantalisingly inadequate) has usually been thought to be a story definitively shaped by Euripidean tragedy, his all too completely lost *Protesilaus.*[31]

The quest for 'the origin' of Latin love elegy has often been put in too narrow terms. Such a literary genre as the epigram or the narrative elegy could be 'the' origin of the developed elegy of Propertius or Ovid only in a restricted sense, since their poems are so different from the epigrams (in

---

[28] The point is missed by P. Veyne in his brilliantly unsympathetic treatment of the poem: *L'Élégie érotique romaine* (1983) 17f.

[29] O. Ribbeck, *Die römische Tragödie*[2] 567.

[30] We do not know exactly what events were portrayed in the various Latin plays whose names have come down to us: the *Hecuba* and *Andromacha Aechmalotis* of Ennius (Ribbeck thought Polyxena's death came in the latter: *Röm. Trag.*[2] 139), the *Troades* and *Hecuba* of Accius (Ribbeck 416ff.). See conveniently F. Bömer's Commentary on Ovid *Metamorphoses* 13.429-622. He remarks on the use made by Ovid of different tragedies of Accius. Cf. also MacL. Currie in *ANRW* 2.31.2701ff.: 'Ovid and the Roman stage', with full bibliography.

[31] See the cautious discussion by H. Jacobson, *Ovid's Heroides* (1974) 195ff. It is not clear whether there really existed a *Laudamia* by Accius (ib.).

length and complexity), and from what we actually know of Hellenistic elegy (in tone and purpose). Comedy made its important contribution in the idea of a world of impoverished lovers and exacting *meretrices*, stylised and possessed of a certain dignity yet still close to real life; and in many of the incidents and motifs which take place in that world. Thus the braggart soldier of Plautus who so often serves as a rival to the lover – wealthy, stupid, a dupe – has with great plausibility been seen as the ancestor of the praetor, enriched overseas, who disrupts Propertius' happiness in his poem 2.16.[32] The 'praetor', who at one point in the poem seems to be called *barbarus* and an ex-slave, is less a portrait of a real person than a literary creation drawing on the upstart and rootless soldiers of comedy. The connection is of particular interest for several reasons. First, Menander is far less stereotyped in his creation of soldiers than Plautus:[33] sometimes, as in the *Perikeiromene*, Menander's soldiers can be quite sympathetic. Insistence on a Greek original is thus unconvincing. Secondly, the attitude of Plautus to this intrusive warrior is in line with the attitude of Roman elegy generally to war and to those who are enriched by it:[34] that such disgusting characters are the very antithesis of love and the love poet. The theme is important enough in these poets for this to be much more than a trivial point of resemblance. The rejection of war and the soldier, the contrast between *militia* and the life of love, is one of the pervasive elegiac subjects, and comedy helps to colour it – even to the point where real acquaintances of the poets, going abroad in the army, are treated on the assumption that their sole motive is the *avaritia* of the comic mercenary. Thus Propertius to Postumus (3.12.5 *omnes pariter pereatis avari!* 'May the greedy all perish at once!'), and Horace to Iccius (*Odes* 1.29.1 *Icci, beatis nunc Arabum invides / gazis?* 'You have your eye on the treasures of the Arabs, have you?').

It may also not be too bold to see in Roman comedy an important source of the characteristic naughtiness of elegy. Plautus went far beyond his Greek models in making his plays embody drastic reversals of proper values and hierarchies. The triumphs of slaves over their masters, and the accompanying language of 'free man at the mercy of slave', a striking feature of most of Plautus' plays, was not Menandrian.[35] Nor was the

---

[32] J.C. Yardley, 'Comic influences in Propertius', *Phoenix* 26 (1972) 134-9: he thinks specifically of the *Eunuchus* as the source of Prop. 2.16.

[33] E.g. A.S. Gratwick in *Cambridge History of Classical Literature* 2.109. The prominence of soldiers 'reveals a Plautine predilection': E. Segal, *Roman Laughter* 124.

[34] Prop. 3.4 and 3.5: *arma deus Caesar dites meditatur ad Indos ... pacis Amor deus est, pacem veneramur amantes*; Tibull. 1.1.49ff., 1.10, etc.; Ovid *Amores* 3.8.9ff., 3.15.5, *Ars* 2.713ff. Propertius makes the *lena* who urges his mistress to emulate Menander's Thais go on to recommend that she should not scorn the *miles non factus amori*, the soldier not cut out for love (4.5.43-50). The link between comedy and contemporary life is made quite clear.

[35] Cf. Gomme-Sandbach on *Perikeiromene* 272, E. Lefèvre in *Herm.* 108 (1979) 311.

humiliation of the *senex*, which in Plautus' later plays assumes an almost ideological intensity: the grave and reverend signor, the pillar of the Senate, who lays down the law and settles the affairs of his clients with a grave face – he is not only outwitted but disgraced.[36] Our sympathies lie with the sons: for them a life of love and frivolity, however much public opinion and *rumor* may condemn it, is appropriate and graceful.[37] The *senes severiores* struggle vainly to interfere with the amours of the young, and a comic father can count himself lucky if he is only cheated of the money to buy his son's mistress, without being exposed and disgraced in addition, like the old men in *Asinaria, Bacchides, Casina, Epidicus, Mercator,* and *Phormio.*[38] It is not only a matter, for the Augustan love poets, of echoing specific motifs of all this, as when for instance Tibullus dwells on the humiliations of the superannuated lover, or Propertius suggests that one of the advantages of a common whore over a woman like Cynthia is that

> *differet haec numquam, nec poscet garrula quod te*
> *astrictus ploret saepe dedisse pater*   (Prop. 2.23.17-18).

'She will not ... wheedle from you a present which your tight-fisted father will often lament that you gave her.'[39] More generally important is the reversal of proper values. As the glorious calling of Roman military service is tainted in the elegists by the repulsive absurdity of the comic soldier, so the respectable life of *frugalitas* and *parsimonia*, of private investments and public duties, is scorned by the elegist no less than it is by the *jeunesse dorée* of comedy.

> *Ista senes licet accusent convivia duri:*
> *nos modo propositum, vita, teramus iter.*
> *illorum antiquis onerentur legibus aures;*
> *hic locus est in quo, tibia docta, sones*   (Prop. 2.30.13-16).

---

[36] *Epidicus* 189, 522; *Casina* 536; *Asinaria* 871. 'If old men like this go after whores, what becomes of the state?' *Mercator* 985. Cf. also *Bacchides* 1207 ('these old men have shown that they were debauchees all the time'), *Asinaria* 857 ('he looked so virtuous, too!'), *Casina* 562; Terence *Phormio* 1000ff. Cf. E. Segal, *Roman Laughter* 24ff.; E. Burck in *A und A* 21 (1975) 12-35; MacCary and Willcock in their edition of Plautus *Casina* 9, 'We have then a reversal of traditional roles on three levels: the young triumph over the old, the slaves triumph over their masters, and the women triumph over the men'; Lefèvre in *Hermes* 105 (1977) 441-54, 106 (1978) 518-38.

[37] Explicitly, e.g. *Mercator* 1015, *Mostellaria* 1141-58; Ter. *Andria* 152, 443ff.; *Adelphoe* 101ff., 149ff.; *Hecyra* 684ff.; Pherecrates fr. 71K.

[38] 'There can be no doubt that the utter humiliation of old gentlemen was a subject which Plautus in his later plays liked more than any other': E. Lefèvre in *Herm.* 108 (1979) 337. Also J.M. Cody in *Herm.* 104 (1976) 461.

[39] F. Leo, *Plautinische Forschungen* 145, compares Plaut. *Mercator* 46ff.; Ter. *Heaut.* 99. Good examples of Propertian poems visibly influenced by comedy: J.C. Yardley in *Phoen.* 26 (1972) 135ff.; more speculative, id. in *CQ* 30 (1980) 240ff.

'Heartless old men may denounce our parties, but let us, my darling, just lead the life we have chosen. Let their ears be wearied with archaic legal language: this is the place for the delightful sound of the flute.' Commentators on such passages do not always find it necessary to refer to comedy, but the whole contrast of lives – youth and irresponsibility, age and dreary cares – reflects that world.[40]

The rejection of sage counsel is another aspect of the life of the elegiac lover,[41] as is the notoriety and shame which he must suffer.

> *'Tu loqueris, cum sis iam noto fabula libro,*
> *et tua sit toto Cynthia lecta foro?'*
> *cui non his verbis aspergat tempora sudor?*   (Prop. 2.24.1-3).

' "Do you speak, when your book has made you a scandal, and your Cynthia has been read all over the forum?" Who would not have sweat on his brows at such words?' The elegiac lover boasts of the disgrace which in comedy is more formidable. In Plautus a young man can be told

> *neque mei neque te tui intus puditumst factis quae facis,*
> *quibus tuom patrem meque una, amicos, adfinis tuos*
> *tua infamia fecisti gerulifigulos flagiti*   (Plaut. *Bacchides* 379-81).

'You have felt no shame before me or before yourself for your actions, by which you have made your father and me, your friends and relations, all notorious thanks to your disgrace.'[42] The weight of a tyrannical public opinion[43] is defied by the lover of comedy; it is but a step to the delight in disrepute of the elegist, and to Ovid proclaiming himself as 'the poet of my own naughtiness', *ille ego nequitiae Naso poeta meae* (*Amores* 2.1.2). Even the idea of the subjection of the lover to the woman, and to a disreputable woman at that, is by no means unknown to comedy.[44] 'A cheap slave-girl has enslaved me' complains the soldier in Menander's *Misoumenos*.[45] Plautus' Pseudolus remarks that no concerted action against the pimp Ballio, their common enemy, can be expected from those who are forced by their love to be slaves:

[40] Cf. for instance Ter., *Andria* 151ff., 188f.; *Hec.* 683ff. Humorously reversed: Plaut., *Merc.* 550ff.

[41] Propertius 1.1.24 *et vos qui sero lapsum revocatis amici* ... 3.24.8 *quod mihi non patrii poterant avertere amici;* Horace *Epode* 11.25 *unde expedire non amicorum queant / libera consilia nec contumeliae graves.* Cf. Plaut. *Trin.* 669 *minus placet magis quod suadetur,* and the abortive dissuasion at *Bacch.* 367ff.

[42] Plaut. *Bacch.* 375-81, *Curc.* 499-504, *Most.* 144, *Trin.* 263; Ter. *Ad.* 92, *Eun.* 238, *Heaut.* 1037; D.C. Earl in *Historia* 9 (1960) 236. Menander *Dysc.* 243, *Peric.* 167, *Sam.* 459, represents public opinion as a much less formidable thing than it was at Rome.

[43] See the first appendix to Chapter Eight.

[44] R.O.A.M. Lyne, in his important article 'Servitium amoris', *CQ* 29 (1979) 123, cites *Bacchides* 92 and *Pseudolus* 15: those passages are not handled again here.

[45] Fr. 2 K. Cf. Propertius 1.9.4 *et tibi nunc quaevis imperat empta modo,* 'Now a woman you have just bought orders you about'.

> *illine audeant*
> *id facere, quibus ut serviant*
> *suos amor cogit?* (Plaut. *Pseud.* 205-6)

'Give me whatever commands you like, any way you like' is the language
of a formerly recalcitrant man surrendering to a meretrix:

> *dic, impera mihi quid lubet quo vis modo* (*Truc.* 676).

At the end of the *Bacchides* the two fathers abandon themselves to the
enticements of the two girls with words of complete self-surrender:

> *ducite nos quo lubet tamquam quidem addictos* (*Bacch.* 1205).

'Take us off as if we were your slaves.' The soldier Thraso surrenders
himself at discretion to Thais in the *Eunuchus*:

> *GN. quid nunc coeptas, Thraso?*
> *TH. egone? ut Thaidi me dedam et faciam quod iubeat. GN. quid est?*
> *TH. qui minus quam Hercules servivit Omphalae?* (Ter. *Eun.* 1025-7).

'I'll give myself up to Thais and do what she bids me ... Just as much as
Hercules was the slave of Omphale.' So much is this sort of thing the
regular small change of amorous talk that an old man who has bought a
pretty slave-girl naturally talks in these terms to her:

> *PA. amabo ecastor, mi senex, eloquere – LY. exquire quidvis.*
> *PA. cur emeris me. LY. tene ego? ut quod imperetur facias,*
> *item quod tu mihi si imperes ego faciam ...* (Plaut. *Merc.* 504-6).

'Tell me please, my dear, why have you bought me?' 'Why? So that you
will do what you're commanded to do; and so that I shall do anything you
command me to do, too ...'

These resemblances between Comedy and Elegy are more than verbal
echoes. They relate to central ideas and attitudes of the genre. Horace in
his hexameter poems and epodes shows an easy familiarity with Roman
comedy, however superior he feels to its technical laxnesses. Augustus
admired it, and Horace tells us that the plays continued to be acted with
success in his time.[46] The Augustan poets do not, in their more ambitious
works, admit to any acquaintance with them; but it is evidently unlikely
that they can really have been unfamiliar. Rather it is to be seen as part
of the pose of the self-conscious poet. Himself a fastidious and aesthetic
person, writing in the most reputable genres, using an exquisitely chosen
vocabulary and style, he is acquainted only with literary models of the

---

[46] The great poets of the second century B.C. provide the lion's share of the quotations
not only in Cicero but also in Varro; cf. H.D. Jocelyn, *The Tragedies of Ennius* 53f., C.O.
Brink, *Horace on Poetry* 3.84.

same distinguished kind: not Cicero but Callimachus, not Plautus but Philetas.

Tragedy, too, had something to contribute. To the withdrawn and ironical treatment of myth characteristic of the Hellenistic elegy it could add the possibility of more passionate mythical narrative, concentrating on the heroines. From Propertius' Antiope and Tarpeia to Ovid's *Heroides* and Virgil's Dido, it is tragedy which gives the poets the perspective in which to see the ladies of mythology.[47] Above all it is Propertius who is receptive to this, and whose poetry is permeated through and through by these stories. The fashionably cool attitude taken to their Latin predecessors by the Augustan poets, whose own work (once Caecilius Epirota and Remmius Palaemon had begun to make it the subject of school instruction)[48] became standard and classic, unfortunately helped to push Roman tragedy into oblivion. So effective was the process that the shattered fragments which survive hardly ever allow us to see how far the Augustans used the plays. In the special case of Virgil, Macrobius preserves some precious tragic parallels, and chance has given us some comparatively extensive citations by Cicero which show the use of Ennius' tragedies in the *Aeneid*.[49] Occasionally we can see a connection elsewhere: thus the episode of Tereus, Philomela and Procne in the sixth book of Ovid's *Metamorphoses* is shown by Bömer to draw on two tragedies of Accius, the *Tereus* and the *Atreus*.[50] But for the most part the influence of tragedy must remain a matter of general conjecture. A respected Latin poetic form dealt in elevated language with the emotions of the human heart, and especially those of love: for tragedy after Euripides was almost as soaked in the passion of love as comedy.[51]

A last point is the existence at Rome of the *fabula praetexta*, tragedies on Roman themes. Among the very few of which we know anything, one, from the pen of Ennius, had as its theme the rape of the Sabine women, that favourite subject of Ovid.[52] Another, the *Brutus* of Accius, dealt with the rape of Lucretia and the expulsion of the kings from Rome. That story began with the prince and his friends coming back unexpectedly

---

[47] Cf. J.P. Boucher, *Études sur Properce* 227ff. The overlap between the list of mythical heroines who occur in Propertius, and those who were the subjects of tragedies, is striking.

[48] H.D. Jocelyn, *The Tragedies of Ennius* 54. He makes the point that the tragedies composed by Ovid and Varius must have 'remained deeply affected by what they read at school'. F. Bömer, Commentary on *Metamorphoses* 12-13, p. 197, remarks on 'the fact that Ovid knew the old Roman drama well, especially Accius'.

[49] Ennius frr. 25, 27 Jocelyn; M. Wigodsky, *Vergil and Early Latin Poetry* (1972) 76-9. Wigodsky brings out the difficulty of isolating echoes of Roman from Attic tragedies in Virgil (ib. 90ff.).

[50] Bömer, Commentary on *Metamorphoses* 6-7, p. 117: 'the main emphasis' comes from Accius; cf. G.K. Galinsky, *The Metamorphoses of Ovid* 132. So too on *Met.* 3.511ff. see Currie in *ANRW* 2.31.2717 (influence of Pacuvius); on Ennius *Alexander* and Ovid *Heroides* 16 and 17, H. Jacobson in *Phoen.* 22 (1968) 229-303.

[51] The heady combination of love and death was common in these tragedies, and is shown by a glance at a list of names – Alcestis, Canace, Deianeira, Haemon, Laudamia, Oenone, Phaedra, Philomela. Pasiphae, too, was a tragic heroine.

[52] Cf. p. 135.

from the war to see how their wives are behaving in their absence, a motif familiar in comedy and beloved by elegy;[53] it contained a speech by Lucretia describing what happened that dreadful night (fr. 5 R). The *Brutus* is known to have been performed, with great éclat, in 57 B.C.[54] Such works are highly suggestive. They represent a model for the treatment of Roman figures with the full stylistic and literary panoply of Greek literature, and in a form which dwelt not primarily on war and conquest, like Ennius' *Annales*, but on the heart.[55] The assimilation of a loving and suffering Roman woman to the great figures of mythology must have taken an impetus from the form, and the hint was not thrown away on Propertius.

It is a pleasing example of the blending of the two worlds that he made his lovelorn Tarpeia, as she considers betraying her country for her passion, take the Greek heroine Scylla as a model – and the Sabine women as another (Prop. 4.4.39, 57). The orators included in the same breath examples from Roman history and from Greek myth: thus for instance Cicero lists as justified homicides M. Horatius, Servilius Ahala, Scipio Nasica, and Orestes; and as instances of violent anger Thyestes, Aeetes, Dionysius of Syracuse, and the Tarquins. He illustrates the theme of subduing grief by a series of instances consisting of a speech from a comedy by Terence, an utterance of Odysseus in Homer, and the death of Pompey. The assimilation of Roman history with Greek poetry is evidently complete.[56] Just so Propertius puts Marius and Jugurtha in the same couplet as the Homeric beggar Irus and the historical King Croesus, and includes Romulus in a list of otherwise Greek *exempla* (*cur exempla petam Graium?*), and imagines the *belles du temps jadis* as including not only the beauties of Troy and Thebes but all the pretty girls of olden Rome.[57] That feat of stylisation, by which Roman subjects were raised to the same level of dignity and poetic significance as those of Greece, has many aspects. The Catalogue of Italian tribes and places in *Aeneid* 7 is an example of it, as is Horace's naming of his nurse and his village in a context of inspiration by Calliope and Phoebus.[58] The

---

[53] Ovid *Fasti* 2.727; Livy 1.57.9. In comedy: Ter. *Heaut.* 277ff. In elegy: Prop. 1.3, 2.29, 3.6; Tibullus 1.3 *fin.* (reversed, Prop. 4.8). In Greek myth, Procris and Cephalus, Ov. *Met.* 7. 715ff., 826ff. (each of the spouses tries to check on the other). The motif underlies the second half of the *Odyssey*. An instance from life: Harriette Wilson, *Memoirs* 173f.

[54] Cic. *Pro Sest.* 123.

[55] F. Leo, *Geschichte der röm. Lit.* 89 regards Naevius' *praetextae* as 'the truly decisive moment, the first appearance of a self-directing literature following in the wake of the Greek'. Cf. also A. Gratwick in *Cambridge History of Classical Literature* 2.94.

[56] Cic. *Pro Milone* 8; *Tusc.* 3.26-7; ib. 65-6. Cf. also *pro Sest.* 48: Erecthei filiae ... C. Mucius ... P. Decius ... *de Divin.* 1.29: P. Claudius ... Agamemnon ... Crassus ...

[57] Prop. 3.5.15f.; 2.6.19; 2.28.53-6. Compare, in Ovid, the list of amorous rivers, which includes the Anio, at *Amores* 3.6.25ff., and the list of exiles in *Ex Pont.* 1.3.61ff. – Rutilius Rufus, Diogenes, Patroclus, Cadmus ... Propertius 2.32.31ff: a list of gallant ladies, including Helen and Catullus' Lesbia, concludes *quod si tu Graias es tuque imitata Latinas* ... – for Cynthia has both Roman and Greek models.

[58] Horace *Odes* 3.4.1-24.

exaltation of Cynthia to quasi-mythical status, the transfiguration of the life of mundane pleasure to a kind of sublimity, was surely assisted by these Roman tragedies. It makes a fitting conclusion to the argument of this book that the inextricable fusion of Greek and Roman in the contemporary world of the Augustan poets, and also the conviction that poetry and history were essentially akin, were both reflected back into the most distant past. In that perspective there had never been any opposition of principle between Greek and Roman, between literature and life.

Select Bibliography

Albrecht, M. von — 'Die Kunst der Spiegelung in Vergils *Aeneis*', *Hermes* 93 (1965) 54-64
'Vergils Geschichtsauffassung in der "Heldenschau",' *WS* 80 (1967) 156-82
'Mythos und römische Realität in Ovids Metamorphosen', *ANRW* 31.4 (1981) 2328-42

Alfonsi, L. — *L'Elegia di Properzio* (Milan 1945)

Anderson, W.B. — 'Gallus and the Fourth Georgic', *CQ* 27 (1933) 46-55

Anderson, W.S. — 'Vergil's second *Iliad*', *TAPA* 88 (1957) 17-30

Balsdon, J.P.V.D. — *Roman Women* (London 1962)
Life and Leisure in Ancient Rome (London 1969)

Bayet, J. — 'Les premières "Géorgiques" de Virgile', *RPh* 4 (1930) 128ff. = *Mélanges de littérature latine* (Rome 1967) 197-242
'Catulle, la Grèce et Rome', Entretiens Hardt 2 (Geneva 1953) 3-39 = *Mélanges* 85-117

Berchem, D. van — 'Cynthia ou la carrière contrariée', *Mus. Helv.* 5 (1948) 133-41

Bethe, E. — *Ahnenbild und Familiengeschichte bei Römern und Griechen* (Munich 1935)

Bignone, E. — *L'Aristotele perduto e la formazione filosofica di Epicuro* 1 (Turin 1936)

Binder, G. — *Aeneas und Augustus: Interpretationen zum 8. Buch der Aeneis* (Meisenheim 1971)

Blümner, H. — *Die röm. Privataltertümer* (Munich 1911)

Blumenthal, F. — 'Die Autobiographie des Augustus', *WS* 35 (1913) 113-30, 267-8

Boardman, J. — *Greek Gems and Finger Rings* (London 1970)

Bömer, F. — Commentary on Ovid's *Metamorphoses* (Heidelberg, 1969-)

Boucher, J.P. — *Etudes sur Properce* (Paris 1965)

Bowersock, G.W. — *Augustus and the Greek World* (Oxford 1965)

Boyancé, P. — 'Properce', Entretiens Hardt 2 (Geneva 1953) 169-209

Bramble, J.C. — '*Cui non dictus Hylas puer?* Propertius 1.20', *Quality and Pleasure in Latin Poetry*, edd. A.J. Woodman and D.A. West (Cambridge 1974) 81-93

Brink, C.O.   *Horace on Poetry*, 3 vols. (Cambridge 1963-82)

Brödner, E.   *Die röm. Thermen und das antike Badewesen* (Darmstadt 1983)

Brooks, R.A.   'Discolor aura', *AJP* 74 (1953) 260-80

Brunt, P.A.   *Italian Manpower* (Oxford 1971)

Buchheit, V.   *Vergil über die Sendung Roms* (Heidelberg 1963)
                  Der Anspruch des Dichters in Vergils Georgika (Darmstadt 1972)
                  'Vergilische Geschichtsdeutung', *GB* 1 (1973) 23-50

Burck, E.   'Römische Wesenszüge der Aug. Liebeselegie', *Hermes* 80 (1952) 163-200 = *Vom Menschenbild in der römischen Literatur* (Heidelberg 1966) 191-221
                  Review of G. Luck, *Die röm. Liebeselegie*, *Gymn.* 70 (1963) 898-94 = *Vom Menschenbild* 238-43
                  'Die Rolle des Dichters und der Gesellschaft in der aug. Dichtung', *A und A* 21 (1975) 12-35

Cairns, F.   *Generic Composition in Greek and Latin Literature* (Edinburgh 1972)
                  Tibullus (Cambridge 1979)

Cichorius, C.   *Untersuchungen zu Lucilius* (Breslau 1908)

Clausen, W.V.   'Callimachus and Roman poetry', *GRBS* 5 (1964) 181-96
                  'The interpretation of Virgil's *Aeneid*', *HSCP* 68 (1964) 139-47

Clay, J.S.   'The argument of the end of Vergil's Second Georgic', *Philologus* 120 (1976) 232-45

Cody, J.M.   'The *senex amator* in Plautus' *Casina*', *Herm.* 104 (1976) 453-76

Coleman, R.   'Gallus, the *Bucolics*, and the ending of the Fourth *Georgic*', *AJP* 83 (1962) 55-71

Colin, J.   'Luxe oriental et parfums masculins dans la Rome alexandrine', *RBPh* 33 (1955) 5-19

Connor, P.J.   'The actual quality of experience: an appraisal of the nature of Horace's *Odes*', *ANRW* 31.3 (1981) 1612-39

Copley, F.O.   *Exclusus Amator*, TAPA Monograph 17 (Madison 1956)
                  '*Servitium amoris* in the Roman elegists', *TAPA* 78 (1947) 285-300

Crabbe, A.M.   'Catullus 64 and the Fourth *Georgic*', *CQ* 27 (1977) 342-51

Crook, J.A.   *Law and Life of Rome* (London 1967)

Crowther, N.B.   'Nudity and morality: athletics in Italy', *CJ* 76 (1980-81) 119-23

Cumont, F.   *Les religions orientales dans le paganisme romain*[4] (Paris 1929)

Recherches sur le symbolisme funéraire des Romains (Paris 1942)

Cunningham, M.P. Review of H.P. Syndikus, *Die Lyrik des Horaz*, *CP* 72 (1977) 75-79

Currie, H. MacL. 'Ovid and the Roman stage', *ANRW* 31.4 (1981) 2701-42

Dahlmann, H. 'Der Bienenstaat von Virgils Georgica', *Abh. Ak. Mainz* 1954.10

D'Arms, J.H. *Romans on the Bay of Naples* (Cambridge, Mass. 1970)

Degrassi, A. 'Virgilio e il Foro di Augusto', *Epigraphica* 7 (1945) 88-103

Della Corte, F. 'Le *leges Iuliae* e l'elegia romana', *ANRW* 30.1 (1982) 539-58

Dihle, A. *Studien zur gr. Biographie* (Göttingen 1956)

Doblhofer, E. 'Horaz und Maecenas', *ANRW* 31.3 (1981) 1922-86

Dodds, E.R. *The Greeks and the Irrational* (California 1951)

Dörrie, H. *Pygmalion* (Opladen 1974)

Dover, K.J. *Greek Homosexuality* (London 1978)

Drew, D.L. *The Allegory of the Aeneid* (Oxford 1927)

Duckworth, G.E. *The Nature of Roman Comedy* (Princeton 1952)

Earl, D.C. 'Political terminology in Plautus', *Historia* 9 (1960) 235-43

Ehrenberg, V. *Alexander and the Greeks* (Oxford 1938)

Elliger, W. *Landschaft in griechischer Dichtung* (Berlin 1975)

Essen, C.C. van 'L'architecture dans l'Enéide', *Mnem.* 7 (1939) 225-36

Faerber, F. *Hero und Leander* (Munich 1961)

Fantham, E. *Comparative Studies in Republican Latin Imagery* (Toronto 1972)

Fedeli, P. *Il primo libro delle elegie di Properzio* (Florence 1980)

Fleischer, U. 'Musentempel und Octavianehrung im Proömium zum 3. Buch der Georgika', *Herm.* 88 (1960) 280-331

Fogazza, D., ed. *Domitii Marsi testimonia et fragmenta* (Rome 1981)

Fontenrose, J. 'Propertius and the Roman career', *Univ. Calif. Publ. in Class. Phil.* 13 no. 11 (1949)

Fraenkel, E.D.M. 'Das Reifen der horazischen Satire', *Festschrift R. Reitzenstein* (1931) 119-36
'Some aspects of the structure of *Aeneid* VII', *JRS* 35 (1945) 1-14 = *Kleine Beiträge* (Rome 1964) 2.145-71
'The *Culex*', *JRS* 42 (1952) 1-9 = *Kleine Beiträge* 2.181-97
Horace (Oxford 1957)
Elementi Plautini in Plauto (Florence 1960)

	'Zum Text von Aeneis 6.852', *Mus. Helv.* 19 (1962) 133-4 = *Kleine Beiträge* 2.142-4
Fränkel, H.	*Ovid: A Poet Between Two Worlds* (California 1945)
Frank, Tenney	*Economic Survey of the Roman Republic* (Baltimore 1933-)
Fraser, P.M.	*Ptolemaic Alexandria*, 3 vols. (Oxford 1972)
Friedlander, L.	*Roman Life and Manners* (English translation of *Die Sittengeschichte Roms*), 4 vols. (London 1908-13)
Funke, H.	'Porcius Licinus fr. 1 Morel', *Rh. M.* 120 (1977) 168-72
Gagé, J.	'Auguste écrivain', *ANRW* 30.1 (1982) 611-23
Galinsky, G.K.	*The Herakles Theme* (Oxford 1972)
	Ovid's Metamorphoses (Oxford 1975)
	'Vergil's *Romanitas* and his adaptation of Greek heroes', *ANRW* 31.2 (1981) 985-1010
Gelzer, T.	Edition of Musaeus, Loeb Classical Library (London and Cambridge, Mass., 1975)
Geymonat, M.	'Vergil, *Buc.* 2.20', *Mus. Crit.* 13-14 (1979) 371-6
Gigante, M.	*Civiltà delle forme letterarie nell'antica Pompei* (Naples 1979)
Ginouvès, R.	*Balaneutikè* (Paris 1962)
Green, Peter	'Caesar and Alexander: *aemulatio, imitatio, comparatio*', *AJAH* 3 (1978) 1-25
Griffin, A.H.F.	'Ovid's *Metamorphoses*', *G and R* 24 (1977) 57-70
Griffin, J.	*Homer on Life and Death* (Oxford 1980)
	'Caesar qui cogere posset', *Caesar Augustus*, ed. F. Millar and E. Segal (Oxford 1984) 189-218
	The Mirror of Myth (London, forthcoming)
Grimal, P.	'Auguste et Athénodore', *REA* 47 (1945) 261-73; *REA* 48 (1946) 62-79
	L'Amour à Rome (Paris 1963)
	Les Jardins romains (Paris 1969)
Guillemin, A.	'L'élément humain dans l'élégie latine', *REL* 18 (1940) 95-111
Hanfmann, G.M.A.	*Roman Art* (London 1964)
Hardie, C.G.	*The Georgics: A Transitional Poem*, 3rd Jackson Knight Memorial Lecture (Exeter 1971)
Heinze, R.	*Virgils epische Technik*³ (Leipzig 1914)
	'Ovids elegische Erzählung', *Berichte d. sächs. Ak.* 71.7 (1919) = *Vom Geist des Römertums*³ (Stuttgart 1960) 308-403
	Von den Ursachen der Grösse Roms (Leipzig 1921) = *Vom Geist* 9-27

	Die augusteische Kultur (Leipzig 1930)
Henig, M.	*Handbook to Roman Art* (London 1983)
Henrichs, A.	'Horaz als Aretaloge des Dionysos: *credite posteri*', *HSCP* 78 (1978) 203-211
Herter, H.	'Die Soziologie der antiken Prostitution', *JAC* 3 (1960) 70-111
Hickey, William	*Memoirs*, ed. P. Quennell (London 1960)
Higgins, R.A.	*Greek and Roman Jewellery* (London 1961)
Hillscher, A.	'Hominum literatorum Graecorum ante Tiberii mortem in urbe Roma commoratorum historia critica', *Jahrb. f. klass. Phil. Suppl.* 18 (1882)
Hollis, A.S.	Edition of Ovid, *Ars Amatoria* 1 (Oxford 1977)
Hopkins, M.K.	'The age of Roman brides at marriage', *Population Studies* 18 (1965) 309-27
	Death and Renewal in the Roman World (Cambridge 1983)
Horsfall, N.M.	'Doctus sermones utriusque linguae?' *Échos du Monde Classique* 23 (1979) 79-93
	'Some problems in the "*Laudatio Turiae*",' *BICS* 30 (1983) 85-98
Hubbard, M.E.	*Propertius* (London 1974)
Hubaux, J.	'Parthenius. Gallus. Virgile. Properce', *Miscellanea Properziana* (Assisi 1957) 31-38
Hunter, R.L.	*A Study of Daphnis and Chloe* (Cambridge 1983)
Huzar, E.	'The literary efforts of Mark Antony', *ANRW* 30.2 (1982) 639-57
Jacobson, H.	*Ovid's Heroides* (Princeton 1974)
Jacoby, F.	'Zur Entstehung der röm. Elegie', *Rh. M.* 60 (1905) 38-105 = *Kleine Philologische Schriften* 2 (Berlin 1961) 65-121
Jenkyns, R.	*The Victorians and Ancient Greece* (Oxford 1980)
	Three Classical Poets (London 1982)
Jocelyn, H.D.	*The Tragedies of Ennius* (Cambridge 1967)
Jucker, H.	*Vom Verhältnis der Römer zur bildenden Kunst der Griechen* (Frankfurt 1950)
Kähler, H.	*Seethiasos und Census, die Reliefs aus dem Palazzo Santa Croce in Rom* = Monumenta Artis Romanae 6 (Berlin 1966)
Kajanto, I.	'The significance of non-Latin cognomina', *Latomus* 27 (1968) 517-34
Kassel, R.	'Dichterspiele', *ZPE* 42 (1981) 11-20
Kenney, E.J.	'Love and legalism: Ovid, *Heroides* 20 and 21', *Arion* 9 (1970) 388-414
Kienast, D.	'Augustus und Alexander', *Gymn.* 76 (1969) 430-56
Klingner, F.	*Virgil* (Zürich 1967)
Knauer, G.N.	*Die Aeneis und Homer* (Göttingen 1964)

* Knoche, U.

'Erlebnis und dichterischer Ausdruck in der lat. Poesie', *Gymnasium* 65 (1958) 146-65

Kraggerud, E.

Aeneisstudien = *Symb. Osl.* Supplement 22 (Oslo 1968)

Kroll, W.

Studien zum Verständnis der röm. Literatur (Stuttgart 1924)
Die Kultur der ciceronischen Zeit (Leipzig 1933)

La Penna, A.

Orazio e l'ideologia del principato (Turin 1963)
Orazio e la morale mondana europea (Florence 1969)
'Estasi dionisiaca e poetica callimachea', *Studi in onore di V. De Falco* (Naples 1971) 227-38
L'integrazione difficile: un profilo di Properzio (Turin 1977)

Lane Fox, R.

Alexander the Great (London and New York 1974)

Lattimore, R.

Themes in Greek and Latin Epitaphs (Urbana 1942)

Lefèvre, E.

'Plautus-Studien III', *Hermes* 107 (1979) 311-39

Leo, F.

Plautinische Forschungen² (Berlin 1912)
Geschichte der römischen Literatur I (Berlin 1913)

Lilja, S.

Homosexuality in Republican and Augustan Rome, Commentationes Humanarum Litterarum 74 (1982), Helsinki

Lintott, A.W.

'Imperial expansion and moral decline in the Roman republic', *Historia* 21 (1972) 626-38

Lloyd-Jones, H.

'Modern interpretation of Pindar', *JHS* 93 (1973) 109-37

Luck, G.

Edition of Ovid, *Tristia* (Heidelberg 1977)

Lyne, R.O.A.M.

'Propertius and Cynthia: elegy 1.3', *PCPS* 196 (1970) 60-78
'*Servitium amoris*', *CQ* n.s. 29 (1979) 117-30
The Latin Love Poets (Oxford 1980)

McDermott, E.A.

'Greek and Roman elements in Horace's lyric program', *ANRW* 31.3 (1981) 1640-72

MacKay, A.G.

Houses, Villas and Palaces in the Roman World (London 1975)

McKeown, J.C.

'Augustan elegy and mime', *PCPS* 205 (1979) 71-84

Macleod, C.W.

'A use of myth in ancient poetry', in *CQ* n.s. 24 (1974) 88-91 = *Collected Essays* (Oxford 1983) 165-8
'Propertius 2.26', *Symb. Osl.* 51 (1976) 131-6 = *Collected Essays* 196-201

Malcovati, E.

Cicerone e i poeti (Pavia 1943)

Marrou, H.I.

Histoire de l'éducation dans l'antiquité⁶

	(Paris 1965)
Meincke, W.	*Untersuchungen zu den enkomiastischen Gedichten Theokrits* (Diss. Kiel 1965)
Michel, D.	*Alexander als Vorbild für Pompeius, Caesar und M. Antonius* (Brussels 1967)
Nadeau, Y.	'The lover and the statesman', *Poetry and Politics in the Age of Augustus*, edd. Woodman and West (Cambridge 1984) 59-82
Nethercut, W.R.	'Recent scholarship on Propertius', *ANRW* 30.3 (1983) 1813-57
Nisbet, R.G.M.	'Notes on Horace, *Epistles* 1', *CQ* n.s. 9 (1959) 73-5
	Edition of Cicero, *In Pisonem* (Oxford 1961)
Nisbet, R.G.M. & Hubbard, M.E.	Commentary on Horace, *Odes* I (Oxford 1970)
	Commentary on Horace, *Odes* II (Oxford 1978)
Nock, A.D.	'Notes on ruler cult', *JHS* 48 (1928) 21-43 = *Essays on Religion and the Ancient World* (Oxford 1972) 133-59
Norden, E.	'Vergils Aeneis im Lichte ihrer Zeit', *NJbb* 7 (1901) 249-82; 313-34 = *Kleine Schriften* (Berlin 1966) 358-421
	Ennius und Vergilius (Leipzig and Berlin 1915)
	'Orpheus und Eurydice', SB Berlin (1934) 626-3 = *Kleine Schriften 468-532*
	Edition of Aeneid VI⁴ (Darmstadt 1957)
Oksala, T.	*Religion und Mythologie bei Horaz* (Helsinki 1973)
Otis, B.	*Virgil: a Study in Civilized Poetry* (Oxford 1963)
	'Propertius' Single Book', *HSCP* 70 (1965) 1-44
	*Ovid as an Epic Poet*² (Cambridge 1970)
	'A new study of the *Georgics*', *Phoenix* 26 (1972) 40-62
Otto, A.	*Die Sprichwörter und sprichwörtlichen Redensarten der Römer* (Leipzig 1890)
Parry, A.	'The two voices of Virgil's *Aeneid*', *Arion* 2 (1963) 66-80
	'The idea of art in Virgil's *Georgics*', *Arethusa* 5 (1972) 35-52
Perret, J.	*Les Origines de la légende troyenne de Rome* (Paris 1942)
	Review of G.N. Knauer, *Die Aeneis und Homer*, *REL* 43 (1965) 125-30
Petersmann, G.	*Themenführung und Mottvenentfaltung in der Monobiblos des Properz* = *Grazer Beiträge* Suppl. 1 (1980)
Pichon, R.	*Index Verborum Amatoriorum* (Paris 1902)

Pöschl, V.   *Die Dichtkunst Virgils* (Wiesbaden 1950) = *The Art of Vergil* (Ann Arbor 1962) 'Die Dionysosode des Horaz (*c.* 2.19)', *Hermes* 101 (1973) 208-30

Puelma Piwonka, M.   *Lucilius und Kallimachos* (Frankfurt 1949)
Du Quesnay, I. le M.   'From Polyphemus to Corydon', *Creative Imitation in Latin Literature*, edd. D. West and T. Woodman (Cambridge 1979) 35-69

Ribbeck, O.   *Die römische Tragödie* (1875)
Richter, G.M.A.   *Ancient Furniture* (Oxford 1926) 'Who made the Roman portrait statues – Greeks or Romans?', *PAPhA* 95 (1951) 183-208

Richter, W.   'Divus Iulius, Octavianus und Kleopatra bei Aktion', *WS* 79 (1966) 451-65

Rieks, R.   'Virgils Dichtung als Zeugnis und Deutung der röm. Geschichte', *ANRW* 31.2 (1981)

Riewald, P.   *De Imperatorum Romanorum cum certis dis ... aequatione* (Diss. Halle 1912)

Rohde, E.   *Der griechische Roman*⁴ (Hildesheim 1960)
Ross, D.O.   *Style and Tradition in Catullus* (Cambridge, Mass. 1969) *Backgrounds to Augustan Poetry* (Cambridge 1975)

Rostovtzeff, M.I.   *Social and Economic History of the Roman Empire*² (Oxford 1957)

Rowell, H.T.   'Vergil and the Forum of Augustus', *AJP* 62 (1941) 261-76

Rudd, N.   'Horace', *Cambridge History of Classical Literature* 2, ed. E.J. Kenney (Cambridge 1982) 370-404

Russell, D.A.   'Plutarch, *Alcibiades* 1-16', *PCPS* 192 (1966) 37-47 *Plutarch* (London 1973) 'Rhetors at the wedding', *PCPS* 205 (1979) 104-117

Russell D.A. & Wilson, N.G.   Edition of Menander Rhetor (Oxford 1981)
Ryder, K.C.   'The *Senex Amator* in Plautus', *Greece and Rome* 31 (1984) 181-9

Schachermeyr, F.   *Alexander der Grosse* (Vienna 1973)
Schadewaldt, W.   'Sinn und Werden der vergilischen Dichtung', *Das Erbe der Alten* 20 (1931) 69-95 = *Hellas und Hesperien* (Zürich 1974) 2.701-22

Schanz, M. & Hosius, C.   *Geschichte der röm. Literatur* (Munich 1935)
Schefold, K.   'Antwort klassischer Sagenbilder auf politisches Geschehen', *GB* 4 (1975) 231-42

Scott, K.   'The identification of Augustus with Romulus-Quirinus', *TAPA* 56 (1925) 82-105 'Octavian's propaganda and Antony's *De sua*

	ebrietate', *CP* 24 (1929) 133-141
	'The political propaganda of 44-30 B.C.', *MAAR* 11 (1933) 7-49
Segal, C.P.	'Orpheus and the Fourth *Georgic*', *AJP* 87 (1966) 307-25
	Landscape in Ovid's Metamorphoses, *Hermes* Einzelschriften 23 (Wiesbaden 1969)
Segal, E.	*Roman Laughter* (Cambridge, Mass. 1968)
Silk, E.T.	'Notes on Cicero and the *Odes* of Horace', in *YCS* 13 (1952) 145-58
	'Bacchus and the Horatian *recusatio*', *YCS* 21 (1969) 193-212
Simon, E.	*Ara Pacis Augustae* (Tübingen 1967)
Skard, E.	'Die Heldenschau in Vergils Aeneis', *Symb. Osl.* 40 (1965) 53-65
	'*Concordia*', *Römische Wertbegriffe* (Wege der Forschung 34, 1967, ed. H. Oppermann)
Skutsch, O.	'The structure of the Propertian *Monobiblos*', *CP* 58 (1963) 238-9
Smith, K.F.	Commentary on Tibullus (New York 1913)
Solmsen, F.	'Propertius and Horace', *CP* 43 (1948) 105-9 = *Kleine Schriften* 2 (Hildesheim 1968) 278-82
	'Propertius in his literary relations with Tibullus and Vergil' *Philologus* 105 (1961) 273-89 = *Kleine Schriften* 2.299-315
Sordi, M.	'Timagene di Alessandria: uno storico ellenocentrico e filobarbaro', *ANRW* 30.1 (1982) 775-97
Stinton, T.C.W.	*Euripides and the Judgment of Paris* (London 1965)
Strasburger, H.	'Der Einzelne und die Gesellschaft im Denken der Gr.', *HZ* 177 (1954) 227-48
Stroh, W.	*Die röm. Liebeselegie als werbende Dichtung* (Amsterdam 1971)
Strong, D.	*Roman Art* (London 1970)
Sullivan, J.P. ed.	*Critical Essays in Roman Literature: Elegy and Lyric* (London 1962)
Susemihl, F.	*Geschichte der griech. Literatur in der Alexandrinerzeit*, 2 vols. (Leipzig 1891)
Süss, W.	*Ethos* (Leipzig 1910)
Syme, R.	*The Roman Revolution* (Oxford 1939)
	Tacitus, 2 vols. (Oxford 1958)
	'Bastards in the Roman aristocracy', *PAPhS* 104 (1960) 323-7
	History in Ovid (Oxford 1978)
Taeger, F.	*Charisma*, 2 vols. (Stuttgart 1957-60)
Taylor, L.R.	'Freedmen and freeborn in the epitaphs of Imperial Rome,' *AJP* 82 (1961) 113-32
	The Divinity of the Roman Emperor (Middletown 1931)

Thompson, D.   'Allegory and typology in the Aeneid',
                                Arethusa 3 (1971) 147-53
Toynbee, J.M.C.   *Death and Burial in the Roman World*
                                (London 1971)
Treggiari, S.   'Cicero, Horace, and mutual friends',
                                Phoenix 27 (1973) 245-61
Troxler-Keller, I.   *Die Dichterlandschaft des Horaz* (Heidel-
                                berg 1964)
Trumpf, J.   'Über das Trinken in der Poesie des Alkaios',
                                ZPE 12 (1973) 139-60
Tsantsanoglu, K.   'The memoirs of a Lady from Samos', *ZPE*
                                12 (1973) 182-95
Usener, H.   'Milch und Honig', *Rh. M.* 57 (1902) 177-95
                                = *Kleine Schriften* 4 (Leipzig and Berlin
                                1912) 398-416
Vessberg, O.   *Studien zur Kunstgeschichte der röm.*
                                Republik (Lund 1941)
Veyne, P.   *L'Elégie érotique romaine* (Paris 1983)
Vollenweider, H.M.-L.   'Verwendung und Bedeutung der Porträt-
                                gemmen für das politische Leben der röm.
                                Republik', *Mus. Helv.* 12 (1955) 96-111
Weaver, P.R.C.   *Familia Caesaris* (Cambridge 1972)
Webb, S. & B.   *Soviet Communism: A New Civilization?*
                                (London 1935)
Weiler, I.   *Agonales in Wettkämpfen der gr. Mythologie*
                                (Innsbruck 1969)
                                Der Sport bei den Völkern der alten Welt
                                (Darmstadt 1981)
Weinstock, S.   *Divus Julius* (Oxford 1971)
Whitaker, R.   *Myth and Personal Experience in Roman*
                                Love Elegy, Hypomnemata 76 (Göttingen
                                1983)
White, P.   'Amicitia and the profession of poetry in
                                early Imperial Rome', *JRS* 68 (1978) 74-92
Wigodsky, M.   *Vergil and Early Latin Poetry, Hermes*
                                Einzelschriften 24 (Wiesbaden 1972)
Wilamowitz-Moellendorff, U. von *Antigonos von Karystos* (Berlin 1881)
Wilkinson, L.P.   *Ovid Recalled* (Cambridge 1955)
                                'Greek influence on the poetry of Ovid',
                                Entretiens Hardt 2 (Geneva 1956) 223-43
                                'Propertius III.4', *Studi in onore di L.*
                                Castiglioni 2 (Florence 1961) 1091-1103
                                The Georgics of Virgil (Cambridge 1969)
                                The Roman Experience (London 1975)
Wille, G.   *Musica Romana* (Amsterdam 1967)
Williams, G.   'Poetry in the moral climate of Augustan
                                Rome', *JRS* 52 (1962) 28-46
                                Tradition and Originality in Roman Poetry
                                (Oxford 1968)
                                Edition of Horace, *Odes* III (Oxford 1969)
                                Figures of Thought in Roman Poetry (Yale
                                1980)

Wilson, Harriette
Wimmel, W.

Wippert, O.

Wiseman, T.P.
Yardley, J.C.

Zielinski, T.

Technique and Ideas in the Aeneid (Yale 1983)
Memoirs, ed. L. Blanch (London 1964)
Hirtenkrieg und arkadisches Rom (Munich 1973)
Tibull und Delia, Hermes Einzelschriften 37 (Wiesbaden 1976)
Alexander-Imitatio und röm. Politik in der rep. Zeit (Diss. Würzburg 1972)
Cinna the Poet (Leicester 1974)
'Comic influences in Propertius', *Phoenix* 27 (1973) 134-9
'Paulus Silentiarius, Ovid, and Propertius', *CQ* n.s. 30 (1980) 239-44
Cicero im Wandel der Jahrhunderte (Leipzig 1912)
Horace et la société romaine du temps d'Auguste (Paris 1938)

Index

General

Passages discussed

CPSIA information can be obtained at www.ICGtesting.com
Printed in the USA
LVOW06s0956250314

378843LV00001B/76/P